From Subservience to Strike

*Industrial Relations in
the Banking Industry*

John Hill

University of Queensland Press
St Lucia • London • New York

© University of Queensland Press, St Lucia, Queensland 1982

Typeset by University of Queensland Press
Printed and bound by Hedges & Bell Pty Ltd, Melbourne

Distributed in the United Kingdom, Europe, the Middle East,
Africa, and the Caribbean by Prentice-Hall International,
International Book Distributors Ltd, 66 Wood Lane End, Hemel
Hempstead, Herts., England.

National Library of Australia
Cataloguing-in-Publication data

Hill, John, 1940–.
    From subservience to strike.

    Bibliography.
    Includes index.
    ISBN 0 7022 1830 8.

    1. Australian Bank Employees Union – History.
    2. Trade-unions – Bank employees – Australia –
    History. I. Title.

331.88'113321'0994

Library of Congress Cataloging in Publication Data

Hill, John, 1940–
    From subservience to strike.

    Bibliography: p.
    Includes index.
    1. Australian Bank Employees' Union – History.
    2. Trade-unions – Bank Employees – Australia – History.
    3. Bank employees – Australia – History. I. Title.
    HD6894.B262A925   331.88'113321'0994   82-2684
    ISBN 0-7022-1830-8   AACR2

Contents

Photographs

Acknowledgements

This story was only made possible by the foresight, persistence, and enthusiasm of the late R.D. ("Barney") Williams, federal secretary of the ABOA from 1950 until 1973, and probably Australia's foremost white-collar union leader. His interest in the ABOA's history was initially apparent when, shortly after becoming federal secretary, he sent the union's early clutter of records and correspondence to the National Archives of Business and Labour in Canberra. Later, as the ABOA's fiftieth year approached, it was he who pressed for a history to be written. Once begun, the task was both facilitated and made more absorbing by the willingness with which Barney Williams recalled events of earlier years, read drafts, and made constructive criticism and suggestions. I trust his belief that this should be an analytical rather than descriptive narrative and one that portrayed the ABOA's faults and failures as well as its successes has been confirmed.

John Sanders, Keith Salter, and Lachlan Riches of the federal office were always willing to provide records, answer questions, read drafts, and make union resources available. I appreciate that the urgency and pressure of everyday union affairs did not always make this easy. Division officials in Victoria and other states similarly helped and freely made available the records and journals of the now merged state unions. Numerous bank officers, many of them now elderly, endured my questioning, shared their memories with me, and suggested further fruitful avenues of investigation.

Most private banks have been willing to scan their records, and a number of bank archivists and librarians allowed me to read their collections. In particular ANZ archivist Fred Holt provided splendid assistance in my search through that bank's extensive and well-managed records. Similarly, Michael Saclier of the Archives of Business and Labour made available the copious quantitites of ABOA material. The writing of this history formed part of a doctorate of philosophy, and my joint supervisors, Dr Tony Dingle and Professor John McCarty of the Department of Economic History at Monash University, patiently schooled me in some of the mysteries of economic history, read my tedious early drafts, and made a myriad of suggestions on style and structure. I also hope I have vindicated at least some of the faith both they and my colleagues have provided. My thanks to Bev Goodall and Denise Mudie who typed innumerable drafts and skilfully produced this final version.

Finally, words do little justice to my debt to my family. They always believed the task was possible, and this enduring confidence has made it so.

Abbreviations

AAESDA	Association of Architects, Engineers, Surveyors and Draughtsmen
ABA	Associated Banks Association, which after restructuring in 1954 became the Australian Bankers Association
ABC	Australian Bank of Commerce
ABEU	Australian Bank Employees Union
ABOA	Australian Bank Officials' Association
ABOF	Australian Bank Officials' Federation (also known as the BOF)
ACA	Australasian Clerical Association, which in 1923 became the Federated Clerks' Union (FCU)
ACSPA	Australian Council of Salaried and Professional Associations
AEU	Australian Engineering Union
AIBR	*Australasian Insurance and Banking Record*
AISF	Australian Insurance Staffs' Federation, which in 1975 became the Australian Insurance Employees Union (AIEU)
ANZ	Australia and New Zealand Bank
AWU	Australian Workers' Union
BOA	Bank Officials' Association, which in 1938 became the ABOA, and in 1978 the ABEU
BOASA	Bank Officials' Association of South Australia
BOAWA	Bank Officials' Association of Western Australia
BOF	Bank Officials' Federation (also known as the ABOF)
BOG	Bank Officers' Guild [of England]
BNSW	Bank of New South Wales
CBA	Commercial Bank of Australia
CBC	Commercial Banking Company of Sydney
CBOA	Commonwealth Bank Officers' Association
CPD	*Commonwealth Parliamentary Debates*
CPEO	Council of Professional Employees Organization
CWCA	Council of White Collar Associations
ES&A	English, Scottish and Australian Bank
FCM	Federal Council Minutes
FCU	Federated Clerks' Union

MOA	Municipal Officers' Association
NBA	National Bank of Australasia
NSWIOA	New South Wales Insurance Officers' Association
NUBE	National Union of Bank Employees [United Kingdom]
QNB	Queensland National Bank
SABOJ	*South Australian Bank Officials' Journal*
SBSA	Savings Bank of South Australia
SSB	State Savings Bank [of Victoria]
SSBOA	State Savings Bank [of Victoria], Officers' Association
UBOA of NSW	United Bank Officers' Association of New South Wales
UBOA of Q	United Bank Officers' Association of Queensland
VCMM	Victorian Committee of Management Minutes
WEB	Women's Employment Board

1 The Banks, and the People Who Worked in Them

This is the story of the formation, growth, successes, and failures of a union of Australian private trading bank employees and of some of the major industrial relations events surrounding this. It is a story of individual leaders who dominated the growth of banking unionism in Australia, and of the union members, whose attitudes and inhibitions were also so important. Yet it is not a detailed account of the internal operations of a trade union, but rather a story emphasizing how economic, social, industrial, geographical, and political factors influenced the formation and development of a trade union.

In Australia today one union,[1] the Australian Bank Officials' Association (hereafter referred to as the ABOA), covers employees in the private banking industry. However, only since the early sixties have private bank employees enjoyed a common union. Before this, five separate unions existed. In Victoria in 1919, E. C. Peverill, a bank clerk with the National Bank of Australasia (the NBA) was instrumental in forming the Bank Officials' Association (the BOA). This union also covered Tasmanian bank officers, and after 1949 some South Australian officers. Branches of the BOA were also established in both South Australia and Western Australia. By 1921, separate state unions had been formed: the Bank Officials' Association of South Australia (BOASA), and the Bank Officials' Association of Western Australia (BOAWA). In 1919, K. H. Laidlaw, a Queensland bank clerk, formed the United Bank Officers' Association of Queensland (the UBOA of Q). In the same year, H. F. Rawson, another bank clerk, initiated events that eventually resulted in the formation of the United Bank Officers' Association of New South Wales (the UBOA of NSW). While the BOA was registered in the federal Arbitration Court, the other unions were registered in various state courts.

The Nature of the Australian Private Banking Industry

The structure and nature of the Australian private banking industry was important to the evolution of banking unionism.[2] They influenced the timing of union formation, the reactions of both employers and employees to unionism, and the effectiveness of unionism. The development of

Australian banking up till the late nineteenth century was characterized by four features:

1. *The large number of banking or quasi-banking enterprises.* The term *banking* was in fact used loosely in early times to cover companies involved in highly speculative lending on mortgages covering land and other even less liquid assets, various types of building societies and land banks, as well as those engaged in more traditional banking activities. By 1891 there were in Melbourne alone sixty-four "banks" soliciting funds from the public.[3] Between 1860 and 1889 the number of Australian bank branches had increased from 71 to 1,212; their capital backing had increased fourfold and accumulated reserves some seventy times over.[4] Intensive competition led to a profusion of new branches, initially in the country but later also in urban areas. It also resulted in a high level of price competition, through variations in interest charges on advances and fixed-interest deposits, and even the payment of interest on current account deposits.

2. *The extent of overseas ownership and control.* The establishment of overseas owned and controlled banks resulted from the large and relatively rapid economic expansion that began in mid-century with the discovery of gold and continued with the development of the pastoral and later agricultural industries. Local capital resources and banking expertise were inadequate to support and service the demands placed upon them. Not surprisingly, much of the early impetus to Australian banking was provided from London. By 1870 four London-based banks operated in Australia: the Bank of Australasia; the English, Scottish and Australian Banks; the Union Bank; and the London Chartered Bank. Together they accounted for a third of total deposits and advances.[5]

3. *The development of an extensive branch structure.* The proliferation of bank branches was a result of the nature and location of Australian economic development. With mining and later pastoral and agricultural activities occurring rapidly and often simultaneously in many parts of the country, there was an urgent need for banking services which was filled by the larger London and colonial banks through the establishment of branch offices.

4. *Lack of government intervention.* Government intervention into the banking industry was almost non-existent. Colonial banking legislation was minimal, and there was no central bank to regulate the activities of individual banks. Most issued their own notes, the gold backing for which was, at least theoretically, at their own discretion. There were no government-owned trading banks to provide competition. Although some colonial governments had established savings banks, these were relatively insignificant, the main form of saving being in the form of fixed-interest-bearing deposits held with the trading banks. By 1880 just on half of Australia's total money stock was held in this latter form and less than 10 per cent with savings banks.[6]

In the period 1830 to 1880, Australia had experienced relatively steady economic growth, certainly when compared with the two decades that followed. The banks, as providers of capital and preservers of savings had similarly expanded, so that by 1880 the industry picture was one of a highly competitive two-tiered structure. In the first tier, and dominant in terms of most banking criteria, were a dozen or so larger banks. Each had a considerable number of branches spread through the colonies and carried out the more traditional banking activities of lending on relatively safe collateral, accepting funds on fixed deposit, and issuing notes to the public. The second tier contained the fringe banks, building societies, land banks, and other companies involved in a range of lending and speculative activities. These were generally smaller, considerably younger, and generally confined to a single city or state.

The 1880s witnessed a rapid upsurge in public and private investment, much of which was basically speculative. Public investment was stimulated by the rapid growth of the urban sector which accompanied manufacturing development and urban population increases. The use of borrowed capital for railroad construction, communications systems, and similar social infrastructure was so rapid and extensive that between 1889 and 1891 the average indebtedness of colonial governments almost doubled.[7] The private sector concentrated so much on land and construction investment that in the twelve months following March 1887, Melbourne city property prices increased by 50 per cent and suburban property prices by more than 200 per cent.[8] More building societies and land banks, relying largely upon frequent injections of London capital, sprang up. The increasingly competitive environment and the often doubtful motives of the proprietors meant that the operations of many of these companies were clouded in uncertainty and even illegality. They lent freely, advancing large sums on flimsy assets and to the most dubious of schemes. By 1888 there were almost seventy "fringe banks" in Melbourne, and twelve new banks of issue had been formed since 1877.[9] The boom was sustained by huge injections of British capital made possible by unfavourable lending conditions in Britain and high interest rates in Australia. The *Australasian Insurance and Banking Record* estimated that by 1893 more than £300 million had been invested in Australia by the British. "The burden is a heavy one, and will be hard to carry without pinching . . . we are of the opinion that one half of the borrowings might easily have proved just as effective."[10]

By the early 1890s the seeds of disaster sown a decade earlier began to spring forth. It was the banking industry that bore the initial shock as the seemingly inexhaustible supply of London funds suddenly dried up. Some fraudulent companies who had been using capital inflow to pay dividends and make interest payments immediately closed down, and panic quickly spread as depositors tried to retrieve their money. Even in normal times the industry would not have been able to cope with such a run, but now with most banks' ratio of cash to deposits abnormally low, few had any chance of weathering the storm. Even the larger, more broadly based banks, whose conservative attitudes normally prevented them entering speculative areas, found that competitive pressures had forced them to lend on projects that had either collapsed or were in imminent danger of doing so. In more normal times they could have expected funds from their other banking activities to offset at least partially the sudden liquidity drain. However, several poor seasons and a fall in export prices, accompanied by a high level of farmer indebtedness based on illiquid collateral, complicated the situation further.[11] The effects were dramatic. Of the sixty-four banks open in mid-1891 in Victoria, all but nine had closed two years later.[12] Those that remained open were generally the largest, most diversified, and cautious. Thirty-four of those that shut never reopened, and most of the others were only able to do so aftery carrying out reconstruction schemes, a process that froze and frequently whittled away customers' deposits for long periods. It was estimated that more than ten million pounds worth of deposits had been tied up by these bank suspensions.[13]

The traumatic events of the early 1890s had a major influence on the subsequent development of the banking industry, for they shaped the attitudes of employers, employees, and the public and did much to determine the future structure of the industry. There was a shift in emphasis from profit-making to security and safety. Cash reserve ratios were raised and priority was given to increasing the volume of funds held in London as a hedge against future drains on liquidity. There was also a change in lending policy away from illiquid assets such as land towards more easily convertible assets. Greater security was now demanded before loans were advanced. While in earlier years the banks had stimulated economic development, they now preferred to lend to proved projects rather than risky new ventures. Senior bankers who had seen supposedly secure banks demolished in the turmoil of 1893 now urged their staffs to act with the utmost caution and give priority to the preservation of the reputation of their bank and the safety of its funds. Most staff, with the evidence of unemployment all around them, required little persuasion to follow such directives. Public attitudes also changed. Bank closures had swept away millions of pounds of customer deposits. The bewilderment and distrust of depositors took several forms. For some it led to a generalized and violent antipathy to the whole banking system, and in the politically turbulent 1890s these feelings were crystallized in the demands of various political groups. From others came a demand for government control over banking. These were to reach partial fruition with the establishment of colonial, and later state savings banks and the formation of the Commonwealth Bank in 1911. This resulted in a significant loss of business for the private banking sector as savings deposits rose from 9 per cent of total money stock in 1890 to 20 per cent in 1900 and 41 per cent in 1911.[14]

The main structural consequence of the 1890s depression was a decline in the number of banking companies in existence. By 1900 there were only twenty, and four of these (the Bank of Australasia, the Union Bank, the Bank of New South Wales, and the Commercial Banking Company of Sydney) handled almost half of total deposits and advances.[15] By 1914 their number had fallen further, yet they operated almost fourteen hundred branches throughout Australia.[16] It was during these years that the foundations of the present oligopolistic private banking structure was laid. The Associated Banks Association of Victoria (the ABA), became an important avenue of bank co-operation and collaboration, as the banks agreed not to compete with each other on interest rates or bank charges. Competition was limited, by agreement, to non-price areas and took the form of an expansion of branch banking. Whereas the decade to 1900 had been one of net branch closures, the years between 1900 and 1914 saw 569 new branches opened, an increase of over 40 per cent.[17] Most new branches were in rural areas. The surviving smaller banks took the initiative here. Aware that larger banks already had well-established branches in provincial towns, they opened new branches in rural areas, thereby hoping to gain a competitive edge. The larger banks then felt compelled to open branches in the same areas to prevent loss of business. The net effect was a rapid increase in the number of rural branches, many of which were never profitable because they were poorly sited, while others rapidly became unprofitable as emphasis swung towards urban development. Some banks also expanded their operations into states in which they had not formerly been represented. The NBA moved into Queensland, the Commercial Banking Company of Sydney (CBC) into Victoria, and the English, Scottish and Australian Bank (ES&A) into Tasmania.

The structure of the banking industry was further modified by the increasing involvement of the federal government. In 1911 Treasury took over the note issue. The private banks accepted this quietly, but realized its broader implications when the Fisher Labor government "resorted to the printing presses" and effectively reduced the 25 per cent gold backing. Legislation was also passed to create a bank with both central and normal trading bank functions. Again few saw any threat to private bank autonomy, particularly when Denison Miller, the first governor of the new Commonwealth Bank, made it clear that he would pursue normal commercial bank operations rather than regulatory central bank activities.[18] Apart from holding the federal government account, the new bank appeared to be at a disadvantage in its efforts to compete with the private banks. However, two factors brought about a rapid increase in its size, competitiveness, and importance. First, it was able to generate a rapid growth in funds through the development of its savings bank function. By establishing agencies in post offices and promising government backing for all funds deposited, the bank effectively exploited community mistrust of private banks. By the beginning of 1920 there were almost half a million

Commonwealth Bank savings accounts with total balances of almost £18 million.[19] The second factor was the outbreak of war in 1914. The bank organized export finance for primary industry and also mobilized war loans. By the end of the war, although it was still not acting as a central bank, the Commonwealth Bank had established itself as an integral part of the banking system. By 1920, private banking was dominated by eight banks, each trading in more than one state, and four of them London owned. There were also several smaller banks, generally confined to a single state, which were soon to be swallowed up by the larger banks.

The Bank Officer and His Work

> The Bank Clerk is a flower which blooms best in a branch. In the city he is outcrowded by botanical magnates of more vigorous growth. There he blushes unseen, but in a country town, great or small, bear in mind he is a person of no little importance. You will know him by his straw hat, and his most characteristic occupation in business hours is strolling nonchalantly about with a few dark oblong books under his arm, wearing the air of a proprietor of things at large. And no wonder! For in the leaves of those dark oblong books he carried the commercial heart of the town and district.[20]

The attitudes of bank management and employees were crucial to the question of union formation. Bank officers were held in considerable public regard, and there was an ample supply of recruits in spite of a rigorous, tedious, and poorly paid branch apprenticeship. Consequently, the banks were able to ensure their employees were prudent and conservative and would continue to be subservient to the banks' every wish and action.

Nowhere was this reflected more than in recruiting policies, where the industry's conditioning influenced the methods of recruiting and new entrants. All recruits were, of course, male and, having completed the fourth year of secondary school, were from a rather exclusive group. Most recruits had attended private schools, came from non-urban areas, and had fathers whose occupations lay in the professional, self-employed, and farmer categories. Less than 20 per cent of recruits' fathers were clerks or tradesmen, and almost none had fathers who were manual labourers. So the banks clearly drew their recruits from a quite specific socio-economic group. This was despite the attitudes of a growing proportion of parents in lower socio-economic groups who sought more prestigious jobs for their sons. As F.D. Klingender says in *The Condition of Clerical Labour in Britain,* "In pre war days the 'superiority' of the clerical worker was still not in question. Nor was the desire of the workman to see that his son should, if it could be contrived, 'rise' from working class employment to the black coated occupations."[21] The community viewed banking as a most desirable form of employment, for it had the effect "of advancing in the scale of social improvement, and to places of trust and emolument, numerous young gentlemen of high character and intelligence, who otherwise would have remained in comparative obscurity, and lingered out an inglorious existence on a bare competency".[22] There is little doubt that this also mirrored the Australian experience. E.C. Peverill, founder and first secretary of the BOA, elaborated on these community attitudes: "To give an idea of how respected bank officers were . . . when I was in Mildura the Mayor wouldn't plan a reception without first checking to see if I could attend . . . because I was the manager of the National Bank and he wanted the Bank represented at all functions."[23]

Recruitment was usually carried out by branch managers. Hopeful youths applied to the local manager and were interviewed, and a recommendation was passed on to head office. A bank officer in this period commented: "The bank was mighty particular about who they took on . . . even to the extent of going into the family history of the applicant. The standing of one's parents in a town or district counted for a great deal."[24] The financial health of the recruit's family was also of importance, for the recruit, a probationer for up to two years, and not receiving salary, had to be supported by his family. This "patronage system" resulted in employee docility, passivity, and commitment to management ideals and objectives. These attitudes were strengthened by an awareness that the recruit was joining a career industry and that it was vital to retain his employer's good will. Clearly, then, it was a very specific type of recruit who entered the industry. Selected from the small proportion of students with relatively high educational qualifications, largely from private schools and with a professional or farming background, they were already imbued with conservative values and entered the industry with attributes amenable to a high level of managerial control.

Following a probationary period, spent largely in carrying out routine office jobs, the recruit was given the task of maintaining ledgers and learning other specific banking skills. After some years the now not so young clerk graduated to the shop front of the bank — the teller's cage. Here his education continued, but in a somewhat different manner to that of other "apprentices":

> Unlike the grocer boy who exudes an untoward flavor of spices and currants, and the barman who quickly comes to resemble unduly his rotund casks of beer, he deals not with the crude substance of trade, but with its refined essence. Crisp polished lucre, (misnamed filthy), which leaves no stain on delicate fingers. Gaily painted notes, bills of exchange and cheques, which verily were often the shadow rather than the substance of wealth.[25]

A period as branch accountant normally followed, a task including the supervision of staff and their activities. Always to the forefront was the fervent hope of promotion to branch manager, for most officers the pinnacle of a banking career. The major tasks of the manager were the granting of overdrafts, the maintenance and expansion of branch business, and general liaison with customers. In larger branches a number of officers, such as bill security exchange, remittance, and draft clerks, were required to carry out more specific duties; these tasks required considerable expertise but were frequently allocated to officers considered unsuitable for accountant or managerial posts.

Because of the type and variety of banking tasks, they were invariably learned on the job. A result of this was the establishment of a strictly observed occupational hierarchy, which further extended the formal attitudes and relationships in the industry. As a retired officer commented, "It was the accepted thing for a junior or other lowly officer to raise his hat when passing a senior officer in the street, and at all times those seniors had to be addressed as 'Sir'."[26] Many clerks' tasks were of a routine nature, requiring relatively easily learnt skills and little training. However, the nature of the industry ensured an inordinate emphasis upon attention to detail and meticulous recording of transactions. A constant fear of tellers was the fear of overpaying customers, for they had to make up shortfalls from their own pockets should their cash be "short" at closing time. As one bank officer noted, "There is, perhaps, no work more trying upon the nerves than bank work; there is the ever present fear of error, which may become a veritable life destroyer."[27]

This, coupled with the frequent monotony, the segmented nature of the work, lack of contact with other workers, and the nature of the supervision, meant that this early period of "on the job" training was viewed with distaste by bank recruits. The standards required were unrelenting. Take, for example, these excerpts from the UBOA of Q journal detailing the qualities apparently expected of a teller:

> Having arrived at this stage of his career he should have learned the lessons of control, patience, etc. — It is necessary that he be imbued with a knowledge of human nature, that he be of a kindly courteous disposition, bright and cheery, combined with a deferential manner . . . The opportunities open to the Teller for increasing and improving the business of the branch are second to none. Bank tellers and all other officers should always act in all their dealing with the customers as if they were conducting the business on their own account . . . It is well also to see this officer taking an interest in the affairs of the community . . . his affiliation with a local church, with sporting organisations . . . in any amateur theatricals . . . with any musical debating or literary society all tend to his own betterment and redound to the credit of the institution for whom he is working. The reading of good literature and a course of study along banking lines, is not only recommended, but is urged as most necessary to his future advancement, and absolutely essential to his future.[28]

Banks formalized the tasks of their officers so far as they were able. For example, the *N.B.A. Book of Regulations* contained more than six hundred rules. However, some areas of banking practice, the setting of overdraft limits, cashing cheques for favoured customers, and lending policy, could not be explicitly formulated, and so the officer was expected to use his "discretion and common sense". This often meant that he was placed in a difficult position because of a conflict between financially cautious regulations and the need to show branch profitability. While his career prospects depended on his ability to show a profit in his branch, he was aware that a poor assessment of a customer could slow his promotion or even bring his career to an end. In such situations the rule book was of little help, and in fact only highlighted the bankers' dilemma.

> It is necessary that due care and caution be exercised, particularly by managers or other senior officers when their advice is sought by customers or others in regard to investments. Cases have occurred where advice has been given by officers who have either been influenced by the optimism of others, or have failed to properly appraise the exact position, and as a result of their statements, and/or recommendations, customers have entered into transactions which have eventually resulted in loss. Subsequently the customers have contended that their loss was due to inaccurate representations by or influence of the banks representatives.[29]

Additionally, there were the ethics of the profession to maintain: "Legitimate competition is desirable and good for all trade, the honorable profession of banking is degraded by the tactics of men who stoop to the level of the butcher boy canvassing for orders."[30]

Banks expected their staff to put the interests of the bank above all else. In discussing the reporting of irregular activities, the general manager of the NBA insisted:

> Officers must not be deterred from doing their duty in this connection by reason say of personal friendship, seniority of officers to be reported upon, mistaken sense of loyalty to a fellow officer and suchlike. The duty involved is clear and well defined, and loyalty lies in the direction not of a brother officer, but of the institution, whose interests they are expected to serve and protect.[31]

Loyalty to the bank was assumed into the officer's private life. He was expected to avoid debt at all times. An officer in the Bank of Australasia inadvertently overdrew his trading account, and although he had an unblemished record of fourteen years service and repaid the amount involved as soon as the error was realized, he was nevertheless dismissed.[32] The banks also operated what amounted to a marriage ban. The general principle was that officers should not marry until their salary reached a specified level; otherwise they would "not be able to maintain themselves, their wives and families in a manner befitting their association with the institution employing them".[33] Any staff ignoring such regulations were treated as single people when being transferred from one branch to another and also jeopardized their chances of promotion. There was no form of application for transfer or promotion. Staff inspectors carried out annual staff inspections, and promotion depended on their assessments and the reports of branch managers. As one more cynical clerk noted:

> When you see your omnipotent Manager shrivel into insignificance, the Chief Clerk show a quickened interest in office routine and the junior diligently overtaking his arrears of indexing, you may know that the Inspector has arrived. Like foolish virgins your ledgers are unchecked; like unjust stewards your tills do not balance; and if his coming be in the morning, it is heavy odds that, though you may have been an exemplar of punctuality for the last six months, you will be late on that fateful day.[34]

The inspectorial procedure epitomized the banking hierarchy; communication and control was centralized in the capital city head office. A bank officer summed up the frustrations felt by many of his colleagues:

> In all industry there never was a class of employee which had so little liberty as Bank Clerks. Hitherto, not only have their services been bought, and at a very low rate of pay, but their individual liberties, freedom of speech and action have been suppressed in every conceivable way. They must not take an active or intelligent interest in politics . . . they must not even give expression to their convictions (one of the Bank's customers might hear them). . . . Although not chattel slaves, they have become, indeed, the property of the Bank . . . Clerks must not go to the races, they must not reside at hotels, they must not help towards the progress of the community as a municipal councillor or occupy other public positions which make for the welfare of the State. They are not permitted to invest any surplus money which they may be fortunate to possess in any undertaking which is not approved by the Bank.[35]

The question of bank officer salaries brought further frustrations and reflected the extent of the bank's dominance. Before 1910 there is no evidence that individual banks used uniform salary scales. Certainly their actions in starting probationers on small or even no salary[36] and in paying widely varying yearly increments, allowances, and bonuses to some clerks and not to others meant that, in practice, salaries for clerks doing similar work varied even within banks. Of greater importance were the salary differentials between banks. During this period salaries paid by colonial banks were consistently higher than those of the English-based banks. The main reason for this was that the English-controlled banks based their salaries on English salary levels, which were considerably lower than those paid in Australia. Some order was brought to the banks' salary structures following the state registration of the United Clerks Union of New South Wales in 1909. This union prepared a general wage and salary claim designed to cover "all persons wholly or partially employed upon clerical work".[37] While this posed no direct threat to the salary autonomy of the banks — for the union had no members in banks, nor did it attempt to recruit there — it did stimulate considerable discussion in the press. "A bank clerk is a bank clerk everywhere, and the duties are so uniform that a wages scale could be fixed that would operate equitably all round."[38] Quickly rejecting any inference that unions rather than employers should set salaries, the banks responded by developing more uniform salary scales. This culminated in 1913 when the CBC established a seventeen-year salary scale for its officers.[39] This scale, providing for an initial annual salary of fifty pounds, increasing by diminishing increments to a maximum of three hundred pounds, reflected the "needs basis" wage concept espoused by various industrial tribunals. It ran counter to the actual industry situation, where all officers were required to attain ever-increasing levels of skill and responsibility. The introduction of a semi-automatic scale, of crucial importance in later years when both federal and state courts implicitly accepted the existence of a lengthy scale in the industry, was one the banks were later to regret. Other banks then introduced similar scales, bringing some uniformity both within and between various bank's salaries.

In the latter years of the First World War the banks' practice of also paying a bonus (normally between 2.5 per cent and 10 per cent) further confused the salary picture. Not only did the level and frequency of bonuses paid to a particular officer grade vary, but frequently there was also considerable variation in bonuses granted to different employees. In 1921 the *Bankers Bulletin* noted: "During the last ten years, the Bank of Australasia has paid eight bonuses to the Union Bank's two."[40] Many employees recognized this bonus system for what it was — an acknowledgement that salary levels were too low: "Our bonus plan was no good, because we knew that it was not a real bonus but was in lieu of salary. It took both of these to put our salary schedule near par with salaries paid in business."[41] Clearly, then, bank officers' salaries did little to compensate for the onerous and demanding nature of their employment.

Why 1919?

By the end of the First World War, unions had been formed in most blue-collar industries, but they had not as yet made significant inroads into private-sector white-collar occupations. In 1913 an attempt by an NBA clerk to form a banking union was aborted when his plans were revealed and he was summarily dismissed. For some years this served as a warning to other bank officers, but finally in 1919 bank unionization occurred. Various developments stimulated union formation. First, and most important, was the decline in real wages of bank staff, both absolutely and relative to blue-collar workers. Secondly, working conditions became increasingly onerous. A third development, linked to the second, was a change in attitude on the part of those who had seen military service and were now rejoining the banks. Fourthly, the industrial relations structure in Australia provided a positive incentive to union formation, as did the establishment and growth of banking unions in other countries immediately after the war. An additional factor was the emergence of individuals willing and able to take on leadership roles.

The first reason, reduced bank officer purchasing power, stemmed from a reduction in the size and frequency of wage increments paid to officers, upon which was superimposed a relatively rapid inflation rate resulting from the Australian government's wartime deficit financing. Appendix 2 provides the results of an examination of bank officer salaries. For example, between 1900 and 1919 the average annual increment for clerks was £13 12s. but between 1917 and 1919 this fell to only £5 10s.[42] For clerks whose income aspirations were based upon regular and substantial increments, this decline was worrying. Alternatively, salary increases came by way of promotion. In earlier years, rapid branch expansion had necessitated significant increases in the number of accountants and managers and thus increased promotion prospects. For example, in Victoria between 1900 and 1914 the number of branches grew from 408 to 526, an increase of 22.2 per cent. However, between 1915 and 1919 the number of branches in Victoria actually decreased by three, largely as a result of wartime manpower restrictions.[43] A comparison of promotion rates for bank clerks entering in 1890 and those entering in 1900 shows that more than half of the earlier intake had gained promotion before their sixteenth year of service, while the 1920 intake took twenty years to reach that situation.

It was the relatively rapid rate of inflation of the 1910 to 1919 era, culminating in dramatic increases in 1918 and 1919, that brought a significant decline in real incomes. Between 1910 and 1919 retail price increases were of the order of 75 per cent, and between 1917 and 1918 alone they increased by almost 30 per cent.[44] When these inflation rates are applied to only slowly increasing money wages of the period, the extent of the decline in bank officer purchasing power is apparent. Table 1 of appendix 2 indicates this decline. For those clerks who had entered the industry in 1890, the decline in purchasing power between 1910 and 1919 was a staggering 30.4 per cent, while for the 1900 intake it was 10.3 per cent. The 1910 entrants increased their purchasing power by more than 50 per cent, but this was a function of very low starting salaries. Even here the table reveals that not only did the real wage of this youngest group of clerks remain virtually static throughout the early war years, but it too declined in 1918 and 1919. Between 1914 and 1919 the real income index fell by 30.6 per cent for the 1890 intake, 22.2 per cent for the 1900 intake, and 3 per cent for the 1910 intake.[45] Even more markedly, between 1917 and 1919 these figures were 18.9, 13.9, and 20.7 per cent.

The banks were not only aware of the situation but felt it proper that their employees (and particularly senior employees) should bear some of the consequences of the rapid rate of inflation. "Men above a certain remuneration do not spend it all in living and consequently the necessity to adjust their remuneration on the increased cost of living should not be in anything like the proportion of junior officers."[46]

Table 2 of appendix 2 indicates that the real incomes of accountants also fell significantly between 1910 and 1919, the 1880 intake's real income falling by almost 30 per cent, that of the 1890 intake by nearly 17 per cent, and the 1900 intake by almost 15 per cent. Of even greater concern was the rapid decline, averaging 18.6 per cent, that took place between 1914 and 1919. In 1918 and 1919 the real wage index for the 1880 intake tumbled from 84.4 to 70.9 per cent, the 1890 intake from 95.1 to 83.3 per cent, and the 1900 intake from 98.6 to 85.1 per cent. Of interest is the real income situation of accountants who entered the industry in 1880 and who in 1919 were earning almost 30 per cent less in real terms than they had ten years earlier. These officers had been in the bank for nearly forty years and had been passed over for promotion. Those who did not measure up to the bank's rigorous though subjective promotional criteria were not compensated for their lack of ability or luck.

Branch managers suffered similarly. Table 3 of appendix 2 reveals that the real incomes of all three groups of managers fell between 1910 and 1920, by 21.8, 20.1, and 26.8 per cent respectively. These figures highlight the dilemma facing younger branch managers in charge of smaller, often only marginally profitable branches. While there was no formal link between branch profitability and salary increases, the all-important inspectorial report system meant that in practice promotion was largely determined by the manager's ability to earn a profit. The relatively static money wages earned by the 1900 intake managers demonstrates this point. It is supported by the editor of a union journal who noted that in earlier years a manager's salary "would depend largely on his luck, but it was no uncommon thing to find managers of fairly large country branches on a salary of £160 to £190 per annum."[47]

Bank officers were also concerned about declines in their salaries relative to other workers. Peverill's claim that he was prepared to work on the wharves, "where I would have been better paid",[48] reflects this. Table 4 of appendix 2 illustrates the extent of this real wage erosion between unskilled workmen, skilled tradesmen, and clerks, accountants, and managers. The nature of the narrowing differential for skill as a result of the non-adjustment of margins for price increases during the war has been discussed elsewhere,[49] and is obvious from a comparison of the second and fourth columns of table 4, where the unskilled worker is seen to increase his real wage considerably in relation to the skilled worker. However, of more immediate interest is the extent to which the real wages of different groups of bank officers declined relative to all blue-collar workers. Table 4 shows that in the period 1910 to 1919, bank clerks, accountants and managers lost salary relativity almost continuously to the unskilled worker. It shows that the largest declines occurred in the latter years of the First World War — so that by 1919 clerks were some 18.2 per cent more disadvantaged than in 1910, accountants 18.9 per cent, and managers 22.3 per cent. The combination of industrial pressure and wage tribunal increases received by unskilled workers was responsible for their improved position. Bank officers, conservative, unorganized, and dominated by management, were unable to do this. Peverill wrote: "It is getting harder every month to make the 'screw' go around; we have to pay the increased cost of living, other classes of workers are getting increased salaries but ours are still the same".[50] Table 4 of appendix 2 also illustrates that in 1918 and 1919 bank employees also lost salary relativity with skilled blue-collar workers, so that even the banks realized that "the salaried and clerical classes [were] now the poorest men in the community".[51]

Loss of purchasing power was the dominant factor in the decision of Peverill and his co-conspirators to risk their careers by trying to form a union. Another factor, and one certainly important to the relatively rapid union growth, was the poor working conditions in the industry. The extent of managerial dominance, geographical dispersion of branches, and the emphasis upon individual branch profitability meant that banking work was frequently conducted under parsimonious and restrictive conditions. There is little documented information available relating to working conditions before union formation, but later union records together with the experiences of bank officers provide many examples of the existence and extent of these poor working conditions. Bank chambers, although apparently grandiose, were in fact often of inferior standard, poorly ventilated, inadequately lit and heated, and lacking even rudimentary fittings and services. Peverill recounts how in 1909, when as a junior officer at the Lancefield branch of the NBA, he ran foul of the bank's auditors. He was commanded to sleep on the cold, dank premises to provide security. The manager suggested he buy a rug and provided half a crown from a branch maintenance account. The payment was later challenged by the auditor and Peverill had to make restitution.[52]

The rural bank manager faced additional problems. Not only was his residence usually of the same poor standard as the banking chamber, but he or one of his staff had to remain on the premises throughout weekends and on bank holidays to provide security. One manager later noted: "Of course it's easy to understand the bank's point of view. Each bank has in round numbers 350 managers guarding premises . . . plus they are saving on the cost of a nightwatchman."[53]

Given the nature of Australian branch banking, there has always been a high degree of staff mobility because of promotion and transfers. As most of these involved movement to and from rural areas, the dislocation, particularly to married officers, was often quite severe. Even though a manager was usually provided with a bank house or a house allowance, he was still disadvantaged, both because of the nature of the bank premises and because the allowance did not cover all housing expenses. Widely spread branches meant most officers spent considerable time travelling. This was invariably carried out in the officer's own time, and without recompense. As an officer wrote: "It is one full day travelling from Burnie, and the only opportunity of getting away from here is in the annual holidays, and four days of that are taken up in travelling."[54]

As the industry was highly labour intensive and salaries were by far the largest operating expense,[55] the bank's foremost desire was to maintain staffing at the lowest possible level consistent with branch operation. With a paucity of relieving and emergency staff, this meant that any shortfall of branch staff because of illness, recreation leave, and even resignations usually had to be borne by the remaining staff. This, coupled with heavy enlistment of bank officers during the First World War, resulted in considerable levels of overtime being worked and the frequent postponement of annual leave.

Another reason for bank clerk dissatisfaction lay in bank policy towards employee provident and fidelity funds. The Provident Fund, to which both banks and employees contributed, was designed to provide a pension for the officer upon retirement. The Fidelity Guarantee Fund, required upon entry to the bank, provided them with some security should the officer default with bank funds. The practice was well established, and there was little employee objection to the actual concept, but conflict frequently arose following the resignation or dismissal of an officer. Under the conditions of the "Individual Agreement", bank officers were not entitled to the return of any contributions made to either of the funds. Given that the banks used their extensive powers of dismissal and retrenchment, this was of some significance. An ex-employee of the CBC, dismissed for "incompetence" in 1924, complained, "I have completed 25 years service, and during that period estimate that I have paid the bank in the vicinity of £200 towards the Provident Fund. They refuse to pay me."[56] Understandably, this practice limited labour mobility, for officers contemplating a new career were constrained not only by the lack of a readily transferable set of skills but by the knowledge that they would also forfeit pension rights and contributions.

These bank conditions and attitudes, then, were an important reason for unionization. "[the BOA] has grown out of the discontent of the staffs . . . that no consideration is shown to any but the select few, and in consequence the majority of the men have lost confidence in the administration."[57] By late 1920 union membership among employees of the CBA was 68 per cent, the highest of all Victorian banks and considerably greater than the overall industry union density rate of 52 per cent.[58] This is attributed to the relatively poorer working conditions endured by officers of this bank.[59] One legacy of the 1890s disaster for the CBA was a preponderence of small, relatively unprofitable country branches servicing a large number of even more scattered agencies,[60] and the low level of expenditure on branch buildings, facilities, and equipment made for poorer working conditions. CBA officers reacted by joining the union to obtain some protection and, they hoped, redress.

With the end of the First World War, large numbers of enlisted officers returned to the branches. Here lay further reasons for the formation of banking unions. First was the effect of a long, enervating war. Robin Gollan has noted in *Revolutionaries and Reformists* that "early enthusiasms gave way to war weariness and the community divided on many matters connected with the war — divisions which lasted to the end of the war and afterwards".[61] This resulted in the spread of an attitude of "getting what you can for yourself". Bank employees were among those who felt harshly treated, and one response was to seek union membership to give voice to the discord apparent in Australian society and also as a means of winning some private advantages. Similarly, there was a growing awareness of the naivety of earlier idealistic thoughts of war's end bringing a new society with a more equitable social and economic structure. An early union leader summarized this disappointment when he asked:

> What has become of all the good resolutions we formed during the war about the better social order which was to arise after the end of it — the improved relations between class and class, the establishment of a genuine partnership in industry between capitalist and workmen . . . Certain it is that, from whatever cause, the atmosphere has changed, and that as far as the two parties in industry are concerned, we are back again in the old feud, the old misunderstandings and recriminations.[62]

However, there were more specific links. The disenchantment of organized labour with the exigencies of wartime conditions was crystallized in the two conscription referenda campaigns and the general strike of 1917.[63] The turmoil of this period was evident in the level of industrial disputes, and in 1919 this figure exceeded five and a half million man-days lost.[64] "Workers were impatient to get . . . the better wages which they regarded as their right after the sacrifices they had been called upon to make."[65] The willingness of unions to use their industrial muscle, particularly in the context of the short-lived post war boom, had made the money wage increases discussed earlier possible. To the extent that these gains were seen by bank officers as the result of union organization and action, this too stiffened the resolve of bank clerks to form a union of their own. Large numbers of bank officers had enlisted for overseas service.[66] Their wartime experiences had made them aware of the often restrictive and limiting nature of bank employment, the frequent monotony, and their relatively small salaries. Upon their return to Australia they were disinclined to accept a continuance of these pre-war employment conditions, and to many, union membership was an obvious, even necessary step.[67] W. J. Brown, general secretary of the large Civil Service Clerical Association in England, describes the effect this way: "The war threw clerical workers into the Army in thousands. Contact with workers from all kinds of industries broadened their outlook. When the war ended they returned full of the spirit of revolt."[68] To some returning officers there was an even more specific need for a union, for they believed they had been penalized by their war service: "I am writing to you on behalf of the A.I.F. men who, like myself, on returning to civil life after four or five years active service, find the men who nobly stayed at home have left us far behind in salary and are occupying the positions we might have filled, had we stayed at home and thus avoided a break in our banking careers."[69]

A further important factor in the development of banking unionism in 1919 was the existence of favourable industrial legislation.[70] A brief outline of this legislation is necessary. Australian compulsory arbitration grew out of a number of debilitating strikes in the 1890s. At the heart of these was the question of trade union legitimacy. Employers, using bargaining power provided by the high level of depression-induced unemployment, crushed the nascent union movement. The public, inconvenienced and worried by this industrial warfare, joined union remnants in a call for some form of government intervention. In following years, as various drafts of the federal constitution were debated, colonial governments established several forms of industrial regulation. This usually included the legitimization of trade unions, the compelling of employers to recognize these, and the establishment of some form of tribunal or regulatory body. A brief examination of the systems developed in Victoria and New South Wales highlights the two major forms of state regulation introduced. By 1896 a set of minimum wage laws had been established in Victoria and the framework of a number of wages boards laid down. These boards, with employee, and government representatives, had the task of setting minimum wage rates and conditions.[71] In New South Wales an Industrial Commission was established in 1901. Heading the tribunal was a Supreme Court judge, with other officiating judges to be nominated by registered industrial unions and employers. This judicial approach was in contrast to that in Victoria, where decisions were to be achieved by a majority vote rather than arbitral decision, since determinations had to be reached through a majority vote. With the exception of Western Australia (where a form of compulsory arbitration had been introduced in 1900), the other states initially followed Victoria's lead and established wages boards. However, by 1912 both Queensland and South Australia had introduced forms of compulsory arbitration.

Meanwhile, efforts were being made to formulate a federal constitution, and by 1898 H. B. Higgins had convinced other delegates that some form of constitutional power was required to control strikes such as shearers and maritime strikes of the 1890s, which lay outside the jurisdiction of a single state. Eventually some support came from the recently formed labour-oriented political groups, and the power to legislate with respect to conciliation and arbitration for the prevention and settlement of industrial disputes extending beyond the limits of any one state, was included as section 51.35 of the federal constitution.

In 1904 the first Conciliation and Arbitration Act was passed establishing the Arbitration Court, consisting initially only of a president, Mr Justice R. E. O'Connor. In contrast to state tribunals, the powers of the new court were seemingly circumscribed. Not only did the issue have to be a genuine dispute and of an industrial nature, but it had to exist simultaneously in more than one state. The court could not make a "common rule" binding on all employees and employers in a particular industry, nor could it hand down a decision that lay outside the boundaries or "ambit" of the original dispute. However, a combination of favourable High Court decisions extending the apparently limited jurisdiction of the court, and the desire of Higgins (who became president in 1907), to expand its activities and influence, meant that the significance of the federal compulsory arbitration system grew rapidly. By 1912 there were seventy-two federally registered unions covering almost 280,000 workers, while at the state level, two hundred unions represented only 150,000 workers.[72]

Encouragement provided by the various sets of legislation stimulated union formation and growth. Between 1891 (when data on trade union membership was first collected in Australia) and 1917, the total number of unions grew from 124 (covering 4.1 per cent of the work force), to 389 (covering 48.7 per cent of the work force).[73] However, unionism was very much confined to blue-collar workers. In the federal sphere only four of the ninety-four registered unions could be classed as white-collar. They covered shop assistants, hospital employees, clerks, and some employees in postal and communications areas and represented less than 2 per cent of total union membership.[74] In New South Wales there were four white-collar unions with 2.7 per cent of total union membership.[75] The only Queensland records available reveal that seven white-collar unions existed,[76] and in 1917, in the South Australian court only one white-collar union with 125 members was registered.[77] In the period between January 1917 and September 1919 (immediately before the first bank union registration), nineteen new unions were registered in the federal sphere. Of these, six were white-collar unions, with 4.6 per cent of total union membership.[78] In New South Wales, of the 213 state registered unions, 10 were in white-collar areas and covered 9.73 per cent of total unionists in that state.[79] In Queensland, of the thirty-six new unions registered only four were from the white-collar areas, and in South Australia there were six registrations including one white-collar union — the Australasian Clerical Association.[80] Overall, the number of unions registered at state and federal levels in the period 1917 to 1919 grew by only five, from 389 to 394, though actual union membership increased by more than 10 per cent.[81] This favourable industrial legislation environment was important to banking unionism, as it was to a number of other white-collar unions. Employers were forced to recognize unions, unionists could not be overtly discriminated against, there was a third-party intervener between the banks and their staff, and the resulting awards were legally enforceable. This legitimization and protection encouraged the development of bank industry unions.

Australian banking unionism was also stimulated by the almost parallel development of bank unions in several other countries. This provided encouragement to Australian bank officers gambling their careers upon successful union formation, and the tactics used by these unions to counter employer attacks upon them were also valuable.

After two abortive attempts, the Bank Officers' Guild (BOG) was formed in England in 1918,[82] and at its first conference it was able to announce that it had seven thousand members.[83] There was some co-operation between the BOG and its fledgling Australian counterparts, and the need to proceed slowly and at all costs avoid antagonizing or frightening potential members was stressed. In a letter to the youthful union in New South Wales the BOG secretary said:

> Naturally great care has to be exercised, for, as you know, bank men for years and years have been bound body and soul to the institution to which they belong . . . There are still many bank men apathetic, and others are afraid of joining in because they think they would be penalized. . . . I sincerely hope that a similar association to ours will be set up, and if you can get the right man, not a firebrand, then things, I am sure, will go well.[84]

White-collar unions in both countries faced similar problems, particularly regarding new members. The BOG's vain attempts to combat the banks' tactic of forming internal staff associations to defuse the union were of value to the BOA when Australian banks attempted the same ploy.[85] The refusal of the English banks to recognize the BOG and the limitations this placed on union effectiveness made Australian union leaders determined to utilize Australian industrial law to the full extent. Of the overseas bank officer associations formed at this time, the BOG was the least militant and the most concerned to preserve its perceived professional status and standing in the eyes of the community. In its first circular, the union described itself as "not a militant union, but a *guild*, conciliatory in its methods and broad enough to take in the whole profession from managers to junior clerks".[86] Although diminishing real wages were, as in Australia, the main reason for union formation,[87] the president of BOG chose an alternative justification: "Believe me, if I thought that the Bank Officers Guild was nothing else than an association for getting more money for you, more bonus, I should not be here. [Cheers] But I do realise that the Bank Officers Guild is becoming a force towards the regeneration of society. [Renewed cheers]."[88] This statement was widely publicized in Australia by union leaders anxious to demonstrate the legitimacy of banking unionism to conservative and wary bank officers.

The Irish Bank Officials Association was formed at the same time as the BOG and had similar difficulties in obtaining recognition. However, their methods were more direct, and following overwhelming membership support for strike action they "convinced the banks to give recognition to the Irish Bank Officers Association as being the authorised spokesmen for the bank officers of Ireland".[89] They were also immediately granted salary increases averaging more than 20 per cent, and a twenty-year salary scale. The Society of South African Bank Officials, formed in 1918, also faced similar employer refusal to recognize the union or negotiate with it. Eventually the society members were forced to strike, an action defended by the society, again in terms that were well reported in Australian bank union journals: "When one heard of a strike, one generally regarded it with horror, but the bank strike was different to all other strikes. Therein was involved something more noble, more ideal than the mere question of money — a principle."[90]

In Canada and New Zealand, unions were also being formed. They too provided support and shared expertise with the Australian union leadership. These overseas events were important, for they came at a time when bank clerk timidity and distaste for organized labour were significant barriers to unionization. It now remained for bank officers prepared to accept union leadership to come forward. Those who did this, the actions they took, and the pressures they faced are discussed in the next chapter.

Notes

1. All these employee organizations were called *associations*. However, as "unionism refers to the presence of an organisation, one of whose aims is to represent members individually or collectively on such matters as pay and conditions of service" (R.M. Blackburn, *Union Character and Social Class* [London: Batsford, 1967], p. 14), the term *union* will be used throughout. At pp. 33–36 Blackburn explores the reasons why many white-collar unions call themselves associations. Of these the desire for respectability and a need to avoid identification with the trade union movement are paramount. Both of these characteristics have been consistent with the behaviour of bank unions. In April 1978, in a long-considered and debated move, the ABOA became the Australian Bank Employees Union (the ABEU). Since the mid-sixties the ABOA had also covered employees in state-owned banks. The employees of the Commonwealth Bank of Australia are covered by a separate union — the Commonwealth Bank Officers' Association (the CBOA).
2. For a fuller discussion of the development of the Australian banking industry, see S.J. Butlin, *Foundations of the Australian Monetary System 1788-1851* (Carlton, Vic.; Melbourne University Press, 1953); R.F. Holder, *Bank of New*

South Wales: A History (Sydney, Angus and Robertson, 1970); S.J. Butlin, *Australia and New Zealand Bank* (London: Longmans Green, 1961); and Geoffrey Blainey, *Gold and Paper* (Melbourne: Georgian House, 1958).

3. Butlin, *Australia and New Zealand Bank*, p. 279.
4. *AIBR* 14, no. 3 (Mar. 1890), p. 63.
5. Butlin, *Australia and New Zealand Bank*, pp. 182-83, 185-88.
6. S.J. Butlin, A.R. Hall, and R.C. White, *Australian Banking and Monetary Statistics, 1817-1945* (Sydney: Reserve Bank of Australia, 1971), p. 343.
7. A.L.G. Mackay, *The Australian Banking and Credit System* (London: P.S. King 1931), p. 99.
8. *AIBR* 12, no. 10 (Oct. 1888): 652.
9. Ibid.
10. Ibid., 17, no. 9 (Sept. 1893): 848.
11. Between 1889 and 1893 export prices had fallen by 25 per cent and import prices by 13 per cent. This converted a surplus on balance of trade of £6,024,000 to a deficit of £6,460,000. *Commonwealth Year Book*, 1901-1910, no. 3, p. 596.
12. Butlin, *Australia and New Zealand Bank*, p. 279.
13. *AIBR* 17, no. 1 (Jan. 1893): 1.
14. Butlin, Hall, and White, *Australian Banking and Monetary Statistics*, p. 534.
15. Butlin, *Australia and New Zealand Bank*, p. 325.
16. *AIBR* 38, no. 12 (Dec. 1914): 139.
17. Ibid., 24, no. 12 (Dec. 1900) and no. 12 (Dec. 1914).
18. For a rigorous analysis of the development of the Commonwealth Bank, see L.F. Giblin, *The Growth of a Central Bank* (Carlton, Vic.: Melbourne University Press, 1951).
19. *AIBR* 44, no. 10 (Oct. 1920): 647.
20. *Bank Officials Journal* 2, no. 5 (May 1922): 7.
21. F.D. Klingender, *The Condition of Clerical Labour in Britain* (London: Martin Lawrence, 1935), p. viii.
22. Ibid., p. 1.
23. E.C. Peverill, in *National Bank Monthly Summary*, December 1976, p. 11.
24. W. De Boos, in *National Bank Monthly Summary*, December 1976, p. 13.
25. *Bank Officials Journal* 2, no. 5 (May 1922): 11.
26. Interview with A.S. McNab, 13 April 1978.
27. Letter to editor, *Bankers Bulletin* 1, no. 4 (May 1920): 4.
28. *Queensland Bank Officer*, 7, no. 4 (Jan. 1927): 9.
29. *NBA Book of Regulations* (Melbourne, 1916), p. 87.
30. *Bankers Bulletin* 1, no. 2 (Mar. 1920): 6.
31. *NBA Book of Regulations*, p. 1.
32. For details, see the *South Australian Bank Officials' Journal (SABOJ)*, February 1929, p. 1361.
33. This principle was restated in a "Circular from Staff Manager NBA to all Bank Employees", circular no. 166, 17 August 1926, held in ABOA archives. See also comments by Justice McCawley in handing down the first Queensland award in early 1920.
34. *Queensland Bank Officer*, July 1941, p. 13.
35. *Bankers Bulletin* 1, no. 4 (May 1920): 13.
36. Klingender sums up how the banks could, however, still obtain sufficient recruits. "A junior clerk in a commercial house starting at 16, 17 or 18 years of age, earns less for his age than, for example, a van boy, influenced perhaps by the hope of future success and certainly employment. He may hope to become manager in turn and is thus content not only to work for a nominal wage for two or three years, but for many years to earn no more than, if as much as, an artisan. As in the legal profession, the eminence of a small minority dazzles the

eyes of a large number whose talents might perhaps have been more profitably directed elsewhere" (Klingender, *Clerical Labour in Britain*, p. 13).

37.   United Clerks Union of New South Wales – Log of Wages and Conditions, copy in BNSW archives.

38.   *Australian Star*, 26 October 1909, p. 3.

39.   CBC circular no. 642, to managers and officers in charge of branches, 1 July 1913, copy in ABOA archives.

40.   *Bankers Bulletin* 2, no. 2 (Mar. 1921): 2.

41.   Letter to editor, *Bankers Bulletin* 1, no. 12 (Jan. 1921): 14.

42.   An explanation of the source of bank officer salary data and the techniques used to analyse this are contained in appendix 2 of J. D. Hill "An Analysis of the Formation and Development of the Australian Bank Officials Association, 1919–1973" (Ph.D. thesis, Monash University, 1980).

43.   *AIBR* 39, no. 12 (Dec. 1915), and *AIBR* 43, no. 12 (Dec. 1919).

44.   S. Bambrick, "Australian Price Levels 1890–1970", *Australian Economic History Review* 13, (Mar. 1973): 57. There were several other (and usually higher) estimates of the rate of inflation. For example, the Australian manager of the Union Bank in telegraphing to London said, "the increase in the cost of living is generally regarded as 125 per cent above pre war level" (telegram no. 2835/7, 8 January 1920, in ANZ archives).

45.   Further explanation for the relatively small real income fall of this youngest group of clerks lay in their receipt of a large increment upon reaching their "first adult year of service", which occurred in 1915 and 1916.

46.   Australian manager of Union Bank to New Zealand inspector, 16 June 1920. The Melbourne manager of the ES&A, in writing to London on 19 February 1920, said, "the real sufferers in Australia are the moderately paid salaried men."

47.   *Bank Officials Journal* 2, no. 10 (Mar. 1923): 1.

48.   Interview with E. C. Peverill, 12 September 1973.

49.   K. Hancock, "The Wages of Workers", *Journal of Industrial Relations* 11, no. 1 (Mar. 1969): 17–38.

50.   Reprinted in the *Australian Bank Officer*, June 1969, p. 3.

51.   Extract from half-yearly report of BNSW assistant inspector, northern Queensland, 31 March 1920, held in BNSW archives.

52.   Interview with E. C. Peverill, 10 October 1973.

53.   *Australian Banker*, 2, no. 30 (Feb. 1927): 22.

54.   Letter in ABOA archives.

55.   For example, in 1913 salaries formed on average 73 per cent of the operating expenses of private banks (*AIBR* 38, no. 4 [Apr. 1914] : 301).

56.   *VCMM*, 16 August 1924, p. 268.

57.   Letter from an ES&A officer to the London general manager, 29 October 1919; in ANZ archives.

58.   Appendix 3 and union records.

59.   This point was made by a number of senior bank officers, including E. C. Peverill (12 Sept. 1973) and A. E. Hore (10 Oct. 1973).

60.   In 1920 the CBA, with forty-six country agencies, operated almost half of the agencies in Victoria (*AIBR* 44, no. 12 [Dec. 1920]).

61.   R. Gollan, *Revolutionaries and Reformists: Communism and the Australian Labor Movement 1920-1955* (Canberra: ANU Press, 1975), p. 1.

62.   *Bankers Bulletin* 2, no. 33 (Nov. 1923): iii.

63.   For discussion on these issues, see I. A. H. Turner, *Industrial Labour and Politics* (Canberra: ANU Press, 1965), especially chapters 3, 4, and 6.

64.   *Commonwealth Labour Report*, no. 10, pp. 140–41; no. 11, pp. 150–51.

65.   H. Radi, "1920–29", in *A New History of Australia*, ed. F. Crowley (Melbourne: Heinemann, 1974), p. 369.

66. Butlin (*Australia and New Zealand Bank*, p. 364) estimates that more than 40 per cent of Bank of Australasia and Union Bank staff enlisted. Blainey in his history of the NBA says: "The staff of the National Bank had an extraordinary record of military achievement. More than five hundred officers enlisted" (p. 280). In the Bank of New South Wales, 793 members enlisted, rather more than 40 per cent of the total staff (Holder, *Bank of New South Wales*, p. 594).

67. Early union leaders Peverill (12 Sept. 1973) and Laidlaw (18 Jan. 1974) both made the point that much of their support came from dissatisfied bank clerks who had recently returned from overseas service.

68. *Clerical Labour in Britain*, p. viii.

69. *Bankers Bulletin* 2, no. 1 (Feb. 1921): 5.

70. For a closer analysis of the Australian industrial legislation, the tribunals formed, and their operations, see H.B. Higgins, *A New Province for Law and Order* (London: Dawson, 1968); B. Healey, *Federal Arbitration in Australia* (Melbourne: Georgian House, 1972); O. de R. Foenander, *Industrial Regulation in Australia* (Carlton, Vic.: Melbourne University Press, 1965); J.H. Portus, *The Development of Australian Trade Union Law* (Carlton, Vic.: Melbourne University Press, 1958): E.I. Sykes and H.J. Glasbeek, *Labour Law in Australia* (Sydney: Butterworths 1972).

71. J.M. Fristacky, "Collective Bargaining, Conciliation and Arbitration in Victorian Wages Boards", *Journal of Industrial Relations* 18, no. 4 (Dec. 1976): 309–25, analyzes the development of wages boards in Victoria.

72. *Labour Report*, no. 2, Commonwealth Bureau of Census and Statistics, Melbourne, July 1913, pp. 11 and 16.

73. K.F. Walker, *Australian Industrial Relations Systems* (Melbourne: Oxford University Press, 1970), pp. 46–47.

74. Federal industrial registrar's files, 1917.

75. New South Wales industrial registrar's files.

76. Queensland industrial registrar's files.

77. South Australian industrial registrar's files.

78. Federal industrial registrar's files, 1917 and 1919.

79. New South Wales industrial registrar's files and *New South Wales Year Book 1923*, p. 389.

80. Queensland and South Australian industrial registrars' files. The Queensland union registration figures are artificially inflated by a change in legislation which required some unions to reregister.

81. Walker, *Australian Industrial Relations Systems*, p. 46.

82. Blackburn, *Union Character and Social Class*, p. 132, discusses the formation and development of the BOG.

83. *Bankers Bulletin* 1, no. 10 (Nov. 1920): 24.

84. Letter from J.R. Hannan to Sydney Smith, 10 July 1919, reproduced in *Bankers Bulletin* 1, no. 2 (Mar. 1920): 14.

85. Blackburn, *Union Character and Social Class* pp. 140–46, discusses the successful development of internal guilds in opposition to the BOG.

86. BOG first circular, reproduced in Klingender, *Clerical Labour in Britain*, p. 33.

87. Blackburn, *Union Character and Social Class*, p. 134 says: "By the end of 1917 the cost of living was 85 per cent above the 1914 level, and in the following year this increased to 120 per cent, but no bank was paying more than a 20 per cent bonus on 1914 salaries, and not all were paying this."

88. President of BOG to second annual meeting of BOG. Reprinted in *Bankers Bulletin* 1, no. 9 (Oct. 1920): 17.

89. Reprinted in *Bankers Bulletin* 1, no. 3 (Apr. 1920): 11.

90. From *South African Banking Magazine*, reprinted in *Bankers Bulletin*, 2, no. 2 (Mar. 1921): 21.

2   Some Early Tentative Union Actions

(To the music of the Anglo-French classic, "Inky Pinky Parlez Vous")

Who was it made our prospects bright?	B.O.A.!
Who was it fought a winning fight?	B.O.A.!
It banished the days when hearts were sad,	
And debts depressed us, and times were bad!	
So here's good luck to B.O.A.!	
Who was it formed this brotherhood?	B.O.A.!
Who was it made our jobs seem good?	B.O.A.!
Enabled the bachelor, unafraid,	
To pluck up his courage and wed a maid,	
To raise recruits for B.O.A.!	
Who is it bids us hope for more?	B.O.A.!
Better than ever we had before?	B.O.A.!
No more dodging our creditors then,	
We'll pay spot cash like gentlemen,	
Thanks to the good old B.O.A.!	
What can we do to help along	The B.O.A.?
How can we make it firm and strong,	The B.O.A.?
By getting each man in all the banks,	
To pay his dues and join the ranks,	
And "do his bit" for B.O.A.!	

[*Australian Banker* 1, no. 9 (Oct. 1928): 8]

By early 1919 some clerks had secretly, even fearfully, begun discussing the possibility of union formation. Within two years, Victorian officers had formed and registered a union in the federal Arbitration Court and separate unions had developed in New South Wales, Queensland, South Australia, and Western Australia. In this chapter the formation and early tentative years of the BOA are discussed, along with important events in other state unions.

The Birth of the BOA

In 1917 E. C. Peverill wrote to the NBA general manager from Nhill complaining that he was unable to provide for his family on his present salary, and asking what he must do to obtain an increase. He was immediately dressed down by a bank inspector and told "his request was not even considered, and his letter crude and indiscreet".[1] Over the next twelve months Peverill, frustrated and disillusioned, began hesitantly to consider unionism as a counter to the bank's seeming limitless power. Many years later he wrote: "I really thought I was taking my job in my hands when I suggested starting a union . . . but I always said to everyone that I had nothing to lose because as things stood my job was not paying me enough to bring up a family."[2] In mid-1918 he was transferred to Kew. For the first time he was able to discuss his idea with other clerks.

The following April, Peverill and six other NBA clerks met secretly and made plans to recruit clerks from other banks. Over the next months, and choosing their confidants carefully, they drew together a small band of bank employees prepared to form some type of union. Some legal expertise was needed, for none had even a rudimentary knowledge of industrial law. Peverill later confessed that after an early meeting had resolved to register in the Victorian Arbitration Court it was discovered there was no state arbitration. But who could they turn to for advice? They felt no affinity with other white-collar unions, and an approach to the legal profession would probably be reported to the banks. Finally W. Warrington Rogers, solicitor and uncle of one of the officers, agreed to assist. Furtive recruiting continued, and in July 1919 a group of 145 officers attended another meeting. After Rogers had outlined existing federal and state industrial legislation, the meeting agreed to seek federal registration, which seemed to offer better prospects than the Victorian wages board system.[3] Also the wages board procedure was for personal representation and face-to-face negotiation with management: where would the union find officers willing and able to confront senior bankers? There was also a belief that the Arbitration Court would be more generous.[4]

It remained to draw up rules, recruit more members, and appoint an executive. So far the banks were unaware of what was afoot, but union registration would alert them. Registration required the appointment of a president, but what officer would accept this position? Peverill chanced to meet Meredith Atkinson, head of the Department of Sociology at Melbourne University, a frequent commentator on Australian social and economic affairs and author of two books in which his sympathy for workers and their need to organize was clear.[5] Though he had little understanding of the realities of industrial relations and in his four years of office rarely attended meetings, he did provide respectability, legitimacy, and prestige for the fledgling union. Peverill was referring to this when he said: "It was a great help to the Association in its struggling youthful days to have a man of the professor's type and ability at the helm."[6] At the next meeting in September, 230 bank officers agreed to form "an Association open to all employees, in or in connection with the industry of banking in Australia . . . and that the said Association be called 'The Bank Officials Association'".[7] Atkinson was elected president, Rogers vice-president,[8] and Peverill secretary, and a committee was appointed. Peverill recognized the strong conservatism of most present and emphasized the union's conciliatory approach. The union would have "no strikes, would abide by the Arbitration Court, maintain effective administration and discipline in the industry of banking, and have no affiliation with other bodies".[9]

Peverill was anxious to obtain Arbitration Court protection. Next morning he presented the association's new rules to the industrial registrar along with a list of members. But here lay the seeds of disaster, for the registrar queried the union's federal basis as all members were from Melbourne. Peverill hastily recruited three interstate clerks, one each in Tasmania, South Australia, and New South Wales, and reapplied for registration.

There were eight objections to registration. The first, from the Australasian Clerical Association (ACA), claimed the right to cover branch officers. The BOA committee protested that a "clerks union" could not adequately represent bank employees, and further, "the ACA — a Trades Hall body — is opposing registration but we have no intention of linking up with the Trades Hall".[10] The seven other objectors came from the seven major banks and provided extensive and identical grounds of objection.[11] In a letter to the *Argus,* Rogers criticized these officers and accused them of being tools of the banks.[12] A lively correspondence ensued. In contention was the representativeness of the membership, bona fides of objectors, and whether the banks were trying to ease the burden of the rapidly rising rate of inflation. One of the objectors, F. McNaughton, concluded his letter with the veiled threat that was to become so familiar. "Many privileges and conditions we now enjoy will be lost if once it comes to a hard and fast contract under terms laid down by the Arbitration Court."[13] The banks, particularly those based in London, while steadfastly opposed to the new union, were generally careful not to criticize it publicly.[14] The BOA committee was concerned at this opposition, and informal approaches were made to the banks to determine whether concessions could be obtained without going to court. There is also a suggestion that some committeemen were willing to trade off registration in return for salary increases. Peverill, however, recognized the shortsightedness of this: "After the success of the September meeting there is no way that the BOA can be stopped . . . we have decided to proceed with registration as soon as possible."[15]

The die was cast, and the committee decided on an all-out recruiting drive. Peverill and Rogers travelled to Ballarat and Geelong, and the first country sub-branches, later a feature of BOA organization, were formed. Advertisements for members were placed in the press as the union publicly advertised their existence for the first time.[16] At a large meeting in late

November, Peverill and Atkinson confirmed the union's conservative nature. Peverill said, "Good conditions would promote efficiency and loyalty to the managements. We are not contemplating direct action", and Atkinson added, "The BOA are not out to make things hot for the managements, but to secure rights which as individuals they have been denied."[17] The membership drive was given impetus when on 20 December 1919 the registrar overruled all objections and granted registration. The union now had 474 Victorian members and one each from Tasmania, South Australia, and New South Wales[18] – truly a federal body!

It was already plain that the refusal of many senior officers to join the union was a significant constraint on membership growth. This was worrying to the union, for they were particularly anxious to recruit branch managers who had such control and influence over their staff. In early 1920, with fewer than 10 per cent of managers unionized,[19] The BOA invited all city and suburban managers to attend a special meeting. Less than 25 per cent of them came and spent most of the meeting wrangling over drawing up a set of claims for senior officers and complaining at the implications of the proposed claim for clerks. While part of this reluctance was based on a belief that union membership was inconsistent with their positions in the bank, there was another pragmatic reason for this unwillingness to join: "Senior men are hanging back under the impression that an award will not increase their salaries, but should they see in the near future that other older men are participants in the salary rises, they will be very eager to join up."[20]

An even more immediate problem was the hostility of the Australian-owned banks.[21] An example of this was the formation of internal staff guilds, which had been successful in minimizing the growth and influence of the BOG. This had been a result of the employers' open encouragement, coupled with the bank officers' perception of his near management role, for "internal guilds have a larger membership since many capable men hesitate to join a body not sanctioned by the directors".[22] NBA general manager E. H. Wreford was aware of this when he wrote to his staff recommending membership of the NBA Officers' Club, guaranteeing "sympathetic and favourable consideration" and offering to meet any club expenses.[23] Peverill immediately authorized the insertion of an advertisement that asked: "Bank Clerks, Are You Awake to your Own Interests? Can you exist on empty promises? Join the Bank Officials Association and begin to live."[24] The inference was clear and the meeting to launch the club was poorly attended, apart from Peverill and a number of BOA members who nominated him for the committee. The chairman refused this nomination, and the BOA members left. A committee was eventually elected, but its lack of representativeness limited its role to a purely social one. A further reason for the success of English staff associations lay in the limitation of that country's industrial legislation,[25] where employers were not compelled to recognize unions. Consequently the banks negotiated with their house associations rather than the BOG and understandably encouraged the development of the former. The BOG secretary ruefully noted: "An internal guild is really of no use whatsoever, for in a difference of opinion between the staff and the directors, the directors views must prevail . . . Place recognition as a just plank in your platform. By recognition only, can the problems of banking employment really receive just and scientific treatment."[26] Australian unions were never seriously threatened by internal staff guilds, for both federal and state industrial legislation forced employers to recognize unions and either to negotiate or to proceed to arbitration.[27]

The banks were successful in inhibiting union growth in other ways, however. Given the crucial nature of staff inspector reports, there was some fear that union membership might adversely affect this report. As one union secretary reported, "In a bank where the membership is very low we made inquiries and found that they were afraid to join, and two instances were quoted. They were firstly, that a branch manager had warned a junior from joining; secondly that a vacancy was under review carrying promotion, and the officer who was entitled to it was a member and this had been mentioned by the inspector to the management."[28] Fear of retribution was strong. A further statement from Wreford could only have confirmed the doubts of some already apprehensive officers. He warned his staff that the BOA would "promote discord, unpleasantness and hostility, where the best interests of all would be better served by an atmosphere of friendliness, goodwill and general co-operation, conditions which are more likely to be promoted by the NBA Officers Club rather than by the Clerks Association."[29] Suspicions of bank discrimination and pressure were also raised by the knowledge that of the fourteen original committeemen only four remained twelve months later. Six had resigned entirely from the BOA, and the other four had been transferred to country branches in shifts that were not consistent with normal career patterns.

By mid-1920 the BOA was tenaciously established in the banking industry. Despite bank attempts to discourage membership, some 1,264, or 44 per cent, of Victorian officers, mostly younger clerks, had joined.[30] The next goal was to win salary increases. Before discussing this, it is necessary to review briefly the formation of other state banking unions.

Union Formation in Other States

The BOA's early development was relatively smooth compared with events in New South Wales. In early 1919, ten officers of the Bank of Australasia had met in Sydney to discuss their increased work loads and rapidly falling purchasing power. Agreeing that some organized action was needed, they invited the secretary of the New South Wales Division of the ACA to the next meeting. He addressed officers from four banks but could not cajole them into joining his union. Instead, they approached Sydney Smith, secretary of the Railways and Tramways Officers Association, who agreed to help form a union and obtain state registration. In May 1919 a meeting attended by officers from all the major banks formed the UBOA of NSW. Commenting on this a year later, the *Bankers Bulletin* reported on the implications of the meeting's attitude of moderation:

> It is hardly possible that any association of men was ever launched with such a unanimous desire to approach the employers in a fair minded, gentlemanly spirit; there being no stop work meetings, no red flag, no explosive bombs, no talk of strike, and no bitterness of any sort (applause). The directors of the Banking Companies were thought to be gentlemen, and as such they were to be asked to make advances in the salaries of the officers, so that they might be enabled to maintain their families in reasonable decency; but alas, time proved that the stop work system was one that would have commanded more respect.[31]

Smith warned of the dangers of meekness, which meant "starvation screws and the aroma of genteel poverty".[32]

As with the Victorians, the burning question was what bank employee would risk his career by accepting the office of president? Harold Crawford, an inspector with the New South Wales Railways, was eventually persuaded to accept, though like Atkinson he was largely a figurehead. Smith became general secretary, an appointment crucial to the development of all Australian banking unions for the next decade. Ambitious and egotistical, he was a skilled court advocate extensively versed in industrial legislation, and already a "white-collar union entrepreneur" of some note. A senior Australian banker gave warning of Smith's involvement: "The Secretary of the Association, a Mr. Sydney Smith (not a bank official, nor has he ever been connected with banks), is regarded as an extremist, and unfortunately he appears to exercise a considerable influence in the association which will be difficult to combat."[33]

Again the local banks actively opposed the union's formation, and this culminated in the BNSW's dismissal of H. F. Rawson, one of the union's initiators. The bank, having heard of Rawson's involvement, transferred him to their Dubbo branch. On querying this, he was told that his latest staff reports were most unfavourable and a change of branch was necessary. These adverse reports were in sharp contrast to those of his previous twenty years of service, and Rawson felt sure his union activity was the real reason for his transfer.[34] He refused to transfer and in September 1919 was dismissed. This ruthless attitude of the BNSW, the largest and most powerful Australian bank, had a significant impact on union membership. An inspector wrote: "We do not think any member of this Division has joined the United Bank Officers Association of Queensland ... If it would have been any use, a petition asking that the Bank of New South Wales be excluded from any award of the Court would have been signed by 95 per cent of the members of our staff, at any rate in North Queensland."[35] The union, as yet unregistered, could offer Rawson little help. Smith wrote to the bank, but his appeal was rejected out of hand.[36] Clearly registration and hence access to the Court of Industrial Arbitration was vital to any successful union action, and in the interim Rawson became a paid union official.[37]

By September 1919 union membership stood at more than eight hundred but registration was proving difficult, with the BNSW and the CBC objecting strenuously. Officers from these banks were so wary of victimization and reprisals that the state industrial registrar agreed not to force the union to disclose the names of members from either bank. Then rejecting a claim that the UBOA of NSW was not a bona fide union of "workmen", he granted registration. In April 1920 the two banks and the ACA successfully appealed against this decision,[38] though the registrar indicated that only minor rule changes were required to achieve registration. The following month the UBOA of NSW convened a special conference to amend their rules and reapplied for registration. The original objectors were now joined by the other banks, who claimed that the union was not a legitimate representative of bank employees because the key personnel, Smith and Crawford, were not bank officers. The registrar refused the appeal and in granting registration commented:

> It was stated by the Bank's counsel that the General Secretary is really a promoter of the union . . . and that the Association is due to his initiative . . . I am satisfied that the Secretary's connection with the Association is a result of an invitation to him to accept that position, and to help towards foundation . . . I am satisfied that the officers are under the control of the Association . . . and I cannot now say that the present appointments make the association other than a bona fide one.[39]

On 19 July 1920, after twelve months of bitter and expensive conflict, the UBOA of NSW was finally registered. Though the banks appealed yet again, Smith was confident enough to plan a huge celebration dinner attended by more than two thousand bank officers and state political leaders. These latter invitations illustrated Smith's attempts to exploit the sympathies of the new state Labor government. These political approaches were in sharp contrast to the BOA's apolitical stance and resulted from Smith's determination to carve out a career in union advocacy, for which favourable industrial legislation was important. The early UBOA of NSW experiences had convinced him that political support was needed to offset the banks' influence and dominance. Also, whereas the BOA was faced with a conservative federal government, the New South Wales union could expect some support from the Labor Party when in power.

Later in 1920 the union held its second conference. With registration secured and fears of victimization somewhat reduced, Crawford resigned as president and was replaced by James Nicholas, manager of a suburban

BNSW branch. Smith's stratagem succeeded when he was offered the full-time secretary's position. The employment terms he insisted on indicate his dominance over the executive and his calculated determination to advance his own interests: "A minimum salary of £550 . . . the right to claim 35½ hours per week to be worked during such times as he considers wise; three weeks annual leave, and all public holidays; the right to private practice in Court or before Tribunals; to hold office with any other body and that his position be a permanent one."[40] He concluded by magnanimously declaring that "he would not accept the position of secretary to any other Association without telling the executive".[41] Union membership was stimulated by Smith's willingness to confront the banks.[42] By June 1920 the union had 2,017 members, more than 65 per cent of New South Wales' private bank employees.[43] Two other union actions had also helped. In late 1920 the union obtained an interim award guaranteeing minimum adult rates[44] and a bank promise to expedite a full award hearing.

Early in 1921 Smith instituted a case for Rawson's reinstatement.[45] After exhaustively examining the evidence, Judge Thomas Rolin ordered Rawson's reinstatement. In his scathing condemnation of the BNSW's actions he said:

> I find that Hilder, the Metropolitan Inspector, did in April 1919, warn, and in effect, threaten, Rawson that his connection with the formation of an association of bank clerks might get him into trouble. . . . I find that the conduct of all the officers of the bank concerned in the removal of Rawson was of such a character as might have then, and may now, reasonably raise a strong suspicion in the minds of his fellow employees that Rawson was being punished for his conduct in promoting the Association, and the conduct of those officers does establish a precedent which the employees of the bank feel, and reasonably feel, is prejudicial to them: and I find that Rawson's connection with formation of the Association was in fact the real, though indirect, cause of his ultimate dismissal.[46]

At a time when banks and their managers were seen as veritable pillars of society and bastions of immaculately conservative and fastidious financial empires, these were strong words indeed. Indeed, they brought the considerable wrath of the Establishment upon the union's head, much of this through the columns of Sydney's daily press. On numerous occasions Smith protested at the "gross impropriety" and the "inaccuracy of reports" and warned his members of the "partisan nature of Sydney's news rags".[47]

In New South Wales and in other states where it was widely reported, the Rawson case result removed much of the fear that had accompanied union membership. It also proved to employers that registration did provide considerable protection and that the traditional employer–

employee relationship had irretrievably changed. Rolin confirmed this in his concluding remarks:

> If however, this Court can — as I hold it can — look at other considerations than those which may be looked at in the other Courts, then in my opinion this Court is entitled to look at the whole circumstances of the case. If it were otherwise, an employer could always act in this fashion with regard to an employee of whom he wished to get rid of. Assume a case in which an employer desired to punish an employee for his connection with unionism: instead of dismissing the employee, he degrades him — that is to say, removes him from a higher to a lower position in his service, and on the employee refusing to accept the change, dismisses him. If the argument urged is right, the Court would be powerless.[48]

UBOA of NSW membership swelled further, and Smith found it easier to gather evidence for the coming award hearing, which was to be the first significant arbitration case conducted by any bank union.

Registration of a bank officer union actually occurred first in Queensland in September 1919 and was largely due to the endeavours of one man, K. H. Laidlaw.[49] Since joining the Queensland National Bank (QNB) in 1903, Laidlaw had worked in various country districts where he saw unionism at work. In 1907, during a shearers' strike, he met an AWU organizer. Excited by the possibilities, he joined the union and asked the organizer to apply to have the QNB pay him AWU award rates. The bank's reaction was swift; resign from the union or the bank, and Laidlaw chose the former. In 1914 he again suggested unionization, this time as members of the ACA, and again the bank issued its ultimatum.

In 1919 he was transferred back to Brisbane on a salary of £190 a year. Thirty, yet unable to marry because of the "marriage ban", he resolved to try once more. Laidlaw was now fully aware of the possibility of dismissal, yet the alternative of declining purchasing power and a dictatorial employer was equally bleak. After informal discussion, the state industrial registrar revealed that a registration application needed twenty signatures. Laidlaw drew up a set of rules based on those of a public service union and invited twenty-two bank clerks to a secret meeting. Conscious that an invalid registration application would jeopardize the jobs of his co-conspirators, Laidlaw invited V. A. C. Partridge, secretary of the Public Service Association. The rules were confirmed and the following morning the application lodged and quickly approved by the industrial registrar. The choice of state court registration was simple. "State applications could be heard in a matter of weeks," he recalled in 1974, "whereas in the federal court it took months before you could get into court. Also, the Victorians were having a great deal of trouble because the banks were able to employ senior counsel to appear against them, whereas in Brisbane I only had to combat industrial advocates." Bank employees flocked to join the UBOA of Q. In Laidlaw's branch, all but one of the sixty-five staff had joined within three days, and in a week more than five hundred Brisbane officers were members. On the morning following news of the union's registration, Laidlaw's branch manager issued yet another ultimatum — withdraw the application or be dismissed. This time Laidlaw refused and was sacked, only to be quickly reinstated once the bank realized that he had the state court's protection.

The next step was to seek an award. As this was the first award for Australian bank officers and contained several important precedents, it warrants brief discussion. Laidlaw and Partridge drew up a claim for a fourteen-year salary scale, a classification system for senior officers,[50] extensive allowances, and recreational and sick leave. The banks responded by seeking to restrict the claims to clerks earning less than three hundred pounds a year, limiting the scale to eight years, and deleting classification. This impasse resulted in the case coming before the Queensland Industrial Court in March 1920. This tribunal, headed by Justice T.W. McCawley, was considerably influenced by the Theodore Labor government, and the banks' disquiet was increased by McCawley's introductory statement:

> It is curious that this should occur in institutions whose business is so intimately concerned with the inflated currency. The financial condition of the banks is not such as to justify the failure to pay reasonable salaries. Notwithstanding the competition of the Commonwealth Bank, their disclosed net profits have doubled since 1906 and their capital and reserve funds have increased by 30 per cent.[51]

He declined to include a classification system, but warned the banks that if they did not grant substantial increases to senior officers he would welcome a further union approach. The banks, anxious to avoid classification, hastily agreed to this.[52] Allowances were brought into line with the Public Service and maximum weekly hours fixed. Confirming the banks' worst fears about interfering industrial tribunals, McCawley volunteered: "Seeing all would benefit by the award, don't you think it would be better that all should join the union. . . . even if you made membership compulsory what harm would it do to the banks?"[53] The banks disagreed, claiming this would allow the unions to engage whom they pleased, irrespective of ability or service. These award terms were an important victory, not only for the UBOA of Q but for other unions contemplating award applications. Though other courts would be less favourably disposed to organized labour, the gains made and the apparent lack of victimization of clerks involved was heartening. Understandably, many bank officers had until now contemplated membership with some trepidation. The union's journal noted: "Before this, anyone taking an active part in union affairs was a marked man, and injured his prospects for advancement."[54]

In early 1920 Laidlaw became full-time secretary of the UBOA of Q. His earlier skirmishes and damning evidence before Judge McCawley had made his bank job untenable. "My days were numbered in the bank," he recalled in 1977, "and rumours kept flying that I was to be promoted to a country branch to get rid of me." In the next few years Laidlaw used his rapidly accumulating expertise to organize and register unions in several other white-collar areas, including nursing, insurance, and commercial travelling. His continued rejection of Trades Hall overtures, a determinedly apolitical, pragmatic, and often expedient stance, was attractive to conservative white-collar groups. Even his lack of legal qualifications was an asset, for it allowed him to appear before the State Industrial Court while legal counsel was prohibited.

In South Australia, bank officer union development lagged behind the eastern states. Eventually Peverill and Rogers, anxious to confirm the BOA's interstate nature by recruiting South Australian officers, contacted a number of Adelaide officers, and a few joined in early 1920. Later that year a branch of the BOA was formed,[55] and again the organizers were forced to look to an outsider, E. G. Heal, a public accountant, as president. Peverill continued as secretary, and Henry Heaton, an economics lecturer at Adelaide University, became vice-president. Within two months, membership, encouraged by Queensland events, was more than six hundred. Employees of the Savings Bank of South Australia (SBSA), a state-owned bank whose salaries and conditions were inferior even to those of the private banks, were to the fore.[56] This was in contrast to Victoria, where BOA rules did not allow the recruitment of State Savings Bank officers.

Peverill also made the first moves towards union formation in Western Australia when he wrote to L. B. Fox suggesting he recruit Perth bankers for the BOA.[57] In December 1919 Fox and five other clerks met and discussed union formation with James Payne, secretary of the Postal Officials Union. Recruiting was difficult, and it was not until July 1920 that 250 clerks met and agreed to form the Western Australian branch of the Australian Bank Officials' Federation (BOF).[58] Fox had the foresight to invite three leading Perth citizens to attend. Dr A. J. H. Saw, a member of the state's upper house, was elected president, Dr J. S. Battye, the state librarian, and A. J. Hardwick, a prominent accountant, became vice-presidents, and Fox became secretary. Saw was merely a figurehead until his resignation in 1928, but Battye became an influential union figure for many years. Again these outsiders provided much-needed legitimacy. "The mere fact that these gentlemen are willing and have associated themselves with our Association and expressed themselves in sympathy with its aims and objectives is surely proof enough that these aims and objects are founded on high and right minded principle."[59] They were also, perhaps mistakenly, seen as "carrying some weight with the banks".[60]

As in Victoria and New South Wales, there was some bank antagonism. Fox eventually buckled under continued bank pressure and in June 1921 stepped down in favour of W. Y. Cooke, a local accountant and former banker. Queensland secretary Laidlaw mentioned Fox's invidious position when announcing Cooke's appointment. "All the states now have Secretaries who are beyond the hand of victimisation."[61] Preston also recounts how, on the morning following the first public meeting, he was called before the general manager of the BNSW in Perth and told that if he valued his promotion in the service he should resign from the association and have nothing more to do with it. However, word of the Queensland successes eventually filtered through, and union membership grew steadily. In late 1921, as a result of the banks' refusal to continue to pay federal rates, and growing dissatisfaction with the BOA's now clearly incompetent leadership,[62] the union obtained registration in the state court.

As noted earlier, Tasmanian bank officer unionization resulted from the BOA's need to satisfy the interstate requirements of federal registration. As a result, the branch was run from Melbourne, and little thought was given to the needs of Tasmanian members. In early 1921, however, the BOA committee, reluctantly responding to rumours of discontent among these members and also to an abortive attempt by the Australasian Clerical Association to obtain a wages board determination for Tasmanian bank officers, agreed to the appointment of E. A. Brooke, a part-time accountant, as branch secretary.

Later in the year, Rogers visited the island and spoke at a number of meetings, one of which was chaired by the mayor of Launceston. Already the branch had 190 members, a reflection of Brooke's enthusiasm and preparedness to spend time organizing. Over the next few years, this enthusiasm, fuelled by the BOA's agreement to pay him ten shillings for every officer enrolled, was to allow the branch to achieve high rates of unionization. Certainly the Victorians showed little interest in Tasmanian events, at least in part daunted by thoughts of the sea voyage across Bass Strait.

The First Agreement and Its Aftermath

Bank Officers are apt to forget the remarkable influence of the BOA in forcing the banks to raise salaries so exceptionally in 1919 and 1920. Bonuses were also given freely in order to show liberality. Feverish haste was made in some banks to readjust and raise salaries so as to prevent exposure of the low remuneration to bank officers.[63]

By late 1920 almost half of all Victorian bank officers were in the BOA (see appendix 3). A reflection of the union's diligent recruiting was that more than 70 per cent of bank employees were in rural areas and so more difficult to unionize (see appendix 1). Initially circulars outlining unionization benefits had been sent to all branches, and this was followed up with the formation and encouragement of a sub-branch network. In urban areas this was on a bank institution basis, while in the country, sub-branches were established in major provincial towns.

One factor encouraging unionization was the BOA's pressing for improved salaries. Earlier in the year a log of claims had been drawn up by the executive in conjunction with a branch managers' committee and a bank messengers' representative.[64] The claims included an eighteen-year scale, rudimentary classification system, reduced hours of work, overtime payment, and annual leave. A twelve-year scale for females was included as an afterthought, to ensure that males would not be replaced by lower-paid females.[65] The banks rejected all these claims, and the BOA applied to Arbitration Court president Higgins for a compulsory conference. In August 1920 the BOA delegation, led by T. C. Maher,[66] met the banks' staff inspectors. The BOA had also made the claim on behalf of their South Australian branch and encountered trouble when the SBSA refused to attend the conference, claiming they could not be covered by an Arbitration Court award. Justice Higgins directed the union to have the jurisdiction issue determined in the High Court, but Maher was reluctant. He convinced the impatient Victorians this would delay salary increases, and outraged SBSA officers by summarily jettisoning them by reducing the claim's coverage. The day after the conference Maher and Bank of Australasia staff inspector George Healey reached amicable and swift agreement on terms somewhat less than the Queensland award. A fourteen-year male scale starting at £75 and rising to £300 and an eight-year female scale running from £65 to £160 were established. Weekly hours were fixed at forty, though staff could be asked to work an extra four hours without overtime. Clerks with less than ten years service were to receive two weeks annual leave and longer-serving officers three weeks. These terms were submitted to the court for certification, but Higgins refused, arguing that clause 5, which allowed the banks to pay less than award rates to officers they deemed inefficient, was inimical to bank officers' interests. Ever anxious to protect and expand the court's influence, Higgins claimed, "This means simply that the bank is at liberty to go back to individual contract again with the individual employee."[67] Eventually, under strong persuasion from Maher, and disclaiming any responsibility, he certified the agreement.

Tables 1, 2, and 3 of appendix 2 indicate the significance of the agreement's impact upon salaries, and in the euphoria that followed its announcement, the limitations and omissions were briefly obscured. The banks, however, had read it more closely. As one general manager wrote: "It will be seen that most of the objectionable clauses in the 'log' have been removed. It will also be noted that several wholesome provisions safeguarding the banks have been embodied. . . . On the whole I am satisfied with the arrangement that has been made and other banks have also expressed themselves as quite satisfied."[68]

Though the banks were soon to regret their ready agreement to the introduction of an incremental scale, they were not very perturbed by the salary increases. "Substantial as the increases appear I am convinced that they do not represent an unreasonable remuneration to the staff in view of the steadily increasing wages awarded by the Arbitration Courts and Wages Boards."[69] This rather sanguine acceptance was also based on a knowledge that they could readily recoup extra salary expenses. Earlier in the year the same manager had informed London: "I do not anticipate any difficulty in being able to increase our interest rate accordingly, even if all the demands in the log are granted."[70] They had also avoided the imposition of a classification system, under clause 5 had retained control over salaries of "inefficient" officers and could still use bonus payments to discriminate between staff.[71] They were also pleased the issue had not been arbitrated. Not only had an unseemly court appearance been avoided, but the agreement's terms were "probably more moderate than would have been obtained had the dispute been heard in open court".[72] The agreement only covered BOA members, but the banks paid the new rates to all their staffs. "To have placed members of the Association – under compulsion – on a better footing than others of the staff would have been a direct incentive to join the Association."[73]

How did bank officers fare from their first tussle with the banks? Tables 1, 2, and 3 of appendix 2 summarize salary situations before and after September 1920. A striking feature of table 1 is the increase in clerks' real wages, a result of significant money wage increases and a reduced rate of price increases. In 1920 real wages of the 1890 intake increased by 5 per cent and the 1900 recruits by 17 per cent. These clerks, having now been in the banks' employ for more than twenty years, were not even covered by the new scale. Their salary increases were a result of the larger increases granted to young clerks on the scale which effectively pushed up the whole industry salary structure. This occurred because of the banks' need to avoid anomalous salary situations with their accompanying declines in morale and productivity. The salary increases of the youngest clerks illustrate the impact of the new scale. Their money wages increased more than 28 per cent between 1919 and 1921 and purchasing power by more than 53 per cent.[74] Table 2 shows significant real and money wage increases for all three groups of accountants. The 1880 intake's real wage increase of nearly 20 per cent was lower because many of these officers, considered by the banks to be mediocre, had been denied promotion and received smaller salary increases. Salaries of the three groups of managers in table 3 again all show significant real and money wage increases. Money wages between 1919 and 1921 increased by an average of almost 20 per cent. Without any classification system, this too resulted from scale increases pushing up the floor of the industry's wage structure.

Ostensibly, the agreement was most successful. Closer analysis, however, reveals problems that were to lead to considerable conflict within the union and would limit its effectiveness. These centred on the relative salary improvements of younger officers, both within occupational groupings and more importantly between them, as accountants and managers saw their historical salary advantage eroded by the clerks' gains. This, plus the early abandonment of classification, the existence of clause 5,[75] and the satisfaction with which the banks accepted its terms, indicate that the agreement was in fact a poor one. Why had Maher been able to conclude it so hastily and with such glaring inadequacies? Certainly the union had wanted to avoid a court appearance and delay and expense that might be involved. Maher, like Sydney Smith in New South Wales, believed that an upsurge in white-collar union growth was imminent and that astute, successful "white-collar entrepreneurs" would be keenly sought after.[76] Certainly Smith and Maher were right on the first score, for between December 1920 and the end of 1922 the number of white-collar unions registered at the federal level grew to twenty-nine (19.3 per cent of the total), representing 16.3 per cent of total union members.[77] Similarly in New South Wales the number of registered white-collar unions had doubled to twenty (10.4 per cent of the total), with white-collar union members forming 13.6 per cent of total union membership.[78] In both Queensland and South Australia the number of white-collar unions also increased, by five in the former and three in the latter.[79] So Maher's eagerness is understandable, and his domination of the BOA executive made his unilateral action possible. For a time he must have congratulated himself on his tactics. Within a few months he had been appointed BOA secretary (replacing the inept F.P. Naylor) and had also become secretary of the newly formed Municipal Officers Association.

Maher's glibness had not hidden the agreement's inadequacies from the other bank unions, who now feared its impact on the decisions of their own state courts. In New South Wales it was caustically described as:

Of a very bad odour blown over the border by an illwind. . . . In many cases men are already receiving more salary than is provided for in the Agreement. . . . It would have been bad enough if the influence of the Agreement had been confined to Victoria, but, like the octopus its tentacles reach out into the other states. . . . it would appear the company paying the lowest standard of salaries has been permitted to call the tune.[80]

Maher's opportunism also helped destroy possibilities of an early amalgamation of the five bank unions. The events, ill will, and recriminations
arising from attempts to do this are an important part of the BOA's early
history. The reasons why this amalgamation was not achieved for forty-
five years lie substantially in the events of the early twenties.

Early BOA leaders had soon realized that their choice of federal registration was indeed fortuitous, for with this came the potential to expand
coverage and to increase union power and authority, options generally
not open to state-registered unions. The Victorians had already settled on
a desirable structure. The BOA was to be the central body with the various
state unions as branches. Accordingly, the BOA had amended its rules to
establish a federal council which drew delegates from these state branches.
Branches were formed from existing members in Victoria and Tasmania
and overtures made to South and Western Australia.[81] The UBOA of NSW
and the UBOA of Q flatly refused similar approaches, which was not
surprising given the ambitions of Smith and Partridge. Maher's enthusiasm
for amalgamation then waned till Smith touted the ABOF. A senior
banker accurately summed up the position:

> It would appear the organisation has emanated from Sydney, that it is
> merely that of the UBOA of NSW under a different name and that the
> present action has been taken as a result of their rejection by the Indus-
> trial Court. . . . the Sydney organisers who have worked up the ABOF
> are jealous of the BOA whose headquarters are in Melbourne and whose
> officials are not of so militant a type.[82]

Once the UBOA of NSW obtained registration, Smith lost interest and
refused to attend another conference where all other union leaders agreed
to amalgamation in principle. Conscious of Maher's ineptitude and
expediency, they agreed: "A strong Federation through Australia shows
united actions among employees. A weak association may at any time
come to a weak agreement which would be detrimental to all states."[83]
There was also recognition that in an industry with varying state salary
levels, interstate transfers would create anomalies, a view the banks con-
curred with.[84] Most importantly, the decision was a reaction to the
rumour: "In the very near future the whole of arbitration will be a
Commonwealth concern."[85] If this came about, a federally registered
amalgam of unions would be preferable.

The Victorians' plan was rejected in favour of the formation of yet
another body, the Bank Officials Federation (BOF). The Victorian and
Tasmanian BOA branches would become BOF branches along with the
other states. This was a body blow to Maher, who was also defeated by
Partridge in the ballot for BOF secretary. Maher then convinced the
Victorian delegation not to join the BOF on the spurious grounds that
should the BOF prove unsatisfactory they would only have recourse to
a wages board. In the meantime, rules for the BOF had been formulated
and application made for federal registration. There were three objectors;

the banks, the BOA, and the UBOA of NSW. Though even the most naive of bank-officers-turned-union leaders realized that amalgamation had become a rather cynical pursuit of increased union and personal power by "industrial agents" Smith, Maher, and Partridge, they were still shocked. "The actions of Victoria and New South Wales came as a thunderbolt to the rest of the BOF executive," stated the *Queensland Bank Officer* of July 1921. The registrar upheld the BOA's objection that bank officers could conveniently belong to it; this, together with Partridge's resignation, aborted this amalgamation attempt. Not surprisingly, Maher's crass suggestion to South Australia and Western Australia that they now join the BOA was contemptuously ignored, and both moved to obtain separate state awards.

Smith's reluctance was a result of plans for expansion of his "union empire". He planned to register federally a union of bank officers from the fast-growing Commonwealth Bank, and to expedite this he had formed the Commonwealth Bank branch of the UBOA of NSW.[86] Federal registration was strenuously opposed by the bank, led by the governor, Denison Miller, and also by the BOA, who argued that they could cover Commonwealth Bank employees. Miller told Smith he "would not receive any delegation from the Association as such, but would be glad to meet representatives of the Bank staff, provided that an application for registration in the Commonwealth Industrial Court was withdrawn".[87] The objections were successful, but in October 1921 when the persistent Smith applied again, only the bank objected. For Smith and Maher had met and decided on an allocation of the spoils. "Syd Smith met Maher of the BOA and settled an agreement whereby the UBOA of NSW took the Commonwealth Bank and the BOA were to have the savings banks."[88] In spite of Miller's continuing trenchant opposition and harassment of members, federal registration was granted. Smith had won a considerable victory; the UBOA of NSW's membership potential was significantly increased, and he now had access to the Arbitration Court. However, the determination of Miller and his successor, Sir James Kell, to brook no interference in the bank's operations, and their domination over the irresolute branch executive, resulted in a series of internal agreements rather than arbitration confrontations in the court. The less able Maher was unable to persuade State Savings Bank employees to join the BOA, for they were justly suspicious of his motives and ability to protect their interests.

The South Australian branch, under considerable pressure from disenchanted SBSA members, was considering forming a separate union. They had appointed A. G. Johnson, a private accountant, as part-time secretary and invited Laidlaw to help boost recruitment and to advise on state registration. When word came of the BOA's intention to levy all South Australian members one pound, they decided to seek separate state registration, which was granted the following month. This, plus senior officer unrest arising from imperfections of the first Agreement, forced the BOA to prepare a fresh log of claims. Maher, anxious to recruit senior officers and worried at rumours they would form a separate body, reminded them that new claims would not be successful without their support.[89] Smith was also pressing Maher to lodge a new claim, for "the current New South Wales case would be strengthened by the BOA claiming new rates and a classification system".[90] But Maher was so tardy that the New South Wales award was handed down months before he even served the BOA claims. If this procrastination grew out of a hope that the results could be used as leverage for the BOA, he must have been disappointed, for no classification system was included by the New South Wales court. Victorian senior officers were incensed on learning that the banks offer of a twenty-five year scale had been rejected in favour of higher rates in the early years of the scale. One disgruntled member wrote: "I was absolutely dumbfounded at such an offer having been so declined . . . it was a criminal neglect of the interests of senior officers."[91] Maher, anxious to placate these officers, hurriedly replied: "Let there by no misapprehension that the Association is designed to draw a line of demarcation between employer and employee, or to antagonise the clerk against the executive head. Perish the thought that such a state of affairs should be brought about. The Bank Officer has certain rights and prerogatives, and to protect, or if necessary, enforce these is one of the primary objects of the BOA."[92]

Convinced the banks would never concede classification, the BOA committee overrode Maher's objections and decided to approach the court. Union subscriptions were doubled and a levy struck to provide fighting funds. T. W. Ratten, an associate of Maher's, was appointed assistant secretary with express instructions to pursue unfinancial members and to comb rural areas for more members. In anticipation of a challenge to the union's "interstateness" following the secession of South Australia and Western Australia, Maher scurried to Tasmania to reassure secretary Brooke that the Victorian dominance of the BOA Federal Council was not detrimental to Tasmanian interests. Thus prepared, the BOA served a claim which included extension of the scale to forty years, significant scale increases, and classification. The banks offered to negotiate using the New South Wales award as a basis. In taking the initiative in this way, the banks pleased Maher, who had little wish to prepare evidence for an arbitration hearing. The banks' offer was also appealing to those committeemen who had lost their earlier courage and were apprehensive about appearing in court. In the negotiations that followed, Maher again proved his inefficiency and lack of awareness of his members' needs. The banks, who had been willing to pay New South Wales rates, suddenly "found that possibly something less than the New South Wales rates might be accepted".[93] The salary scale was extended to eighteen years, and adult officers received an average 4 per cent increase, while junior rates remained unchanged. The banks were permitted to pay the increases "partly as salary and partly as allowances so as to protect the pension funds".[94] Hours of work were extended, "which should materially assist in reducing overtime".[95] Maher's explanation to his sullen membership only confirmed his incompetence. "In fact when at one stage something definite was agreed to, the BOA had granted a 'quid pro quo' by giving way on another point. This appeared to settle the matter, but on the eve of settlement the clause was struck out by the banks, and our point which was conceded was retained."[96]

There was also sharp criticism from the state unions, whose chances of improving their salaries were now slim. This together with the shambles of the first agreement and the duplicity of the amalgamation discussion brought the state unions' wrath upon the hapless Victorians. "It has been the sorry experience of bankers in Australia that most unfortunately the Victorian Association has deliberately committed breaches of good faith with all associations in other states, and the final climax was reached when a most ill considered and misconceived settlement was made an award."[97] The state unions had every reason for resentment. For example, in December 1921 BOAWA had negotiated rates considerably better than the new BOA scale. But before these were confirmed the BOA result became known. The banks withdrew their offer and substituted the Victorian scale. Infuriated, the Western Australians "decided to apply to the Commonwealth Court for the deregistration of the BOA".[98] The South Australian Industrial Court actually adopted the BOA rates, as the president, Dr Jethro Brown, indicated:

> Now in deciding upon the proposed new scale, I am not left to drift about in a sea of troubles without any pilotage for guidance or anchorage for steadiness. I have the best of all assistance, and starting point in the first Federal Agreement made on the 2nd September 1920, between the B.O.A. and respondents who are parties to this dispute. And still better I have assistance in the shape of the Consent Award of February 28th 1922 between the same parties.[99]

So concluded the first BOA attempt to improve the lot of bank officers, which had promised so much but yielded much less. In addition, Maher's sloth and deception, together with the timidity and conservatism of other executive members, had created problems which were to inhibit the union's efficiency and which brought conflict both internally and with these other state unions.

In all states other than Tasmania, separate unions of private trading bank officers were now firmly established, and the prospect of a more broadly based union would not re-emerge for forty years. The internal structure of the BOA, consisting of two state branches, Victoria and Tasmania, was now determined. Each had a committee of management, composed of representatives from each institutional sub-branch, the number of representatives dependent upon the membership of the relevant sub-branch. Elections for these positions were provided for but rarely required. In turn, the branches were each to provide two representatives to Federal Council, whose executive (president, vice-president, and treasurer), were to be elected at the BOA Annual Conference. However, for more than fifteen years the influence and authority of the incumbents was so great that no elections were required.

On the surface, this union structure provided for a considerable Tasmanian voice, but in reality they were largely ignored, and the Tasmanian branch committee played but a minuscule role in BOA affairs. In part, this resulted from the obvious geographical problems which required that a Victorian member acted as the single Tasmanian proxy at Federal Council meetings. In addition, however, not only was the Federal Council dominated by Victorians, but almost without exception these same men also formed the Victorian branch committee of management. As a consequence Federal Council and Victorian branch committee meetings were usually held virtually simultaneously. Not only did this ensure that the Tasmanian influence was small indeed, but in later years this joint membership of the Victorian branch committee and Federal Council by several influential bank unionists was to markedly affect and impair the BOA's performance.

The ability of Tasmanian members to participate in BOA affairs was in fact even further restricted. Under BOA rules, policy was to be laid down at the Annual Federal Conference, composed of delegates from both branches. Conference was also to elect Federal Council members, whose task it was to implement Conference policy. However, such was the intertwined nature of the BOA's leadership that right up until the Second World War brief meetings of Conference were held throughout the year, quite often at the conclusion of Federal Council or Victorian branch committee meetings. Obviously there was little opportunity for the Tasmanians to participate or even express their views when the BOA's policies were being determined.

To the Court at Last

> The letter lay there white upon my blotter
> For me, and as I read it I grew hotter.
> That it was from Head Office, was quite plain,
> I groaned, and then I read it through again.

"I have pleasure in advising that the Board, having squashed the Bankers Union's last Award have reduced your salary back to where it used to be a year ago today, and besides that you will pay a 3 per cent levy for our Court expense was heavy. Since the union caused the fight, this is only just and right.

"Please don't ask us to relieve you when you're ill — we won't believe you. All leave due by Award is hereby stopped: allowances, of course, will all be dropped. We think your staff too many for the work you have to do, and as we're rather short of staff, we'll cut you down by two.

"You wouldn't pay your union fees, each levy caused a fuss, as the unions smashed thro' lack of funds, you can pay those fees to us. In short, conditions now will stand, as before the union took a hand."

> Four times I read this letter through,
> and wondered what on earth I'd do.
> With joy I woke — it wasn't true,
> then it dawned on me "your subscription's due".[100]

The Victorians were unworried that all chances of amalgamation or united approach had disappeared. But they were concerned at the increasing dis-content of senior officers who continued to lose salary relativity to younger officers still on the scale. There was voluminous correspondence outlining anomalous situations. "The Manager, the accountant, the teller and the ledgerkeeper, each with widely varying responsibility and skills were earning within a few pounds of each other."[101] Dissatisfaction crys-tallized in a meeting attended by nearly a hundred managers. They elected a subcommittee to investigate various types of classification and told Maher to circularize all Victorian managers requesting salary histories and urging them to join the BOA. Maher was eager to help, for George Benwell, newly appointed Victorian branch secretary, had prepared some worrying membership details: while the unionization rate was now more than 56 per cent, the proportion of managers in the union was only 40 per cent (see table 1).[102] More serious, however, was the implication that the preparedness of a branch's staff to join the union was influenced by whether or not the manager was a member.[103] The last column of table 1 lends support to this argument. In banks where a larger proportion of

Table 1. *Manager and Staff Union Density in Major Victorian Banks — August 1922*

	Managers			Other Staff		
	Total Number	Number BOA Members	Percentage BOA Members	Total Number	Number BOA Members	Percentage BOA Members
Bank of Australasia	56	9	16.1	403	175	43.4
Union Bank	42	16	38.1	344	212	61.7
B NSW	40	2	5.0	220	96	43.6
ES&A	72	48	66.7	498	312	62.6
Victoria	113	39	34.5	447	230	51.5
NBA	127	31	24.4	698	401	57.4
CBA	97	77	79.4	506	334	66.1
	550	222	40.3	3,116	3,116	56.5

managers were members, the overall density rate was also the highest
(ES&A and CBA). Concomitantly, in the BNSW and the Bank of Australasia both the rates of manager and staff union density were considerably
lower. This relationship became known as the "manager-member effect".
Maher too was convinced that the attitudes and intentions of senior
officers were crucial to further growth, for the rapid membership increases
of the union's first two years had now slowed considerably.

First reaction to Maher's circular came from an unexpected quarter.
Sir John Grice, NBA chairman of directors, challenged his patently false
statement that most managers were BOA members. In a further circular to
all NBA managers, Grice said:

> Managers are desired to inform this Department . . . whether or not
> they are members of the body referred to. The bank would prefer that
> its managers were not members of the Association, but it neither desires
> to seek to prevent them from joining it, nor has it any idea of penalising
> those who may do so. The desire of the Chief Manager to know
> whether or not the statement is correct, is the sole reason for the
> present inquiry, and managers are therefore asked to respond to it
> promptly.[104]

The union attacked Grice in the press, contending that union membership
was no concern of his and that the circular was intimidatory: "To say that
in one sentence the bank would prefer its members not to join, and to
immediately proceed to say that it did not want to prevent members from
joining, could only be interpreted by managers as a wish or command that
they should not become unionists. Such action was a paltry juggling with
the casuistry of words."[105]

In spite of this, Grice's tactics were successful, and further manager
meetings organized by the union were poorly attended. The suggested
classification system of the senior officers' subcommittee was incorporated
into claims served on banks in late 1922. The banks through the ABA told
the union that the claims were absurd. This participation of the ABA in
award discussion was recognition of the need for a co-ordinated defence
in the face of persistent union demands, and an indication of the banks'
hardening attitudes.

Early in 1923 Maher wrote to the ABA suggesting discussions, but over
the next few months they made only negligible concessions. The ABA
refused to consider classification despite Maher's assurance: "The actual
classification of the officers, and the manner in which the banks are to
deal with their administration, is not sought to be altered."[106] In despera-
tion the BOA sacrificed classification for all but managers, but the banks
wanted more. They felt confident that Maher's distaste for the court
would eventually make an agreement on their terms possible. They were
right. Maher had just persuaded Federal Council to agree when news came
of Smith's attempt to register federally the branch managers and senior

officers division of the UBOA of NSW, and to cover senior officers in all states. Maher and the BOA were appalled at the implications of this. They would lose members, but worse would lose the "manager-member" effect. Also, the legitimization of union existence and actions, largely provided by senior officers, would disappear.[107] The union now had no choice but to continue the fight for classification, for as Smith gloated: "Our activities will make the BOA do a bit of work on behalf of the senior officers."[108] The tenor of his circular to all senior officers is summed up by the purported comment of two managers: "You will find material benefits have been obtained for juniors while in these Federal awards the senior officers have been entirely neglected. . . . on the results of the past activities of the B.O.A. you will not obtain benefits worthy of your standing . . . whilst you are members of the B.O.A., whose constitution embraces men identified with junior positions, messengers, watchmen and cleaners."[109] Smith concluded by playing on senior officers' perceived status: "This association stands for you and officers having control of others, also for those of equal status to you, but does not include unclassified officers, juniors or other employees." In a further circular he exploited their desire to keep their union membership secret: "Mr. Tom Maher, is objecting to a separate registration of such an association for managers and has produced your name in Court, showing you are a member of his association."[110]

Smith's actions resulted from his ambitions as a white-collar entrepreneur. In the battle for control of a nation-wide union, Maher would be the only real opposition, for Laidlaw, Heal, and Cooke had neither the skills nor the pretensions for such a position. The registration application was heard in March 1923. The BOA and the ABA objected, with the latter arguing that bank managers were employers so that the court lacked jurisdiction. The real though unstated bank objection was somewhat more pragmatic and based on their assessment of the relative militancy and skills of Smith and Maher. In reality they had little to fear, for the new body's few members made success unlikely. Smith had hastily wired Laidlaw, urging him to form a senior officer branch, but Laidlaw saw through it. "It is hard to fathom what real gain the new branch would be other than to open up another source of revenue for the New South Wales Association by mulcting all senior officers for a further annual subscription."[111] The application was refused, not on jurisdictional grounds but because the BOA was already covering some senior officers.[112]

Maher triumphantly reported Smith's defeat and was immediately instructed to approach the court for an early hearing of the claims already served. But then came the bombshell. On 8 August 1923 Federal Council met urgently to discuss a charge by Tasmanian secretary Brooke that subscriptions forwarded eight months earlier had not been acknowledged. Maher's explanation was unsatisfactory, and while the staid bankers on the executive could tolerate his bumbling ineptitude, they were outraged by this financial malpractice and forced his resignation. Dismay soon replaced anger as they realized that their own laxness had allowed Maher to dominate, and now who could take over the impending case? But they reckoned without the indefatigable Smith; just three days after Maher's resignation they received his offer of assistance. The BOA executive immediately appointed him acting federal secretary and Victorian branch vice-president so that he could appear in court. Already secretary of the UBOA of NSW, which included the rapidly expanding Commonwealth Bank branch, Smith had now achieved a considerable power base. With access to the federal Arbitration Court and most state courts, he was to be the dominant bank union leader for the next decade.

Smith soon found that Maher had made no preparations for the case; nor had he collected any evidence. Benwell was set to work. Smith was anxious to avoid a repetition of delaying tactics used by the banks in New South Wales and also aware that they planned to challenge the court's jurisdiction, claiming that banking was not an industry. Accordingly he invited the banks to test this immediately in the High Court and in return offered to allow them to use legal counsel in the Arbitration Court.[113] The case began in September 1923, and as agreed, the banks at once challenged the court's ability to hear the claims. They also objected to Benwell's requests for them to tender salary histories and positions of senior officers since 1913, with their counsel arguing that these were trade secrets, and that if officers disclosed them to the court they would be violating their secrecy oath. But deputy president Sir John Quick told the banks that some information would be required, though names need not be mentioned. Disturbed at the court's firmness, the banks suggested negotiations and made minor concessions. Smith, seeing this as stalling tactics, called a mass meeting, where more than seven hundred members resolved to press on with arbitration. Meanwhile the banks' challenge was heard by the High Court in conjunction with a similar one brought by the insurance companies, who were in dispute with the AISF.[114] In a majority decision handed down in December 1923, both banking and insurance were considered industries because they constituted the financial side of the industrial system.[115] The High Court also confirmed that a dispute could exist between the banks and managers.

When the Arbitration Court case recommenced in March 1924, Smith spent considerable time trying to prove that bank officer purchasing power had declined for ten years. The banks not only opposed this but argued that the scale should be abolished or at least reduced to fourteen years because there were so many "hacks" in the industry incapable of carrying out tasks expected of officers at the top of an eighteen-year scale. Their objections to classification were numerous and included reduced staff flexibility and inability to promote on merit rather than seniority. They also denied that managers needed salary increases to compensate for entertainment, donations, and subscriptions required to maintain custom, because they got their "amusement from them . . . and . . .

managers got the benefits in the long run by send offs from the towns-people and testimonials, and whilst they were there the farmers gave gratuities to bank managers."[116]

In April Justice Quick announced his decision. The eighteen-year scale was retained and increased by twelve pounds a year for all adult officers. In supporting bank arguments about mediocre or "hack" officers, Quick rejected claims that officers with twenty, twenty-five, and thirty years of service should receive stated salary minima: "Some of these officials have reached stationary positions in the service, beyond which they cannot hope to go . . . this may be their misfortune rather than their fault, but if such a clause were inserted it might lead to them being retired early, which would probably be worse than ever for them."[117] In refusing classification he accepted the bank arguments and confirmed the union's fear that the unwillingness of many managers to join the BOA or to appear in court limited possibilities of success.[118] To the BOA's consternation, he added that branch managers, the "visible embodiment of the bank" and direct representatives of their employers, ought not to appear in court alongside clerks as "members of a common labour organisation".[119] There was considerable criticism of this by senior officers, but one commentator noted (with some satisfaction): "The managerial brigade have themselves to blame . . . for less than half of them have joined the B.O.A., whether because of an inherent belief that their employers would advance them for their so-called loyalty, or whether they had an objection to association with their fellows."[120]

Another example of the union's continuing conservatism came after a new committee member suggested approaching the Victorian Trades Hall Council to convene a meeting of white-collar unions and that the union should publicly voice dissatisfaction with the new award. He was told that "the Association must keep away from Trades Hall influence and a public demonstration would only prejudice managers".[121]

With dissatisfaction among senior officers still mounting, and Vice-President Rogers openly talking of setting up a senior-officer union, some immediate action was needed. Smith organized a deputation of representatives from thirteen white-collar unions to the attorney-general, Littleton Groom. Smith's strategy was to exploit the Bruce government's growing concern at the overlap between the Arbitration Court and the state courts. After emphasizing that they were not complaining about the court's awards, Smith gave the attorney-general the false impression that white-collar unions would prefer to use the federal jurisdiction, and all that prevented this was the court's refusal to include managers and supervisors in awards. But Groom was unimpressed by Smith's glibness, and the deputation returned empty-handed.

Again results had been disappointing, even though Smith had orchestrated the union's first arbitration appearance. Little had been done for senior officers, and the banks still retained almost complete control over their employees.

The Union Itself

What significant changes had occurred in the BOA? Between 1919 and 1924 Victorian branch membership had grown from 473, or 16.8 per cent of the state's private bank employees, to 2,435, or 56.2 per cent (see app. 3), largely as a result of the salary increases discussed in this chapter. Complementing and aiding this membership growth was a significant increase in the industry's work force as a result of urban branch expansion.[122] The banks' extensive recruiting campaign had resulted in the proportion of officers aged twenty or less growing from 17.2 per cent to 23.5 per cent.[123] This aided union growth, for younger clerks did not have the same inhibitions towards union membership as did many older officers.[124] The union had taken several other initiatives. They enthusiastically promoted the annual BOA Ball and "smoke nights". The Bankers' Club, established some years earlier by the BOA in the union offices, enabled members to meet in a convivial and relaxed atmosphere. It was well patronized, though some members may have found their pleasures inhibited by the "prohibition of alcohol, women, dice games, dogs and bicycles" in the club.[125] An orchestra and athletic and rowing clubs were formed, and football, cricket, and tennis teams representing each major bank played regular fixtures. All these activities were fully reported in the *Bank Officials Journal,* which also emphasized the need for bank officers to improve their banking skills and strongly recommended further study. The *Journal* was an important communication and information device, laying emphasis as it did on social notes, articles on banking practice, short stories, and lengthy lists of member transfers and promotions. Later in 1924 Smith, wishing to concentrate his work in Sydney, persuaded the UBOA of NSW and the BOA to produce a joint journal, *The Australian Banker* which was to endure until 1941. His other centralizing tactics were not so successful, and Benwell incurred Smith's wrath after pointing out to Federal Council that he had been told to forward all union correspondence, minutes, and records directly to Smith in Sydney. The union objected, and Smith was forced to maintain two offices, and at least for some time to commute between the two states. Smith's bombastic, high-handed attitude resulted in considerable conflict with Rogers and Benwell, and the latter lost no opportunity of informing the Federal Council of missing minutes, wayward accounts, and unanswered mail. After the resignation of Meredith Atkinson earlier in 1924, L. P. Harrison, an ES&A branch manager, had become president of both the Victorian branch and Federal Council. Cautious and extremely conservative, he was to hold both these positions until 1938. Smith continued as secretary of the federal body, and Benwell was confirmed as full-time Victorian secretary. In Tasmania, E. A. Brooke remained as secretary while the president's position changed frequently. Brooke's constant harrying of both the Victorian branch executive and the Victorian proxies representing Tasmania on Federal Council was the only factor preventing their total subjugation by the Victorian branch.

The end of 1924 is an appropriate point to draw breath following five years of eventful and at least partially successful union activity. There had been three salary increases which favoured younger officers, and the establishment of minimum working conditions and standards had eliminated some earlier abuses. A few difficulties had been overcome; a modicum of bank officers' distaste for unionism had been dispelled; moves to establish rival unions countered; and a limited form of interstate coordination established. Many problems remained, and others were shortly to surface as the economy began its long downswing into the Great Depression. Bank officer optimism would have been shattered had they known that the union's next Arbitration Court appearance was to be an unsuccessful attempt to avoid the 10 per cent salary cuts of 1931.

Notes

1. Interview with E.C. Peverill, 12 September 1973. Much of this section relies on several interviews with Peverill.
2. E.C. Peverill, *National Bank Monthly Summary,* December 1976, p. 10.
3. In fact, when the next year a Tasmanian wages board covering bank and insurance employees made an award, the Commercial Bank of Tasmania successfully applied to have this set aside (*Bank, Solicitors and Insurance Wages Board Award* ex parte *Commercial Bank of Tasmania Ltd* [1920] 16 TAS. L.R.30).
4. The Tasmanian experience also bears this out. For example, the twenty-one year rate awarded was £169 (federal award £200). "This was but to be expected when the General Manager of one of the banks represented employers on the Board" (*Queensland Bank Officer* 2, no. 5 [July 1921] : 12).
5. M. Atkinson, *The New Social Order: A Study of Post War Re-Construction* (Melbourne: Macmillan, 1919); M. Atkinson, ed., *Australia, Economic and Political Studies* (Melbourne: Macmillan, 1920).
6. E.C. Peverill in the *Australian Bank Officer,* June 1969, p. 24.
7. BOA Committee of Management minutes, 24 September 1919.
8. A compelling reason for Rogers's appointment lay in the Court's refusal to allow legal counsel before it. However, as an executive member, Rogers could represent the union.
9. *Bank Officials Journal* 1, no. 1 (June 1921): 10.
10. W.W. Rogers addressing general meeting, 20 November 1919, *Argus,* 21 November 1919, p. 8.
11. Declarations nos. 12 to 19 to industrial registrar, 28 November 1919, held by industrial registrar, Melbourne.
12. *Argus,* 2 December 1919, p. 8.
13. Ibid., 3 December 1919, p. 17.
14. See, for example, the exchange of letters and cables between the superintendent of the Bank of Australasia and London: confidential cables nos. 557 and 567, and confidential letter no. 454, 24 September 1919, in ANZ archives.
15. E.C. Peverill to D. Farrell, 3 December 1919, letter in ABOA archives. Atkinson had also sought to pacify older officers who had suggested negotiations rather than registration. "Everything possible has been done by the committee,

but without avail, to arrive at an amicable understanding with the management" (*Argus,* 20 Nov. 1919, p. 8).

16. *Argus,* 21 November 1919, p. 13.
17. Report of meeting reprinted in the *Argus,* 22 November 1919, p. 8.
18. BOA Committee of Management Minutes, 19 December 1919, p. 23.
19. BOA monthly circular, no. 2 (Apr. 1920): 2.
20. *Bankers Bulletin* 1, no. 4 (Sept. 1920): 7.
21. The London-based banks, with some experience of unionism, seemed less concerned. This was a result of their success in countering the BOG and a belief that "the union would largely be made up of young and irresponsible clerks, as well as older incompetent malcontents . . . and that the main bulk of staff will remain loyal" (superintendent, Bank of Australasia, to London, letter no. 567, 24 September 1919, in ANZ archives).
22. *Bankers Magazine* 107, no. 900 (Mar. 1919): 300.
23. Circular letter from Wreford to all Victorian and Riverina NBA officers, 10 December 1919, copy in ABOA archives.
24. *Argus,* 27 December 1919, p. 14. This brought the banks' wrath upon him. He was summoned before Wreford, accused of labelling as empty promises the proposed bonus, and threatened with further repercussions.
25. Blackburn, *Union Character and Social Class,* pp. 140–46, and Klingender, *Clerical Labour in Britain,* pp. 33–40, discuss the development of internal staff guilds in England.
26. J. R. Hannan to UBOA of NSW, 10 July 1919, letter reproduced in the *Bankers Bulletin* 1, no. 2 (Mar. 1920): 13.
27. But most banks were apparently unaware of the implications of this legislation. See, for example, letter from C. J. O'Sullivan, Australian manager ES&A, to London, 6 December 1919, in ANZ archives.
28. *Bankers Bulletin* 1, no. 1 (Mar. 1920): 13.
29. Reprinted in Blainey, *Gold and Paper,* p. 311. Note also Wreford's slighting reference to the BOA as a clerks association.
30. Compiled using data from ABOA archives.
31. *Bankers Bulletin* 1, no. 4 (May 1920): 4.
32. Ibid., p. 15.
33. Australian manager of Union Bank to London, 11 October 1919, confidential letter no. 2748, in ANZ archives.
34. An extract from the branch manager's report justifies his suspicion: "Fraternises with staff familiarily, and though I have no proof, I think that he was a prime mover in calling a meeting of officers to form the association" (report of manager, Pitt Street branch of BNSW, on H. F. Rawson, June 1919, reprinted in *The Rawson Case, an Historical Document* by H. W. Foster [Melbourne: ABOA, 1968], p. 12).
35. Half-yearly report of assistant inspector, North Queensland, 31 March 1920, held in BNSW archives.
36. See Sir Charles McKellar to Sydney Smith, 22 August 1919, reproduced in the *Bankers Bulletin* 1, no. 5 (June 1920): 11.
37. Curiously the bank, after granting him six months' salary as an "act of grace", paid five hundred pounds into his current account.
38. The secretary of the ACA is reported as saying: "Bank clerks are snobbish and that is why we are opposing them in the Courts" (*Bankers Bulletin* 1, no. 3 [June 1920]: 4).
39. UBOA of NSW application for registration judgement, 13 May 1920, New South Wales industrial registrar.
40. Minutes of UBOA of NSW 1920 Annual Conference, 18 October 1920. The average senior branch manager's salary at this time was £370 per annum.

41. A month or so later he did inform the executive of his appointment as president of the New South Wales Insurance Officers Association.
42. And by his threats of legal action against those promoting rumours of links between Smith and the then militant Australian Workers Union. These allegations of his involvement with manual workers were designed to alienate conservative and status-conscious bank officers, but Smith's quick action nipped this in the bud. See, for example, *Bankers Bulletin* 2, no. 16 (May 1922): p. 2.
43. *Bankers Bulletin* 1, no. 5 (June 1920): 10.
44. *United Bank Officers Association of New South Wales* v. *Australian Bank of Commerce and Ors* (20 AR 303).
45. *United Bank Officers Association of New South Wales* v. *Bank of New South Wales* (21 SR 593).
46. *UBOA of NSW* v *BNSW*, p. 596.
47. *Bankers Bulletin* 2, no. 16 (May 1922): 2.
48. *UBOA of NSW* v. *BNSW*, p. 599.
49. Much of the material in this discussion is from an interview with Laidlaw on 18 January 1974 and later communications. D. Murphy, *Ken Laidlaw: A White Collar Union Leader* (Brisbane: ABEU, 1979), also provides a competent analysis of Laidlaw's industrial career.
50. Classification was set to be a contentious issue for years. It was a union attempt to set minimum salaries for accountants, managers, and senior clerks in administrative positions, whose skill and experience could not be encompassed by a chronological salary scale. Because of the bank's tardiness in providing salary increases to officers above the scale, they invariably suffered declining salary relativities compared with younger offices advancing steadily through the scale. The banks opposed classification, it limited their control over senior officer salaries, increased salary costs, and they believed opened the way for further union interference into salaries and promotion decisions. They also feared that continuing guaranteed salary increases would reduce motivation and productivity.
51. *United Bank Officers Association of Queensland* v *Bank of Australasia and Ors* (5 QIG 381) at p. 382.
52. See, for example, Australian manager Union Bank to London, 31 December 1920, confidential letter no. 2760, in ANZ archives.
53. *United Bank Officers Association of Queensland* v *Bank of Australasia and Ors* (5 QIG 381) at p. 387.
54. *Queensland Bank Officer* 1, no. 2 (Mar. 1920): 5.
55. The organization retained the title Bank Officials' Association (South Australian Branch) until 1929, when it became the Bank Officials' Association of South Australia (BOASA).
56. By October 1920, SBSA officers comprised more than 27 per cent of membership (*Bank Officials' Association Bulletin*, October 1920, p. 1).
57. Most of the material relating to the formation of a bank officers' union in Western Australia has been destroyed. A significant part of the information in this section has come from tape recordings made in 1969 by L.H. Preston, a life member of the union until his death in July 1973.
58. The unregistered BOF was an organization created to facilitate the amalgamation of all Australian banking unions. Events surrounding its short ill-fated career are discussed later in this chapter. The Western Australian union became the Bank Officials' Association of Western Australia (BOAWA) in 1928.
59. L.B. Fox to Sydney Smith, 16 July 1920, reprinted in the *Bankers Bulletin* 1, no. 7 (Aug. 1920): 18.
60. Preston tapes.
61. *Queensland Bank Officer* 2, no. 5 (July 1921): 12.
62. See, for example, "How It All Began", *Westralian Banker,* no. 100, (Jan.

1933), p. 1: "It meant we were dependent upon the BOA absolutely and they had to be referred to for every action we decided to take."

63. *Bankers Bulletin* 2, no. 24 (Jan. 1923): 11.

64. Few bank officers felt any affinity with the lowly messengers. They had been included in claim discussions because of a fear they might otherwise be recruited by another union, who would then have a foothold in the industry. Once their membership was guaranteed, the BOA did not pursue these claims. FCM, 6 May 1920, p. 50.

65. FCM, 6 May 1920, p. 50.

66. Maher, secretary of the Commonwealth Public Service Clerical Association, appeared because Peverill had just been transferred to Wangaratta. The union had gladly accepted Maher's offer of assistance. Ambitious and devious, Maher had already conducted a number of cases before the court. Peverill's transfer ended his active union involvement, for he spent the next twenty-one years in NBA rural branches. It was generally accepted that this was a direct result of his union activities and clash with Wreford. Later, Peverill was justifiably angry after the BOA had appointed Maher as secretary on £450 per annum and granted Maher and Rogers honorariums of 150 guineas as a "small recognition by the members of their excellent and unselfish efforts since the Association was formed" (VCMM, 26 Oct. 1920, p. 89). He claimed £600 for past services, but the union, after seeking legal advice, rejected him out of hand (VCMM, 9 Oct. 1923, p. 259).

67. *Bank Officials Association* v *Bank of Australasia and Ors* (14 CAR 591) at p. 593.

68. Superintendent of Bank of Australasia to London, confidential letter no. 619, 17 September 1920, in ANZ archives.

69. Australian manager ES&A to London, 12 October 1920, letter in ANZ archives.

70. Ibid., 6 May 1920.

71. See, for example, superintendent of Bank of Australasia to London, confidential letter no. 619, 17 September 1920, in ANZ archives.

72. Australian manager of Union Bank to London, letter no. 2737, 3 September 1920, in ANZ archives.

73. London manager of Bank of Australasia to Australia, confidential letter no. 495, 30 September 1920, in ANZ archives.

74. This real wage increase is much larger than for any other group. This is partly the result of the extremely low starting wage (£63/10/0 in 1910) and the relatively large money wage increases accruing to bank clerks in the earlier years of service. There was obviously a significant advantage in being on the scale.

75. The banks were not slow to "assess" officers. The *Bankers Bulletin* of April 1922 reported, "In one bank alone more than one hundred members have been denied their Agreement scale" (*Bankers Bulletin* 2, no. 15: 8).

76. This had been his reason for volunteering to help the union. He believed it would be easy to show his worth and win increases that appeared substantial in this, the union's first case.

77. See Walker, *Australian Industrial Relations Systems,* p. 46; Commonwealth Labor Report no. 14; and federal industrial registrars' files.

78. New South Wales industrial registrar's files.

79. Queensland and South Australian industrial registrars' files.

80. *Bankers Bulletin* 1, no. 10 (Nov. 1920): 3.

81. These structural changes were purely cosmetic. Victorians continued to dominate Federal Council, and the Tasmanians were indifferently represented by Victorian proxies. The Victorians thought so little of the Tasmanian branch that two months after the first agreement was made, secretary E. A. Brooke knew nothing of what was in it (VCMM, 26 October 1920, p. 87).

82. Australian manager of Union Bank to London, letter no. 2726, 2 July 1920, in ANZ archives.
83. *Queensland Bank Officer* 1, no. 3 (Mar. 1920): 1.
84. See, for example, Australian manager of Union Bank to London, letter no. 2726, 2 July 1920, in ANZ archives.
85. For discussion of this, see *SABOJ*, January 1921, p. 15. In South Australia this fear was averted when the Industrial Disputes Act of 1922 was allowed to lapse. A section of this Act dealt with the proposed abolition of the South Australian State Industrial Court.
86. The development of unionism in the Commonwealth Bank is treated in detail, though unfortunately rather descriptively, in "Conciliation Can Work: A History of the Commonwealth Bank Officers Association", by C. L. Mobbs (Sydney, 1968).
87. Mobbs, *Conciliation Can Work,* p. 8.
88. *Bankers Bulletin* 2, no. 9 (Oct. 1921): 3.
89. See, for example, *Bank Officials Journal* 1, no. 1 (June 1921): 1.
90. FCM, 28 September 1921, p. 150.
91. M. R. Gibbs, BOA committeeman, to Sydney Smith, reproduced in *Bank Officials Journal* 2, no. 1 (June 1922): 8.
92. *Bank Officials Journal* 2, no. 2 (July 1922): 1.
93. Australian manager of Bank of Australasia to London, letter no. 693, 31 December 1921, p. 1, in ANZ archives.
94. Ibid., p. 3.
95. Ibid., letter no. 704, 10 March 1922, in ANZ archives.
96. *Bank Officials Journal* 1, no. 10 (Mar. 1922).
97. *SABOJ,* September 1923, p. 150.
98. *Queensland Banker* 3, no. 1 (Jan. 1922): 1.
99. South Australian State Industrial Court, No. 13 of 1921, p. 2.
100. *Bankers Bulletin* 2, no. 25 (Feb. 1923): 8.
101. FCM, 21 August 1922, p. 279.
102. If the CBA figures are excluded, this falls to 31 per cent. There are sound reasons for doing this, for as pointed out in chapter 1, this bank had an atypically high manager unionization level.
103. Certainly bank union leaders were convinced that non-member managers either openly or covertly dissuaded their branch staff from joining (interviews with Peverill, 13 September 1973, Laidlaw, 18 January 1974, and Hore, 11 October 1973). Peverill tells of a manager in a branch of the Bank of Australasia who not only forbade any discussion of unionism but directed all BOA members on his staff to resign from the union.
104. Circular from Sir John Grice to all NBA managers, August 1922, copy in ABOA archives.
105. Letter from T. C. Maher, *Age,* 24 August 1922, p. 13.
106. T. C. Maher to ABA, 5 February 1923, copy in minutes of ABA in ANZ archives.
107. The importance the BOA executive placed upon this is indicated in a misleading journal article outlining membership rates. "Percentage of managers financial to September 30, 1923 – 97 per cent" (*Bank Officials Journal* 3, no. 4 [Dec. 1923]: 6). The intent is rather obvious, for while practically all manager members were apparently paid-up members, the proportion of Victorian and Tasmanian managers actually unionized was less than 43 per cent (BOA files in ABOA archives).
108. *Bankers Bulletin* 2, no. 28 (June 1923): 4.
109. Circular to all bank managers, accountants, and senior officers in Victoria and Tasmania, February 1923, reprinted in the *Bank Officials Journal* 2, no. 14 (July 1923): 9.

110. Circular no. 2 to all bank managers, accountants and senior officers in Victoria and Tasmania, March 1923, reprinted in *Bank Officials Journal* 2, no. 14 (Aug. 1923): 7.
111. *Queensland Bank Officer* 4, no. 2 (Apr. 1923): 4. Laidlaw knew that all but one shilling of the one guinea subscription was destined for UBOA of NSW coffers.
112. Branch managers and senior officers branch of the UBOA of NSW, application for registration judgement, 24 May 1923, New South Wales industrial registrar.
113. The banks had discussed the possibility of a High Court challenge some years earlier (see, for example, superintendent Bank of Australasia to London, confidential letter no. 619, in ANZ archives). They chose to do so now because Smith's arrival made it likely that the claims would go to arbitration and there would be stiffer opposition. As one Australian manager wrote: "The demands and inquisitions of the various clerks' unions have intensified . . . there is further evidence that the Associations will not hesitate to challenge and endeavour to interfere with our internal administration on the slightest pretext — the unions' paid executive [Smith] who lives by agitation will see to that" (Australian manager of Union Bank to London, 13 October 1923, letter in ANZ archives).
114. The BOA executive were concerned that this joint hearing would strengthen the view that banking was a similar industry to insurance, with its lower salaries and certainly less community prestige and status. But Smith was particularly anxious to proceed, for he was also president of an organization of insurance workers in New South Wales and so could only benefit from the forging of closer links with the banking industry.
115. *Australian Insurance Staffs' Federation and Bank Officials Association v Accident Underwriters Association and Bank of Australasia and Ors* (33 CLR 517).
116. *Bank Officials Association v Bank of Australasia and Ors* (19 CAR 272), transcript p. 176. This patronizing statement enraged many senior officers. In one of the first *Journal* letters signed rather than contributed under a *nom de plume*, N.C. Graham, manager of Prahran branch of Bank of Australasia, said, "As one who has spent a lifetime in the service of the Bank I hung my head in shame to think that such pauperising evidence should be submitted to strengthen its cause" (*Bank Officials Journal* 3, no. 9 [May 1924] : 4).
117. *Bank Officials Association v Bank of Australasia and Ors* (19 CAR 272) at p. 275.
118. Ibid., p. 278.
119. Ibid., p. 279. Quick was forced to modify his statement after the Australian manager of the Union Bank, concerned that senior officers would again try to form a separate union, wrote to him (letter in ABOA archives).
120. Editor of *State Savings Bank Journal*, reprinted in *Bank Officials Journal* 3, no. 8 (Apr. 1924).
121. FCM, 14 April 1924, p. 8.
122. City and urban branches increased by 42.4 per cent in the period and country branches by only 6.4 per cent (see app. 1).
123. Data from 1921 Commonwealth Census, Order 4 of Class 3. This includes officers in the State Savings Bank and Commonwealth Bank officers based in Victoria. Figures for 1924 from BOA archives.
124. J. Shister, "The Logic of Union Growth", *Journal of Political Economy* 61 (Oct. 1963): 421, notes "ceteris paribus, the younger workers will show a greater propensity to unionise".
125. *BOA Bankers' Club Rules,* 1923, copy in BOA archives.

The first Bank Officers Conciliation Committee in Australia meets in Conference, August 1926, in Sydney.

First annual smoke night of Bank Officials Association held in the Masonic Hall, Melbourne, Wednesday 25 February 1920.

Bank Officials Ball — St Kilda Town Hall, 1923.

Professor Meredith Atkinson, University of Melbourne. First Victorian Branch and General President – 1919–23.

L.P. Harrison (Manager, London Bank of Australia, Fitzroy – merged with ES&A Bank Limited, 1921). He succeeded Professor Atkinson as the Victorian and General President 1923–38.

Delegates to interstate Conference on "Depression Policy" held in Melbourne on Monday 18 August 1930.

3 Doldrums and Depression: 1925–34

Ye Bankers of Old England,
  Who sit at home at ease;
List to the cry for help that comes
  From far off Southern Seas:
"Advance Australia money" –
  So we don't have to sow,
But merely reap the benefit
  of the money that we owe.

Australia has a motto,
  'Tis known throughout the world:
"Advance Australia money"
  On our banner is unfurled.
What is a thousand millions
  On which to come and go?
Just put another one in front,
  And add another O.
And we'll pay you what you lend us
  With the money that we owe.

Australia needs no bulwarks,
  No towers along the steep;
What Australia needs is money,
  So we can eat and sleep;
And journey out to Randwick,
  Then see the Easter Show,
And buy a Yankee motor car,
  To Yankee pictures go –
And we'll pay you what you lend us
  With the money that we owe.

"Advance Australia money" –
  If you decline with thanks,
Don't think that it will make us save,
  We've always got the Yanks.
"Advance Australia money" –
  "Advance Australia fair" –
You can't advance too much, my lads,
  "Australia will be there."
And don't be scared, my bonny boys,
  Of course you always know –

We can pay you what you lend us
With the money that we owe.

[*Australian Banker* 5, no. 6 (June 1930): 12]

On the Coat-tails of the UBOA of NSW

For several years following 1924 the BOA executive was content to wait upon the results of an award case conducted by the UBOA of NSW.[1] That the union in fact waited for more than five years is an indication of both Smith's domination and the BOA's continuing distaste for appearing before the Arbitration Court.

This attitude and its longer-term implications demand a brief discussion of the UBOA of NSW's approaches to the New South Wales Industrial Arbitration Court. In contrast to the BOA, the New South Wales union showed keen interest in political events, and particularly state elections. While this can be partly attributed to earlier difficulties in obtaining state registration, an additional factor was their expectation that victory by a Labor government in the looming New South Wales state election would bring favourable industrial legislation. This prospect was even sufficient for some bank officers, historically supporters of non-Labor political parties, to consider changing their allegiance. The union's journal reported on the general meeting and Smith's comment: "The return of the Labor Party to power in New South Wales seemed assured, when amendments to the Industrial Arbitration Act would be passed, and many of our troubles overcome. This statement was received with such enthusiasm that the impression was gathered that the meeting was living in hope that this would be fulfilled."[2] Smith asked all candidates specific questions relating to the Industrial Arbitration Act and the retention and scope of state arbitration. Their answers were printed in the journal and the unfavourable responses of Nationalist Party candidates emphasized.[3] There was understandably some jubilation when the Lang Labor government was re-elected, for in the mean-time the union had filed a claim for improved wages and conditions. This included scale extensions and increases, a comprehensive classification system, and other significant gains which the New South Wales union now had high hopes of achieving.

However, the opposition of the non-elected New South Wales Legislative Council meant that the proposed industrial legislation was not introduced until early 1926,[4] when the Industrial Arbitration Court was replaced by the state Industrial Commission headed by A. B. Piddington, QC. The banks were greatly worried, for his 1920 report on the federal basic wage advocating an increase of more than 50 per cent had "stamped him as idealist".[5] Among the numerous legislative changes was the extension of the tribunal's power to hear salary claims up to £750, and the introduction of industry conciliation committees. Further delays occurred while the composition of the banking conciliation committee was determined. The UBOA of NSW was represented by the president, L. A. Downey, the general secretary, Sydney Smith, and two Sydney branch managers. The banks' representatives were four senior staff inspectors from the major banks. N. G. McWilliam, a barrister, was appointed as independent chairman and so had the near impossible task of reconciling the interests of the dour bankers and the ebullient, aggressive Smith.

For three months the hearing of evidence continued,[6] until Smith requested that an interim award salary be made.[7] McWilliam refused, arguing that retrospectivity was possible under the act and that the salary issue was closely related to the question of classification and so could only be settled after that had been determined. Considerable delay followed after the banks then successfully challenged the legal basis of the committees. With the government embroiled in the redrafting of its industrial legislation, Piddington then reconsidered and offered to bring down a limited award based on evidence already given. The banks reluctantly agreed, and in June 1927 an interim award was made. The eighteen-year scale was retained with an average increase of 3 per cent across the scale. In line with the new state child endowment legislation, family allowances were also included. All officers earning less than £750 per annum were to receive an additional £35 for each child under fourteen years of age, or if at school under the age of sixteen. The UBOA of NSW was delighted and claimed that Piddington had recognized that banking salaries should reflect the "high ideals of our profession".[8] The BOA, bravely ignoring that the family allowance had been made possible by New South Wales legislation, informed their members that as federal awards were based upon a three-children standard, they could expect their salaries to increase by more than 33 per cent.[9] The banks for their part were horrified: "If Mr. Piddington deals with the other claims of the Association in the same absurdly liberal manner, the serious consequences to the banks are obvious."[10] They were equally quick to point out that some increase in interest rates would be required to offset the wage increases.[11] Although the new scale was now some 7 per cent better than the BOA scale, Smith, wanting no complications from the federal arena, commanded the BOA to wait until the issues of classification, hours and conditions, and female salaries had been determined. All of these benefits, he glibly told them, would then be readily translated to the federal award.

Consequently there was consternation among both unions the following month when all deliberations of the state Industrial Commission were suspended pending a royal commission into its operations and in particular the actions of Commissioner Piddington. In the words of one senior banker, he had "considered himself not so much a judge as a Commissioner more or less bound to give effect to the will of the Parliament of the day".[12] The royal commission continued until October 1927, when the charges were finally rejected. However, union hopes that the long-delayed case would now be finalized were quickly dashed, for before Piddington could hear further evidence, the increasingly erratic and controversial Lang government was replaced by a Nationalist government led by Thomas Bavin, with whom Smith had frequently clashed in earlier years. The antagonism was still there, for Smith had recently asked Bavin what the Nationalist government's attitude towards the existing industrial legislation would be. Bavin retorted that "if bank officers wanted all these rights the best thing they could do was to go to the Labor Government".[13]

The Nationalist government quickly introduced further industrial legislation. The right of the conciliation committee chairman to vote was removed, but even more importantly the control of the state Industrial Commission was vested in three judges rather than Piddington alone. This meant that union evidence already presented was worthless and a new case would have to be prepared. All banking unions were downcast, for though the UBOA of NSW had made some gains, the BOA and other unions' three-year wait had been in vain. Bereft of leaders capable of organizing an effective arbitration case,[14] the BOA had little choice but to continue to wait on New South Wales developments. The poor results of an agreement negotiated in the insurance industry by the Australian Insurance Staffs' Federation (AISF) provided further reason for their procrastination: "It was felt that the acceptance of such a small increase over the previous award, would probably prejudice our new claims in as much that the last case of the ABOA was practically taken in conjunction with that of the Insurance Staff Federation."[15] With Benwell's skills limited to routine office operations and lengthy, relaxed country recruiting tours, Harrison and the new vice-president, Lindsay McLosky, were left to run the union, now interrupted only infrequently by Smith's peremptory commands from Sydney.

The only real opposition to Smith's directive to the BOA to wait upon the finalization of the UBOA of NSW claims came from Western Australian vice-president J. S. Battye. On an earlier visit he had attacked Smith for his eagerness to confront the banks in the courts and claimed that better results could be obtained by negotiation.[16] Battye summed up the views of several committeemen regarding Smith's "interference" when he commented that the negotiators ought to be men who were actively engaged in banking work: "They should not have in conference men who are seeking, not so much to further the ends of bank officers . . . as they are seeking to further from a public standpoint their own ends."[17] He argued that as all banking awards were shortly to expire, a combined approach to negotiate a single award was more appropriate. But his idealism had outstripped his industrial relations expertise. For in advocating a combined approach he was playing into the banks' hands, who believed that any move to award uniformity would assist them "in resisting the extravagant claims of the New South Wales Association".[18] Smith reacted savagely, accusing Battye of "attempting to introduce tricks of diplomacy" and of "caution and discretion coloured by ulterior motives in place of the candid, frank attitude on the part of [union] executives".[19] The BOA then tentatively approached the banks with a view to fixing a new award. This was not so much a victory for Battye over Smith (although the BOA did notify the banks that "the Association would not be represented by its General Secretary"),[20] but rather an indication of the simmering discontent of senior officers. Discussions followed, and Battye optimistically reported, "sympathetic consideration will be given to the salaries and conditions of senior men."[21] However, Norman Bell, the bank's arbitration officer, dashed these hopes immediately: "The report is misleading to managers and gave them false hopes of increments."[22]

Battye retired to the West, his faith in negotiations severely bruised. Senior officers, constrained by their inherent conservatism, could do little other than bemoan their straitened circumstances. The BOA leadership was now left ample time for the mundane and often inane issues such as collection of unpaid subscriptions and seemingly endless discussions whether the Bankers' Club should apply for a liquor licence. Even the fatal shooting of a young bank officer brought but a meek BOA protest at the lack of security in the growing number of one-man branches and agencies.[23] After a muted request to the banks to improve security was rejected, the union half-heartedly set about soliciting contributions towards the establishment of a suitable memorial. In early 1926 there was a brief flurry of activity when the BOA suggested to the State Savings Bank of Victoria Officers' Association (SSBOA) that they should join the BOA. However, the SSBOA refused the offer, pointing out there were few advantages in joining an organization so clearly in the doldrums and so clearly dominated by Smith, whose crudeness and antagonism was far from their conception of the ideal of a white-collar union leader.

In other states there had also been few changes, for they too had waited on New South Wales developments. The Tasmanian branch remained under the domination of the Victorians, though their high level of unionization was more a result of boisterous and well-funded sub-branch meetings held in various towns than of any great feeling of loyalty to the BOA. Leadership changes had been minimal. Laidlaw and Heal were now firmly entrenched. In Western Australia, the incumbent W.Y. Cooke had relinquished the secretary's position in favour of his business partner A.F. Stowe, though in practice E.S. Saw, another accountant, did most of the work on a part-time basis. Yet despite this inactivity, these state unions were characterized by high levels of union density, in all cases exceeding 75 per cent, some 10 per cent above the BOA level. This reflected the continuing inability of the BOA to satisfy the demands of senior officers and hence to recruit them.

Some Gains, Some Losses

By the late 1920s there were signs that Australia faced a serious economic crisis. The Nationalist government's reactions included a number of amendments to industrial legislation. It believed that demands for increasing levels of protection by Australian secondary industry to maintain international competitiveness arose at least in part from attempts to maintain profit levels in the face of extensive union wage claims. Additionally, the industrial unrest resulting from employer resistance was impairing government plans for sustained economic development. In an attempt to contain this industrial strength, the government took several initiatives.

In late 1926, Prime Minister Bruce, aware that some union gains were a result of their being able to "build on" claims already granted in another sphere (precisely the BOA's rationale), sought through referendums to extend the industrial powers of the Commonwealth at the expense of the states. The complexity of the proposal combined with strong union opposition, including that of all state banking unions, ensured the defeat of this proposal. State bank union resistance was predictable given the relatively poor 1924 federal award and the declared intention of the Arbitration Court not to provide a classification scheme.[24] The BOA's opposition was also influenced by their dependence upon the results of the current New South Wales case. As well, the BOA executive, with limited expertise and determination, did not relish the prospect of responsibility for all banking arbitration cases. Most importantly, Smith too was opposed, for this would have removed much of his New South Wales power base. In 1927, further amendments to the Arbitration Act reflected a continuing government concern with escalating labour costs and were designed to reduce trade union bargaining power by penalizing the use of the strike. The Court was also to be required to take economic issues into account; given the increasingly unfavourable economic climate, this could only mean wage reductions rather than increases.

As the confrontations continued through 1928 and early 1929, the Nationalist government became increasingly obsessed with the need to restrict union power. Organized manual labour, convinced that unionism was threatened, fought back savagely. In the resultant turmoil it became apparent that neither of Bruce's goals of industrial peace or economic prosperity were achievable, and in 1929, as economic conditions worsened, he abandoned his earlier approach and proposed legislation that effectively gave the states full responsibility for the regulation of wages and working conditions. The BOA, a federally registered union, understandably viewed this seriously and notified the government of "its strongest protest at the abolition of the Arbitration Court".[25] Smith, stunned by the government's proposal, for it threatened his own livelihood and ambitions, took the first train to Canberra to lobby ministers. Local parliamentary members were approached and urged to oppose the legislation. The UBOA of NSW also objected, for they were worried that this would increase the delays in the state arena and that should Premier Bavin's pronounced antipathy to white-collar unions and their access to arbitration be translated into action, then they too would be left without protection. The dependence of the Western Australian and South Australian unions upon the federal award prompted them also to oppose the plan; BOASA passed a resolution disagreeing with the "oft expressed opinion that compulsory arbitration in Australia has failed, or is responsible for the industrial depression now being experienced throughout the Commonwealth".[26]

As the federal election precipitated by the proposed legislation grew closer, the question of the political stances of banking unions came to the fore. For the UBOA of NSW there was little problem, union members having already accepted that "on political matters the Executive could give some guidance to the members".[27] There was no such freedom in Victoria, though Smith in responding to numerous letters requesting advice and clarification was able to assert: "the announcement of the P.M. to abolish federal arbitration, the refusal of the Victorian Premier to substitute any satisfactory system in its place . . . are of such vital importance that it calls for the serious consideration and activity of all bank officers in upholding what they have secured at such great price in the past."[28] In an appeal to members, the union's journal, after listing the favourable responses of Labor candidates towards Arbitration Court retention, reminded members: "Bankers must decide on election day whether we stand on the rock of the Arbitration Act or forsake it for something which may not prove to be as sound a footing. Failure to vote retention may mean a reversion to old conditions. Support the candidate in favour of Federal Arbitration."[29] However, it is unlikely that many bank officers would have even seriously considered this, and there was some relief when, following defeat at the polls, the proposed legislation followed the Bruce government into oblivion.

A casual observer might question Bruce's economic wisdom in seeking legislative change to cut wage costs in a period of apparent prosperity. From 1925 to 1929 export prices and volumes had been maintained at high levels and unemployment was only marginally higher than earlier years. Rapid expansion of social infrastructure was made possible by large quantities of readily accessible overseas funds.[30] The banking industry eagerly participated in all of this. Between 1925 and 1929 total Australian branches increased by 10 per cent, in contrast with the five years preceding 1925 when there was net branch closure.[31] Yet this increased activity did not signal increased profits, for between 1926 and 1929 bank profits were stagnant.[32] There were two major reasons for this. First, the private banks had not participated to any significant degree in the provision of public capital in the period as it had largely come from overseas sources. Second, although the proportion of urban branches was increasing (from 24 per cent in 1920 to 27 per cent in 1925 and nearly

34 per cent in 1929),[33] most branches were still in rural areas. However, the predominance of government spending programmes in urban areas and increasing tariff protection for burgeoning urban-based secondary industries meant that most economic expansion was now concentrated in these areas. Illustrating this structural shift is the fact that by 1926, for the first time, manufacturing employed more workers than primary industry.[34]

The increasing inflexibility of the Australian banking structure was reinforced by the growing inability of farmers to repay their debts, which was compounded by the rapid decline in Australian export prices during late 1929. This terms-of-trade decline was intensified by an equally rapid fall in export sales, coupled with an increase in imports. By the end of 1929 the Australian trade balance was in considerable deficit, and overseas loans had ceased. The resultant balance-of-payments crisis was intensified by an increasing level of interest payments on overseas borrowings. By now the banks were thoroughly alarmed, as much of this deficit would have to be financed through their quite inadequate holdings of London sterling. For although the lessons of 1892 had been well learned and sterling balances were at much higher levels, they were insufficient in this abnormal situation. In fact the deficit was so great that even the compulsory acquisition of the banks' gold reserves did little to reduce it. In addition, the banks faced an acute domestic liquidity strain, as their cash reserves fell following a reduction in the community's saving ratio and an increased demand for advances. As revenue generation through increased lending was clearly impossible, the liquidity drain could only be halted by cost cutting, which in this labour-intensive industry really meant reducing staff costs.

In the four years following 1929, the banks used a variety of techniques to cut staff expenses. Included in their repertoire were branch closures and retrenchments, salary cuts by way of the Arbitration Court, "assessment" and salary reductions for inefficient officers, non-payment of annual salary increments, and giving "rationed" officers the options of resigning or taking large amounts of unpaid leave. After the gains of the previous decade, these were new and frightening challenges for banking unions. Even more seriously there were threats to their very existence. None came under greater pressure than the BOA, whose mediocre and inhibited leaders were largely unable to protect their members.[35] Smith, still engrossed with the continuing UBOA of NSW case, work for other unions, and a considerable drinking problem, was increasingly unwilling to devote time to BOA affairs. There was internal union conflict, between different unions and particularly in the BOA between different banks. Prospects of united opposition to the banks vanished as unions scrambled to negotiate separate state and bank agreements. The earlier procedure of unions using other awards to improve their own situation was now reversed. It was the banks' turn to fragment union membership, winning concessions from one group then using these to force other unions to agree to wage cuts or to the removal of earlier-won conditions of work.

The first specific bank response to the worsening economic conditions came late in 1929 when the banks asked the New South Wales Industrial Commission to reduce salaries to pre-1927 levels and to abolish the family allowance. The Industrial Commission refused, arguing that there had been earlier agreement that no other salary issue would be heard before the results of the long-running case were handed down. This finally occurred in mid-1930 when the interim scale was confirmed, with the top of the scale forty-eight pounds above the federal rate. A classification system was also introduced, so that when the family allowance was added "officers on the scale in N.S.W. were receiving on an average £100 per annum more than officers in other states rendering identical service".[36] Smith's satisfaction was tempered by legislative amendments proposed by the Nationalist state government, so as to deny Government Savings Bank employees similar terms of employment to those enjoyed by trading bank officers.[37] A measure of Premier Bavin's hostility towards Smith and the UBOA of NSW and his determination to reduce public service costs was shown in his insistence on the changes despite strong union objections. This culminated in a general meeting where "political action was threatened in the fighting speeches, many speakers being admittedly former Nationalist supporters".[38] In other states the banks had already cut the salaries of some "over-award" officers, and in Queensland they twice successfully approached the state court to reduce salaries in line with state basic wage falls, much to the consternation of Laidlaw, who to date had been smugly content with its determinations.

These events paled into insignificance, however, when in July 1930 the banks refused to renew the South Australian agreement, which meant that no further increments would be paid in that state. BOASA was able temporarily to invoke the 1923 award (though with lower salary rates), but it was obvious that the banks now intended a full-scale assault on salaries. BOASA secretary Heal desperately appealed to other bank unions for help, and an interstate conference was hastily convened. Here there was seemingly general agreement on the need to form a single union to combat the banks' attacks, and all unions other than the UBOA of NSW agreed to join the BOA as state branches.

The decision was made not out of respect for the quality of the Victorian leadership but rather because of the need for any Australia-wide union to hold federal registration. Individual union leaders too had different reasons for again contemplating amalgamation. To Harrison and Battye it was an opportunity to bring about amalgamation rather more easily than they had earlier thought possible. Heal, secretary of a union now without an award, saw an opportunity to apply the federal award to South Australia. Laidlaw also saw at least some short-run advantages in federal arbitration in view of the recent state basic wage cuts. "As far as we are concerned," he wrote to Harrison, Federal Council president, "to approach our State Court would be suicidal and would invite reductions similar to the public servants of between 10 and 20 per cent."[39] In addition, recent federal Arbitration Act amendments had allowed an expanded role for industry conciliation committees. The scheming Laidlaw believed that after carefully choosing the committee members, the union could use the committee to its advantage: "We can get a claim before that committee and we should be able to juggle matters for quite a time, and even if we can't get any increases at present, we may certainly stop some decreases."[40] Further explanation for empire-builder Smith's uncharacteristic ambivalence over the proposal lay in his knowledge that the amalgamation would not enhance his power and influence as general secretary of the BOA, for the conference had insisted that the state unions should retain their financial and decision-making authority.

The conference then drew up claims based on the Piddington award, and the BOA agreed to serve it on behalf of the other unions. Battye, the tireless proponent of negotiations, favoured a meeting with the ABA, but only Charles Wren and C.J. O'Sullivan from the ES&A were prepared to attend. This "cast quite a gloom over the conference as it was felt that arrangements satisfactory to all might have been made".[41] The earlier optimism was further shattered when it became evident why the ES&A managers had come. They told the conference that large-scale retrenchments and branch closures could only be avoided if yearly salary increments were suspended indefinitely (appendix 2 reveals the extent of these increments). For clerks, the average increment between 1924 and 1930 had been £16 11s, for accountants £16 19s, and for managers £16 10s. The 1929–30 increment for the same occupational groups was £10 2s, £23 5s and £16 10s;[42] significant wage increases indeed in a labour-intensive industry facing falling profit levels. Conference rejected this request for the "lost year of service" (as this suspension of increments became known), but the issue was to recur frequently in the near future.

Over the next few months the states waited for the BOA to serve the claims, but the Victorians had already changed their minds. Harrison, in writing to an impatient Laidlaw, explained that the issue had been discussed at the annual meeting of the Victorian branch and that members had decided not to serve the log.[43] The union minutes, however, deny this and again highlight the Victorian leadership's refusal to consult the rank and file: "Mr. McLoskey (Vice President) informed the meeting that no action would be taken on the matter of any new award until such time as the banks lodged a counter claim against our existing award."[44]

For most clerks the important question was not amalgamation, anyway, but employment security. As Harrison explained, "The opinion is that any move to increase salaries at this time will probably result in a large number of dismissals from the ESA on account of depressed business."[45] His fear of ES&A retrenchments was soundly based, for although all banks faced similar problems, the ES&A could retrench staff more readily because the majority of their branches, almost 70 per cent in fact,[46] were in urban areas. Given that urban branches normally operated with larger staff establishments than rural branches, there was greater scope for retrenchments without forcing branch closure. As well, the ES&A's urban concentration and hence relatively smaller need to protect rural loans allowed for a more economical distribution and allocation of labour.

By the end of 1930, fear of unemployment dominated ES&A employees' thoughts, and there was growing rank-and-file pressure to appease the banks by granting the "lost year of service". This culminated in a meeting of ES&A staff which demanded that the BOA agree to the suspension of increments for twelve months. The union, fearful of creating a precedent and disturbed by the influence of senior management and non-members at the meeting, refused. As Benwell reported: "The decision was certainly taken under duress and no officer could be expected to stand up and say anything to the contrary."[47] A number of ES&A officers then took the extreme step of resigning from the union. In the next six months eighty-five officers, or 16 per cent of total ES&A membership, resigned, only fifteen being a result of retrenchment,[48] which prompted Harrison once again to urge increment suspension. He became so insistent that finally he was told to leave all executive meetings when the issue was being discussed.[49] In New South Wales, Smith, content with the new state award, was prepared to sacrifice officers' increments rather than risk being taken into court by the banks, and he wrote to other unions urging them also to concede. Laidlaw comments on Smith's reasoning: "I suppose you also realise what a good wicket New South Wales would be on if automatic increases were withheld for twelve months. Our members are on a maximum of £390 and New South Wales had £430 and Family Allowance. If there are to be any sacrifices, let them give up Child Endowment."[50]

In South Australia, Heal, still fuming at the BOA's failure to serve the claims and under strong attack from his own members, resolved to make a separate agreement with the ES&A incorporating the "lost year of service". He wrote to Laidlaw complaining that the BOA, by failing to serve the log, "had sold South Australia a pup . . . and were leaving the banks to their policy of attacking and slaughtering one state union at a time".[51] Heal added that he was going to Melbourne to make an agreement. Laidlaw, desperate to maintain a united front, cabled Harrison: "Heal considers South Australia let down . . . is coming to Melbourne to negotiate separately. Do what you can to intercept him as I feel certain he is looking for a loophole to crawl out of and will let us down."[52]

A further conference was held in Melbourne, and after much bitter argument its members agreed to approach the ABA with the offer of increment suspension as long as all retrenchments ceased and all retrenched officers were reinstated.[53] The banks, however, stated that this was insufficient, for they had envisaged "a scale running up to the fourteenth year at reduced rates and nothing beyond that; late in life clause to be omitted, overtime to be based on four weekly period, no classification and no assurance that retrenchment would not then follow. As a matter of fact from their point of view their right to retrench must be preserved."[54]

Laidlaw, already convinced that the banks were "using the present depression for all they are worth to defeat our associations",[55] effectively spoiled the possibility of agreement by maliciously suggesting that "as a gesture of bona fides the general managers and executive officers should take a lead by reducing their own salaries".[56] Then, a senior banker's chilling comment that in fact "the present was not a period of depression but part of a well ordered arrangement to return the industry to pre-war levels"[57] stimulated some discussion of officer rationing. Conference agreed that any bank announcements of further retrenchments would be countered with a union offer that for the next twelve months all officers would take double recreation leave without pay. Armed with this unsatisfactory compromise, Harrison returned to face continuing unrest provoked by salary cuts for officers above the scale. This led to the union suggesting an application for a preference-in-promotion clause. The banks, unaware that the Arbitration Court would be most unlikely to infringe upon their managerial prerogatives anyway, opposed the proposition bitterly and refused even to discuss the issue. The bewildered union executive, almost as a last resort, called a general meeting. The rank and file, now more concerned with continuing employment rather than increments, attempted to force the adoption of additional claims requiring preference to unionists in employment as well as promotion, and protection of male employees at the expense of females.[58] However, the BOA executive, now unwilling to antagonize the banks in any way, were reluctant to present the claim. Using the ploy that the opinions of country members were needed, they decided upon a postal ballot, but in the face of a serious union rift, organization of this ballot ended abruptly.

The BOA leadership has been thrown into panic by news that the ES&A sub-branch had decided to call upon all ES&A officers to resign from the BOA because of its failure to agree to the suspension of increments. The preference issue was quickly forgotten as the BOA, in most uncharacteristic haste, entreated ES&A officers not to resign. A further meeting of ES&A officers rejected the union's argument but gave them one last chance to agree to their bank's demands. Annoyed at this impudence, the BOA executive refused, falsely arguing that the respondent to the award was the ABA, not individual banks, and hypocritically complaining that ES&A country members had not been consulted. The ES&A sub-branch then convened another meeting and refused to allow Smith and Benwell to attend. The union, wary of the bank's role, wrote to the meeting's organizers: "The object of this meeting is obviously to put pressure upon younger members. Mr. Docker, Assistant to the General Manager, this day informed Messrs. Smith and Benwell that the bank does not desire its officers to resign from the Association. This should be made known to the meeting."[59]

Benwell was finally permitted to speak. He received a hostile reception and came away suspecting that the real question was one of union membership rather than the "lost year of service". He then warned the organizers: "Resignations obtained under the pressure that you and the Bank are exerting will not be treated by the Association as voluntary acts . . . and the matter will be brought before the Arbitration Court at the earliest possible moment."[60] Benwell's fears were confirmed when the union received a message from Docker denying he had said "it was not his wish that members should resign from the BOA".[61] Smith then sought a compromise. Returning to Sydney and using the argument that any court action could jeopardize the New South Wales award, he convinced the UBOA of NSW to agree to the "lost year of service" for ES&A officers and then urged the BOA executive to follow suit. However, their equivocation was mercifully relieved when the ABA indicated that they did not approve of separate agreements, and again the issue faded.

That which replaced it was of even more consequence. In early 1931 the banks made application to the Arbitration Court to reduce all salaries by 10 per cent. This application arose from an application by the Victorian and New South Wales railway commissioners to vary awards in the railways industry. A Full Court inquiry into the basic wage followed. They were encouraged in this by views held in influential quarters that the Australian wage structure was too high relative to her trading partners. The court refused to alter the method of computing the basic wage but, accepting the lack of employers' "capacity to pay", ordered the reduction of award wages by 10 per cent.[62] To the union's argument that a reduction in workers purchasing power would only worsen the depression, the court expressed the classically orthodox view that this was merely transferring the purchasing power to the employers, and that in their hands this surplus "would operate as a stimulus of general industrial activity, thus giving work to men now unemployed, with consequential benefit to all industries".[63]

The banks immediately sought an order to vary banking industry awards. Once more the reluctance and inability of the BOA to prepare and fight an arbitration case was apparent. BOASA had instructed Heal to go to Melbourne to protect their interests, and Smith came down from Sydney. Heal reported: "On arriving in Melbourne Mr. Smith and myself found everyone was prepared to take the 'cut' and that no case had been prepared against it . . . [We] briefed a KC and instructed him to prepare a case against any reduction . . . in view of the apathy of the Federal Council we considered we should fight against any reduction as it would prejudice every other state."[64]

In court, the banks' counsel argued that bank profits had fallen sharply and that a reduction in wages in line with the fall in the cost of living was required to reduce their costs.[65] The BOA's counsel leant heavily on the concept of banking as a career industry as he attempted to show why salaries should not be reduced. He pointed out that the acceptance by officers of relatively low salaries was because of the security of tenure, the incremental salary structure, and the promotional prospects in the industry, all of which were now in some doubt. The unwillingness of the union to accept the salary cut brought considerable media comment; the *Argus* commented:

> There is general recognition of the fact that everyone in receipt of a regular income must make some contribution in response to a general appeal. It would be grossly unfair, for instance, if the civil servant contributed substantially to the relief of the situation while the bank clerk performing similar duties made no contribution. The trend of wages and salaries is downwards. Even if the banks' profits permitted them to pay high salaries, the wise course would be to reduce salaries and allow the banks to pass onto the public the benefits of their lessened expenses. It must be sufficiently in evidence that those who have their money invested in banks have necessarily made their contribution in some form before this.[66]

The BOA, incensed and shocked by this, its first public criticism, authorized "any action which may be necessary to bring the *Argus* before the Court for contempt".[67]

This editorial had been inspired by the notoriously conservative bias of the *Argus* and the paper's vigorous promotion of the Premiers' Plan of June 1931. Arising from the clash between the mildly expansionary plans of Labor government treasurer E.G. Theodore and the deficit-avoiding goals of the Commonwealth Bank, the private banks, and imported government advisers, the Premiers' Plan was a resounding victory for proponents of deflationary policies. In return for interest rate reductions, mortgagee relief (supposedly so that fixed-income earners would share the burden of adjustment to depression conditions),[68] and support for a conversion loan to finance the large government deficit, the state and federal governments agreed to reduce government expenditures by 20 per cent and to increase taxes.

In spite of evidence of significant declines in bank profits, advances, and deposits, the court chose to reserve its decision until the final results for the financial year were known. In July 1931, as the downward profit trends continued,[69] the court brought down its judgment. It "could see no valid reason why bank officers should not be included in the rule that all participate in the effort to re-establish affairs on a new level".[70] Accordingly they ordered a 10 per cent cut in all award rates for Victorian and Tasmanian officers. But to the banks' chagrin the court could make no order regarding officers above the salary scale, and these were quantitatively of greater importance. For example, though the cut reduced the

Bank of Australasia's salary bill by £8,500 per year, had the cut been applied to all officers, the annual saving would have been in excess of £20,000.[71] While the CBA and NBA immediately cut all over-award salaries by 10 per cent, other banks, particularly those with branches in other states, were reluctant to do so. BNSW general manager A. C. Davidson had written earlier in the year: "The senior officers in this Bank are earning a net salary much lower than the man holding the same position before the War. With this in mind I think it is unjust to ask for any sacrifice from such men on the same percentage with those who have gained large benefits as the result of unsound policies pursued by the various Industrial Courts."[72] However, within months all banks had overcome their scruples and applied salary reductions to all officers. It is doubtful whether they were greatly heartened by the knowledge that directors of at least one bank were "voluntarily surrendering 10 per cent of their remuneration".[73]

A perplexing problem for the banks was how to extend these salary reductions to the state unions, and most particularly to New South Wales and Western Australia, where còst of living falls had not been reflected in award reductions. The BNSW sought to negotiate a separate agreement with the bank's sub-branch in New South Wales, at least one meeting of which was addressed by Davidson. Here it was unanimously resolved: "that this meeting of officers of the Bank of New South Wales expresses its willingness to share in the sacrifices demanded by the position as disclosed by the General Manager".[74] Possibilities of a separate agreement were given further impetus when the beleaguered Government Savings Bank closed, victim of a classic "bank run" initiated by Premier Lang's threatened loan repudiation. More than a thousand officers faced retrenchment, and even the strong though officially denied rumours of an amalgamation with the Commonwealth Bank were of little comfort. Then came the not unexpected failure of the Primary Producers Bank and, following many retrenchments, the absorption of the Australian Bank of Commerce by the BNSW. As the possibility of a separate agreement strengthened, the ABA, dominated by the Melbourne-based banks, intervened; their usual antagonism towards the BNSW was heightened by Davidson's independent and aggressive attitudes. They too were concerned at the unwillingness of the New South Wales Industrial Commission to vary the award, but believed that given that body's emphasis on conciliation they would continue to defer a hearing while separate negotiations were continuing. Davidson, however, determinedly went on his way, and a three-month agreement was eventually concluded. All salaries were to be reduced by $8\frac{1}{3}$ per cent and the family allowance restricted to two children. In return, the BNSW undertook to minimize retrenchments.

In South Australia the banks' abil‚ity to reduce staff costs was complicated by a long-running case in the Industrial Court which had begun in October 1930 after BOASA had finally served a claim on the banks.

Several conferences followed where BOASA indicated that they would agree to the "lost year of service" in return for the readoption of the 1925 award salary scale, an end to retrenchment, and the reinstatement of all officers already dismissed. The banks refused, and an exhaustive arbitration hearing began. Soon the banks, now doubly anxious to bring South Australian salaries into line with the reduced federal award, were complaining of "the enormous amount of evidence tendered by the Association with a view to prolonging the hearing . . . the long drawn out delay is very irritating."[75] These union tactics, sponsored by Smith, who had in fact borrowed them from the banks, underwent drastic change when their legal counsel presented an account for nearly three thousand pounds. Frantically but vainly they contacted other states for financial support, then finally placed a levy on their members. When this plus the receipts from the sale of most union assets proved insufficient, they were forced to ask for an interim award based on evidence to date. The court then laid down a 10 per cent reduction on 1925 award rates, so that South Australian salaries again paralleled those of the federal award.[76] In Western Australia the banks' tactic of simply cancelling the agreement was complicated by state legislation foreshadowed in the Premiers' Plan, which provided for a decrease in interest rates. A banker explained how this affected salary reductions: "As a reduction in interest rates does not take effect in Western Australia until October 1, our solicitors consider it would be lacking in force and not politic to approach the Court for a reduction in salaries until that takes effect."[77] At this later time the union agreed to a 10 per cent salary reduction in return for an end to retrenchments.

So by the end of 1931 the banks had succeeded in reducing all salaries by between 8 and 10 per cent. They now turned again to the question of automatic increments. The manager of one bank indicated the extent of the problem: "By means of the general 10 per cent reduction and the reduction of fifty in the number of our staff, salaries have fallen from £247,000 in the half year to October 1931 to £229,000 in the half year just closed (April 1932). This saving however will soon be absorbed by automatic award increases which, in the year to October last, totalled about £17,000."[78] Their bargaining power was considerably enhanced by a new variant of the retrenchment theme: "Eight officers who recently became twenty one . . . were given notice that their services would no longer be required . . . they were also told that the Bank was well satisfied with their work and was very sorry to lose them but the General Managers had decided on a policy that they had to be put off and juniors taken on in their places."[79]

In Victoria the BOA's resolve not to relent on the "lost year of service" had been weakened by the existence of the award clause which allowed the banks to "assess" officers and pay them less than award rates.[80] The banks also continued to reduce the salaries of officers beyond the scale.

For example, in February and March 1931, twenty-one senior officer members (and an unknown number of non-members) suffered salary cuts in excess of fifty pounds per annum.[81] In mid-1931, under pressure from influential senior officers, the BOA served a claim on the banks to the effect that no officer whose salary was in excess of the award could be reduced in salary, grade, or status except by agreement between the union and the bank concerned. In what was known as "Walker's Case",[82] the banks claimed that the court did not have jurisdiction, as the dispute was not of an interstate nature, an argument with which the court agreed. In mid-1932 the BOA, under continuing member pressure, for some banks were now rationing employees quite heavily,[83] again approached the banks. This time they were quite amenable to accepting the banks' conditions — a cessation of increments and a further salary cut. The following clause was inserted in the award.

> Time shall not run during a period from the first day of December 1932, to entitle any male or female employee to receive any increase of salary except that on attaining 21 years of age.
>   The banks shall, for a period of one year from the first day of December 1932, cease rationing and retrenching employees: but this shall not affect the right to dispense with the service of an employee for misconduct or for lack of diligence and efficiency.[84]

The extension of the "lost year of service" to other states was rendered difficult by a number of local factors, including state industrial legislation, and it eventually occurred only in New South Wales. Remarkably, no doubt fortuitously, bank officers in the three smaller state unions had escaped increment suspension.

The net effect of these Depression salary adjustments is apparent in tables 1, 2, and 3 of appendix 2. Of overwhelming importance (and perhaps surprisingly) is that the real wages of all bank officers improved over the course of the Depression. As table 1 indicates, the clerks all made considerable real income gains. This was largely a result of the significant price falls of the early thirties. Remarkably, the money incomes of younger clerks even showed little effects of the 1931 salary cut of 10 per cent. Table 2 shows a similar story for accountants. All benefited from the banks' payment of some increments to senior staff. That the salary increases of younger accountants was relatively greater than that of the older group indicates that a number of these older accountants were, after lengthy service, viewed as mediocre officers and relegated to less important branches. In both cases the 10 per cent salary cut is clear and not disguised by any incremental increase. A further common feature is the money wage stagnation that followed. The salary history of branch managers for this period parallels that of accountants as shown by table 3. Though steady increments were rudely interrupted by the salary reductions in 1931, the considerable price decline also left this group with significantly increased purchasing power.

The extent of the relative real wage improvement only becomes apparent when table 4 of appendix 2 is examined. This table compares bank officer and unskilled and skilled workers money and real wages. Several points are evident. Firstly, in the period 1924–29, while there was some small increase in the real wages of blue-collar workers, these were dwarfed by the increase of almost 20 per cent in bank officer real wages. This reverses the trend found in the pre-unionization era up to 1919 and reflects the importance of regular and substantial increments. Even more significant are the results for the Depression years of 1929–34. While blue-collar real wages fell by 17 per cent for unskilled workers and almost 10 per cent for tradesmen, those of bank officers all showed increases ranging from 9 per cent to almost 20 per cent. The net effect was that while blue-collar workers held less purchasing power in 1934 than they had ten years previously, quite the opposite was true for bank employees.

An examination of unemployment levels reinforces the conclusion that bank officers withstood the effects of the Depression better than blue-collar workers. Between 1929 and 1933 the average rate of unemployment of Victorian trade unionists never fell below 20 per cent.[85] L. J. Louis in *Trade Unions and the Depression* indicates the extent of inroads into blue-collar union membership: "Although the different unions experienced varying degrees of decline, over all they suffered greatly. . . . many disintegrated, some to the point where they continued to exist practically in name only."[86] BOA records show that, between January 1930 and December 1933, 107 officer members were retrenched, which is 3.6 per cent of the average union membership for the period.[87] This was confirmed at the 1933 interstate conference, where it was stated, "No more than five out of every hundred bank officers have been retrenched in the last four years."[88] Further evidence of a low rate of unemployment in the industry is given by the fact that the net reduction in Victorian banking employees between 1929 and 1933 was 333, or 7.5 per cent,[89] from which must be deducted those retiring. So whether measured in terms of real wages or unemployment levels, there is little doubt that bank officers fared much better than blue-collar workers through the Depression.

There were several reasons for this. The importance of regular increments to officers on the scale has been stressed. But what of the senior officers receiving salaries beyond the scale, and apparently at the mercy of the banks? As discussed earlier, the banks were wary of allowing senior officer relativities to be unduly distorted. So paradoxically the automatic salary scale, criticized by so many older officers, was important to the maintenance of their salary situation. The incremental scale is, however, not a sufficient explanation. Credit must also be given to the banks for their generous treatment of some employees. Seldom did they dispense with the services of pedestrian and mediocre officers, choosing rather to "assess" them as inefficient and to reduce their salaries. Bearing in mind the sharp profit decline of the period, these were seemingly generous gestures. In fact they often had little choice, for in general, branches were already operating at minimum staffing levels. Also, larger cuts in senior officer salaries would not have been in the banks' longer-term interests, for larger salary reductions would have further damaged the already wavering morale of those officers most important to the banks' prosperity – the managers and accountants. The banks also realized that a significant problem facing the BOA was the unwillingness of many senior officers to join the union, an attitude that might well change if further salary reductions occurred.

Bank officers had done relatively well through the Depression. This was due to the incremental scale, bank paternalism, initial low staffing establishments, and the vissitudes suffered by blue-collar workers, rather than being the result of the BOA's protective ability or its leaders' endeavours and skills.

A Stagnant, Unresponsive Union

Union density figures indicate that the BOA was given at least some of the credit for protecting bank officers. The proportion of union members in Victorian private banks increased from 56 per cent to 70 per cent between 1924 and 1934.[90] In contrast, membership of all Australian unions fell from almost 50 per cent to less than 43 per cent.[91] However, the BOA union density should also be viewed in the context of density rates in the other state banking unions. On this comparison it fares less well. In Queensland the density rate never fell below 90 per cent, in Western Australia and South Australia it was always greater than 80 per cent, and in New South Wales in excess of 75 per cent.[92] Much of this can be explained by the BOA executives' continued timidity, inaction, and willingness to compromise, which was in contrast to some of the state unions. This not only alienated younger officers but failed to attract the senior officers so desperately needed by the union.

The BOA's problems were compounded when they forced Smith to resign. In this they acted in concert with the UBOA of NSW. Following Smith's appearance in Sydney before a magistrate on charges of conspiracy to defraud an insurance company, the New South Wales union had demanded his resignation. Though the charges were dismissed, and he successfully counter-sued for malicious prosecution, the UBOA of NSW used this to rid themselves of the increasingly embarrassing Smith. A now obvious drinking problem leading to a number of injudicious actions had convinced the union executive, now controlled by officers of the BNSW sub-branch, that Smith must be dismissed. This thrust Harrison to the forefront of BOA decision-making. After retiring from the ES&A he had established a small real estate business while retaining the now paid presidency of both the Victorian branch and Federal Council. This BOA decision was not a result of any belief that he was a good union leader, or even the best available, but that his long service to the BOA required that his inadequate bank pension be supplemented. However, his actions remained dominated by the effects of a lifetime of subservience to the bank. After being controlled by Smith for so many years, he was unable to move into the decision-making role following Smith's departure. Battye summed up the BOA's quandary: "As far as the Federal Council is concerned, I am inclined to think there is room for considerable improvement, both in organisation and management, and it would possibly be much more effective if the President accepted more responsibility and exercised more directive power."[93]

This prevarication had an impact on union membership. BOA records show that approximately twenty of the union resignations in late 1931 were a result of the 10 per cent salary cut,[94] though given the widespread nature of the cuts, these resignations were perhaps illogically based. The aftermath of the meek concession of the "lost year of service" was, however, more serious, when 256 officers, almost 9 per cent of the total Victorian membership, resigned in the first three months of 1933.[95]

A further factor contributing to improved BOA membership density was the changing location of officers, as the banks slowly responded to Victoria's increased urbanization. Between 1925 and 1934 the number of branches located in Victorian city and suburban areas had increased from 174 to 241, or from 27 to 35 per cent of total branches.[96] As urban branches were, on average, larger than rural branches, this meant a significant increase in the number of clerks in urban areas.[97] Because the dispersed branch structure had posed a major recruiting problem for the BOA, any increasing concentration of bank officers aided union recruiting.[98] It allowed Benwell to recruit new members, which in turn increased union revenues. It also encouraged membership by permitting more bank officers to use BOA facilities, in particular the Bankers' Club. Urbanization gave a greater number of bank officers an opportunity to participate in union decision-making, but few took up the opportunity, and elections for institutional sub-branch or Victorian branch delegate positions were rare. A unionist summarized problems still facing the large number of country members:

> We cannot help to remove or retain a member of the committee. . . . we have no part in the election of our officers. . . . we cannot help formulate business for the Committee or voice an opinion on the Association undertaking expensive litigation. . . . our constitution may be altered without reference to country members. . . . we never hear financial reports. . . . levies may be called notwithstanding our ignorance of the cause.[99]

The unrepresentativeness of the BOA Federal Council continued. Tasmania was still treated as "practically an appendage to Victoria. . . . The

Tasmanians appear to have been treated as the tail which wags in the direction of the brain of the dog",[100] even though (or perhaps because) they had a union density rate in excess of 95 per cent for the period.[101] Brooke, the vigorous founding secretary, had been forced to resign following several clashes with the Victorians. He had vainly requested increased Tasmanian representation on Federal Council and more regular visits from executive members. Brooke had frequently condemned the docile Victorians and attacked their obsession, the Bankers' Club, which though subsidized by Tasmanian members obviously could not be used by them. Finally, Federal Council had instructed him to resign for conduct "unbecoming to the union",[102] after he had roundly criticized an influential Tasmanian officer who had refused to pay his subscriptions. This angered the Tasmanians, and the appointment of a new secretary, W. T. Crosby, ex-bank officer and now insurance agent, did little to mollify them. In early 1933, Benwell and S. J. Dangerfield, the Tasmanian proxy on Federal Council, were hurriedly dispatched to Tasmania to prevent mass resignations. Though the complaints were ostensibly based upon the BOA's acceptance of the "lost year of service" and the lack of money for Tasmanian branch recruiting and organizing, the real issue was their lack of involvement in BOA decision-making. The union's failure to rectify this was to have repercussions in the near future.

As the banking industry gradually emerged from the Depression, BOA members had little reason to feel confident that their present leaders could adequately advance, or even protect, their interests in the future. The BOA's leaders were now relatively old, extremely conservative, and after a lifetime of devoted service to their employers, quite unable to provide significant opposition to the banks. For their part, the Depression experiences of the banks had reinforced their awareness of the pre-eminence of salary costs in such a labour-intensive industry. Consequently, though economic conditions were beginning to improve, the banks remained determined to resist salary increases for as long as possible and bitterly opposed inroads into their long-held control of the banking industry.

Notes

1. The banks also recognized the probability of the Arbitration Court passing on gains won at the state level (Australian manager of Union Bank to London, confidential letter no. 3141, 9 December 1926, in ANZ archives.
2. *Australian Banker* 1, no. 5 (Jan. 1925): 9.
3. See, for example, *Australian Banker* 1, no. 9 (May 1925): 1–4.
4. Industrial Arbitration (Amendment) Act, No. 14 of 1926.
5. Superintendent of Bank of Australasia to London, confidential letter no. 919, 13 May 1926, in ANZ archives.
6. So concerned was the BOA that they instructed Benwell to attend as an observer. Laidlaw was also frequently in attendance, obviously anxious to translate

any gains made here to the Queensland award, through the compliant Queensland Industrial Court.

7. In fact, Smith had misjudged the role of the conciliation committee. "Unfortunately the proceedings have developed on lines which we did not think would be followed . . . i.e. that our case must be properly proved by evidence, and this involves considerable time, and no doubt exhausts the patience of our members" (annual report of general secretary to UBOA of NSW annual conference, 23 February 1927, reprinted in *Australian Banker*, 2, no. 31 [March 1927] : 7).

8. *Australian Banker* 2, no. 35 (July 1927): 1. This was a strange statement given that salary increases for most officers were now related more to the number of children they had rather than the type of work they performed.

9. Ibid., p. 2.

10. Australian manager of Union Bank of London, confidential letter no. 3190, 9 June 1927, in ANZ archives.

11. Ibid.

12. Australian manager of ES&A to London, 21 September 1927, letter in ANZ archives.

13. *Australian Banker* 2, no. 38 (Oct. 1927): 2. The publishing of these comments was designed to encourage bank officers to vote for the retention of Lang's ministry. In addition, Lang's statement that he favoured earlier closing hours on Saturday morning, something long desired by bank clerks, was prominently published.

14. Rogers, the only executive member with court experience, had resigned in protest at Smith's bellicose dominance of the BOA.

15. FCM, 12 October 1927, p. 177.

16. *Australian Banker* 1, no. 9 (May 1925): 7.

17. Ibid., p. 8.

18. Superintendent of Bank of Australasia to London, confidential letter no. 877, 23 July 1925, in ANZ archives.

19. *Australian Banker* 1, no. 10 (July 1925): 1.

20. FCM, 7 January 1926, p. 121.

21. *Australian Banker* 2, no. 21 (May 1926): 1.

22. Reported in VCMM, 8 June, p. 116.

23. However, the union did object to the banks requiring "escorting officers chaining the bag containing the cash to their wrists" (superintendent of Bank of Australasia to London, 20 June 1925, letter in ANZ archives).

24. For an example of this opposition, see *Australian Banker* 2, no. 25 (Sept. 1926): 19.

25. FCM, 4 September 1929, p. 243.

26. *SABOJ*, December 1928, p. 1340.

27. Minutes of 1926 UBOA of NSW annual conference.

28. *Australian Banker* 4, no. 19 (Oct. 1929): 2.

29. Ibid., p. 17. L. J. Louis, *Trade Unions and the Depression* (Canberra: Australian National University Press, 1963), p. 14, notes that "such was the intensity of the issues, that many of the non-political white collar and public service organisations took the extraordinary step of appealing to their members to 'vote for the retention of arbitration', that is for Labor."

30. C. B. Schedvin, *Australia and the Great Depression* (Sydney: Sydney University Press, 1970), analyses the reasons for what was a misleading sense of prosperity, the false responses and structural effects it engendered, and the traumatic economic consequences that followed in the early thirties.

31. *AIBR* 49, no. 12 (Dec. 1925), and *AIBR* 53, no. 12 (Dec. 1929).

32. Net profit of Australian banking banks in 1926 was £6,449,000 and in 1929 £6,359,000 (*AIBR* 63, no. 12 [Dec. 1939] : 958).

33. See appendix 1.
34. M. Keating, "Australian Work Force and Employment 1910/11 to 1960/61", *Australian Economic History Review,* September 1967, pp. 150-70.
35. Louis, *Trade Unions and the Depression,* p. 17, argues that most if not all Australian trade unions were totally unprepared for the crisis of the early 1930s and were able to do little to ease the misery and deprivation suffered by members.
36. Secretary's report to annual general meeting of BOASA, 10 December 1930, copy in ABOA archives.
37. In contrast to Victoria, where State Savings Bank employees had formed a separate, though unregistered union (the SSBOA), the New South Wales Government Savings Bank employees were members of a branch of the UBOA of NSW — further evidence of Smith's earlier preoccupation with a personal white-collar union "empire".
38. *Sydney Morning Herald,* 13 May 1930, p. 7.
39. K. H. Laidlaw to L. P. Harrison, 23 September 1930, letter in ABOA archives.
40. Ibid.
41. *Westralian Banker* 5, no. 10 (Oct. 1930): 4.
42. Appendix 2, tables 1, 2, 3.
43. Harrison to Laidlaw, 13 October 1930, copy in ABOA archives.
44. Minutes of annual general meeting of Victorian branch of the BOA, 24 September 1930, p. 10, copy in ABOA archives.
45. Harrison to Laidlaw, 13 October 1930.
46. AIBR 54, no. 12 (Dec. 1930).
47. Benwell to Laidlaw, 20 October 1930, copy in ABOA archives.
48. Union records.
49. FCM, 4 February 1931, p. 36.
50. Laidlaw to E. G. Heal, 7 November 1930, letter in ABOA archives.
51. Heal to Laidlaw, 29 October 1930, letter in ABOA archives.
52. Laidlaw to Harrison, 3 November 1930, telegram in ABOA archives.
53. This, the unions argued, should be seen as "their contribution towards the stabilisation of the present financial crisis in Australia" (FCM, 20 November 1930, p. 302).
54. FCM, 20 November 1930, p. 304.
55. Laidlaw to Harrison, 14 October 1930, letter in ABOA archives.
56. FCM, 20 November 1930, p. 303.
57. *SABOJ,* January 1931, p. 85.
58. VCMM, 18 December 1930, p. 27.
59. BOA solicitors, Blackburn and Tredinick, to meeting organizers, Messrs Higgins and Von Bertouch, 28 January 1931, copy in ABOA archives.
60. Benwell to Messrs Higgins and Von Bertouch, 29 January 1931, copy in ABOA archives.
61. Letter reprinted in *Australian Banker* 6, no. 2 (Feb. 1931): 18.
62. *Australian Railways Union* v. *Victorian Railway Commissioners and Ors* (30 CAR 22).
63. Ibid., p. 23.
64. BOASA minutes, 11 March 1931, p. 264.
65. *Bank Officials Association* v. *Bank of Australasia and Ors* (30 CAR 482).
66. *Argus,* 12 June 1931, p. 6.
67. FCM, 3 July 1931, p. 334. The union also wrote to the industrial registrar complaining that the article was misleading and created some dissatisfaction and disrespect for the court (BOA to industrial registrar, 25 June 1931, copy in ABOA archives).
68. Schedvin, *Australia and the Great Depression,* p. 259, notes: "although elaborate plans were taken to ensure that everything was cut by 20 or 22½ per cent.

... In the event, however, the average cut in deposit rates in 1932 was only 11 per cent".

69. By 1931 the net profit of Australian trading banks had fallen from £6,359,000 in 1929 to £4,404,000 (*AIBR* 63, no. 12 [Dec. 1939] : 958).

70. *Bank Officials Association* v. *Bank of Australasia and Ors* (30 CAR 482) at p. 483.

71. Superintendent of Bank of Australasia to London, 24 July 1931, letter in ANZ archives.

72. Davidson to general manager of Bank of Adelaide, 6 January 1931, letter in BNSW archives.

73. Australian manager of Union Bank to London, confidential letter no. 3528, 17 September 1931, in ANZ archives.

74. Meeting of UBOA of NSW, BNSW sub-branch, 15 July 1931, copy of minutes in ABOA archives.

75. Australian manager of Union Bank of London, confidential letter no. 3519, 27 August 1931, in ANZ archives.

76. *Bank Officials Association of South Australia* v. *Australian Bank of Commerce and Ors* (12 SAIR 115).

77. Australian manager of Union Bank of London, confidential letter no. 3519, 27 August 1931, in ANZ archives.

78. Superintendent of Bank of Australasia to London, confidential letter no. 1387, 27 May 1932, in ANZ archives.

79. *Queensland Bank Officer* 12, no. 11 (Jan. 1931): 8.

80. For example, in May and June 1931, fifty-five BOA members were "assessed" and endured salary reductions ranging from £20 per annum to £105 per annum (from union records in ABOA archives).

81. From union records in ABOA archives.

82. *Bank Officials' Association* v. *Bank of Australasia and Ors* (30 CAR 616).

83. For example, by August 1932 the CBA had rationed ninety-one officers (VCMM, 9 August 1932, p. 151). Rationing took two forms. Banks would employ some nominated employees for, say, three weeks in every five, or have them work on only certain days of the week. This latter form of rationing was most frequently practised in urban areas.

84. *Bank Officials Association* v. *Bank of Australasia and Ors* (31 CAR 679) at p. 681.

85. Commonwealth Bureau of Census and Statistics: Labour Report No. 25 (1934), p. 147.

86. Louis, *Trade Unions and the Depression*, p. 142.

87. ABOA archival material and appendix 3.

88. Minutes of 1933 interstate conference at Melbourne, copy in ABOA archives.

89. From material in ABOA archives.

90. See appendix 3.

91. K. F. Walker, *Australian Industrial Relations Systems* (Melbourne: Oxford University Press, 1970), p. 46.

92. From various union journals and minutes.

93. Letter from J. S. Battye in *Queensland Bank Officer,* 13, no. 6 (Aug. 1932): 9.

94. BOA records.

95. Ibid. These resignations are disguised in appendix 3 (for the 1933 membership is only 33 less than that of 1932), because the union, alarmed at the slump in membership, had instructed Benwell to carry out a four-month recruiting programme throughout the state.

96. See appendix 1.

97. Union records show that at December 1927 the average number of staff in

Victorian rural branches was 2.85, and that of urban branches 5.15 (from records in ABOA files).

98. R. M. Blackburn, *Union Character and Social Class: A Study of White Collar Unionism* (London: Batsford, 1967), p. 56, suggests that the lack of opportunity to join a union, rather than a positive disinclination to do so, is a major impediment to white-collar union growth. This is supported by the example of the union densities of three Victorian banks in 1932. The ES&A, with only 46 per cent of its branches in rural areas, had a union density of 63 per cent; the Bank of Australasia, with 79 per cent, and the BNSW, with 90 per cent of its branches in rural areas, had union density of less than 38 per cent (compiled from data in appendixes 1 and 3 and BOA records).

99. Letter to editor, *SABOJ,* January 1934, p. 202.

100. Letter from J. S. Battye in *Queensland Bank Officer* 13, no. 6 (Aug. 1932): 9.

101. For example, in October 1931 more than 97 per cent of Tasmanian bank officers were in that branch of the BOA (*Australian Banker* 6, no. 10 [Oct. 1931] : 18.

102. FCM, 10 December 1928, p. 222.

4 Timidity, Blunders, and Change: 1935–46

I am still finding this Victorian lot to be weak kneed and exasperating. Take this letter for example, which arrived today. How can even I 'gird up the loins' of such timid mice. . . .

"All through my career it has been an unpleasant fight for leave, and often to avoid open rupture I have, I blush to confess, sacrificed both health and holiday to be the cheerful obedient officer."

With employees like that, what hope is there of convincing the banks we are serious!

[Sydney Smith to K. H. Laidlaw, 9 February 1938]

In the Doldrums

The BOA drifted aimlessly through the mid-1930s, still dazed by the disasters of the Depression all about them and with few answers to the mounting criticism of its performance. With slowly returning prosperity and receding fear of unemployment came agitation for restoration of the 1931 salary cut and the "lost year of service". Senior officers complained of the continued reduction in their salary relativities, particularly because their pension entitlement was based on salary levels immediately before retirement. The BOA, hopeful of the formation of a banking conciliation panel, was unwilling to go to the court. They apparently ignored the uncertain constitutional basis of these panels and the Nationalist government's reluctance to amend the Arbitration Act to allow their introduction.

A major cause of unrest was the excessive levels of overtime officers were forced to work. This overtime, a result of the virtual cessation of recruiting since 1929,[1] placed officers under strain and reduced branch morale. K. H. Laidlaw observed: "Many managers are working late into the night, rather than face the consequences of putting in for overtime for staff . . . other managers in order to show larger profits, are causing their own staffs to be harassed by not applying for additional staff and are even allowing transfers of staff without replacement."[2] A branch manager claimed that "if he submitted claims for overtime to headquarters, he was immediately a marked man, and even his staff might entreat him not to submit them, being themselves fearful of the result".[3]

The BOA executive rather feebly washed their hands of the issue, declaring that the award allowed for overtime anyway (which neatly avoided the question of non-payment) and that "health inspectors are appointed to carry out the task of policing working conditions".[4] The overtime problem was perhaps insoluble in the short run, anyway, for most branches lacked sufficient experienced staff; a considerable lag would follow even an extensive recruiting campaign. This was made evident in March 1935 when C. J. O'Sullivan, manager of the ES&A, "admitted that his Bank was breaking the award, not only in Tasmania, but in Victoria also, and suggested that the Association should take a reasonable view and fall into line with the Banks' decisions".[5] The BOA, with the AISF, whose members had similar problems, lobbied for the appointment of an arbitration inspector to police awards, and Arthur Blakely, minister for home affairs in the earlier Scullin ministry, was appointed. But when the banks were eventually prosecuted in July 1935 for non-payment of overtime, it was Laidlaw who led the way. The CBA was fined on several counts of failing to pay overtime, and this was extensively publicized in all journals. Laidlaw in particular was jubilant: "Not only is the practice of working overtime without payment illegal, but it also shows very clearly how it is keeping others out of employment."[6]

In an attempt to counteract falling membership,[7] a growing level of unpaid union dues, and considerable membership apathy, lethargy, and lack of interest, the BOA again discussed the possibility of obtaining compulsory unionism, for which there was little precedent in the federal jurisdiction.[8] The BOA had, however, noted the Queensland experience and naively sought to follow it. In 1929 the UBOA of Q had asked its members whether they favoured compulsory unionism and had received overwhelming approval.[9] Nothing had been done, perhaps because the union already represented more than 90 per cent of Queensland bank employees. In 1934, in the face of declining membership and what Laidlaw saw as victimization of some unionists, the union applied for and was granted compulsory unionism by the compliant state court. A senior banker hinted at the difficulties that would face a similar application in the federal jurisdiction: "This decision is typical of the attitude of the Queensland Courts, which obviously reflects the policy of the State Legislature."[10] In Victoria the membership slide was only halted in late 1935 when Benwell, now acting general secretary following Smith's departure, willingly shook himself free of office tasks and spent two months touring rural branches recruiting members. This relaxed "spin through the rural areas", as Benwell described it, was spoiled when he crashed the union car in north-east Victoria and spent three weeks in hospital.

The BOA had actually been shaken from their torpor earlier in 1935 when a general meeting of senior officers rebuked the executive for its inaction and demanded the union make a claim for the return of the "lost year of service". Senior officers in particular were affected, for while clerks on the scale had been granted 2½ per cent of the 1931 reductions, those above the scale were dependent upon their employers for salary adjustment. The banks used this opportunity to discriminate even further between officers, a factor compounded by varying practices between banks. For example, by mid-1935 senior officers in the Bank of Australasia had been returned much of the reduction, while those in the CBA remained on their 1931 salaries. These older officers were upset not only because of the extra limitation of their purchasing power and the reduction in their salary relativity compared to the more junior officer, but because of their reduced pension entitlements. However, the leadership continued to stall and finally only acted after the Tasmanian branch again threatened to leave the BOA. They complained that the BOA executive showed "weakness insomuch as they didn't fight strongly enough for increases in salaries and have failed to go to Court for restoration of the Lost Year of Service . . . and that no member of the Federal Council had visited Tasmania since 1932".[11]

Benwell was instructed to prepare a case for the court and to accompany Harrison on a good-will mission to Tasmania. As a result, the claim for the restoration of the "lost year of service" was eventually brought before the court in May 1935. The union argued that the increment deferral had been a temporary measure and that the banks could now afford to return it. Justice Dethridge agreed that there was now some industry capacity to pay the extra increment. He also confirmed the fears of the banks when referring to the marginally better BNSW agreement with the BOA and a new agreement between the BNSW and the UBOA of NSW which had returned the increment. "The best evidence of what is fair in such cases is that of amounts actually paid or agreed to be paid without legal compulsion by employers in the industry in question."[12] Accordingly, he ordered that the "lost year of service" be returned. An indication of the extent of this was the average increment for younger clerks in 1935 was £40 14s.[13]

By mid-1936 the BOA again faced growing criticism. The unwillingness of the union even to protest at continuing high levels of overtime, forced deferral of already accrued recreation leave, and frequent transfers on short notice led to the point where mass resignations seemed imminent. In the ES&A, for example, the sub-branch had disbanded and unpaid BOA dues exceeded three hundred pounds.[14] There were also signs that members wanted a greater say in the union's affairs. Concern was expressed that Federal Council and the Victorian branch executive, still largely made up of the same individuals, were now dominated by Vice-President McLosky. McLosky had tried to fill the gap created by Smith's departure, but he was aloof and arrogant, knew little about industrial relations, and seemed concerned only with senior officer needs. At the 1936 Victorian branch annual meeting, McLosky proposed several rule changes that would materially increase the power of the incumbent branch committee − and, *de facto,* of the Federal Council − and though opposed by three younger officers − H. Dwyer, J. Dufty, and H. Showman − was successful. This accession of power was important, for over the next few months a number of decisions were made which were to cast Federal Council in a most unfavourable light.

The Tasmanian branch, again threatening secession, finally forced Federal Council to prepare claims. Totally unimpressed by Harrison and Benwell, they also insisted on the appointment of a secretary with legal skills. When McLosky demurred, T.W. Stanwix, Tasmanian branch president, was dispatched to Melbourne with the ultimatum that if a permanent general secretary were not appointed, Tasmanian bank officers would seek union membership elsewhere. This, of course, would have placed the BOA's registration with the Arbitration Court in considerable jeopardy. This threat was given even greater credence by the well-reported inclusion of J.S. Bell, of the UBOA of NSW executive, in a Tasmanian branch deputation to the Labor premier of that state, A.G. Ogilvie, requesting the abolition of Saturday morning banking.

A Doomed Foray to the Arbitration Court

In October 1936 the BOA reluctantly filed the claim. Continuing sluggish economic conditions, which limited branch expansion and promotion, had created another group of disgruntled officers: those languishing at the top of the salary scale. A banker recognized the problem and suggested an explanation:

> The majority of these are accountant/tellers and while they may be capable of increased responsibilities, positions in which they could gain higher and more varied experience . . . these do not often become vacant . . . From a close study of the position for years past I think there is no doubt . . . that unionism has to a considerable extent destroyed ambition and initiative. Many officers reach the maximum award salary and when they see little chance of going further they are apt to despair of the future with the result that they stagnate and in the course of time become disgruntled.[15]

With a court appearance imminent, the BOA finally appointed solicitors to represent them, and vainly offered a brief to R.G. Menzies. They also advertised for a general secretary and finally, with reluctance, had to appoint the only applicant − Sydney Smith − on a short-term basis. Delays due to the union's lack of preparation were exacerbated by the Arbitration Court's preoccupation with basic-wage deliberations. Smith, quickly back into stride, convinced McLosky that the pre-election climate was a suitable time to lobby for an additional judge. In July 1937 a deputation from the BOA and Smith's New South Wales insurance union waited on Attorney-General Menzies. Smith confidently reported: "Our arguments so impressed the Attorney General that he asked us if we knew of a suitable man for the position."[16]

As the case preparation continued, there were growing signs of tension among the unions' representatives. Initially this was due to the general secretary's bombastic and supercilious attitude towards counsel T.W. Smith and solicitor Bryan. Smith wrote to Laidlaw: "They have no industrial men here in Melbourne, and the one McLosky picked [T.W. Smith] now refuses to appear in Court with me on the grounds that I am older than he is, more experienced, and a man of a dominant nature who would not sit quietly and listen to any tommy rot spoken in Court . . . Just fancy that charge against me!"[17] There was also disagreement over tactics to be adopted. Sydney Smith was adamant that the issue should be decided in the court, where his talents could be on full display. However, the union's counsel believed that the banks would be unwilling to go to court because of their sensitivity to public opinion, particularly since the Depression: "I notice in other business dealings they are very loath to take their customers to Court, and this would apply with greater force so far as their employees are concerned in view of the atmosphere in the community."[18]

As regards the claims, T.W. Smith argued that because of the difficulty in obtaining classification, the union should first obtain increases on the scale.[19] But Sydney Smith and McLosky insisted that the case could not be split for fear of further antagonizing senior officers. Further distractions arose when the BNSW sub-branch suggested that their agreement with the bank should be renegotiated. Under Davidson, the BNSW had actively fostered these sub-branches as a tactic to subvert the union and to increase the *esprit de corps* of "Wales" officers. In some states this management aura was so strong that the BNSW staff were only willing to join the union if a sub-branch existed.[20] The BOA referred the proposed agreement duplicating New South Wales salaries to their counsel. He warned, "Agreements are very dangerous documents, binding as they do employees in the future unless exceptional changes take place in the economic and other conditions of the industry."[21] He added "There is no doubt that the approval by the officers of individual banks of proposals which fall short of our present claim will have a most damaging effect upon our chances of success before the Court." But under considerable pressure, and at McLosky's insistence, the BOA finally agreed to endorse the agreement. Again the Victorian banks were upset.[22] The relatively small increases in the agreement indicate that their disapproval was based more on pique than on a fear that their case would be prejudiced.

Chief Justice Dethridge had already begun hearing evidence on scale rates and had indicated that he wanted to hear evidence at first hand rather than through the medium of assessors. The union, frustrated by this delay and Dethridge's refusal to continue while the BNSW negotiations were proceeding, and needing to show an increasingly restive membership some results, then asked the court for an interim award on the scale. The banks reluctantly agreed as long as no retrospectivity was granted. The male scale was increased by approximately 13 per cent at the sixth year running down to 6 per cent at the eighteenth year.[23] The banks were unperturbed: "For sometime past the Federal scale has been less than was being paid under awards in other states and the increase was therefore fully expected."[24]

This capitulation was the final straw for some members, coming as it did on top of the union's approval of the BNSW agreement, which contradicted the decisions of two general meetings. Rebellion was in the air when in early December the Victorian branch met to select Conference delegates. Where normally a handful of members attended, on this occasion the BOA rooms could not accommodate the five hundred who came, and the meeting was postponed until the next evening. So well had the rival groups lobbied that the results of the first BOA elections ever held were inconclusive. The young rebels – Dwyer, Dufty, and Showman – were soundly defeated, as were McLosky's nominees. Those elected, R. H. Trangmar, A. Whitlock, and C. Larner, could be identified with neither group. In a further rebuke to McLosky, the architect of the recent BNSW agreement, the meeting resolved that all delegates must support branch policy.

In spite of this eventful preliminary, Conference was its normal dull self until the question of court representation was raised by John Cook, the new Tasmanian president, who had opted to attend personally rather than use the Tasmanian proxy. He again reminded Conference of the possibilities of a Tasmanian secession and unfairly argued that T. W. Smith's performance had been inadequate and, as little evidence had been prepared, Sydney Smith would need extra assistance. Conference, aware that relationships between the general secretary and counsel had deteriorated even further, and sensing an opportunity to allocate blame for the hasty interim award and the chaos that preceded it, agreed to dispense with T. W. Smith's services. Cook was prepared for this eventuality and suggested that the Tasmanian premier, A. G. Ogilvie KC, might accept the brief, for his efforts to obtain the early closing of banks in Hobart had won him a reputation as "a keen critic of the banks".[25] After Cook outlined Ogilvie's lavish demands – two hundred pounds retainer, a hundred pounds on the brief, and thirty guineas a day – Smith broke the stunned silence with strong support for the proposal, an action seemingly at odds with his earlier attitude and statements. He had succeeded in having T. W. Smith taken off the case, so why would he voice approval for another? In fact Smith was repaying a debt incurred in his capacity as president of the New South Wales Insurance Officers Association, which for some years had competed with the AISF to recruit insurance workers. In early 1937 the membership battle had extended to Tasmania and Smith had won a resounding victory "with the very helpful co-operation of the Premier".[26] Conference directed Smith and McLosky to go to Tasmania to interview Ogilvie and, if satisfied, to offer him the brief.

Flushed with victory, Cook aired further Tasmanian grievances and even nominated an opponent for Harrison. However, Harrison again avoided contesting an election when no seconder for Cook's motion came forward. So ended the first BOA conference that had done anything more than ratify the actions of its entrenched leadership. The ageing leadership was relieved, mistakenly seeing an end to this divisiveness and controversy, which they felt hardly benefitted a staid and respectable organization of bank officers.

Ogilvie's acceptance of the brief, together with the news that Justice H. B. Piper, the new appointee to the Arbitration Court, would start hearing their case shortly, heartened the executive. It also convinced them to resist CBC efforts to make an agreement similar to that of the BNSW. It was therefore shattering to McLosky and Harrison to learn that Ogilvie, while in Sydney on other business, had begun negotiations with the CBC for a separate agreement. Though he was instructed to break off all discussions, no executive member voiced doubts whether this indicated that Ogilvie might lack industrial relations expertise. Ogilvie's earlier promise of compulsory unionism for Tasmanian bank officers should also have provided early warning of his industrial naivety. Disillusionment soon followed, however, when it became clear that his state duties, political commitments, and a large Hobart legal practice would severely limit his preparations. McLosky again sailed for Tasmania to determine Ogilvie's intentions. He returned to state delicately: "Our counsel apparently has not yet mastered the complicated issues of this case."[27] It was obvious that the only alternative to further postponement was the briefing of new counsel; however, the apparent benefits of "Mr. Ogilvie's presence which means prestige and that is what the Association is buying – flare [sic] and prestige",[28] won the day, and it was agreed to apply for an adjournment.

The case recommenced in early March, but the illness of the banks' counsel, Ogilvie's continued absence, and the desire of Judge Piper to hear senior officers at first hand ensured that the hearing would be lengthy. The question of evidence had been complicated by Sydney Smith's circular to senior officers seeking information on salaries, promotion, and duties. The banks objected, citing the secrecy oath taken by all officers, and the BOA was inundated with officers' pleas not to use material already forwarded. Judge Piper convinced the banks that some information was vital, and they agreed to send a further circular to senior staff requesting similar detail but concluding, "Whether or not officers, whether members of the Association or not, furnish this information is entirely a matter for their personal discretion."[29] Smith, though, had the last word: "Quite a number have not responded to the request consequently those who have not done so, have their names under review to be subpoenaed to give evidence. . . . similar steps will be taken in the case of non members."[30]

Ogilvie's opening address was disastrous. After earning McLosky's wrath by showering criticism upon the BNSW, he accused the banks of causing the Depression. This led to a spate of union resignations, and forced the BOA to publish a retraction.[31] He also stated, perhaps with some urging from Smith, still with expansionist dreams: "It is the desire of the claimant organisation that Your Honor's Award should apply throughout Australia . . . all organisations throughout Australia had participated in the preparation of the statement of claim, and were all desirous of a uniform award."[32] The UBOA of NSW immediately forwarded a strong protest, sending a telegram to the BOA on 4 April which ended:

> We have made clear to you many times that we do not desire a Federal award for New South Wales, nor have we, as has been suggested, any desire for affiliation with your organisation. If you persist with your application against the express wishes of this Association, we will oppose the matter in court, and will not co-operate with you in your claim for an award. We regard this as a deliberate attempt to extend your operations to New South Wales, and we resent the fact that we have been kept in ignorance of your action.

Then both the UBOA of NSW and the UBOA of Q appeared before Judge Piper and made it clear that they had no desire to be joined in the federal award and that Ogilvie did not have permission to represent them, none of which did much for the credibility of the BOA or the embattled Ogilvie. The case ground on for two months as the BOA produced an interminable number of managers, accountants, and senior clerks. Judge Piper was particularly interested in the responsibilities of officers outside bank hours. "A bank officer at any time in his career is expected to be versatile in social activities in the community, and use all his talents in the community life to the advantage of the bank."[33] The case then shifted to Sydney so the judge could appraise himself of comparative salaries and conditions, and evidence was taken from a number of senior officers selected and schooled by Smith. Ogilvie and Smith also made another crude attempt to establish the federal award for all Australian bank officers. The UBOAs of New South Wales and Queensland immediately forward strong protests and threatened to oppose them in the court.[34] They later appeared before Judge Piper to restate that Ogilvie did not have permission to represent them.

Back in Melbourne again the court became preoccupied with the link between the court's basic wage and the incremental salary scale. Ogilvie tried to establish a basic wage for the industry by arguing that a twenty-one-year-old officer should receive a salary greater than the basic wage. The banks objected, claiming that this question could only be resolved by a Full Bench, to which Judge Piper agreed.

Later in 1938, with the case bogged down in legal argument and the banks yet to begin their evidence, two hundred members attended a special meeting, ostensibly to approve further rule changes. Dufty attempted to force the executive to answer a series of questions relating to the conduct of the case, but Harrison refused to allow discussion of any issues not on the agenda. He was forced to relinquish the chair, and his replacement, McLosky, in appealing for harmony and order, agreed to allow these questions after the rule changes had been disposed of. The speed with which this was done indicated that most of the members at the meeting were there for other reasons. Harrison and McLosky refused to answer all but three of the twenty-four questions asked by Dufty.[35] The questions that remained unanswered revolved around the reasons for and propriety of Ogilvie's appointment, his conduct of the case, and reasons for the lengthy postponements and exorbitant court costs. Three questions brought particularly angry reactions from McLosky: Did any person receive remuneration for obtaining Ogilvie's services? Was he engaged against the advice of the union's solicitors? Was it known that Ogilvie had not looked at the brief before he arrived in Victoria? Dwyer then moved a motion of no confidence in Federal Council, "owing to their mismanagement and their neglect of the interests of members generally".[36] A passionate speech by Smith, who argued that such a resolution would irreparably damage the union's arbitration case, eventually persuaded Dwyer to withdraw this. Sensing the pessimism that underlay the meeting's anger, Smith seized the initiative and suggested that the BOA should seek a partial award covering scale increases only, to which the meeting agreed.

For some time Smith had known that the union's case was going badly. Ogilvie's mediocre performance was now worsened by his impatience to return to Tasmania, and his relationship with solicitor Bryan had deteriorated further. During the negotiations the feud between Ogilvie and Bryan had flared again when Bryan disagreed with acceptance of these terms. "[Bryan] went behind my back and spoke to Mr. Harrison and other representatives," Ogilvie complained to the Federal Council. "Mr. Harrison then said they would not accept the New South Wales Award."[37] Ogilvie issued an ultimatum: either Bryan left the case or he did. Bryan was dismissed.[38] The length of the case and Ogilvie's lavish demands had exhausted BOA funds and accumulated liquid assets, and Justice Piper had indicated the case would proceed well into 1939, for the banks were adamant they would never concede classification.

Unknown to Smith, the banks too had been quite anxious to settle, for there was concern that further argument would not dispel thoughts that Ogilvie had, "before a young judge, new to such cases and argument raised certain issues against the banks which our counsel felt, rightly or wrongly, had impressed the Judge's mind very strongly in favour of claimants".[39] Senior bankers were also anxious to "avoid any further publicity in which the banks might be involved owing to their activities being brought into public notice through legislation in prospect",[40] a reference to the central banking legislation then being framed by the Lyons government. There was also a fear that further delay might convince Judge Piper to make the salary increase retrospective. The banks immediately offered the New South Wales award terms as total settlement. Though this was an increase at the eighteenth year of £13 (to £412) and proportionately smaller increases through the scale, it offered little to senior officers, other than a minimum rate only £3 above the top of the scale. However, Smith and Ogilvie soon assuaged the fears of Harrison and McLosky, and in early October the tentative agreement was ratified by Justice Piper as a consent award.[41]

Union members were angered, not only by the insignificant salary increases that had been gained at such great cost but by what they saw as the supine attitudes of their leadership. This forced the executive into hasty rationalizations. Justice Piper's supposed role in forcing the agreement was emphasized, and his statement that "if the parties were not able to come to a settlement, he would force them into a compulsory conference presided over by himself",[42] freely quoted. Smith also sought to explain the inadequacy of the consent award as being a function of "the international position, the prospects of a recession and other factors",[43] vagueness that only further antagonized the rank and file.

Open Revolt

The poor result, following some years of growing unrest, set in motion a challenge to union leadership which was to influence the future of the BOA profoundly. The challenge took place at the annual meeting of the Victorian branch in late 1938. A year earlier McLosky had nominated for the presidency but withdrew when Harrison assured him that he would step down when the case was finalized. Harrison, though increasingly frail, changed his mind; McLosky, anxious not to split the conservative vote, again did not stand. Harrison's opponent was Dwyer, who had shown at several earlier meetings that he could muster considerable support from the growing number of suburban officers. To combat this, Harrison and McLosky had insisted on postal voting,[44] and Harrison also used the journal to solicit support. In bravely ignoring the recent ineptitude and blunders, he wrote: "It will be during the next two years that those who have had the practical experience of meeting the difficulties and problems of improving your salaries will require all that experience in preparing an efficient case. . . . Your leading counsel, the General Secretary, and other officers of the organisation are convinced that those who have been carrying the responsibilities should carry on their work . . . in order to meet with and bring about success in your interests."[45]

However, Dwyer won convincingly by 349 votes to 180.[46] The elections for four vice-presidents did return McLosky and his supporter

A. E. Hore, but also Dufty and Showman.[47] With Dwyer now in the chair, the meeting proceeded smoothly until Dufty criticized McLosky's domination of Federal Council and moved that all Federal Council positions be declared vacant and fresh elections held. In the heated discussion that followed, the continuing conservatism of bank officers was apparent, for the recurring issue was the effect of this bickering upon the image and prestige of the ABOA.[48] Finally Dufty was persuaded to withdraw his motion.

The following month the Victorian committee held a ballot to appoint conference delegates, and the comfortable success of Dwyer, Dufty, and Showman reflected the mood of the rank and file. Further conflict followed over the reform group's proposal that the ABOA publish a separate journal rather than jointly with the UBOA of NSW as had been done since 1924. This was a result of a number of clashes over editorial content, space allocated to ABOA news (and even the captioning of this as the "Victorian" rather than "Federal" section. Most particularly was the editor's refusal to publish Dwyer's election manifesto or a series of reports on the conduct of the case as seen by the Victorian branch. Dwyer and McLosky also clashed again when the latter insisted that all interstate correspondence be forwarded *via* the federal office. This culminated when "Mr. Dwyer spoke in very annoyed terms at receiving a letter relating to an article to be published in the Journal and said he proposed to take legal action in the matter and that he did not trust any of the members of the Federal Council, including the General Secretary".[49] The Victorian branch committee were also increasingly hostile at Federal Council's inaction in the face of a new ploy of the banks.

> It appears that the practice is being developed in the banks of appointing an officer to a position on the understanding that he must prove his efficiency in that position, otherwise he will be rated as inefficient. In these cases officers are chosen at times for positions in which they have not had any previous experience. The main intention is to defeat the anticipated award as the banks consider if a man is declared inefficient at this stage they will be able to withhold from him his rights under the new award. The idea is to put an officer in this position and when he fails, tell him that the bank will retain his services on a certain salary, lower than what he is entitled to. If he refuses, or the Association does not agree, he would be dismissed.[50]

Consequently, when conference convened in mid-December 1938 it was in an atmosphere of strain and hostility. With the existing office bearers Harrison, McLosky, and H. O. Appleby offset by Victorian branch delegates Dwyer, Dufty, and Showman, the Tasmanian delegate would hold the deciding vote. So when the Tasmanian branch decided to send the secretary, Crosby, and to have their conservative proxy, Hore, advise him, then any Federal Council leadership changes seemed most unlikely. Battle was immediately joined when Harrison refused Dufty permission to address the meeting over the circumstances of Ogilvie's appointment. Smith's report was marred by constant interjections and exchanges, which were increased by his attempts to pass over inconsistencies raised by the auditors in Federal Council's balance sheet.[51] The elections followed, and with Harrison not standing for the presidency,[52] McLosky defeated Dwyer four votes to three. The same voting pattern saw Whitlock returned as vice-president and Harrison as treasurer.

Having confirmed their positions, the ruling junta then successfully moved that Conference be adjourned. Dwyer protested vigorously, arguing that this violated an earlier promise to answer the questions on events surrounding the disastrous case. As the Victorian delegate reported: "We felt we were up against arranged silence. We are of the opinion that the business of conference was cut and dried . . . the interests of members made quite subservient to the whims of the executive officers."[53] The ginger group knew they had little hope of gaining control of Federal Council while the three principal executive officers, although members of conference, were not elected representatives of any branch of the ABOA. "Owing to an anomaly in the rules, once they attain these positions, by voting in a block, they are able to remain in office, although they may be quite unrepresentative and out of touch with the views of members generally."[54]

Eventually they saw a chance to remove McLosky, Harrison, and Whitlock, who were all union life members and, on Dwyer's interpretation of ABOA rules, ineligible to hold union office.

> It is a curious fact that all the gentlemen named [i.e., the Federal Executive] are Life Members of the Association, and pay no subscriptions. The latter seems undesirable, as we consider the men in control should have a direct financial interest in the organisation. . . . We are thus faced with the position that the men occupying the chief executive offices may either not be members or unfinancial, and so ineligible for office. If either of these alternatives exist all their actions would be invalid, and may result in serious legal difficulties for the Association.[55]

The Victorian branch referred this to counsel and were bitterly disappointed when told it was considered that life members could be office bearers. Another suggestion, that the Federal Council executive be elected by all members rather than the present collegiate system, understandably foundered when presented to that body. In further undermining Harrison, they queried whether salaried union officers should have other income sources (for some years Harrison had conducted a small estate agency) and whether he should also receive a commission for selling journal advertising space. An indication of the level of bitterness and trivia that had now overtaken the union was Federal Council's decision to send Hore and Whitlock to "visit certain towns to see that the right outlook is presented from the Federal Council's viewpoint and to counteract the present propaganda from the Victorian Branch".[56]

By mid-1939 the ABOA's financial situation was critical. A significant part of the four thousand pounds court costs remained unpaid. Long-accumulated assets had been realized, the Bankers' Club closed, and even the practice of providing free cigarettes at Federal Council meetings abolished. McLosky saw the establishment of new branches as a way to tap new financial sources and approached both BOASA and BOAWA. He suggested they become ABOA branches and adopt the new federal award. This met with stern opposition from the banks, who were anxious to minimize Smith's involvement. Both unions also curtly informed the ABOA that they preferred to maintain their individual status and were preparing claims for improved awards.[57] The one remaining area where costs could be pruned was secretarial salaries. Conference reconvened in May 1939 and decided to terminate Smith's appointment, and in August 1939, after almost twenty turbulent years, Smith finally disappeared from the banking industry. Despite his experience and earlier record of spirited and successful opposition to employers on behalf of a number of white-collar unions, this was now of little moment. Heavy drinking had affected his always erratic and spasmodic nature, severely limiting his effectiveness and increasingly alienating him from the BOA executive and membership. Consequently, on all sides, his departure was marked with relief rather than disappointment, and he was little missed. Conference also decided that the Victorian branch secretary's job should be amalgamated with that of the general secretary and that position re-advertised. So in October 1939, the faithful George Benwell was asked for his resignation. Initially angry and deeply hurt, he was somewhat pacified by the union's sugges-tion that he become an organizer at ten shillings per member, and later that month, complete with the ABOA's Overland car (which he had pur-chased for thirty pounds), Benwell began an extensive organizing tour.

In late 1939 Conference met again in calmer circumstances. Smith, that notorious ruffler of feathers, had gone, the increasing certainty of war had diverted attention from earlier conflicts, and Federal Council's perfor-mance had improved. The Victorian branch was particularly impressed by Federal Council's willingness to prosecute the CBA for its failure to return the 10 per cent reduction of 1931 to a number of senior officers. They had finally taken a case to the Arbitration Court but failed because of senior officer reluctance to give evidence and the court's refusal to intrude on the banks' managerial prerogatives. McLosky then arranged an appoint-ment with Attorney-General Menzies, and within a week all but one officer had received full restoration.[58]

Although internal union conflict had died away, its effects were to fundamentally alter the nature and activities of the union. Younger officers had challenged and entered the ABOA's leadership hierarchy, and the days when Smith and McLosky could ride roughshod over the rank and file were gone. No more could older and generally more conservative union leaders expect to dominate the ABOA's decision-making. Thoughts of real opposition to the banks had hardly begun to crystallize yet, but there was a realization that younger officers could and should take a more active role in the union. Most senior officers, however, still retained a perception of their occupation and its place in society that was increasingly at odds with the changing economic and social environment. One example of this was the attitude towards bank messengers. Though ostensibly they had always been able to join the ABOA, few had done so, for not only had the union never pressed claims on their behalf, but several unfortunate incidents, particularly in the Bankers' Club, had convinced most messengers that they were not really welcome. This belief is supported by a Federal Council minute supporting their membership "because of the fear of the FCU organising them and so gaining a foothold in the industry".[59]

The Problems of War

On the outbreak of the Second World War, the federal government established greater controls over the Australian banking system on "all matters which are necessary or convenient to be prescribed for the more effectual prosecution of the war".[60] These included controls over the export and sale of securities overseas, certain forms of investment, and interest rates. By mid-1940, as enlistments increased despite the industry's reserved status,[61] one problem to emerge was the "make-up" of army pay to the officer's previous salary levels. A number of banks had done this,[62] but others refused, agreeing only to re-employ them again in peacetime. After the ABOA pointed out that National Security Regulations compelled this anyway, the banks demanded that in return for salary make-up, weekly hours of work be increased from forty-two to forty-four and annual leave limited to two weeks. Federal Council rejected the first proposal but gave tacit approval to the second. The UBOA of NSW immediately appealed to the ABOA not to do this. Incredibly, they had just discovered that their treasured "Piddington Award" contained no provision for annual leave.[63] They had just brought a case for annual leave before the state court and felt that any ABOA concession would prejudice this.

This question of make-up pay bedevilled bank-union discussions for some years. At one stage the ES&A and the CBA exploited the naivety of the ABOA executive by announcing they would withhold make-up pay until the end of the war and then pay the difference between the employee's aggregate military and civilian pay, which would have meant a loss to any officer who attained commissioned rank after enlistment. Then in early 1942, when members of the militia were called up for full-time duty, the banks again refused to make up pay. The question of payment of increments normally received by officers on the scale was yet another problem that remained unsolved.

The banks then offered salary make-up in return for a relaxation of female employment award constraints. When Federal Council again equivocated, the Victorian branch were critical, for this would "open the way for supplanting male officers, and evidence could be called for females with the object of lowering the conditions of banking".[64] The Victorian branch pressed Federal Council to ask members whether the banks should be allowed to increase female staff as long as they "continued to absorb the normal number of male staff",[65] a proposal obviously aimed at deferring the whole issue. A number of conferences followed, and finally the union agreed to an award variation in return for the banks' promise to make up salary, to pay it fortnightly rather than twice monthly, and to close earlier on Saturday morning. The award was varied as follows: "If vacancies occur in any positions due either directly or indirectly to the absence of male officers on naval, military or airforce service, then such vacancies may be filled temporarily by the employment of female employees at female rates of pay."[66]

The extension of the war to the Pacific in late 1941 further increased manpower needs. Though the banking industry had already made a significant contribution,[67] the minister for war organization, J.J. Dedman, believed that further manpower savings were possible, and the reservation covering senior staff was withdrawn for all but Commonwealth Bank officers.[68] Dedman then curtly told the banks that some rationalization of branches was necessary. This would release further manpower, and vacated premises would provide badly needed buildings, furniture, and equipment. He claimed that a Commonwealth Bank survey indicated too many bank branches in some Australian towns. He agreed that branch rationalization would be difficult but suggested that banks close at least five hundred branches rather than "have a cut and dried plan imposed on them without regard to the peculiarities of each bank and each town in which concentration takes place".[69]

The rationalization plans incensed the banking unions, and they were only pacified when Dedman, after giving them "secret and alarming information on the progress of the war",[70] emphasized that further manpower was vital to the war effort. Delegates from all unions, meeting for the first time as the Commonwealth Conference of Bank Officers' Associations, then presented Dedman with nine points for the protection of officers involved in branch rationalization. These included granting of absolute preference to union members (perhaps of more importance to the union than union members), absorption by the Commonwealth Bank of all displaced officers both during and if necessary following the conclusion of the war, protection for managers of closed branches, and the establishment of an industry panel of employers and employees to oversee rationalization. They also asked for rationalization to be extended to the Commonwealth Bank, for there was justifiable anger at the protection afforded its employees and the almost moribund CBOA. They felt there was a "tacit understanding between the Commonwealth Bank and its officers that, so long as they did not become unionists within the full meaning of the term, their salaries and conditions would not be worse than those obtained by the ABOA for its members".[71] But Dedman was unshakeable: "I will not agree . . . or be a party to the closing of any branch of the Commonwealth Bank."[72] This was also a reaction to the private banks' action in closing more than seventy unprofitable rural branches, which he saw as exploitation of the rationalization scheme. Dedman's view is unwittingly supported by the comments of a senior banker: "We have closed all branches in Northern Queensland, as we were the last to open and business was very small with little opportunity to increase. I had this in mind several months ago owing to staff difficulties and higher costs of operation . . . I expect to acquire reciprocally a volume of business practically equal to that surrendered."[73] Dedman was furious because the closing of these branches had released only a few officers and had left some country areas without any banking services. Injudiciously he warned that "one method for the releasing of manpower would be nationalization".[74] In spite of later denials that branch rationalization was the first step along a path that inevitably led to nationalization, neither banks nor their employees believed him.

In the face of Dedman's anger, banks other than the powerful BNSW reluctantly nominated four hundred branches to be closed. Most were in "one bank" areas, and Dedman told them to try again. He then asked the Commonwealth Conference of Bank Officers' Associations for ideas to reduce branch establishments. They suggested earlier branch closure, elimination of some free banking services, and a number of technical changes to Australian banking practises. Conference also debated the possibility of increased female employment. After gratuitously agreeing that the female norm of efficiency was 70 per cent of males, they set down a number of preconditions for their employment, the aim of which was to protect male careers and employment. They repeated demands for increased officer protection by way of legislation and for the establishment of an industry panel, pleading, "With the enemy at our gates, it behoves any Government to refrain from breaking pledges which might create disunity in the community."[75]

L. H. Newton, president of the UBOA of NSW, and vice-president S. E. Card, a gifted and ambitious Rural Bank officer, visited Canberra and persuaded Dedman to establish an industry panel with a member from each banking union. This panel was to develop proposals relating to the wartime operations and regulation of the banking industry. The panel met L. J. McConnan, general manager of the NBA and chairman of the ABA, and presented him with a list of points aimed at streamlining the wartime operations of branches. McConnan rejected a request for compulsory unionism,[76] but agreed to "make it known throughout his Bank that there was no objection to officers becoming members of the Association".[77] The panel got little further satisfaction, as McConnan was opposed to overtime for "above scale" officers and believed that the other points were domestic issues for individual banks to resolve. This unsatisfactory experience with direct consultation merely confirmed the views of Dwyer and a growing number of rank and file members that stronger action was needed. Further bank attempts to break down union resistance to increased female employment, blatant breaches of overtime clauses, and their failure to make up pay to militia members all reinforced Dwyer's statement: "Those banks which are seeking to whittle down the privileges to which their employees are entitled should follow a course dictated by reason instead of using the War as an excuse to humbug their officers and to obtain advantages which they would not attempt to seek in times of peace."[78]

To date the powerful BNSW had refused to join any rationalization schemes. Though the spectre of government control dominated Davidson's thinking, he cogently argued that given a little time the banks could alter their banking techniques to release more staff than would rationalization. The bank's refusal had brought the scheme to a virtual halt, for other banks, jealous and wary of the relative size and importance of the BNSW, refused to close branches near that bank's branches for fear of further increasing its trading advantage. The BNSW's obstinance brought some problems for unions, particularly the UBOA of NSW. The *"esprit de corps"* of the bank's staff, fostered by a 5 per cent wartime bonus, was increasingly expressed through their sub-branch, which took a strong line against rationalization; James Peters, its outspoken president, demanded that the union send a protest deputation to Canberra. Card, a Rural Bank officer and so not affected by rationalization, refused, and this was sufficient for the sub-branch to label him as a supporter of bank nationalization, which, in the light of later events was ironic in the extreme. Peters then announced that the sub-branch intended circularizing all New South Wales' officers attacking the "intention of the Minister to cripple the trading banks".[79] He added that unless Card was removed from the union executive, the sub-branch would hinder any future court cases by refusing to provide evidence. Ill will mounted further when the union stated that they would apply for an injunction restraining the issue of the circular.

In Victoria McLosky, rejected by the ABOA rank and file, was now president of the BNSW sub-branch. He wrote to his New South Wales counterpart to discuss the possibility of forming a body to negotiate directly with the bank. The New South Wales sub-branch responded with a plan to "organise a Commonwealth wide body . . . and our ambition to register would be realised at some future date".[80] These BNSW sub-branches were now posing a direct threat to all unions, particularly given the close relationship between sub-branch committeemen and bank management. Often individual officer problems were handled most effectively by the sub-branch,[81] further enhancing employee views of sub-branch leadership. The ABOA, aware of the dangers of "house" associations, acted swiftly by insisting that they should be notified of all sub-branch activities and reaffirming the principle that all sub-branch members should also be union members. McLosky, characteristically, refused to appear when summoned before Federal Council and was censured in his absence.[82]

A further blow to BNSW sub-branches came when the exasperated Dedman promulgated a National Security Regulation empowering him to "issue an order limiting the number of offices, branches and agencies at which a trading bank could operate, and to direct any particular trading bank to close any office, branch or agency".[83] The BNSW was forced to concede and over the following month closed the required number of branches. By early 1943 the rationalization was complete: 545 branches, mostly small, had been closed; approximately eight hundred staff released for other duties; and £35 million of advance and deposit business and ninety thousand accounts transferred.[84] Yet the scheme made little contribution to the war effort, for the administrative burden for banks and the Department of War Organization absorbed much of the released manpower. At another level significant antagonism was generated, because for many employees rationalization was now inextricably linked with the early stages of nationalization, a result of bank propaganda and the confusing formulation and implementation of the scheme. Later, opponents of nationalization plans were able to call upon this nucleus of opposition and swiftly mobilize resistance.

The Second World War had an impact on the industry's work force, in the form of a dramatic increase in the number of female employees. This had implications for the ABOA during and particularly after the war, and is worthy of brief discussion. By 1942, banking employment had been pegged at 55 per cent of pre-war male staff and 90 per cent of total staff. The banks, along with a number of other industries, had recruited a significant number of females.[85] Existing industrial tribunals could not cope with difficulties associated with high levels of female employment. The main problem lay in the tradition of paying females approximately half male rates, for this was insufficient to coax sufficient females into the work force. If rates were increased, however, the whole structure of post-war awards would be altered. There were also questions relating to employment in particular industries, hours of work, and protection of the safety, health, and welfare of females. This exacerbated union fears that lower-paid women working under inferior conditions might supplant males. With these problems in mind, the Women's Employment Board (WEB) was established under Justice A.W. Foster.[86]

In late 1942 bank attempts to employ females on more responsible tasks was referred to the WEB, but the hearing was delayed by legal challenges. Dissatisfaction over the board's structure and fear of "equal pay" and large increases in female rates brought employer protests, while union concern centred on a decline in male job opportunities, erosion of the "family wage concept", and the relative wage advantage afforded single females. So it was not until mid-1944 that the WEB determined that female tellers would be paid forty to eighty pounds per annum above normal female rates, in line with the WEB's bench-mark of paying females in clerical areas at two-thirds of male rates.[87] The board's suggestion that females doing other male tasks should be paid at full male rates, while pleasing some unions anxious to avoid future bank claims that certain jobs had been efficiently done by lowly paid females, was flatly rejected by the banks.

The ABOA had taken a different stance. Restating their long-held aversion to female clerks, they queried whether it was "the Association's first duty to get the highest possible rates of pay for women, most of whom are merely temporarily in the employ of the banks".[88] No doubt this attitude also grew from their disenchantment with the level of female unionization, which in spite of frequent exhortations never rose above 30 per cent, compared with other states where it was in excess of 50 per cent.[89] However, it must be remembered that the ABOA had only permitted female members after 1938. The inglorious history of the ABOA's treatment of female bank officers is discussed in chapter 9.

Throughout all of this, Australian banking unions remained enthusiastic supporters of the war effort. Some offered interest-free loans to the government, and all paid enlisting officers' subscriptions. Union journals reflected the tide of events, initially being full of optimism and details of officer enlistment, which by early 1942 gave way to extensive casualty lists. As invasion appeared imminent, there were frequent explicit and implicit appeals for enlistment by younger officers and for older officers to bear with equanimity the burdens of excessive overtime, modified branch procedures, and cancelled annual leave. Obituaries replaced articles on banking practice, and bankers social jottings disappeared in favour of appeals for union members to assist with fund-raising and the details of production of civilian-produced goods such as camouflage nets and the number of bandages rolled. At the same time the ABOA was determined to prevent exploitation or dilution of award provisions. The character of union leadership had changed, and no more would ABOA leaders consent to the erosion of hard-won conditions, not even in the supposed name of God, King, or Country. In late 1941 the question of payment in lieu of annual leave had precipitated another union leadership crisis after the Victorian Branch censured Federal Council for not demanding penalty rates.[90]

Tension between Dwyer and McLosky increased further when Dwyer opposed McLosky for the general presidency. In almost an anticlimax McLosky, after being roundly criticized at Conference, resigned and severed all connection with the union, and Dwyer, only the third federal president, came to power. Once more the presidency of both the Victorian branch and Federal Council was vested in one man. Dwyer's autocratic and intolerant nature and misuse of authority was to create many problems. Because of the union's constant financial plight, there had been no union secretary since Smith and Benwell had left, and the bulk of the work had been done by executive members during lunchtimes and after work. Finally the union advertised for a secretary. He was to share his time between Federal Council and the Victorian branch and be editor of a new journal, for after years of conflict the ABOA and the UBOA of NSW had decided to publish separate journals. L.W. (Oliver) Lodge, late of the *Sydney Morning Herald* and ex-president of the Australian Journalists Association, was appointed. Mild-mannered, diligent, and an efficient organizer of office routines, yet without any industrial expertise, he was a far cry from the often offensive, negligent, though at times brilliant Smith. Lodge's inoffensiveness and lack of incisiveness and vigour was to tell against him and the ABOA in negotiations with the banks' shrewd and calculating staff inspectors.

More important was the rapid ascent of J.H.O. Paterson, an officer of the CBA, to union leadership. Within a few months of his transfer to Melbourne in 1942 he had been elected vice-president of Federal Council. Paterson had been a lay-preacher while working in country branches and, while not a member of the Labor Party, had a well-developed working-class consciousness. As such he was quite different from any other ABOA leaders before him. In fact, Paterson had few of the inhibitions and reservations about loss of prestige and status still common among many bank employees. Yet as Dwyer became increasingly irrational and ineffective, the ABOA quickly came to rely on Paterson's hard work, coolness, and logic. In the new *Bankers Journal,* Paterson frequently criticized the long-held policy of passivity at any cost, for bank officers undoubtedly suffered "because of their gentlemanly attitude towards their employers".[91] Non-members were attacked, with comparisons being drawn with what Paterson knew many members fondly saw as similar professions. "Both the doctor and the lawyer regard non members of their respective associations as beyond the pale, and as being guilty of unprofessional conduct."[92] As Paterson grew more confident, the journal's tone hardened: "Have we not the courage to realise that, after all, we are just working men, but with immense power in our hands if only we had the courage to use it."[93] Supporting this there were discussions, previously unthinkable, on the merits of Trades Hall affiliation. For this new hard-headed union leadership, wartime controls and the prospect of favourable Labor government legislation made affiliation important: "We would have more direct access to government . . . through the channel which is officially recognised."[94] Others had earlier argued that affiliation offered an opportunity to show the banks that their employees' attitudes were changing: "Many members feel that among the banks' executives, the reluctance of the Association to adopt a militant tone is misinterpreted as a sign of weakness."[95] It was argued pragmatically that in affiliation lay an opportunity of demonstrating to the banks the changing attitudes of bank officers without asking for an individual commitment and expression that would not have been forthcoming from more than a handful. Consistent with this, the union pursued member grievances with greater zeal, and in the year to August 1943 the arbitration inspector recovered more than a thousand pounds in overtime and tea money for members.[96] An earlier indication that the leadership now saw the ABOA more as a union than as a professional association occurred following a discussion between Prime Minister Curtin and the ACTU on the extent of war-induced industrial relations problems. The ABOA, now a member of the Council of Professional Employees Organization, a loose grouping of white-collar unions, was incensed: "It is imperative that if discussions are to cover the whole of the trade union movement then the CPEO must be invited to attend."[97]

In early 1943 Dwyer suggested the formation of a political party to represent white-collar workers. Several meetings were held, but Dwyer's dogmatism prevented any further action. Though this attempt at union politicization was largely a product of Dwyer's restless ambition and ego, there was some enthusiasm from both bank employees and workers in the insurance and clerical areas. For some, formation of a political party that did not have the connotations of manual work, as did the Labor Party, yet provided an alternative to remaining politically represented by the Conservative parties "which the bosses dictated, with disastrous results to bank officers",[98] was an attractive thought. Dwyer's reputation as an aggressive yet inconsistent militant was confirmed by events in Tasmania in 1944. Here the management of both the Launceston Bank for Savings and the Hobart Savings Bank were stoutly resisting ABOA attempts to organize their employees, preferring instead that they join the more conservative Federated Clerk's Union (FCU). It was not, of course, coincidental that FCU award rates were also considerably less than those of the ABOA's award. After the FCU failed to obtain jurisdiction, the banks' management suggested their employees form a separate organization. Dwyer rushed to Tasmania, confronted R.W. Freeman, general manager of the Hobart Savings Bank, bluntly told him he was "placing himself in a most invidious position", and offered the vague threat that the ABOA would report the bank to the attorney-general, Dr Evatt.[99] After further resistance and considerable unpleasantness, the ABOA succeeded in recruiting a few members from each bank. This political activism was certainly not shared by all members, and one reaction was the engineering of the election of G.W. Sneddon, a BNSW officer, as Victorian president in late 1943. The defeat of Dwyer in the ballot for Victorian branch delegates to Conference, which meant he was unable to renominate for Federal Council president, was similarly organized, "the meeting being packed against him by the BNSW".[100] However, if the banks and their supporters in the ABOA believed the way was now clear to swing the union behind the rapidly escalating campaign against nationalization, they were sorely mistaken, for to their consternation Paterson defeated Sneddon for Federal Council presidency. The "banks' man's" failure brought his resignation from the union within a few months.

Paterson's rise to prominence was one of the few encouraging aspects of the ABOA's performance in the period immediately before and during the Second World War. His persistence, determination, and refusal to be cowed by the banks was refreshing, as well as crucial to the union's development. His leadership was to be in sharp contrast to the expediency and selfishness of Smith, Harrison, and McLosky's complacency and ineffectiveness, and Dwyer's bellicose authoritarianism. The onset of the Second World War renders it purely speculative whether the anger of the rank and file culminating in the replacement of McLosky with Dwyer, could have, with better leadership, hastened the development of bank officer militancy. Certainly the privations of war stimulated bank employee discontent. The effects of branch rationalization, excessive work strains arising from manpower shortages, the prospect of increased female employment in the industry, and continuing declines in purchasing power created a ripe source of bank officer dissatisfaction.

In later years similar reasons did result in rapidly escalating militancy. However, in the immediate post-war period, bank employees were caught up in the greatest crisis in the banking industry's history. This arose from Labor government threats and attempts to nationalize the Australian private trading banks. Paterson's attributes were vital to the ABOA's role in these nationalization events. For the first time the union adopted an independent stance, refusing to be influenced or intimidated by the banks. As such, this marked a dramatic shift in the ABOA's philosophy and rationale, and one that was crucial to the union's post-war development.

Notes

1. Between 1929 and 1933 the proportion of Victorian bank officers aged less than twenty fell from 17 to 6 per cent (ABOA records).
2. *Queensland Bank Officer* 16, no. 11 (Jan. 1936): 3.
3. *Australian Banker* 9, no. 12 (Dec. 1934): 10.
4. Report of annual general meeting of the Victorian branch of the BOA, 25 September 1934.
5. Minutes of special joint meeting of Federal Council and Victorian branch committee, 26 March 1935 (FCM, p. 180).
6. *Queensland Bank Officer* 16, no. 6 (July 1935): 4.
7. In the twelve months following June 1934, 274 union members, or almost 10 per cent of Victorian branch membership, resigned (app. 3 and ABOA records).
8. Although the act did contain provision for the awarding of preference, it had only been granted once and on appeal the High Court had overturned the judgment (*King* v. *Commonwealth Court of Conciliation and Arbitration and President Thereof* v. *Australian Tramway Employees Association;* ex parte *Brisbane Tramway Company Limited [19 CLR 43]*.

9. *Queensland Bank Officer* 10, no. 2 (Apr. 1929): 5.

10. Australian manager of ES&A to London, 17 May 1934, letter in ANZ archives.

11. FCM, 12 March 1935.

12. *Bank Officials Association* v. *Bank of Australasia and Ors* (34 CAR 843) at p. 849. This led the banks' arbitration officer to report: "As anticipated, the separate agreements made by some banks with the Association in New South Wales will prove a definite handicap in presenting the case for the banks as a whole in any court" (ABA minutes, 14 June 1935, p. 3).

13. See appendix 2, table 1.

14. *VCMM*, 9 June 1936, p. 59.

15. Australian manager of the Union Bank of London, 23 July 1936, letter in ANZ archives.

16. Private letter from Sydney Smith to K. H. Laidlaw, 19 July 1937, in ABOA archives.

17. Sydney Smith to Laidlaw, 9 October 1937, letter in ABOA archives.

18. T. W. Smith to BOA, 31 July 1937, letter in ABOA archives.

19. Ibid., 6 August 1937, letter in ABOA archives.

20. See, for example, BOASA minutes, 19 June 1937, p. 101, and *Westralian Banker,* no. 176 (May 1939), p. 2.

21. T. W. Smith to BOA, 18 September 1937, letter in ABOA archives. This was sound advice, given what Judge Quick had earlier said. "I accept as a sound proposition that what employers in another bank have been paying, and what employees in that other bank have received and accepted affords evidence of what may be regarded as fair and reasonable rates" (*Bank Officials Association* v. *Bank of Australasia and Ors* [19 CAR 272] at p. 278).

22. See, for example, superintendent of Bank of Australasia to London, confidential letter no. 1899, 8 October 1937, in ANZ archives.

23. *Bank Officials' Association* v. *Bank of Australasia and Ors* (38 CAR 866).

24. Superintendent of Bank of Australasia to London, confidential letter no. 1923, 24 December 1937, in ANZ archives.

25. *SABOJ* 15, no. 7 (Feb. 1938), p. 12.

26. Annual report of New South Wales Insurance Officers Association, 4 April 1938, copy in ABOA archives.

27. Joint meeting of Victorian Committee of Management and Federal Council, 21 February 1938. Ogilvie did gratuitously offer to send his junior partner to stand in for him.

28. Association solicitor T. Bryan to Federal Council, 21 February 1938, letter in ABOA archives.

29. Circular to senior staff, 1 April 1938, copy in ABOA archives.

30. *Australian Banker* 13, no. 5 (May 1938): 27.

31. *Australian Banker* 13, no. 9 (Sept. 1938): 22.

32. *Australian Bank Officials Association* v. *Bank of Australasia and Ors* (39 CAR 1012), transcript 31 March 1938.

33. Ibid., evidence of C. Thompson of ES&A Bank, 5 May 1938, p. 297 of transcript.

34. See, for example, telegram from UBOA of NSW to ABOA, 17 June 1938, reproduced in *Australian Banker* 13, no. 7 (July 1938): 8.

35. See VCMM, 28 August 1938, p. 321.

36. Ibid., p. 322.

37. FCM, 2 September 1938.

38. Interestingly, the Bank of Australasia sub-branch (of which both Dufty and a close sympathizer and supporter W. E. A. Innes were influential members), offered to pay the expenses of retaining Bryan on the case. Apparently they saw him as a partial counterweight to Ogilvie's haste and ill-decisions.

39. Australian manager of Union Bank to London, 19 September 1938, letter in ANZ archives.
40. Ibid.
41. *Australian Bank Officials Association* v. *Bank of Australasia and Ors* (39 CAR 1012).
42. *Australian Banker* 13, no. 11 (Nov. 1938): 22.
43. Ibid.
44. Significantly, *all* votes had to be received through the post (VCMM, 9 October 1938, p. 339).
45. *Australian Banker* 13, no. 10 (Oct. 1938): 12.
46. Minutes of 1938 Victorian branch annual general meeting in VCMM, 16 October 1938, p. 346.
47. However, the cagy McLosky, aware that the battle would be won or lost at Federal Conference, the composition of which was decided by the branch committee, immediately resigned in favour of Smith. At the next meeting of the Victorian branch he reappeared as the representative of the BNSW sub-branch.
48. In another attempt to expand its federal image, the union had recently changed its name to the Australian Bank Officials' Association (ABOA).
49. FCM, 28 October 1938.
50. Ibid., 6 June 1938.
51. The Victorian delegates later reported: "No reflection should be too scathing on an executive which submits misleading figures and an incorrect balance sheet to Conference" (report of Victorian delegates on 1938 Federal Conference, copy in ABOA archives).
52. The final blow to Harrison's prestige had come the previous month when after being told by Federal Council that Harrison and Hore would attend the annual meeting of the branch, the Tasmanians replied that "they did not want Mr. Harrison to come" (FCM, 17 November 1938).
53. Report of Victorian delegates on 1938 Federal Conference.
54. FCM, 11 May 1939.
55. Report of Victorian delegates on 1938 federal conference.
56. FCM, 11 May 1939.
57. Once McLosky told BOASA that their contribution in the first year would be approximately £800 – 50 per cent of subscriptions (£500) and £300 to be joined to the federal award, his case was lost (see BOASA minutes, 19 June 1939, p. 1, and the *Westralian Banker,* no. 177 [June 1939], p. 3).
58. *Australian Banker* 14, no. 4 (Apr. 1939): 24.
59. FCM, 6 December 1939.
60. National Security Regulations, Statutory Rules 1939, No. 91, 13 September 1939. An extensive discussion of influences of the Second World War upon the Australian economy are provided in E. R. Walker, *The Australian Economy in War and Reconstruction* (New York: Oxford University Press, 1947): S. J. Butlin and C. B. Schedvin, *War Economy 1942-45* (Canberra: Australian War Memorial, 1977).
61. This rate of enlistment was so extensive that 8,314 (or approximately 47 per cent of all Australian male staff) had been released for war service by mid-1944 (*Bankers Journal* 3, no. 4 [May 1944]: 9).
62. The willingness of most banks to "make up" may well have been a complementary reason for the relatively high rate of enlistment from the industry. J. J. Dedman, minister for war organization in the Curtin ministry, was later unwise enough to make this point. He was assailed on all sides by unions and banks who resented his remarks "in that they cast an unwarranted slur on a loyal and patriotic section of the community" (minutes of Queensland branch

of BNSW sub-committee, 24 March 1942, reprinted in *Queensland Bank Officer* 23, no. 5 [July 1942]: 15).

63. A fact blandly described by Smith as "an oversight" (Smith to Laidlaw, 9 October 1940, letter in ABOA archives). The granting of annual leave had to date apparently been an act of grace by the banks.

64. *Australian Banker* 15, no. 4 (Apr. 1940): 8. The ABOA's disapproval of female bank clerks and its refusal to pursue their interests are explored in chapter 9. Given the attitudes of the ABOA to female employment, the "conditions of banking" really meant the conditions of employment for male officers.

65. *Australian Banker* 15, no. 5 (May 1940): 36.

66. *Australian Bank Officials Association* v. *Bank of Australasia and Ors* (44 CAR 627) at p. 268.

67. As at February 1942, male employment in private trading banks had fallen by 30 per cent, female employment increased by 31 per cent, with overall numbers declining by 11 per cent (Walker, *Australian Economy in War and Reconstruction*, p. 58).

68. Given the declared nationalization policy of the recently elected Labor government, and the comment by the minister for labour and national service, E. J. Ward, that "Commonwealth Bank employees who remained in reserve could handle much of the work of the private banks" Melbourne *Sun*, 28 February 1942, p. 7), the level of trepidation in private banking circles was not surprising.

69. Dedman's statement to private bank executives, Melbourne, 7 March 1942 (*Bankers Journal* 1, no. 9 [May 1942]: 5).

70. K. H. Laidlaw to BOAWA, 13 March 1942, letter in UBOA of Q files.

71. *Bankers Journal* 1, no. 9 (May 1942): 2. This statement referred to an earlier agreement between the bank and the CBOA. Known as the 1925 Agreement, this included the bank's promise that its employees would be "placed on a footing in respect of salaries and conditions not less advantageous than are provided under awards of the Commonwealth Arbitration Court for bank officers", as long as they refrained from approaching the Court (1925 Agreement reprinted in C. L. Mobbs, "Conciliation Can Work", pp. 24–25.

72. *Bankers Journal* 1, no. 8 (Apr. 1942): 16.

73. Australian manager of ES&A to London, confidential letter no. 432, 10 April 1942, in ANZ archives.

74. *Bankers Journal* 1, no. 8 (Apr. 1942): 7.

75. Minutes of Commonwealth Conference of Bank Officers' Associations, September 1942, p. 7, copy held in ABOA archives.

76. E. J. Ward's promise that he would "do everything possible to compel the non-unionist members of banking staffs to join the organisation" had come to nothing (Ward to ABOA, 8 May 1942, letter in ABOA archives).

77. Letter from L. J. McConnan to ABOA, 17 September 1942 (*Bankers Journal* 2, no. 2 [Sept. 1942]: 12).

78. *Australian Banker* 15, no. 8 (Sept. 1940): 1.

79. Report of special meeting of UBOA of NSW committee, 28 April 1942, in ABOA archives.

80. New South Wales BNSW sub-branch to McLosky, 9 July 1942, copy in ABOA archives.

81. This view has been supported in interviews with a number of bank officers, in particular L. Byrne (7 June 1978) and D. Gaunson [12 June 1978]).

82. FCM, 27 August 1942.

83. National Security Regulations, Statutory Rules No. 84, 17 November 1942.

84. This data is drawn from material held in the ABOA archives.

85. Between December 1939 and December 1942, the number of females employed by the Victorian trading banks increased from 380, or 9.3 per cent of the industry total, to 1,183, or 36.1 per cent (see appendix 3).

86. National Security Regulations, Statutory Rule No. 146, 25 March 1942. C. Lamour, "Women's Wages and the WEB", in *Women at Work*, ed. A. Curthoys, S. Eade, and P. Spearritt (Canberra: Australian Society for the Study of Labour History, 1975), pp. 47–58, provides an analysis of the formation and operation of this board.

87. *Australian Bank Officials Association* v. *Bank of Australasia and Ors* (Women's Employment Board) (52 CAR 303).

88. General president's report, 1944, to Federal Council (*Bankers Journal* 4, no. 2 [Sept. 1944] : 7). They also expressed the fear: "If the banks feel that should they be forced to pay temporary female labour substantial amounts from their now limited profits, this would be detrimental to male officers, particularly those in the Forces, who now enjoy benefits, and may also influence those banks which we know we are seeking to improve Guarantee and Provident funds by more liberal subsidies" (FCM, 7 January 1944, p. 442).

89. Appendix 3 and records of state unions.

90. VCMM, 20 November 1941, p. 478.

91. *Bankers Journal* 2, no. 10 (Aug. 1943): 8.

92. Ibid., 3, no. 1 (Sept. 1943): 8.

93. Ibid., no. 3 (Nov. 1943): 3.

94. Ibid., no. 4 (Dec. 1943): 8.

95. Ibid., 2, no. 3 (Nov. 1942): 6.

96. Ibid., 3, no. 1 (Aug. 1943): 14.

97. Telegram from ABOA to Prime Minister Curtin, 14 May 1942.

98. Minutes of special meeting of white-collar unions, 2 March 1943, copy in ABOA archives.

99. Report of visit to Tasmania by general president, August 1944, in ABOA archives.

100. Paterson to Laidlaw, 15 November 1943, letter in ABOA archives.

5   The Ultimate Challenge: 1946–49

Cabinet today authorised the Attorney-General, Dr. Evatt, and myself to prepare legislation for submission to the Federal Parliamentary Labor Party for the nationalisation of banking other than State
banks, with proper protection for shareholders, depositors, borrow-
ers, and staff of private banks.

[Prime Minister J. B. Chifley, August 1947]

Ever since the First World War the private banks had been concerned at
the growing power of the Commonwealth Bank and also that a federal
Labor government might nationalize them. The changing attitudes of the
ABOA towards nationalization and the implications of this for banking
unionism are worthy of discussion. Not only was the union's response to
nationalization different from that of the other banking unions, but it also
indicated a strengthening of an emerging spirit which, though not yet
definable as white-collar militancy, did reflect the new independence of
the ABOA's leadership and at least part of its rank and file.

Some Nagging Fears

The private banks had always viewed the Commonwealth Bank with
apprehension, for they did not want increased competition, particularly
from a bank not a member of the powerful banking oligopoly. But even
more they feared the increase of the Commonwealth Bank's central
banking role. In reality they had little to fear. Sternly led in the 1920s by
Sir Robert Gibson, the bank emphasized rigidly orthodox deflationary
policies, stoutly resisted any political intrusion, and seemed little interested in expanding its central banking function.[1]

By 1931, however, the bank controlled the exchange rate and had
extensive control over government spending, private bank liquidity, and
interest rates. As a result of the exigencies of the Depression, it was now
clearly moving swiftly towards becoming a fully fledged central bank.
This was encouraged by the Labor government, whose long mistrust of
the private banks was constantly reiterated, and compounded by the
banks' refusal to allow the creation of employment opportunities through

deficit financing.[2] In his policy speech before the 1931 election, Prime Minister Scullin promised to reintroduce proposals to separate the bank's trading bank function from its central banking role so that "increased bank credits could be made available to industry".[3] This increased fears of inflation, summed up by an *Argus* editorial:

> Mr. Scullin concluded his speech without any reference to a fiduciary issue of notes. The verbal dressing which Mr. Theodore employed some months ago has become bedraggled. Accordingly Mr. Scullin dresses Mr. Theodore's old ideas in new garb. The fiduciary issue, however, differs in no way from the proposals of Mr. Scullin to monopolise credit so that politicians may seek their own aggrandisement.[4]

The banks treated the election seriously[5] and provided financial support to numerous anti-Labor groups. The crushing defeat of Labor ended immediate prospects for further Commonwealth Bank expansion, but the old animosities smouldered on.

> Banks were still . . . targets of bitter criticism. . . . [There was] both resentment of the part allegedly played by the banks in the collapse of Labor governments in New South Wales and the federal parliament, the hostility of every debtor who believed his fate could have been avoided with proper bank aid, and of every sufferer from the depression who at least half believed that, even if it had not been caused by the banks, its worst severity could have been averted but for their wickedness and stupidity.[6]

On the question of nationalization, the BOA stood firmly with the banks. When the ES&A issued a circular to all customers condemning nationalization, the BOA resolved "to support the ESA in this matter and that every assistance possible be given to expound the fallacies of the arguments in support of nationalisation".[7] The Victorian branch "urged every bank officer to do all in his power, not only in his own service, but with the public generally, to stop such a proposal being put into effect".[8] An interstate conference in September 1933 had before it letters from Scullin to the new secretary of the UBOA of NSW, W. Panton-Craik, in which Scullin reaffirmed his nationalization plans and outlined how private bank officers were to be absorbed by the Commonwealth Bank. This only incensed union leaders, for even in the unlikely event of the bank being able to do this, the officers would perforce become CBOA members. For full-time union officials — Smith, Laidlaw, and Panton-Craik — nationalization would mean the end of their careers. Consequently the conference resolved to establish a central campaign committee to liaise with the banks, and to offer every possible assistance to them.

In the run up to the 1934 federal election, all cards were on the table after Scullin stated that "Australia was suffering want because of the failure of our banking institutions".

This failure has caused the depression. The banks have done more than any other section to land Australia and the world in the depression existing today. Without credit industry was at a standstill. In the boom period the banks lent thousands on overdraft to inflate for profit, but during the depression deflated to protect their shareholders. Banking should be under complete national control. . . . Every municipality and State and Commonwealth department should be forced to use the Commonwealth Bank.[9]

Harrison warned members that "the policy of the advocates of nationalisation was to strangle the private trading banks. . . . without doubt competent officers would be superseded by political appointees . . . and half of the present officers [would] be unemployed."[10] It is difficult to ascertain whether this aroused members to the same vehement heights as their leadership. However, it certainly alienated sections of the Labor Party, who saw the BOA as "conducting a whispering campaign under the influence of the banks with the object of circulating propaganda to protect the banks' own interest".[11] The BOA's support of the banks was illustrated by their reply to a member who queried why his pro-nationalization letter was not published in the journal. "It was not even considered, and has been consigned to the waste paper basket."[12]

As the election drew closer, BOA executive members were instructed to oppose nationalization "over the air", the union asked permission for some senior officers to go on a public speaking tour,[13] and Benwell and McLosky spent three weeks in rural areas exhorting bank clerks to oppose nationalization. Their efforts may have been of value, for Scullin was "somewhat chastened by the hundreds of enquiries that [had] been directed to him by bank officials".[14] In its final advice before the election, the *Australian Banker,* aware of the politically conservative attitudes of most members, warned: "Should nationalisation be adopted the officers of the nationalised bank would be expected to be loyal to the political controllers of the institution."[15] Throughout the campaign the dominant union theme had been one of support for their employers. Only rarely had the BOA raised fears of loss of employment, yet this was surely the issue of most legitimate union concern.

The Lyons Nationalist government won comfortably, and fears of nationalization again receded. The BOA congratulated itself on its role in the defence of the private banking system, but regretted that "the Associated Banks had refused to refund union expenses incurred in the campaign".[16] In a statement that provides further reason for the keeness with which they had fought the Labor Party, they plaintively complained that "the Association had not received any word of recognition from the Associated Banks".[17] That the banks had not even recognized their assistance further reinforced bank officers' perceptions of their humble positions in the industry.

Later in the thirties, bank unions gave strong support to the banks when legislation to limit their operations loomed. This had arisen from considerable public concern over the private banks' actions during the Depression. This concern had crystallized in the establishment of a royal commission into the Australian banking system.The general manager of the ES&A, in a letter to London on 10 January 1935, outlined reasons why he believed this occurred:

> A great deal of controversy took place on the subject of the need for monetary reform. These discussions took the form in the main of an attack upon the banking system, and as a result the Prime Minister was having a particularly troublesome time in Tasmania with Douglasites and more or less half witted clergymen who strongly advocated the Douglas theories of credit. . . . For political reasons he gave a half hearted promise that if Parliament so willed it, there would be a Commission appointed after the election. We were hoping that the whole matter would drift into the limbo of forgetfulness, but quite recently *The Argus* newspaper in a most ill advised attempt to dispose entirely of the subject began advising the public that such an enquiry was unnecessary. This has proved embarrassing to the Prime Minister and his Treasurer, and as a result he now has to come out into the open and a Commission will be appointed.[18]

Consistent with their long-term acquiescence to the banks, it is not surprising that Australian banking unions made no critical contribution to this inquiry. Rather, they were content to ring the praises of their well-tried system which had stood the test of time and had served the needs of the Australian people sufficiently and well for over a hundred years. The composition of the commission was followed with keen interest by the banks, and they were generally well pleased with the government's choice. Even the appointment of J.B. Chifley was seen as purely political. "He may be a nuisance," wrote the general manager of the ES&A in the letter quoted above, "but I do not think he has sufficient force to cause us any anxiety." These words must have later returned to haunt the writer. The royal commission proceeded relatively smoothly, with the banks eager to prove that they definitely were in competition "and the Commission must not be allowed to think otherwise."[19]

Eventually the commission recommended legislation to empower the Commonwealth Bank to require the private banks to hold minimum deposits with it, and also that the Commonwealth Bank should have the right to call upon the private banks' overseas funds. The banks, unaware that these recommendations were in fact the first of a plethora of central banking regulations that would significantly constrain their future actions, were displeased but not angered, for the origins of the royal commission suggested that some discussion on bank nationalization may have come foward. Only Chifley's dissenting report made any mention of this: "There is no possibility of the objectives being reached or of any well ordered progress being made in the community, under a system in which there are privately owned trading banks which have been established for the purpose of making profit."[20] However, after two years of government procrastination and mild bank resistance, led largely by the BNSW, the legislation was aborted by the onset of the Second World War.

The Second World War further increased the control by the Commonwealth Bank and federal government over the private banks. In mid-1941 the UAP government, concerned at the prospect of inflation, proposed that the banks place their excess funds with the Commonwealth Bank and allow it to control interest rates. The banks agreed reluctantly, hoping to extend the life of the ailing ministry, but also to circumvent allegations of excessive wartime profits. With the fall of the Fadden government in 1941, the new Curtin Labor government immediately imposed these controls by regulation. Fears of nationalization induced by this were heightened by the long dispute over branch rationalization. On 17 May 1941, *Smith's Weekly,* a paper of wide circulation though dubious merit, angered bank unions when in reporting on an interstate conference it claimed there had been agreement to support nationalization and as an initial step to seek amalgamation with the dormant CBOA. At this time, when union nationalization attitudes were significantly influenced by the relative power of BNSW sub-branches, it was not surprising that the UBOA of NSW was already under considerable pressure to declare their support for the banks. Eventually a special conference was held, but after acrimonious debate it merely resolved that the "Association's attitude to nationalisation be deferred indefinitely".[21]

To this time the ABOA, as could be expected, blindly followed the banks in their opposition to nationalization. This attitude, consistent with the bank employees' perception of his lowly place in the banking hierarchy, was a result of years of industry conditioning. While there were grounds for believing that banking employment and promotional opportunities would be prejudiced by nationalization, this argument was seldom expressed by the ABOA. Rather, their opposition was based on some generalized and non-specific fear concerning the "socialist" tendencies of Labor governments. The banks knew their employees well and guaranteed ABOA support by fostering this apprehension.

The Challenge Is Issued

The latter years of the Second World War saw an intensification of nationalization rumours and eventually another Labor government attempt to eliminate the private trading banks. This action, and its preliminaries, destroyed the fragile bonds between the various banking unions and left wounds that took twenty years to heal. On the one hand was the ABOA, and for a time BOASA; opposing them were the other state unions, led by the UBOA of NSW. At this time, the policies of banking unions towards nationalization were still largely a function of the attitudes of their leaders. In Victoria the energetic Paterson, initially federal vice-president and later president, fought doggedly to prevent the ABOA declaring its opposition to nationalization. There is little doubt that Paterson, a long-time Labor sympathizer, favoured nationalization. Yet his oft-repeated argument that the ABOA should defend its members' interests and not those of the private banks was put with sufficient forthrightness and logic to convince most ABOA members that the union must continue to remain outside the maelstrom. In New South Wales, Card was in charge of the UBOA of NSW's anti-nationalization campaign. Initially he had followed a policy not unlike Paterson's, but realization that his industrial and political career prospects might hinge on opposition to nationalization soon ensured his total support for the banks' campaign.

Before the 1943 elections the banks again mounted an extensive campaign, for which they had considerable union support. ABOA secretary Lodge (whose pro-bank leanings, so evident in his journal editorials, had already brought him into conflict with Dwyer and Paterson) encouraged members to express support for the non-Labor parties by hinting that this would be warmly welcomed by their employees.[22] These only ceased after Paterson warned him that his position was in jeopardy.[23] In Western Australia the strong BNSW sub-branch readily convinced the excessively conservative leadership to mount a strong anti-nationalization campaign, and for some months the *Westralian Banker* carried a number of *AIBR* articles condemning further government intervention.[24] BOASA, however, still remained uncommitted, largely because of the dominance of SBSA members. With nothing to fear from nationalization, they saw little point in alienating the federal government on behalf of the private banks.

In New South Wales, agitation by the BNSW sub-branch reached new heights, and the UBOA of NSW committee eventually agreed to hold a postal ballot. Members were asked: "Are you in favour of the nationalisation of banking and the abolition of the trading banks?";[25] 3,406 members opposed the proposal with only 259 in favour.[26] However, in spite of extensive propaganda and a six-week state-wide tour by the president, Newton, the refusal of more than half the members to even vote reflected a considerable lack of interest. Fearful of Labor government recrimination, other state unions asked the UBOA of NSW not to publish these results, but the New South Wales union refused, another sign of hardening leadership attitudes. Card now led the way, for he was aware that Newton would retire shortly and that he could win the presidency. He was anxious to show union critics that earlier charges of nationalization support were false and now used all the union's resources to vilify the Labor government and its nationalization policy. The publication of the New South Wales ballot results brought a flurry of activity in Victoria, and the increasingly irrational Dwyer immediately rushed to Sydney to urge the formation of an Australia-wide union for reasons that few could comprehend. In his absence, Victorian branch president and BNSW employee Sneddon set about mobilizing support for the banks, while Paterson strove equally as hard to ensure the union did not co-operate with what was now a blatantly political campaign by the private banks.

Later in 1944, with the struggle over official ABOA policy continuing and rumours of legislation rife, Sneddon and Lodge hurried to Sydney for further discussion with Card.[27] This resulted in the calling of another interstate conference. Paterson was actually relieved at this news, for not only was he worried that Sneddon might soon convince the Victorian branch committee to take some unilateral action, but his own position was increasingly untenable. Bank pressure and some rank and file agitation had eroded a little of his earlier conviction and made him anxious for direction and confirmation of his opposition to the banks. As he confessed to Laidlaw: "What worries me is that a section of members here and in New South Wales wish to support the banks in their campaign, the section wishing to support the government has not yet appeared."[28] Yet Paterson was fearful that any precipitate change in ABOA policy would be disastrous. This fear was not only a result of his personal political views. His informal discussions with several cabinet members had confirmed that legislation was in the offing and that "even if the union made it clear that they were not attacking the government but only the proposed legislation, it would nevertheless be viewed as an attack on the government, and they would not forget".[29] He was heartened by other advice, however, and wrote to Laidlaw: "Confidential information which has reached us inclines us to the belief that the government if approached would grant us absolute preference, provided of course we had done nothing to oppose their legislation."[30] Paterson used this to encourage his wavering supporters and to resist his own bank's attempts to compromise him by nominating him as their representative on a committee investigating new legislation. This clumsy ploy failed when Paterson, realizing that "his fate was to be turned out and trained as a public speaker to fight for the banks",[31] refused to be co-opted. His newfound determination was decisive, and he managed to firm up the wavering views of most executive members to the point that when the Melbourne *Herald* speculated on the ABOA's anti-nationalization tactics,[32] the union insisted on a retraction. Then when he defeated Sneddon for the federal presidency, the chances of the ABOA supporting the banks' campaign were further reduced.

At the interstate conference, Paterson's growing diplomacy skills and reasoned argument were in evidence, and he persuaded Conference to send a delegation to Chifley seeking protection for unionists following nationalization. For a short time at least, Paterson had convinced the other unions that nationalization was inevitable. This was a significant victory, particularly given the enthusiasm the UBOA of NSW had already shown for the anti-nationalization campaign. In view of this, Chifley's blunt refusal to provide any assurances to the delegation was a mistake, particularly as these union leaders still retained significant control over their membership on this issue.

Chifley's refusal to guarantee the employment of private bank officers following nationalization — an assurance that was eventually given, but all too late (see below) — provided state union leaders with their first tangible argument against nationalization. One can only speculate on the effect that a more placatory statement from Chifley may have had, particularly upon leaders from states other than New South Wales, who as yet did not have the same obsession about nationalization. It is unlikely that they would have recommended nationalization to their membership, but it may well have served to reduce their later antagonism to the Labor government. Chifley's refusal also gave those members who did not blindly accept their leaders' edicts little opportunity to assess the situation more objectively. Though Conference did not immediately commit the unions to an anti-nationalization campaign, time was to show that only the ABOA would withstand the banks' blandishments.

Following this interstate conference, opposition to nationalization grew rapidly in most states. The banks were most active in New South Wales, and the UBOA of NSW's office was bombarded with demands by BNSW members for a declaration of opposition to nationalization. Card's Rural Bank employment was seen as so inconsistent with a defence of the private banking system that the UBOA of NSW committee was forced to move a motion of confidence in him.[33] He did not let his supporters down, and when in early 1945 the union formally resolved to oppose nationalization and to establish a network of provincial committees to facilitate this, Card was stridently in support.[34]

In March 1945, when Chifley eventually introduced the long-feared legislation, the banking unions, apart from the ABOA and BOASA, were totally opposed. In emphasizing that control over post-war inflation would be through control of the credit base rather than the note issue, the legislation outlined how the Commonwealth Bank would expand its central banking function by controlling trading bank liquidity using a system of special deposits. In addition, the Commonwealth Bank's trading role was to be expanded and it was to be empowered to requisition portion of the private banks' overseas exchange. Union reactions were predictable, with the UBOA of NSW, after rationalizing its earlier inaction,[35] leading the way. Their well-organized district "fighting committees" swung into action, disseminating propaganda largely supplied by the banks, and with the banks' permission union members were instructed to publicly oppose the legislation in any way they could. When UBOA of NSW secretary Panton-Craik resigned in mid-1945, Card took leave from the Rural Bank to act as full-time union president and secretary. He now saw an opportunity to further his industrial career and threw himself wholeheartedly into defence of the private banking system.

As unofficial co-ordinator of the unions' anti-nationalization campaign, Card found the ABOA the only stumbling block. Within the ABOA, Paterson was now firmly in control, for at several fiery meetings his logical argument had proved more than equal to the emotive pleas of bank supporters, who had done little more than vilify the Chifley government. Paterson argued that "it would be easy to embark upon a policy of uttering diatribes . . . but such a policy would perform no useful purpose and may render the members of the Association the greatest possible dis-service".[36] Having obtained an appointment with the prime minister, he returned comforted by Chifley's newfound awareness of the difficulties created for bank officers by nationalization and tried to convince the other unions to join an industry panel which would deal with bank employee problems and anomalies. But this was all too late, and their scathing rejection of this proposal only widened the gulf between the ABOA and the state unions.

Further bank and union opposition was in vain. The legislation finally passed through both houses in mid-1945.[37] The issue then briefly faded in importance, the banks intent on servicing post-war economic expansion and the unions preoccupied with problems caused by continuing staff shortages, extensive overtime, and the industry's retention of females.[38]

Battle Is Joined

The nationalization controversy dragged on for several more years, all the time further damaging inter-union relationships. Only the ABOA refused to join the banks in their anti-nationalization and anti-Labor government campaign. For some union leaders, protection and advancement of their members' interests was of secondary importance. At no time was this demonstrated more clearly than by their continued, wholehearted support for the conservative political forces long after all possibilities of nationali-zation had disappeared. In May 1947 the Labor government finally imple-mented section 48 of the banking legislation, compelling all state and local government authorities to bank with the Commonwealth Bank. Upon challenge, the High Court decided that this section was invalid because it interfered with an essential function of state government.[39] Chifley, angry that he had been so easily thwarted, immediately announced that legisla-tion would be drafted to eliminate the private banks, leaving only the Commonwealth Bank and the state-owned banks. Reactions were immediate, and ranged from Laidlaw's dramatic, Churhillian appeal to his members "to remain calm and carry on their banking business in the ordinary way";[40] a prominent federal opposition member's claim, "We can never be sure that it [the Labor Party] will not attempt to socialize the shops or the newspapers, or even heaven knows, the Churches",[41] to strident approval from much of the Labor Party and the left wing press.[42] Chifley's announcement ushered in two years of political turmoil and brought banking unions face to face with their greatest challenge.

Only BOASA's leaders and Paterson had not yet committed their unions to total support for the banks. In New South Wales, Card quickly organized numerous mass meetings and arranged the distribution of further vast quantities of propaganda. So frantic was his activity that the Speaker of the House of Representatives, J. S. Rosevear, was moved to comment that "bank officers were being browbeaten by the employers into opposing the plan".[43]

There had still been little discussion of the impact of nationalization upon bank officers. The legislation as initially framed did threaten private bank employees' salaries, promotion, and perhaps even job security. Yet Card, in arguing emotively though with little clarity, chose to exploit the loyalty that officers held to their banks. Any member questioning the UBOA of NSW's rabid support for the banks was ruthlessly dealt with; Hodson, the CBA delegate, was forced to resign after participating in a meeting at the New South Wales Trades Hall supporting nationalization.[44] In Western Australia the political aspirations of H. M. Malcolm guaranteed BOAWA's increased support for the banks. Malcolm, who was later to stand unsuccessfully as a Liberal Senate candidate, presided over a meeting that authorized the executive to "do all such things as are considered necessary to combat the proposal".[45] Additionally, both he and the BOAWA vice-president, G. E. L. Throssell, were leading members of the Citizen Rights Association and unabashedly used the union to further the aims of this conservative body. In Queensland Laidlaw, in his cautious, pragmatic, and parochial fashion, was not yet prepared to throw full union support behind the campaign. Yet he soon found himself chairman of the Staff Protest Committee, and the UBOA of Q president, W. C. Wood, was seconded to the banks' fighting organization.

It was Laidlaw who restated an explicit rationale for union opposition after Dedman foolishly declared that Australia's banking could be carried out with five thousand fewer officers.[46] Laidlaw claimed Dedman looked upon nationalization as "a method of again releasing a fountain of man-power which he can push about and divert into any channels", adding "Mr. Chifley does not appear to have any concrete scheme for the preser-vation of the seniority of officers taken into the Commonwealth Bank."[47] Dedman's statement, together with the postmaster general's announce-ment that he would employ any surplus clerks,[48] forced Chifley into a long-overdue statement: "All employees of the private banks will be given the right to become members of the staff of the Commonwealth Bank. The proposals to be put to the party will provide protection for the existing rights of these officers and for their conditions of service and emoluments to be not less favourable than those at present enjoyed."[49] But battle lines had already been drawn, and Chifley's attempted reassurance fell on deaf ears.

In Victoria, Paterson's approach of emphasizing protection of members rather than the banks in the event of nationalization was restated and confirmed at a large general meeting in October 1947. The events of this meeting, in establishing a policy that was in total opposition to that of other unions, and perhaps more importantly of the banks, demand brief discussion. Not only did the meeting confirm Federal Council's decision to seek legislative amendments,[50] but several notable conservatives among the union leaders also came out in support of the official ABOA policy. The Victorian branch president, David Gaunson,[51] in opening the meeting, affirmed his personal opposition to nationalization but stressed that the industrial future of bank officers was in the hands of the membership. "See that your Association remains strong and united and not torn asunder by the adoption of political opinions," he said. He also reminded them that "already there were committees working solidly against nationalisation . . . but were any of these organisations greatly concerned about the established rights of bank officers being preserved?"[52] Paterson then outlined ABOA amendments already accepted by Chifley. Of most significance was a Commonwealth Bank Appeals Board to ensure continuity of salaries, promotional prospects, and pension rights for trading bank officers. Paterson then detailed the relative advantages of Commonwealth Bank employment: a higher scale running to twenty-one years, an extensive classification scheme, and superior conditions and allowances.[53] Tasmanian proxy Hore, who was also personally opposed to nationalization, assured the meeting of Tasmanian support and warned members not to allow the union to be "used as a political body, or they would have to take the consequences". Heated discussion followed, and finally the spokesman for the BNSW sub-branch moved that Federal Council be instructed to "take all possible steps to actively oppose the legislation". Their optimism was shattered when this was lost by a two-thirds majority and a resolution confirming the ABOA policy accepted.

Though some disgruntled officers argued that the ABOA's policy resulted from Paterson's persuasive influence, the fact that nine of the fourteen provincial sub-branches from rural areas, where nationalization opposition was greatest, also supported official policy[54] indicates this was not a sufficient explanation. The distinguishing feature of ABOA leaders' and many members' actions was a determination to maintain the union's apolitical stance. Certainly Paterson was a Labor supporter,[55] but his attitude was significantly influenced by a belief that the best protection for his members lay in legislative amendment. Additionally, he and an increasing number of members were convinced that the ABOA must no longer be seen as the fawning, ineffectual, and conservative body of earlier years, and this issue was appropriate to demonstrate that. As he wrote to BOASA president S.V. Barratt: "I don't think that what the other unions are up to will win them many friends amongst the banks when this is all over."[56] Many Victorian officers did oppose nationalization, either individually or as members of the numerous protest and action committees. Most, however, were not ABOA members. Paterson noted, "When you look at how some of these fellows are carrying on then it's no wonder they never joined the union."[57]

An interstate conference hurriedly convened by Card in late 1947 highlighted the conflict between bank unions. After vain attempts to sway the ABOA and BOASA, the conference degenerated into a series of diatribes against the government. Eventually there was agreement that the time was ripe to claim a salary increase from the banks, and a joint salary approach resulted in an offer some twenty-five pounds less than the Commonwealth Bank eighteenth-year rate. R.A. McKell of the Bank of Australasia, the then UBOA of NSW president, was convinced that this should be accepted, and Card's praise for the banks' offer was profuse. With Paterson arguing that less obsequiousness and more determination would bring a better result, the conference ended in acrimony. Paterson, certain that there was "no doubt that at this time they would rather have us onside",[58] continued negotiations alone and was vindicated when the banks agreed to vary the ABOA award to pay the Commonwealth Bank rate of £575 at the top of the scale and to introduce automatic cost-of-living increases.[59]

In the meantime the nationalization legislation had been introduced into parliament in October 1947. In forbidding private banks from carrying on business except while being absorbed by the Commonwealth Bank, it encompassed voluntary or compulsory acquisition of private bank and shareholders assets, the level of compensation available, and a comprehensive set of conditions covering the transfer of private bank employees to the Commonwealth Bank.[60] It was swiftly and remorsefully pressed through both houses, with the government ignoring opposition calls for a referendum and rejecting claims that the new bank would be susceptible to political interference. The government reiterated that as there was little genuine competition between the private banks anyway, fears of abuse of the proposed Commonwealth Bank's monopoly power were unjustified.

The considerable tension between the ABOA and other unions was heightened when the Communist newspaper the *Tribune* published a highly coloured and inaccurate report of Paterson's discussions with Chifley on legislative amendments.[61] Card sought to discredit Paterson and the ABOA by sending all unions copies of this alleged collaboration with "the enemy" and by demanding the ABOA president publicly deny the bizarre details of the article. He refused, as "he did not regard this newspaper as having any influence upon the type of person with whom we have contact, and he had no intention of descending to the gutter to enter into any controversy".[62] This controversy, together with the impending

Victorian state election, galvanized nationalization opponents into even more frenzied action.

In Victoria, the Bank Employees Protest Committee had been formed following the ABOA's refusal to support the banks, and Sneddon had re-emerged as one of its leaders. They had earlier organized a meeting which condemned the legislation and authorized a poll of Victorian employees which allegedly showed that 99 per cent of them opposed nationalization.[63] The holding of this meeting in banking hours with express management approval and the biased nature of the poll raise serious questions about the committee's frequent claims that it spoke for Victorian bank officers because of the ABOA's neglect. The comment of one clerk — "I have yet to hear of any bank officer who has voted for any member of this Committee, donated one penny to its resources, or otherwise assisted it"[64] — lends support to union claims that the committee was largely bank controlled and financed.

In South Australia, Barratt and a fellow SBSA officer, D.W. Simmons, both of whom were later to figure prominently in the establishment of a South Australian branch of the ABOA, still maintained BOASA's non-involvement. However, the BNSW and NBA sub-branches were pressing hard for a change in union policy. They eventually forced a postal ballot on whether its members were in favour "of the Association adopting a definite policy to combat the proposed legislation",[65] but to the chagrin of its promoters the proposal was soundly defeated 725 votes to 376.[66] This prompted Paterson and Gaunson to approach BOASA and suggest amalgamation,[67] so that following nationalization they would be better placed to protect their members.

The events that followed were crucial, not only to BOASA's official nationalization policy, but also the ABOA's future. SBSA members of the BOASA committee, chafing at the SBSA trustees' refusal even to discuss salary and condition issues with them, and impressed by the more vigorous Victorians, urged agreement. However, delegates from the BNSW and the NBA, prompted by Card and no doubt their own banks, convinced other committeemen to wait on legal opinion. This procrastination was successful, for the next month, R.W. Peirce, president of the BNSW sub-branch, was elected unopposed as BOASA president. Barratt and Simmons, accepting the inevitability of defeat, did not nominate, and private bank officers gained control of BOASA. However, at the very next committee meeting, argument whether Peirce's full-time secondment to the bank's anti-nationalization committee was consistent with the current BOASA policy of "no political alignment" brought his resignation. Barratt won the election held at the same meeting[68] but resigned almost immediately, in order to establish the point that the interests of SBSA and private bank officers could not both be satisfied within the existing union structure. The new president was another BNSW officer, D.R. Thomas, and a change in BOASA attitude appeared imminent.

However, not until August 1948, when the High Court declared much of the legislation invalid,[69] were there any further developments. In the light of the decision, BOASA's BNSW committeemen suggested another postal ballot. "Not until the Socialists have been prevented for all time from any further implementation of their scheme, can we say, as bank officers, that the threat to our chosen careers has been removed," *SABOJ* reported. "Not until then, will we be permitted to relax our vigilance."[70] Despite resistance and disaffiliation threats by the SBSA sub-branch, the ballot was held. It saw a substantial majority support the argument that the BOASA executive be "unfettered to deal with any contingency which may arise from time to time".[71] For some months the SBSA sub-branch adroitly steered the union clear of any further commitment, but following Thomas's secondment to the Combined Trading Banks Staff Committee, and the delight with which some committeemen received this news,[72] SBSA members resigned *en masse* from BOASA and formed the South Australian branch of the ABOA. Though it was the nationalization issue that overtly brought about the secession of Savings Bank officers, this decision was really a culmination of many years of discontent with the archly conservative South Australian private bank officers who had at different times controlled BOASA. This secession was crucial to post-war banking unionism and is discussed in the following chapter.

By 1949 the nationalization battle had moved to the political stage. All unions other than the ABOA eagerly joined their employers and numerous other groups in a campaign of unparalleled intensity. The banks now waived earlier instructions forbidding political involvement[73] and released more officers for political work.[74] Numerous examples of the politicization of the union's campaign can be found in union correspondence, journals, and minutes, and it is perhaps not surprising that most historians have assumed that these reflected the views of the rank and file as well as their leaders.[75] In fact, numbers of unionists objected to their unions' political involvement. As one officer wrote: "With others, I have received a telephone call from a representative of a political organisation, operating within the banking industry, abruptly informing me I was expected to attend a certain meeting. I discovered the object of the meeting was to canvas for the Liberal Party."[76]

The Privy Council's rejection of the government's appeal and the Labor Party's statement that nationalization was no longer feasible had little impact on either bank or union campaigns. An increasing number of officers queried this.

Why then, many officers wanted to know, were they being obliged to forego leave and work overtime so that the anti-nationalisation teams could carry on as Liberal election teams? No one can deny the right of any man to campaign for the party he favours, yet when it becomes a matter of pressure being brought to bear on our members to assist in campaigning for one particular party which they may or may not support, it is time for the Association to make a stand.[77]

Card's attacks upon the Labor government and particularly the minister for labour, E.J. Ward, had become so frequent and antagonistic that the Rural Bank and Bank of Australasia sub-branches protested.[78] In one virulent outburst upon Ward, "that charming specimen of socialist manhood", Card accused him of betraying Australia and the Labor Party both before and during the Second World War.[79] There was growing feeling among members that bank employee interests were being sacrificed in this frantic, obsessive support for the banks.[80]

Further controversy flared when Card's intention to enter politics became known, and his motives and actions as union leader in the last three years came under fresh scrutiny. It was generally conceded that Card would win preselection for the blue-ribbon Liberal seat of Evans for the looming federal election, the key issue of which would undoubtedly be bank nationalization. However, circulation throughout the electorate of a pamphlet apparently written by the secretary of the CBC sub-branch destroyed his chances. This circular, after warning Liberal Party members of the dangers of being too closely identified with the banks, urged that Card, "palpably a Banks' Nominee", not be endorsed. "In returning one good turn for another [we] are unthinkingly leaving the Party wide open to a raking attack by Labor. The repercussions may easily be the decisive factor as . . . it is useless to deny that the average middle and lower class wage earner rightly or wrongly distrusts the power of the banks."[81] Though the statement that Card was a banks' nominee was false, the circular had the desired effect, and he was defeated in the preselection ballot by F.M. Osborne and was forced to contest unsuccessfully the safe Labor seat of Watson.[82]

The election brought crushing defeat for Labor, due in large part to emotions stirred by the nationalization campaign. As Chifley's biographer notes:

> First it galvanized the anti Labor parties, from their representatives in Canberra to their branch members in the smallest suburbs and country towns, to a degree unknown since 1931 — or perhaps even 1917. . . . Secondly never before or since, nor for such a sustained period, have the anti Labor forces had anything approaching the campaign funds for their cause which were, directly or indirectly, lavished on them between August 1947 and December 1949.[83]

With the battle over, the participants turned to a reckoning of the gains and costs of the nationalization battle. Most bank employees who had supported the banks had done so either as an instinctive, compliant reaction of support for their employers, a conviction that the existing banking system should be preserved, or in the latter days of the crisis, because they feared the loss of jobs or employment benefits. These motives are readily understood, though the manner in which the banks, anti-Labor political parties, and some union leaders exploited these bank officer fears can be questioned. However, there were some who hoped for more tangible rewards.

> We lined ourselves up with the boss. . . . without need of much encouragement we organised committees, called meetings, got petitions signed, distributed propaganda (and swallowed it), did electioneering and scrutineering. . . . But when the tumult and the shouting died, and we stand with shining countenance awaiting our reward, with thoughts by some of promotion hinted at, by others, of better conditions . . . do we get anything of which we dreamt?[84]

Though criticized by some, these sentiments received considerable support. One clerk, in recalling the rigours of the thirties, asked whether the banks would remember their recent contribution if "peace broke out, the price of wool tumbled, wheat was once more in oversupply, and security values followed on the slide. Would your job be secure? Would your salary avoid a cut?"[85] Certainly the private banks had paid post-war bonuses of 10 to 15 per cent, but these had merely maintained purchasing power, and their emphatic refusal to discuss the abolition of Saturday morning banking was bringing increasing unrest. It was galling to state union leaders to realize that after their much-vaunted victory over the "socialists", Commonwealth Bank officers still enjoyed superior salaries and conditions, and it had been the despised ABOA which had been responsible for most private bank employee salary increases anyway. A. L. May argues in *The Battle for the Banks* that the improved salaries and conditions that occurred in the fifties were "partly as an acknowledgement of their efforts and partly also as a result of their newly discovered strength in combination".[86] He was wrong, for as discussed in the next chapter, increased militancy, initially confined to the ABOA, was alone responsible for these gains. Certainly this union's organizational and tactical skills had been sharpened, but by persistent efforts to maintain the union's independence, not by involvement in the campaign against nationalization.

For the ABOA the nationalization crisis had hastened the emergence of unionists and leaders considerably less conservative and less in awe of their employers than earlier bank officers. The events of the campaign had cemented Paterson's position as ABOA president. Though he may personally have viewed the nationalization result as a loss, the union's rank and file may not have been so sure. Their jobs, future prospects, and status in the community seemed guaranteed, and the union had remained politically uninvolved. However, the salary victory won by Paterson had shown them that strong independent action could wring more concessions from the banks than the traditional unquestioning obedience had. This was a lesson they were to remember well. The nationalization crisis had also created another restive group of bank employees, those disturbed and even angry at the way in which the banks had sought to exploit them for their own political ends, long after all possibilities of nationalization had vanished. These, then, were the bank officers who were in the vanguard of the bitter struggles of the fifties and sixties, struggles that saw the ABOA emerge as the most militant and powerful Australian banking union.The nationalization issue, by stimulating the formation of the South Australian branch of the ABOA, also aided the union's development. Not only was this the first step along the way to an Australia-wide banking union, but the new branch's leaders, Barratt and Simmons, had much in common with the ABOA leadership and were able to provide valuable support.

Perhaps most importantly, the pressures and conflicts of nationalization allowed some ABOA members to resolve what to date had been the fundamental ambiguity of banking unionism. For nearly thirty years bank officers had grappled with the apparent irreconcilability of unionism and their supposed quasi-management role, perceived status position in society, and loyalty to employers. Now for the first time at least some bank officers, in rejecting the appeals and cajoling of the banks, had shown that their employment was not necessarily incompatible with active union membership. The next step in this evolutionary process was outright opposition to and confrontation with employers. Reasons for and examples of this are explored in the next chapter.

Notes

1. The Labor Party, when in power, was faced with a hostile Senate and had little hope of enacting strong banking legislation anyway. This was shown when Treasurer Theodore outlined relatively mild legislation to transfer the banks' central banking functions to a Reserve Bank, leaving the Commonwealth Bank as a government trading bank. The private banks rallied the conservative forces in the Senate and the legislation was defeated.
2. See, for example, Frank Anstey, *The Kingdom of Shylock* (Melbourne: Fraser and Jenkinson, 1916), and J.T. Lang, *Why I Fight* (Sydney: Labor Daily Ltd, 1934).
3. *Age,* 2 December 1931, p. 9.
4. *Argus,* 2 December 1931, p. 6.
5. Each bank contributed five thousand pounds (Australian manager of ES&A to London, 19 July 1934, letter in ANZ archives).
6. Butlin, *Australia and New Zealand Bank,* p. 406.
7. FCM, 13 June 1933, p. 83.
8. Minutes of annual general meeting of Victorian branch of the BOA, 27 September 1933, copy in ABOA archives.
9. *Age,* 30 October 1933, p. 12.
10. *Australian Banker* 9, no. 1 (Jan. 1934): 3.
11. *Labor Daily,* 22 January 1934, p. 1.
12. FCM, 10 April 1934, p. 133.
13. FCM, 12 June 1934, p. 142.
14. Australian manager ES&A to London, 5 July 1934, letter in ANZ archives.

15. *Australian Banker* 9, no. 4 (Apr. 1934): 6. However, one Queensland officer did parochially note: "A city cannot thrive upon Greek fruit shops and Casket agencies alone" (*Queensland Bank Officer* 15, no. 4 [June 1934] : 8).
16. VCMM, 15 January 1935, p. 335.
17. FCM, 18 December 1934, p. 160. In the privacy of his weekly letter to London, one senior banker spoke of the valuable role of bank officers in the crisis. "I feel sure that the advent of 15/16,000 bank clerks into the political arena who carried with them the sympathetic votes of their relations and close friends, had a very important influence in bringing about the return of the UAP" (Australian manager of ES&A to London, 20 September 1934, letter in ANZ archives).
18. General manager of ES&A to London, 10 January 1935, letter in ANZ archives.
19. Ibid.
20. *Royal Commission on the Monetary and Banking Systems* (Canberra, 1937), p. 262.
21. Minutes of special conference of UBOA of NSW, 25 August 1942, p. 1.
22. See, for example, *Bankers Journal* 3, no. 5 (May 1943): 2.
23. FCM, 26 May 1943, p. 371.
24. See, for example, *Westralian Banker* 18, no. 6 (June 1943): 1.
25. Ballot paper for nationalization ballot, 1943, copy in ABOA archives. The wording of the question undoubtedly influenced the results.
26. UBOA of NSW minutes, 7 December 1943, p. 3.
27. The ever suspicious Laidlaw noted: "They seem to get their information in the carpeted portion of the banking chambers" (K. H. Laidlaw to C. Hodson, 21 November 1944, letter in UBOA of Q files).
28. Paterson to Laidlaw, 30 November 1944, copy in ABOA archives.
29. Special Report on Proposed Government Legislation, 28 November 1944, p. 2, copy in ABOA archives.
30. Paterson to Laidlaw, 1 December 1944, copy in ABOA archives.
31. Ibid., 18 December 1944, copy in ABOA archives.
32. *Herald,* 7 January 1945, p. 13.
33. UBOA of NSW minutes, 28 December 1944. The Rural Bank was, of course, already a government-owned bank, and so immune to nationalization.
34. UBOA of NSW Minutes, 13 February 1945.
35. UBOA of NSW *Annual Report, 1944-45*, 18 April 1945, p. 8.
36. *Bankers Journal* 5, no. 5 (May 1945): 1.
37. Commonwealth Bank Act and Commonwealth Banking Act, 1945 (Nos. 13 and 14 of 1945). *Commonwealth Parliamentary Debates,* 29 August 1945, p. 4963.
38. The banks and their supporters had indicated they were reserving their right of challenge for a more suitable time (see, for example, *CPD,* 15 October 1947, pp. 802-3).
39. *City of Melbourne* v. *Commonwealth (The State Banking Case)* (74 CLR 31).
40. *Queensland Bank Officer* 28, no. 6 (Aug. 1947): 10.
41. *Sydney Morning Herald,* 17 September 1947, p. 7.
42. For example, *Tribune,* 28 August, p. 1.
43. *Sydney Morning Herald,* 6 October 1947, p. 1.
44. UBOA of NSW minutes, 1 October 1947.
45. *Westralian Banker* 22, no. 9 (Sept. 1947): 8.
46. *Sun News-Pictorial,* 11 September 1947, p. 3.
47. *Queensland Banker* 28, no. 7 (July 1948): 3.
48. *Sun News-Pictorial,* 9 September 1947, p. 4.
49. *Sydney Morning Herald,* 12 September 1947, p. 3.
50. This decision had been made some weeks earlier, and Paterson had met Chifley twice to discuss these (see FCM, 19 August 1947, p. 658).
51. Gaunson had replaced the ill E. J. F. Roberts, who had earlier defeated Sneddon for Victorian branch presidency. This victory had been made possible by a

change in union voting procedures which reduced the ability of the BNSW and NBA sub-branches to use proxy votes.

52. Report of general meeting of Victorian branch, 1 October 1947, *Bankers Journal* 6, no. 9 (Oct. 1947): 1.
53. Paterson was also at pains to outline how officers transferring from the private banks (where no long-service leave existed) to the Commonwealth Bank would be entitled to include previous service in the calculation of long-service leave.
54. *Bankers Journal* 6, no. 9 (Oct. 1947): 3–5.
55. Paterson was prepared to stand for Labor Party preselection in the Victorian federal electorate of Higinbotham at the 1949 elections. However, the party would not allow this because he was not a member.
56. Paterson to Barratt, 16 December 1947, copy in ABOA archives.
57. Ibid., 3 September 1947, copy in ABOA archives.
58. Ibid., 14 December 1947, copy in ABOA archives.
59. *Australian Bank Officials Association* v. *Bank of Australasia and Ors* (59 CAR 1254).
60. *The Commonwealth Banking Act, 1947*, No. 47 of 1947, *CPD*, p. 2896. 27 November 1947.
61. Tribune, 1 November 1947, p. 6.
62. Paterson to Card, 1 November 1947, p. 6, copy in ABOA archives.
63. *Sun News Pictorial*, 22 November 1947, p. 4.
64. *Bankers Journal* 7, no. 12 (1948): 8.
65. BOASA minutes, 16 October 1947, p. 176.
66. Ibid.
67. The CBA had refused Paterson leave to address BOASA on the issue (BOASA minutes, 10 December 1947, p. 190), so the meeting was rescheduled for a Sunday. This niggardly attitude reflected the bank's antipathy towards the ABOA and Patterson in particular, no doubt because of his refusal to co-operate with their plans.
68. Though the SBSA was highly unionized, the dispersed nature of many branches made it difficult for sub-branch nominees to defeat those from the private banks at meetings held in Adelaide. However, in postal ballots or in committee (where voting strength was proportional to sub-branch membership), the SBSA fared much better.
69. *Bank of New South Wales* v. *Commonwealth Bank of Australasia* (74 CLR 508).
70. SABOJ 28, no. 1 (Aug. 1948): 1.
71. BOASA minutes, 17 November 1948, p. 248. The voting was 612 to 412.
72. BOASA minutes, 13 April 1949, p. 4.
73. *AIBR* 73, no. 9 (Sept. 1949): 451.
74. A. L. May *The Battle for the Banks* (Sydney: Sydney University Press, 1958), p. 111, notes that immediately before the 1949 election more than four hundred bank officers had been seconded to the anti-nationalization campaign.
75. See, for example, May, *Battle for the Banks*, p. 105; Blainey, *Gold and Paper*, pp. 362-72; Holder, *Bank of New South Wales*, pp. 883-89; and Butlin, *Australia and New Zealand Bank*, pp. 429-31.
76. *Bankers Journal*, 7, no. 12 (Dec. 1948): 8.
77. Ibid., 8, no. 11 (Nov. 1949): 18.
78. UBOA of NSW minutes, 13 January 1949, p. 4, and 8 February 1949, p. 6.
79. *The Banker* 6, no. 12 (Nov. 1947): 11.
80. Membership interests were now sadly neglected. An example of this concerned proposals for the abolition of the five-day week, which for years

had been a goal of bank unions. The UBOA of NSW had joined the "No Saturday Work Campaign" some time earlier but then resigned, "in view of the fact that a number of the organisations represented were affiliated with the Trade and Labour Council, and therefore, committed to actively supporting the Federal Labor Government's Nationalisation of Banking programme" (UBOA of NSW *Annual Report*, 1948-49, p. 12.).

81.   Circular headed "Evans Electorate", copy in UBOA of NSW annual conference minutes, 1949, p. 3.

82.   Osborne, brother of the general manager of the CBC, was nominated at the last moment, apparently with considerable though covert support from the private banks. In spite of Card's eagerness to support their cause, they clearly believed there were political and industrial risks in having an ex-secretary of a banking union in federal parliament.

83.   L. F. Crisp *Ben Chifley* (Melbourne: Longmans, 1961), p. 340.

84.   *Westralian Banker* 25, no. 8, (Aug. 1950): 9.

85.   Ibid., no. 11, (Nov. 1950): 5.

86.   May, *Battle for the Banks*, p. 130. May provides a detailed analysis of the nationalization issue. However, the concentration on events after August 1947, emphasis on the reactions of the banks, and incorrect assumption that all unions and employees supported the anti-nationalization campaign of the banks detract from this analysis. For example, he seeks to explain ABOA opposition by arguing that State Savings Bank employees with nothing to lose from nationalization, had dominated union decision-making. This is incorrect, for these officers did not even belong to the ABOA but to their own union, the SSBOA.

6 The Fifties — a Time of Change

No longer is the term "bank clerk" regarded as an appropbrious epithet — no longer in billiard rooms do we hear the phrase "all side and no screw, like a bank clerk".

[*Australian Banker* 14, no. 9 (Sept. 1939): 11]

The new, more resolute and vigorous ABOA philosophy, which emerged so tentatively in the immediate post-war era and strengthened in the nationalization crisis, developed and extended at a significant pace throughout the fifties.

Post-War Changes

In the immediate post-war period, several banking industry changes and events encouraged the development of a new and decidedly more militant attitude among many bank officers. Work loads had increased because of serious staff shortages and there was a growing awareness that employees in other industries were enjoying superior wages and conditions. Heightening the sense of injustice felt by bank officers was the community's lessened respect and regard for bank employees. The ingredient required for this unrest to manifest itself in stronger union opposition was skilled, committed, and professional leadership. This in turn was made possible by the formation of a new ABOA branch. It is there that the story of the fifties really begins.

In 1948 Paterson had invited BOASA to join the ABOA and so better protect its members following nationalization but had been rejected. SBSA officers, strongly represented in BOASA,[1] favoured the proposal, for his visit had coincided with increasing discontent in the SBSA, a result of the intransigence of the bank's trustees and this "refusal to recognise the Association other than in a Court case".[2] Any thoughts of secession were constrained, however, by a BOASA rule preventing resignations while a case was in progress,[3] and since early 1948 the union had been in dispute with the banks over female salary rates. Finally, in mid-1949, and in the face of BOASA's support for the banks' political opposition to the Labor government and the leadership changes already discussed which this brought, the South Australian branch of the ABOA was formed with Barratt as president and Simmons as secretary. Almost six hundred SBSA officers and two far sighted and courageous private bank officers, R.D.Gell and K.Yates, resigned from BOASA and joined the new branch, amid angry BOASA cries of "body snatching" (which the ABOA later had to disprove before the industrial registrar).[4]   This was a crucial event in the ABOA's history, for it strengthened the union's "interstate" nature and at the same time added to its membership and coverage.   This also brought significant union structural and decision-maiing change.   Federal Conference, the ABOA's policy-making body, had formally been held in Melbourne as a number of short, infrequent meetings with a Victorian acting as the Tasmanian proxy.   Now, with an extra branch, and at the insistence of Barratt and the outspoken Tasmanian president, G.I.A. Hodson, Conference was scheduled for specific times, so that all branches could be directly represented in proportion to their membership.   Though the Victorian branch still supplied some 70 per cent of all delegates, these new arrangements would obviously inhibit what to date had been their almost total control over the ABOA's policy and operations.

In early 1950, at the first of these new-style conferences, the ABOA elected another general secretary, for in late 1948, after several quite undistinguished years and constant vacillation, Lodge had finally resigned.   Paterson had struggled on as ABOA president, secretary, and journal editor in spite of being transferred from a city to a suburban branch by the CBA.   Paterson wanted to be full-time ABOA secretary, and it was only after a considerable time that he was convinced that he should remain president and that a new secretary should be appointed. The position was to be filled at this first full ABOA Conference.   Most delegates favoured T.W.Sheedy, an ex-bank officer and lately ABOA organizer, whose geniality only partially concealed a lack of self-discipline, expertise, and application.   The other candidate was R.D.("Barney") Williams, a private accountant and ex-employee of the State Savings Bank of Victoria.   By a strange quirk of political fate, resulting from family links and his long, faithful, and skilled services to the Labor Party, Williams was a commissioner of the same bank. Conservative Conference members Gaunson, Hore, and the Tasmanian Hodson, although aware of Sheedy's shortcomings, strongly opposed Williams. They feared he would politicize the union and manoeuvre it into areas and actions that would infringe the ABOA's long-maintained apolitical stance.[5]   That the Labor Party might benefit from any such manipulation further stimulated their opposition. William's strongest supporter was H.W.Foster, who himself had only recently become prominent in the ABOA. After joining the NBA in Victoria, he had been transferred to Queensland and then in the mid-forties back to Bendigo. Here he gained recognition by revitalizing the provincial sub-branch, and on his transfer to Melbourne in 1947 he was

soon elected to Federal Council, where his militancy, working class sympathies, and purposeful eloquence were soon evident. At Conference,
Foster lobbied Barratt and Simmons, who having just escaped the stultify-
ing grasp of the SBSA trustees were initially horrified at the thought of a
Savings Bank commissioner becoming ABOA secretary. But Foster won
them over, and their support gave Williams victory by seven votes to six,
a result that in hindsight was probably the single most important event
in the ABOA's history.

During the preliminaries, much had been made of Williams's Labor
Party involvement,[6] and that this had not automatically precluded him
provides some measure of changing ABOA leadership attitudes. There is
also some evidence that this reflected the views of an increasing number
of members and was particularly strong among returned servicemen who
found the restrictions of bank employment galling. Though politically
most officers probably still supported non-Labor parties,[7] there had been
several signs of admiration for more militant stances. Some approval was
given to a successful strike by Irish bank officers, and the sympathetic
public response was remarked upon.[8] On the local scene there was growing
criticism of the ABOA's earlier, largely ineffectual approaches to the
banks. With the rejuvenation of a number of provincial sub-branches came
"complaints that the Association was not sufficiently active in the presentation of new claims".[9] For the first time the accepted practice of union
members resigning upon appointment to senior bank executive positions
was challenged. It was argued that these resignations were a result not of
possible conflict of interest but because "resignations from the Association
are published in the *Journal* and are so known by the powers that be".[10]

There was, however, a more immediate cause of unrest, one that
concentrated and intensified bank officer dissatisfaction. This was the
issue of salaries, where steadily increasing prices were eroding purchasing
power, particularly of those not receiving annual increments.This decline
was highlighted by the relative improvement in the salaries and conditions
enjoyed ,by Commonwealth Bank employees. With Labor government
approval, the Commonwealth Bank's salary scale had been extended to
the twenty-seventh year of service. In the face of Chifley's threat to bring
it under the control of the Commonwealth Public Service, the bank had
also 'introduced a classification scheme covering all employees. Private
bank employees were further unsettled when this innovation was also
applied to employees of the Victorian State Savings Bank. They had
always believed themselves superior to savings bank officers, whom they
felt needed less skill and experience to carry out their largely routine tasks.
That savings bank employees now enjoyed significant salary advantages
made a mockery of trading bank officers' supposedly elitist position.

In spite of these rumblings, the private banks had initially resisted
union salary claims, arguing that National Security Regulations still prohibited wage increases. However, following an interstate conference of

bank unions, where agreement was reached to mount a united campaign, the banks agreed to seek authority to increase bank officer salaries to a point where the marginal component was 25 per cent. The top of the scale thus became £485, an increase of £18.

This did little to pacify private bank employees, and increasingly there were calls to members to "wake up to the fact that they [were] purely and simply workers . . . amongst the poorest paid workers", and to "stop being 'the mugs' in the community" with regard to "salaries, hours of work or anything else".[11] Increasingly came membership demands for ACTU affiliation as the wages and conditions of blue-collar workers continued their relative improvement. The traditional meekness of bank officers came under increasing scrutiny, for as one writer pointed out: "As long as we are 'moderate' we can expect to have secret reports, no houses, a stationary standard of living in an advancing economy, long working hours, etc. Our hope of obtaining long service leave or even the minor item which everyone except shops and banks have – 'Saturday Closing' lies in militancy. . . . moderation is for mice, militancy is for men."[12] Such were the fresh winds of change that one senior officer bemusedly asked: "I wonder what has happened to the members and the executive since the War. It would appear they have been eating red meat, for I have never seen such a virile and determined Association in my long membership."[13]

Yet the banks were still regarded with awesome deference by many officers and with fear by others. Paterson explained why most *Journal* letters critical of the banks were unsigned. After suggesting that some officers sought to curry favour by signing letters sympathetic to the banks, he explained, "On the other hand a bank officer expressing views, equally honestly held, but which may be in conflict with those of his employer, is scarcely to be condemned for his discretion in using a non-de-plume."[14]

A further factor encouraging a more critical approach by bank officers to their employers and jobs was the worsening staff situation. To the paucity of suitable recruits, a result of the low birth rates of the thirties, was added the high wastage rate of returned servicemen. Some of this latter group just did not return to the industry; others, on taking up their careers again, found themselves employed on jobs that provided neither satisfaction nor sufficient recompense.[15] To this was added the unrest of others at the uncertain hours, Saturday morning work, frequent dislocating and expensive transfers, poor housing, and broken and inadequate annual leave. Many of these opted for new careers in the expanding Australian economy, casting aside the supposed status, security, and pensions that had earlier inhibited labour mobility. This resignation rate, coupled with industry growth and the opening of a large number of urban branches,[16] had brought serious staff deficiencies and provided banking unions with considerable potential bargaining power. Paterson, ever aware of the continuing importance of the manager-member relationship discussed earlier, noted how this bargaining power could be developed: "Every junior of today is certain of at least branch managership irrespective of his qualifications for the position. The banks will not be in a position to pick and choose as before. The scramble for juniors today means the scramble for managers in the future. What we must do is ensure we recruit all of these juniors, for this will guarantee more members in the future."[17] To facilitate this, Cec. Rial, a retired bank clerk, was appointed assistant secretary with primary responsibility for recruiting, and Tom Sheedy became a full-time organizer. However, other banking unions were still myopically absorbed with opposition to the Labor Party, and only the ABOA would prove capable of exploiting this advantage.

Another subtle change was occurring in the industry, one that worked to the ABOA's advantage by breaking down some of the reserve and conservatism of bank employees. Increasing competition between banks and from other new financial institutions, the heightened emphasis on individual branch profitability, and most particularly the continually growing competitiveness of the Commonwealth Bank had added new pressures. The mass of new banking regulations brought further complexities. A recently retired branch manager lamented:

> Banking was once a clean cut affair, there was no work at high pressure with an inadequate staff, no pressure from above to build up business . . . no brickbats if he lost an account, and no losing a night's sleep worrying what your divisional inspector would say, how caustic, sarcastic or intimidatory he would be. . . . Now the race goes to the salesman, the showman, the man who attracts or acquires by devious means a mass of new business . . . who now also wallows in a bog of highly technical and changing resolutions evolved by government experts and his superiors.[18]

The public too had seen how banking had changed, and to the despair of those bank officers who craved the status and prestige formerly derived from banking employment, had withdrawn much of the esteem formerly accorded bank employees. One astute officer summed this up: "The manager has lost his former eminence in the business world. Now a financial inferior, he is scorned, criticised and pushed in the ruck. . . . The public have not been slow to realise the fall in the manager's standing, and have been quick to appreciate how vulnerable he is to the threat of loss of business, of promise of new accounts."[19] Other disillusioned officers came to doubt the whole rationale of their changing employment, and one remorsefully commented: "I have given service on behalf of the Bank only where there was a profit to be made."[20] These changes, by stimulating further questioning of the banks' and their employees' roles in society, served to crystallize the unions' legitimacy and purpose for more bank officers. Membership figures show a dramatic increase, and it seems likely that these changes, plus the ABOA's firm stance on nationalization, had contributed to this. Victorian branch union density rose from 67 per cent

in 1939 to 83 per cent in 1950 (see app. 3). This now compared favourably with 82 per cent in Western Australia, 87 per cent in New South
Wales, and 86 per cent in South Australia.[21]

The ABOA's post-war adjustment, a new branch, fresh, aggressive, and
professional leadership, and improved organization and administration all
reflected the changing mood of bank officers. This was to make for a
fascinating and turbulent decade of union development and actions.

New Campaigns and Tactics

The ABOA fought three salary campaigns during the fifties. They were
more vigorous than those of earlier years and contained several new
features. They also provided further proof that the character of union
leadership and membership was changing. The union's rationale and
approach to the employers changed significantly, Barney Williams recalled
in July 1978: "We aimed to follow a pattern which in itself did the best
to extract as much from the Court, and then scream dissatisfaction and
involve the rank and file in a salaries campaign and win new salary
standards by consent." The strike, the ultimate measure of rank-and-file
involvement, did not occur until the end of the sixties, but this earlier
period was an important incubating period. These campaigns provided
union leadership with valuable tactical experience in the harnessing and
exploitation of bank officers' discontent with their employment
conditions, as well as demonstrating to members the benefits of more
belligerent and committed leadership.

In early 1949 the New South Wales court begain the first investigation
into banking industry salaries since the infamous "Ogilvie Case" more than
ten years earlier. The UBOA of NSW's case hinged on an earlier bank offer
of a 10 per cent salary increase and extension of the scale and a request
that bank staff be compensated for the abolition of the family allowance
in 1937. Justice A. J. De Baun, formerly the union's counsel, refused to
consider this latter claim and further dented union optimism by stating
that he would set an amount for the top of the scale, regardless of its
length. Worried by the internal union wrangles and anomalies that a
twenty-five-year scale under these terms would bring, the UBOA of NSW
hastily opted to retain the eighteen-year scale. Then when De Baun made
it clear that the terms of the UBOA of NSW's poor 1947 consent award
would be of considerable relevance to his decision,[22] it was apparent that
Card's obsequious support for the banks during nationalization had not
been in the union's long-term interests.

The scale handed down in September 1949[23] did nothing more than
add the 10 per cent bonus earlier offered. With inflation beginning to

escalate, the unions' ready acceptance of the suggestion that the award should run for three years only further heightened rank and file dissatisfaction within the UBOA of NSW and other unions awaiting the results. The ABOA, poised for an Arbitration Court appearance, was particularly vexed, and Paterson told members: "It must be expected that the judgement given will have an effect upon the thoughts of industrial authorities in the Federal Court."[24] More than ever he was convinced that the ABOA should use quite different tactics.

The banks immediately offered the New South Wales terms to other unions, and in their normal fashion, union leaders in Queensland, South Australia, and Western Australia gratefully accepted. But in Victoria a series of meetings angrily rejected the banks' offer. At the Victorian branch's 1949 annual meeting, Federal Council was instructed: "No agreement should be reached with the banks which does not include the five day week, long service leave, no exceptions to overtime, and a scale of salaries not lower than that of the Commonwealth Bank."[25] So closely did this log parallel salaries and conditions in the Commonwealth Bank that the Labor MHR Clyde Cameron suggested, rather tongue in cheek, that the government should, in the interests of equity and fair competition between the banks, "intervene in this case in support of the employees of the banks and in opposition to the wealthy interests that own and control them".[26]

This rank-and-file determination arose not just from the ABOA's new sentiments but also from changed salary relativities, this time in the insurance industry. Here the AISF, with only minimal effort, had been able to conclude a new agreement which introduced a twenty-year scale, and in paying £590 in the eighteenth year eliminated the historical salary advantage previously enjoyed by bank employees.[27] The ABOA's immediate reaction was to serve new claims based on Commonwealth Bank salaries and conditions.

The hearing of these claims began in May 1950 before Conciliation Commissioner Murray-Stewart. The ABOA, anxious to deny the banks the use of professional advocates, entrusted the case to Paterson, who had taken three months leave from the CBA, and the new secretary, Williams. From the outset it was clear that the banks would resist strongly, and SBSA actions reflect this. Unhappy at the thought of the decidedly more militant ABOA rather than BOASA representing their employees, they shocked the union by asking the commissioner to exempt the bank from any award made. They argued that he lacked jurisdiction over a state instrumentality and that the issue could be more appropriately dealt with by a state court. The commissioner deferred his decision on this, an early indication of his later procrastination, uncertainty, and confusion. The SBSA's action followed an earlier visit to Victoria by BOASA's president and secretary to complain at the ABOA's proposed coverage of all South Australian officers. Paterson and Williams, protesting their innocence, agreed to alter the claim so as to exclude South Australian trading bank officers. In the light of later events, this was clearly a first attempt to bring about the absorption of BOASA. When the BOASA president, underrating the ABOA's new secretary, suggested that he confine award coverage to Victoria and Tasmania, he was told "in quite blasphemous terms, that after such an infamous proposal the ABOA would take steps which could only end in the annihilation of BOASA".[28]

In his opening address, Paterson stressed that he represented a union with frustrated and angry members in three states. With the superior Commonwealth Bank salaries and conditions in mind, Paterson was anxious to prove that the work performed by trading bank officers was the equal of that done by Commonwealth Bank officers. He even drew upon editorials of the ABOA's long-term media combatant, the *Argus*, which had argued for parity because "it would clearly be wrong if the competition of the private banks [with the Commonwealth Bank], were subsidised in any way at the expense of employees salaries".[29] In a well-prepared case, Paterson then used numerous witnesses to support the major claims: scale extension and increases, an improved and expanded classification system, the abolition of Saturday morning work, and the introduction of long-service leave.

Just as he completed this, Commissioner Murray-Stewart, whose grasp and understanding of much of the evidence had been noticeably impaired, was forced to adjourn the case. There was further delay after the Arbitration Court president urged commissioners to defer any decisions that might constrain the Full Bench's basic-wage deliberations. Consequently it was not until August 1950 that the case recommenced against a backdrop of growing staff antagonism to what they mistakenly saw as employer-inspired delays. In their evidence, the banks partially countered the ABOA's claim for classification by agreeing to apply the recently negotiated New South Wales manager rates, based upon branch size rather than years of service. Long-service leave claims were rebutted on cost grounds, and in what was to be a well-trodden path, Saturday morning closing was seen as inconveniencing traders and customers. The banks strenuously resisted scale extension, arguing that this would only exacerbate problems of officers "sitting back and resting on the scale".[30] Towards the end of the lengthy hearing, the commissioner announced that SBSA employees could be covered by federal awards. Though doubting that the commissioner's decision grounds were valid, Paterson and Williams were delighted. They had worried that an adverse decision, by leaving SBSA members at the mercy of the bank and BOASA's incompetence and lack of interest, would result in the withering away of the South Australian branch.

With Commissioner Murray-Stewart again incapable of comprehending the evidence, a further five-month delay ensued. Finally, in February 1951, he called the parties together, but instead of an award he placed before them a number of draft suggestions, which were "so garbled that even matters on which the parties had reached consent before him were still treated as in dispute, and showing that scant consideration had been given to evidence".[31] In this "reading to the minutes", the ABOA had fared badly. There was no scale extension or improvement in overtime allowances, though the accountant's position had been added to the classification system. The abolition of Saturday morning work was seen as beyond the court's jurisdiction, and although the commissioner believed he had the power to award long-service leave, he did not "intend to impose this obligation on the banks".[32] The top of the scale was increased to £778, still some £37 less than the eighteenth year in the Commonwealth Bank, where the scale ran to £895 at the twenty-seventh year. The commissioner's suggestions, which he refused to amend despite Williams's strong argument, ignored the changed work-value considerations that had been put forward. The banks were pleased with the result: "The outcome of the case may be regarded as very satisfactory and . . . is not likely to involve any important or costly changes."[33]

The ABOA rank and file were angry now and needed little urging from Williams. More than twelve hundred metropolitan members flocked to a mass meeting. The meeting's mood can be judged from the "thunderous applause which greeted a country member's suggestion that the executive should have called a 'stop work' for two or three days to give all members a chance to attend".[34] A motion from the floor calling for strike action was soundly defeated, but Commissioner Murray-Stewart was censured and Federal Council was instructed to "immediately confer with the Prime Minister to request that the case be transferred to another Commissioner". The meeting also directed Federal Council to approach the banks again to seek salary parity with the Commonwealth Bank. Later that evening Williams broadcast the meeting's results to country officers, and the following day again spoke during peak listening time to remind the public that bank officers were "in a militant mood, seeking simple justice and determined to obtain it".[35] More letters, public addresses, and meetings followed, and later in the month the banks agreed to further negotiations. A measure of their recognition of the ABOA's new determination was the decision to have general managers, rather than staff inspectors, meet ABOA representatives.

The Commonwealth Bank's continuing willingness to pay better salaries was now a considerable problem for the private banks, for not only was their employees' discontent increased but recruiting was made difficult. Although the Commonwealth Bank's higher salaries resulted partially from the political factors mentioned earlier, they were also a result of increasing profitability, coupled with the relative ease with which the Bank's governor, unencumbered by any board or co-director, could be convinced to permit salary increases. The private banks approached the Commonwealth Bank, and it was settled that they would pay equivalent rates and that the Commonwealth Bank would "not further increase the scale and refrain from general bonuses".[36] The banks then agreed to pay Commonwealth Bank rates to the eighteenth year, but told the ABOA that this would be at the expense of future bonuses. The Sydney banks, however, convinced the others to oppose these new rates being written into the award.[37] The ABOA protested that "in the event of an economic change the banks would be able to revert to the Court figures",[38] but Commissioner Murray-Stewart refused to write in the higher rates. Officers on the scale were reasonably satisfied with the new rates, but senior officers were disappointed at the scale's brevity and the still limited classification system.

Though far from satisfactory, this sojourn in the court was important to future campaigns. Any lingering thoughts that the banks would repay officers for services rendered during the nationalization campaign had been dispelled, a little more of the earlier timidity and hesitancy had disappeared, and older members' faith in the Arbitration Court's power and willingness to safeguard their interests had diminished. Most importantly, Williams and Foster now knew that the salary issue was one that would unite the membership and from which previously unknown levels of commitment and militancy could be extracted. As a writer to the *Bankers Journal* noted: "In future, our policy should be a series of general meetings backed up by a publicity campaign which the banks particularly dislike, as this is a cheaper and more effective method of gaining our objectives than futile and protracted pleadings before the Arbitration Court."[39] In summarizing the campaign, Williams urged all members to remember that "betterment of working conditions and salaries [would] only be obtained by resolute and persistent action through unity".[40] Referring again to the seven-week Irish bank officers strike and emphasizing "the strike should be at the end of the industrial road", he was yet fulsome in his praise for the firmness, courage, and steadfast purpose they had exhibited.

The Murray-Stewart case also hastened Paterson's resignation from the presidency. He was in poor health, a result of the rigours of running the union almost singlehanded since the war, and Williams's heartening court performance and positive action since then had reassured Paterson that the ABOA's future lay in good hands. He also knew that the nature and style of the industry's industrial relations was changing. A more volatile and outspoken membership and the sterner resistance of employers facing escalating labour costs and previously unheard of intrusions into their managerial preserves required industrial tactics that Paterson had neither familiarity nor affinity with. Though still prepared to defend implacably the new ABOA philosophy and actions, he had of late preferred to work behind the scenes, assessing attitudes, persuading, cajoling, and conveying offer and counter-offer. Even the Murray-Stewart case had been forced upon him, and its events and results merely confirmed his distaste for the centre stage of arbitration. Reinforcing his decision was realization that involvement of the rank and file, perhaps even to the point of direct industrial conflict, was now a necessary and vital adjunct to court appearances. Unlike himself, both Foster and Williams were remarkably at ease both in the boisterous atmosphere of mass meetings and in confrontations with the banks.

Early in 1953 Paterson retired and Foster became president, cementing an already close alliance with Williams.   They had similar industrial attitudes and possessed complementary characteristics and strengths. Foster's ideological radicalism and intellectual skill was tempered by Williams's pragmatism, political astuteness, and contacts. In turn, Williams's courage, organizational skills, and diligence were supported by Foster's reasonableness and creative, fertile mind. Both were fine public speakers and debaters, in the hurly-burly of mass meetings, the formality of the Arbitration Court, or the as-yet still restrained atmosphere of Federal Council. There was now no challenge to Williams's position. He had overcome his biggest hurdle, the animosity of politically reactionary bank officers towards his active involvement in Labor Party politics. That this had happened in the context of the anti-Communist hysteria of the early fifties says much for his success and the respect in which he was now held.

Williams had encouraged several organizational changes. Federal Council membership was enlarged to eight members, and as Victorian branch secretary he streamlined its operations, leaving the day-to-day matters in the hands of Cec. Rial, assistant state secretary and treasurer. The gregarious branch president, Hore, much more at home at a smoke social than before the Court, need little prompting to extend his development of the provincial sub-branches.   These meetings were well attended, both because of the guaranteed conviviality and for the chance to hear the latest union news.   The provincial sub-branches became a feature of the ABOA's organization, contributing to the increased union density and member involvement. Williams also worked hard at reducing the internal union conflict of earlier years and in this was helped by the advent of a rudimentary classification system, which stilled some senior officer discontent. So though beset by the logistical problems of organizing a union still with most its members working in small dispersed locations, [41] Williams had significantly strengthened the ABOA's "sinews of war".

In the years immediately following the Second World War, most Australian white-collar unions continued along in their generally timid and conservative fashion, with individual unions giving scant heed to the possibilities or need for joint action or even co-operation with other white-collar unions. However, the shock of an employer application to the Arbitration Court for Basic Wage reductions, a lengthening of the forty-hour week, and abolition of cost-of-living adjustments convinced Foster and Williams to initiate a series of meetings of representatives for several white-collar unions to consider preparation of a joint defence. Unions representing salaried employees in the banking, insurance, state Public Service, local government, state instrumentalities, the police force, and some technical and professional occupations began to meet on a regular basis from September 1952. Williams, already an enthusiastic advocate of white-collar union co-ordination, amalgamation, and closer co-operation with the ACTU, ensured that the ABOA was one of the first unions to join this loose grouping, known as the Kindred Organizations. However, divergent philosophies and varying levels of militancy, leading to significant differences of opinion regarding tactics and possible co-operation with the ACTU, prevented the development of any firm policy or initiatives.[42]

Early in 1954, in the face of apparent court indifference to the inflation-induced unrest of white-collar unionists, the remnants of the Kindred Organisations became the basis for another body, the Council of White Collar Associations (CWCA). E.J.Gillespie from the AISF was president, Williams became secretary, and J.F. Foley, vice-president of the Victorian branch of the ABOA, treasurer. Though early meetings emphasized the purely advisory capacity of the CWCA, Williams and Foster saw it as the focal point in the battle for improved salaries and conditions. Conscious of the support provided to blue-collar unions by the ACTU, they were now mulling over plans to establish a peak organization to co-ordinate and strengthen white-collar unions. An obvious problem was that the leaders and some members of the ABOA were considerably more aggressive and militant than those of other white-collar unions, and to encourage these unions to adopt similar philosophies and tactics at this stage would have invited resistance and antagonism.

However, chances of increasing co-operation between white-collar unions was given impetus by the events of the 1954 "margins case", conducted by metal trades unions with the support of the ACTU. This had resulted from further employee discontent over declining salary margins — that salary component over and above the Basic Wage which compensated the worker for skill, experience, necessary qualifications, or unpleasantness. This unrest was widespread, being shared by all those blue- and white-collar unions representing skilled workers. In brief, margin reductions were a result of regular Basic Wage increases as the Arbitration Court sought to compensate wage-earners for rapid price increases resulting from the dismantling of wartime controls.[43] These Basic Wage increases were of proportionately greater benefit to lower income earners (generally unskilled labour), because the Basic Wage was a larger proportion of their total wage. Supplementing this was the inability and at times unwillingness of the court to maintain the real value of margins. On one hand were constitutional limitations on their freedom to do this; on the other, fear that a significant increase in the money value of margins would merely add to inflationary pressures.

Foster and Williams seized on the margins controversy to instigate another salary campaign. They drew up several tables and diagrams which together with numerous articles dramatized the story of bank officer margins erosion. Through 1954 the *Bankers Journal* contained many letters bewailing the shrinking of margins and suggesting various remedies. These ranged from "warning off" prospective recruits because of poor industry conditions and salaries to the need for ACTU affiliation and even work stoppages and full-scale strikes. The campaign was given impetus following Commissioner G. A. Mooney's statement in bringing down an award for trustee officers. He claimed banking industry salaries were too high, owing to the banks' earlier willingness to pay rates equivalent to those of the Commonwealth Bank because "those banks were in mortal fear of nationalization", and that it would be "quite wrong for any arbitrator to place any weight . . . on any such agreement".[44] Williams used the rank and file's discontent over this to convince the executive to issue an extensive set of claims on the banks.

The court's hearing of these claims, which included margins restoration, scale extension, improved classification, and the five-day week, was delayed by the metal trades margins case. Earlier, Commissioner J. M. Galvin had refused to award the metal unions marginal increases, but continuing industrial unrest, exacerbated by the court's abolition of cost-of-living adjustments, led to the reopening of the case. Significant demonstrations of the metal union's industrial muscle convinced the commissioner to hand down a judgment that increased the metal fitters' margin by two and half times its 1937 level, that being the date of the last full inquiry into the industry's wage levels. The commissioner concluded by saying: "This might be used to afford general guidance to all authorities acting under the Conciliation and Arbitration Act . . . or other salary fixing tribunals . . . where the wage or salary may properly be regarded as containing a margin".[45] He further boosted the optimism of white-collar union leaders and members by adding:

> We desire to emphasise that the manner in which we dealt with these references and the observations which we have made as to our reasons should not be read as determining claims which may be made for increases in salary or wage rates for many highly paid employees . . . such employees may, we think, generally speaking have benefitted less by the improvements which have been awarded since the last war and may have suffered far more by the loss in real value of their margins which the fall of the value of money has brought about.

The ABOA then used this decision to seek restoration of margins based on the 1949 De Baun judgment, which, if successful, would have required an increase of £135 at the top of the scale. But their hopes were rudely shattered by Chief Justice Sir Raymond Kelly's statement to another white-collar union claiming margins increases: "I hope the view that the question of fixation of salaries for career and professional occupations . . . is of such importance that the Court should be afforded the opportunity of propounding the principles of assessment to be followed".[46]

The ABOA, shocked at the court's reversal and exasperated by the state unions' refusal to join the margins compaign, prepared and issued a pamphlet to all Australian bank officers. This outlined action to date, the involvement of the CWCA and the ACTU, as well as the ABOA's proposal to escalate the campaign. The results of the case, it said, "will decide your standard of living, your family's happiness and your status in the community".[47] The pamphlet concluded with an appeal to officers in other states to "get your Association to support the ABOA in every way . . . to give support both moral and financial". Most state unions reacted angrily, viewing this as a blatant ABOA attempt to spread its influence.[48] A letter given prominence in state union journals and directed at Williams told him, "the wording of your circular leaves one with the impression that your organisation would like to join forces with the wharfies".[49] BOASA, its old wounds still far from healed, advised its members to "totally ignore the propaganda sent out by the ABOA . . . for it was done in an underhand manner".[50] This was too much for Williams, and under a banner headline "South Australia BOA Leaders Show Their True Colours" he reviled them for their apathy and their willingness to "live like a leech on the efforts of other Associations and unions".[51] Only in Western Australian was any support forthcoming. Here J.J. Williams, a younger, less conservative committman and future president, recommended that members should make a donation to the ABOA's campaign.[52]

With their case still delayed, the ABOA, supported by the CWCA, asked for an interim award. Commissioner A.S. Blackburn, conscious of the test-case nature of this application, referred the whole matter to a Full Bench. There were two important questions to be decided: (1) Did bank salaries include a margin?[53] and (2) Were the metal trades decision principles applicable to white-collar workers, and if so, what was the nature of this nexus? Further delays followed after the Full Bench decided to initiate a full work-value inquiry, and Williams and Foster could contain themselves no longer. Declaring that "it had cost the ABOA and the CWCA affiliates nearly £2,000 in legal fees — to get no result at all",[54] they demanded an interview with the attorney-general, Senator J.A. Spicer. While this interview was ostensibly concerned with the court's delays, ambivalence, and procrastination, Williams and Foster were able to impress on the attorney-general the extent of dissatisfaction of white-collar workers and unions.

In Victoria, continuing rank-and-file agitation finally elicited a further offer from the banks, but even the promise of retrospectivity failed to convince union members that the rates offered, with £1,150 at the top of scale, should be accepted. The issue was resolved when the New South Wales court, influenced by unrest generated in the federal sphere, brought down an award which, in setting the top of the scale at £1,180, effectively brought the award rates up to the "adopted rates" already being paid. Williams accepted the same terms on behalf of the ABOA, for he was conscious of the congestion in the Arbitration Court and feared that any margins judgment would be based on the inferior 1938 rates. In proceedings before Commissioner Webb to ratify this consent award, [55] the UBOA of NSW objected to the ABOA's application to cover bank officers in the Australian Capital Territory. The ABOA, which also sought to cover bank officers in the Northern Territory, refused to amend its claim and threatened to take the whole issue back to the rank and file. The commissioner then readily agreed to ratify it. Though in terms of increased membership this victory was of little importance, further extension of the federal award was subsequently to prove significant.

The ABOA's two salary campaigns of the early fifties had resulted in demonstrations of bank officer militancy never before seen. In the immediate post-war period, Paterson had been forced to stimulate and nurture any fleeting signs of dissension in order to demonstrate to the banks that union members were concerned about particular issues. This leadership initiative was no longer as necessary, for the ABOA rank and file, spurred on by what they believed were salary injustices, had now given signs that they were more prepared to protect their own interests. Increasingly, the task of Foster and Williams was to mobilize and channel this unrest in ways that would maximize the ABOA's bargaining power. Their establishment of a peak organization of white-collar unions showed an awareness of the changing nature of industrial relations in these areas and the need for co-operation and co-ordination.

A Taste of Victory

The final ABOA salary campaign of the decade took place against a backdrop of continuing Arbitration Commission wage restraint.[56] The commission was still disinclined to compensate workers for inflation-induced real wage declines, choosing instead to base wage increases on the economy's capacity to pay. In an era of balance-of-payments crises, the commission's obsession with keeping down the cost of exports and import replacements meant that few wage increases were generated within the commission. It was only the willingness of ABOA rank and file to join in a strenuous salary campaign outside the commission which made significant salary increases possible.

Through the late fifties there were a number of issues that further
increased bank employees' restiveness and left them eager to support more
aggressive leadership tactics. As well, there was an increased urgency and
frequency about their demands, in contrast with the almost apologetic
tone of pre-war claims. Events of early 1957 provide an example of this
new insistence, after the union requested Commissioner J.H.Portus to
vary the award to increase salaries for officers engaged in savings bank
work and to introduce penalty rates for Saturday morning work. The
Victorian branch held several general meetings while these claims were
being considered but failed to sway either the banks or the commissioner.
The rank and file were disgruntled and the ABOA office was flooded with
letters demanding further action. Williams responded to this by using
salary rates in the Melbourne and Metropolitan Board of Works and the
Victorian Public Service to show the extent of recent salary relativity loss
endured by bank officers. He also revived the argument that bank
employees needed salary increases to retain their supposed relatively high
community standing, adding, "In these days of high competition it has
been freely admitted that all banks expect all officers to play their part in
retaining and acquiring business".[57]   After the banks rejected this, the
union responded with a claim that trading bank salaries should retain
parity with those in the Commonwealth Bank, where scale rates had
recently been increased again. This equality, maintained since 1951 was,
the union claimed "one which the then Chairman of the Associated Banks
and the then Chief Manager of the National Bank assured us would
continue".[58] Again the banks refused, and their employees had one more
grievance to add to an already long list, one that Williams and Foster
continually reminded them of. As a writer to the *Bankers Journal*, when
urging the necessity for stronger action, commented:

> The bank employee of today presents a degrading spectacle. He has be-
> come nothing more than a fugitive from economic extinction. His
> entire life is governed by the need to try and make ends meet. Many of
> his necessities must be done without, and if not that, then by some
> devious means he must discover where and how he can get these at a
> "cut price". He is constantly devising ways and means of finding where
> even his food can be purchased as cheaply as possible. He has been
> forced to become a hunter and a discoverer of bargains. If married, his
> wife in many cases has been forced into this miserable scheme, and in a
> number of instances to seek employment to try and assist family finan-
> ces. Truly a sorry spectacle! This glamourised bookkeeper – this
> Cratchit of the clerical world – this plaintive impoverished parvenue
> who haunts the purlieus of pauperism.[59]

The frequency of similar if somewhat less passionately expressed
reminders to bank officers of their straitened circumstances, together with
signs of growing support from senior officers,[60] gave impetus to final

preparations for what was to be the ABOA's most vigorous and intensive salaries campaign to date.

This campaign had really begun following the formation, in October 1956, of the Australia Council of Salaried and Professional Associations (ACSPA) out of the CWCA and the Salaried Employees Consultative Council of New South Wales. This latter organisation, formed in 1931 as the Public Service Defence Council, to defend public servants against the effects of the Premiers' Plan, had suffered from the same problems as had the CWCA, being limited both by the single-state origins of its constituents and by their significant differences in militancy and aggression levels. Over a period of a few months, Victorian and New South Wales members of these two organizations formed ACSPA state divisions, as did enthused white-collar unionists in other states. Each division had seven executive members, so that the ACSPA federal committee contained forty-two members. This committee then elected the federal executive consisting of the federal president, one vice-president from each state division and a secretary, assistant secretary, and treasurer.

ACSPA's founding president was P. D. Allsop, federal president of the Association of Architects, Engineers, Surveyors and Draughtsmen of Australia (AAESDA). Williams in his usual thorough fashion had earlier canvassed the field for a suitable president and had decided that Allsop should lead the new organization.

ACSPA's federal secretary was, of course, the indefatigable Williams, and he proved more than willing to commit his union's resources to the new organization. His services (and he was to spend more than half his time on ACSPA affairs), were made available on an honorary basis; space was provided in the ABOA's Hardware Street premises, and later, when finances were strained because of the refusal of some unions to pay all or some of their affiliation fees, Williams was able to convince the ABOA to make additional contributions. An assistant federal secretary and research officer, A. McD. Richardson, formerly secretary of the Federation of Scientific and Technical Workers' Association, was appointed. Though not good at delegating authority in the ABOA, Williams was content to leave at least some of the day-to-day operations of ACSPA to Richardson, while concentrating upon developing plans and strategy for the eventual creation of one peak organization covering all Australian blue- and white-collar unionists by having white-collar unions join the ACTU. Even at this early stage Williams saw ACSPA not as an end in itself but rather as merely a necessary step along the path to this ultimate goal.

While the ACSPA constitution placed significant emphasis upon co-operation at the industrial level, the involvement of J. S. Baker, secretary of the Australian Third Division Telegraphists' and Postal Clerks' Union, as publicity officer ensured that ACSPA was also constantly supplied with innovative and novel ideas in a number of non-industrial as well as industrial areas. Baker also ensured high levels of publicity for the new types of union activities carried out by ACSPA. In part at least, this move into non-industrial areas resulted from Baker's and Williams's belief that ACSPA's survival required a strategy quite separate from that of the ACTU. This grew from a recognition that ACSPA's industrial actions would be considerably more constrained by rank-and-file conservatism than was the ACTU. However, it also reflected a realization that some apparently non-wage issues could be used to stimulate enthusiasm for industrial initiatives once ACSPA gained credibility. Baker was quick to realize that in this regard ACSPA could tap certain illustrative and publicity skills held by its members, and that these might evoke quite positive reactions from white-collar workers.

Just as Foster was Williams's ideal foil in the ABOA, so Baker's vision and ideas, and Allsop's steadiness and pragmatism, were to supplement Williams' energy and commitment within ACSPA. Baker's other significant contribution to ACSPA was to publicize and refine a method for the historical measurement of salaries and wages developed by Richardson. This became known as the "ACSPA formula", and affiliates were encouraged to use it as the basis of future wage claims.

In May 1957 ACSPA had held a "margins conference" attended by representatives of more than sixty white-collar unions, and here the "ACSPA formula" was developed. Wage claims of affiliates were to be based upon three criteria: the restoration of purchasing power, an equitable share of national productivity increase, and compensation for increased taxation. These claims were to be pursued before the Arbitration Commission and backed up with external campaigns similar to those already carried out by the ABOA. Conference also decided to use the ABOA claims as the spearhead of the campaign and authorized expenditure up to ten thousand pounds for this purpose.[61]

In January 1958 the ABOA served its claim. As well as containing scale increases in line with the ACSPA formula, it asked for a lengthening of the scale and a broader classification system. After some delay this test case was listed for hearing before a Full Bench in August 1958. Meanwhile the ABOA–ACSPA campaign was gaining momentum. Pamphlets were issued, the media flooded with material, mass meetings held, and petitions to both state and federal parliamentarians collected from employees and even some customers. The ABOA funded the secondment of Simmons to ACSPA, where his economic and organizational experience was valuable. The increase of ACSPA affiliation fees facilitated further expansion, including the appointment of an assistant secretary to take some of the burden from the overworked Williams.

In contrast with the ABOA's key role in ACSPA were the continued refusal of all state bank unions except BOAWA to join ACSPA and the UBOA of NSW's decision to go ahead with a separate salary claim not based on the ACSPA formula, which severely embarrased the ABOA and ACSPA. Late in 1958 the UBOA of NSW, after ignoring the appeals of the ABOA and ACSPA, had served a claim for scale increases. An indication that the New South Wales union's leadership had not adjusted to the changing industrial climate was given by Card's editorial comment following the breakdown of negotiations: "It is regrettable that our 'old world' taste for quietly adjusting our affairs with the banks should have received a snub".[62]   The New South Wales court eventually brought down a new scale, which even Card and McKell admitted was "most disappointing".[63]   This result, with an increase of only eighteen pounds at the top of the scale, was largely a product of Card's failure to produce witnesses capable of providing evidence of a material change in the nature of bank officers' work since the last arbitrated case. This decision, a further sign that the ABOA award was rapidly becoming the pace-setter for Australian banking salaries and conditions, was to be a crucial factor in the events of the early sixties when the ABOA accelerated its amalgamation attempts.

In the short run, however, the refusal of the UBOA of NSW to adopt the ACSPA   formula, which would have at least allowed the New South Wales court to look more closely at the question of declining margins and purchasing power, reduced the credibility and impact of the ACSPA campaign. Coming on top of extensive delays in the Arbitration Commission, where seventeen "white-collar" cases were listed for hearing, it forced the ABOA to apply for an interim salary increase. Williams's worst fears were realized when the banks responded with an offer identical to the New South Wales decision. The union executive rejected this out of hand, with Williams warning the banks that some of their employees were talking about strike action. In reporting the banks' offer, he reminded his members of the recent air pilots' strike and their startling salary gains.[64]

In April 1959 the campaign's next stage was launched, with "April Means Action" as its motto. More than thirty meetings throughout the state attracted almost five thousand members. To publicize the Melbourne meeting, Williams arranged for derelicts carrying sandwich boards to patrol the city's main streets for two days. The boards, announcing the date and location of the meeting and proclaiming "Money Money Everywhere and Not Enough to Live On",[65] stimulated enormous interest and some controversy, for this way of doing things struck not only at the very heart of the banks' distaste for publicity but also at that of some of their employees. To those union members who considered this tactic "degrading, lacking in taste and beneath the dignity of bank officers",[66] Williams curtly replied that "it was more degrading for some bank officers to have to send their wives to work to make ends meet".[67] Williams always viewed the working wife, perhaps even the working female, with some distaste. In chapter 9 it is discussed just how this attitude prejudiced his work on behalf of female bank officers — the "sheilas", as he so often called them.

The sandwich boards served their purpose, and more than two thousand officers crowded into Kelvin Hall, where motions supporting the ACSPA campaign were overwhelmingly passed and "sixty seconds of sustained applause greeted his [Williams's] next words, "We've got a right to withhold our labour if it's not being paid for at a decent rate".[68] The meeting was widely reported in the media, with comments such as Foster's "as a group we are all living far worse than the plumber because the banks have taken advantage of our orderliness and loyalty"[69] receiving prominence. The tenor of the meeting was such that even when Foster questioned the basis of the Australian economic system and why its resources should be controlled by a few individuals, he was vociferously cheered. The meeting authorized the union executive to "take whatever action they thought appropriate in an endeavour to win salary justice"[70] and rejected a proposal that "should the executive decide on positive action the matter should then be put to a secret ballot of the whole financial membership".[71] This latter decision not only confirmed the membership's trust and confidence in Williams and Foster but guaranteed them tactical flexibility and the element of surprise so important to successful industrial confrontation. In addition, it reduced the ability of the banks, either directly through the medium of staff circulars or indirectly by way of sympathetic branch managers, to put pressure on their employees.

The response of the banks was to issue a circular that accused the union of "publishing material in its monthly journal, by pamphlet and in the press, the effect of which has been to engender feelings of unrest and dissatisfaction".[72] With some justification they then argued that delays in the Arbitration Commission were due to the ABOA's desire to test the ACSPA formula before a Full Bench, and had the union been content to have its claim dealt with by a single commissioner, the salary question may have already been settled. However, few members were prepared to accept this reasoning.

The following month Williams told another packed meeting that the banks had now agreed to retrospectivity to May 1958 for any award made before the end of the year, but would not increase their offer. This, plus Commissioner E. A. C. Chambers's statement that an early hearing could be expected, appeased most of the members who had demanded direct action. With the case about to be heard, unionists contributed more than £3,500 to a campaign levy,[73] and in another departure Williams organized and publicized a meeting of bank officers' wives. More than fifty attended and passed several resolutions relating to maintenance of standards of living and declining purchasing power. They further embarrassed the banks, unused to such industrial tactics, by demanding they send a staff inspector to the next meeting.

During procedural discussions in the commission, ACSPA leaders soon realized that any case for margin increases must involve the ACTU. Williams approached the ACTU, and after consultation with the president of the Arbitration Commission, Sir Richard Kirby, it was decided to proceed with a combined ACTU–ACSPA case for all workers in private industry. However, neither the ACTU nor Kirby would agree to the use of the "ACSPA formula", preferring to use the traditional benchmark of the metal fitters' wage. In August 1959 a Full Bench began hearing the matter, the first time white-collar unions had been directly involved with manual unions in arbitration proceedings. The union case proceeded smoothly, with the ACTU arguing for a restoration of the purchasing power of margins and ACSPA adding that their affiliates must also receive an increase to maintain the wage relativities previously established by the commission. Late in 1959 the commission decided on a 28 per cent margins increase for the metals industry and suggested to white-collar unions that they should confer with their employers in the light of this decision.[74]

The banks, however, refused to accept any nexus between the metal workers' margin and that of their employees, and negotiations soon broke down. A mass meeting of ABOA members then authorized the executive to take whatever steps were required to obtain the full flow-on of the marginal increase. With feelings running high, Commissioner Chambers agreed to arbitrate and varied the award to grant a 20 per cent marginal increase to officers with ten or more years of service, but nothing for younger clerks and females.[75] He argued that the ABOA claims had only been part heard and that younger employees had done relatively better than older officers between 1937 and 1955. Williams immediately responded that as the case had been about declining salary margins, then this decision, by providing for lower marginal increases to bank officers, only perpetuated this decline. Williams had no difficulty in evoking an angry response from the younger clerks who had been discriminated against, and sensing that the banks were weakening under this and the barrage of publicity, he suggested further negotiations. He was right, and after brief negotiations the banks agreed to new scale rates with the top of the scale at £1,470. Incredibly, this meant marginal increases of 29 to 33 per cent, greater than those received by the blue-collar unions. Also, the range of classified positions was extended, with even higher marginal increases going to senior managers. A remarkable achievement indeed.

The determination and militancy of the rank and file and the organizational skills of the ABOA leadership had been well rewarded, and congratulations flooded in from other banking and white-collar unions. These were a combination of genuine delight at the success of the ABOA's campaign and realization that here lay an opportunity to improve their own salary situation. A brief telegram from the UBOA of NSW, where the top of the scale was now some £170 less than the federal award, merely stated that the New South Wales union would apply for similar rates. Then the following month, when the AISF and other white-collar unions were able to negotiate new salary rates based on the ABOA award, it was apparent that the ABOA was now not only the foremost banking union but also among the leaders of Australian white-collar unions. This was reflected in its prominence within ACSPA; Williams controlled the ACSPA executive, and the ABOA continued to support ACSPA, both financially and logistically. These events also indicate the extent of Williams's pragmatism and instinct for self-preservation. Though usually anxious to promote co-operation among ACSPA affiliates, he was, when he felt it to the ABOA's advantage, always willing to move to separate negotiations with the banks.

For almost fifteen years through the fifties and into the early sixties, the ABOA also fought another long, strenuous campaign on behalf of its members — this was to have Saturday morning banking abolished. These long-running events are of considerable interest, for they too reflect significant changes in post-war union leadership and rank-and-file attitudes. As such they provide an excellent example of the ABOA's maturation as a trade union. Additionally the growing aggression and militancy of the rank and file, shown through the fifties and particularly in the salary campaigns, was an important ingredient in the eventual success of the ABOA's five-day week campaign.

From the union's inception, bank officers, aggrieved that they were one of the few white-collar worker groups forced to work on Saturday morning, had agitated without success for change. Finally, in 1948, in the face of considerable opposition from large retailers who were supported by energetic Victorian newspaper publicity and editorial urging, Paterson did instigate action. In these early stages the ABOA joined with other unions, particularly those representing retail employees, in seeking to abolish Saturday morning work. However, after it became clear that, to be successful, the claim for a five-day banking week had to be separated from that of a five-day shopping week, this initiative dissipated.

In the early fifties, one of Williams's first tasks was to survey public attitudes towards Saturday morning bank closure. The results of this, in confirming that the public wanted branches to remain open, forced the union to take a low profile on the issue until the mid-fifties, when the ABOA was to the fore in the creation of a five-day-week committee, made up of unions whose members were in clerical and retail areas. The task of this committee was to mount pressure on the Victorian Liberal government so as to force legislative change. This was deemed necessary because of the continuing refusal of the Arbitration Court, and later Commission, to adjudicate on the issue, on the grounds that this was not an industrial issue and therefore they lacked jurisdiction.

Throughout the latter part of the fifties, Williams and Foster were able to exploit the now mounting anger of their members at the intractability of the state government, dogmatism of the retailers and the press, the unwillingness of the Arbitration Commission, and the vacillation of the banks over the abolition of Saturday work. While in the short term this unrest brought no change in banking hours, it did provide the ABOA leadership with another issue to maintain and stimulate rank-and-file anger during the salary campaigns of the period.

In hindsight, a key factor in the campaign was a 1957 commission decision to award penalty rates for Saturday morning work. This decision, based on the apparently just-realized fact that most Tasmanian bank officers, as a result of legislative change, had not worked on Saturday morning since 1937, eventually convinced the banks that the cost of staffing branches on Saturdays now outweighed the benefits of maintaining support for the large retailers. Over the next few years this changed employer view was to be crucial as pressure for change mounted.

Events in other states, where strong political pressure had also been mounted by committees similar to that in operation in Victoria, were also important. Throughout the late fifties, South Australia, Western Australia, Queensland, and eventually New South Wales state governments legislated to abolish Saturday morning banking. By 1962 only the Victorian government had not conceded despite the still-growing agitation from bank officers and the now public statement by the banks that they did not want to open their branches on Saturday mornings. The ABOA responded by mounting a strenuous political campaign which culminated in bank officers participating in political meetings and rallies and threatening industrial stoppages, events that were earlier unheard of in the banking industry. Under considerable electoral and industrial pressure, Premier Bolte eventually agreed to an inquiry into Victorian banking hours. The ABOA initially boycotted this but agreed to participate after being told the inquiry was really implemented to provide a political face-saving compromise for the Liberal government and Premier Bolte. This was indeed so, and finally in early 1963, in response to the inquiry's findings, legislation was brought down to extend hours of opening on Fridays and to abolish Saturday morning banking.

As a long-running saga, this issue is eloquent testimony to the changing post-war nature of the ABOA, and consequently the events of the five-day week campaign are examined in some detail in chapter 7.

The Union and the Industry at the End of the Fifties

The 1950s had seen considerable changes in the ABOA. The rank and file's vigorous commitment had allowed the union leadership to use increasingly militant tactics more akin to those traditional to the blue-collar sector, which had borne results. In the face of this, the union's orientation had changed significantly. Gone were attempts to cultivate and maintain the cosy atmosphere of social gentility and superiority. Apart from their working-class sympathies, Foster and Williams knew that urbanization of bank employees, the changing attitudes of bank officers and the wider society, and the exigencies of a harsher industrial climate all dictated that the trappings of another era be dispensed with. Williams had earlier convinced the union to purchase a property in Hardware Street, City. This did not provide facilities for members to while away idle hours with books, billiards, cards, and tobacco as in earlier days. Rather it was the headquarters for Australian white-collar union development, as indicated by the decision to locate ACSPA offices there. In place of the disbanded Bankers' Club came a purchasing scheme and later a credit union for members. The *Journal*'s social jottings and transfer lists gave way to details of industrial events in blue- and white-collar areas. Editorials extolling the virtue of ordered, reasonable, and peaceful co-existence with the banks were replaced by those from Williams's pen which hammered home the continually worsening position of bank officers and suggested a number of remedies, all of them requiring degrees of militancy unheard of in previous decades.

However, these changes had not been reflected in the ABOA's formal structure, for apart from the establishment of the South Australian branch in 1949, this had remained basically unaltered since the early twenties. The major task of the branches remained that of handling day-to-day industrial and organizational affairs. The Victorian, Tasmanian, and South Australian branches continued to have a committee of management each, though the proviso that delegates from each sub-branch were to be appointed on a basis proportional to their membership had been supplanted by reasonably competitive elections of the branch as a whole. Williams was anxious that the Victorian branch committee should contain representatives from all major banks and not be dominated by officers from one or two banks (and particularly not from the NBA or the BNSW). Consequently, he scrutinized the nominations and usually was able to ensure that all, or most, banks were represented by appropriate officers. The election of delegates to the annual Federal Conferences was now also keenly contested, with each branch supplying delegates in proportion to its membership. This meant, of course, that the Victorian branch retained its dominance, both because of its larger membership and the relative militancy and outspokenness of its delegates. For example, at conferences through the 1950s, the Victorian branch regularly supplied more than 70 per cent of the delegates.

Besides determining the thrust of ABOA policy, Conference delegates elected the Federal Executive (which had replaced the Federal Council in June 1954). Federal Executive was composed of the federal (or general) president, vice-president, and treasurer, together with a representative from each of the branches. The task of Federal Executive remained that of implementing industrial policies determined by Conference and to co-

ordinate the activities of the branches. Again the Victorian branch delegates, through their majority at Conference, had formal control of Federal
Executive.

Late in 1957 the retirement of Hore, the amiable Victorian president,
had further hastened the translation of the ABOA into a purely industrial
union. Staunchly conservative in his earlier days, and never imbued with
Foster's idealism or Williams's trenchant opposition to the banks, Hore
had little part in developing the ABOA's industrial tactics. Yet he had
never tried to hinder the union's activists: his fondness for provincial
sub-branch meetings and his at times almost bawdy nature had done much
to break down the image of the union executive as being the preserve of
restrained older members. In the election to replace Hore, Leo Payne
defeated J. H. Quirk and K. H. Remington, a younger officer destined for
higher office. Payne was president for only one year, giving way in 1958
to Quirk. Williams was still deeply involved in ACSPA, and the following
year John Sanders of the Hobart Savings Bank, who had come under
notice for his involvement in the fracas surrounding ABOA attempts to
extend the federal award to employees in that bank, was appointed
assistant federal secretary.[76]

The continuing loyal support of the Tasmanian and South Australian
branches had enabled the ABOA to present a united front to the
employers and was an important factor in the union's increasing bargaining
power. Though not as militant as the Victorians, the two smaller branches
had shown a similar willingness to challenge and oppose the banks. Though
Federal Executive was still numerically dominated by Victorian delegates,
the independence and zeal of leaders and delegates from the other two
branches ensured that, unlike the pre-war Tasmanian experience, these
branches were integral parts of the ABOA. Both branches had union
density rates in excess of 90 per cent.[77] In Tasmania, G. I. A. Hodson was
now branch president; though an endorsed Liberal candidate at several
elections in the early fifties, he was nevertheless a firm supporter of the
union's stronger industrial policies. South Australian SBSA members had
reaped considerable benefits from their ABOA affiliation. Earlier in the
decade the bank had refused to pay the "adopted rates" above the federal
award, but following "discussions" with Barratt, Simmons, and Williams,
it had soon fallen into line. Later, the forced provision of a non-
contributory medical scheme and low-interest housing loans offset some
of the disadvantages of an inferior pension scheme. In 1955 Simmons had
left the industry and W. J. M. Ewing was appointed part-time branch
secretary. Ewing not only maintained the momentum generated by Barratt
and Simmons but within months was playing a leading role in the South
Australian Five Day Week Committee, which shortly afterwards obtained
the abolition of Saturday morning work.

A brief survey of events in other states confirms the ever-increasing
differences between the ABOA and the other banking unions. In New

South Wales the disastrous 1958 case was symptomatic of the union's performance. Card's constantly expressed conservatism and deference to the banks reflected the union's inability to adapt to the reality of post-war industrial relations and prevented adequate protection and representation of its members. He continued to warn of the dangers of nationalization, as if in looking back he could recapture some of the glory of those heady days. Later in the decade, as his fears of a "socialist" government receded, Card vented his political frustrations on the Commonwealth Bank. He incessantly warned of "nationalization by stealth", arguing for the abolition of the special deposits scheme instituted during the war and even more vehemently for the separation of the Commonwealth Bank's trading and central banking functions. So frequent were these diatribes that one officer caustically noted: "A Bank Officials Association should primarily fight the battle of employees. Bank directorates and shareholders can pay their own publicists."[78] As the decade drew to a close it was clear that the effects of Card's egotism and erratic behaviour were now more than offsetting the efforts of the assiduous president, McKell. The losers, of course, were the UBOA of NSW membership, who, bereft of efficient full-time leadership, were now slipping further behind their ABOA counterparts. In response to the UBOA of NSW's apparent lack of interest in industrial matters, membership density in the early fifties fell to less than 70 per cent and, despite the efforts of a full-time organizer, was still less than 75 per cent at the end of the decade.[79]

In South Australia, BOASA's meek, ineffectual image was carefully maintained by secretary Cook and a succession of presidents. The longest serving of these was E.C. Wills, seemingly more interested in the trappings of office than his members' welfare. BOASA's political and industrial attitudes were reflected not only in its public statements and journal content[80] but in the paranoia felt towards the ABOA and in particular the South Australian branch. An additional irritant to BOASA's leadership was their dependence upon the ABOA. Earlier criticisms by Williams of BOASA's parasitic nature were even truer at the end of the fifties, and even the struggle to abolish Saturday morning work in the state was spearheaded by members of the South Australian branch of the ABOA. In late 1959 Cook resigned, his secretarial performance even further impaired by illness. E.S. Johnson was appointed, and over the next few years he developed close links with Laidlaw and Card, further widening the gulf between BOASA and the ABOA.

In Queensland, little disturbed Laidlaw's determination to maintain the insularity of "his" union. His dominance of the UBOA of Q, a result of thirty years of leadership, control over union resources, and the apathy of his compulsorily unionized membership ensured a continuation of his post-war torpor. This isolation from the mainstream of industrial affairs was reflected in his refusal even to discuss union amalgamation, consider membership of ACSPA, or participate in its salary campaigns. When in

1958 ACSPA representatives met the Queensland state government to canvass the five-day week issue, he first ordered then vainly begged them not to include bank officers in discussions. Laidlaw's earlier purpose and initiative had now totally disappeared, and for some years he had been content to ask the state court to incorporate gains made by the ABOA into the UBOA of Q award. An ABOA member, seconded to Queensland, aptly summarized the UBOA of Q's activities:

> [The journal] merely contains lists of transfers . . . and takes approximately two minutes to read. . . . The Association takes no active part in endeavours to improve the lot of bank officers in Australia . . . and for years now, any benefits of consequence which have accrued are largely the results of efforts elsewhere. . . . The UBOA of Q through apathy, a narrow and insular outlook, and a lack of industrial awareness . . . has drifted into becoming a "one man show" — run by a paid official — its General Secretary. There is no leadership, or progressive and informed opinion among its Council members . . . and it has a secularly local and native distaste for assisting, or being associated with parallel efforts in either the trade union movement or that of the white collar worker. For years the UBOA of Q has opposed a federation of all bank officers in the Commonwealth . . . although undoubtedly quite a considerable number of its members would welcome such a move. These people, although they are compelled to join, have no voice in their Association affairs, and the present set up would see to it that their voices were not heard.[81]

Only in Western Australia was there, in the latter part of the decade, any official sympathy and support for ABOA policy and initiatives. In the early fifties BOAWA's president was G. E. L. Throssell, ex-banker turned insurance agent, strong nationalization opponent, and Liberal Party supporter. Part-time secretary Evan Saw, though concerned, could do little to combat BOAWA's inertia. Gains made in the federal arena were eagerly accepted, arguments for protection and compensation for members in remote branches and suffering intolerable conditions were never put, and frequent bank exploitation of overtime and penalty rate provisions went unchecked. The formerly informative and provocative *Westralian Banker* now consisted merely of lists of transferred officers, diatribes against ABOA actions, and reprints of Card's more virulent attacks on the Commonwealth Bank and the socialists supposedly lurking beneath its fast-spreading counters. Between 1950 and the end of 1956 BOAWA union density fell from more than 90 per cent to only 66 per cent,[82] a reflection of the union's lethargy and inept organization. In 1957 Throssell was replaced by J. J. Williams, a bank officer of distinctly less conservative hue, who set about revitalizing BOAWA. A vigorous membership campaign lifted union density to 93 per cent within twelve months.[83] Williams also arranged affiliation with the newly formed ACSPA state division. Then in a gritty display BOAWA issued a claim on the banks in line with the

ACSPA formula. Though events in the federal jurisdiction overtook this initiative, the willingness and tenacity of the union to prepare and present arbitration claims showed an enthusiasm that was to be important in the next few years, as the ABOA unleashed further energies in pursuit of amalgamation of all Australian banking unions.

The decade had also seen significant change in the banking industry. The Commonwealth Bank's expanding competitiveness, the continuance of extensive controls over the banking system, and the changing nature of Australian industrial and commercial spheres all threatened profitability and forced some adaptation by the private banks. These included the restructing of the ABA into the Australian Bankers Association to co-ordinate individual bank actions and maintain the oligopolistic nature of the industry; the entry of trading banks into savings banking; the provision of hire-purchase facilities; and two bank mergers, which by 1959 reduced the number of Australian private trading banks to seven. The implications of these industry changes for bank staff and for the ABOA require brief discussion.

A major reason given for the ever-increasing ability of the Commonwealth Bank to outshine the private banks was its savings bank arm, and in the mid-fifties most trading banks decided to establish savings facilities. They believed this would facilitate greater contact with potential customers and that the funds generated would offset some of the liquidity problems arising from the government's strict application of reserve deposit regulations. The banks were also attracted to the lucrative hire-purchase field, where, unencumbered by government controls, they would be able to increase profitability.[84]

Entry of the banks into savings banking, hire purchase, and various investment services, unit trusts, and superannuation schemes meant that by the end of the decade their staff were increasingly engaged in new, frequently more difficult tasks for which they had little training or experience. This prompted the ABOA to apply to the banks and then the Arbitration Commission for salary compensation, but without success. The resultant employee discontent was heightened when Williams printed one bank's admission that the introduction of savings banking had resulted in extra work for its staff.[85] All of these changes, Williams commented, meant that bank work was becoming "degraded, unbecoming and detrimental to the status of the banks . . . and officers today have to be salesmen, touts, collectors of arrears of hire purchase, and must even rush to get accounts from people who won lotteries".[86] He also attacked the banks' refusal to charge for a number of customer services, for as "a consequence of bank charges being either free or on too low a scale, salaries of bank officers are detrimentally affected and in reality are used as a means to subsidise the costs of trade and industry".[87]

An enduring source of friction had been staff shortages. In the late fifties these were exacerbated by the continuing inability of the banks to attract sufficient recruits, a result of a tight labour market and the relatively poor junior salaries.[88] The urbanization of branch banking contributed to this staffing problem inasmuch as it reduced the potential of the time-honoured recruiting system carried out by country branch managers. Recruiting shortfalls had existed since the war and were now significantly impairing the banks' operations and ability to service Australia's economic expansion. By 1958 more than 50 per cent of Victorian bank officers were less than thirty, and only 17 per cent between thirty and forty-five,[89] the normal ages for appointment to senior positions. In earlier years the degree of upward job mobility provided by the consequent ready availability of promotion would have limited union membership. However the "new breed" of bank officers did not have the same affinity for and trust in their employers; nor did they feel that having achieved branch managership they no longer needed the protection and support of the union. Above all, there was now widespread belief that union membership was not necessarily inconsistent with senior banking positions. For example, in December 1959, when overall Victorian male union density was only 72.3 per cent, more than 87 per cent of Victorian bank managers were members of the ABOA.[90] Some banks considered unilateral increases in juniors' salary rates, but were dissuaded in the face of criticism from other banks, who saw this as "unfair competition for recruits".[91] The ABOA unabashedly made capital from the banks' quandary. They ridiculed the current recruiting methods of "hawking at schools . . . giving guided tours of capital city offices, lunch provided and ten shillings thrown in".[92] Williams also told the banks there would be recruits aplenty if Saturday morning banking were abolished and salaries increased.

Heightened competition and increasing sophistication in the Australian banking industry had also led to structural change through merger. First mooted in 1946 but deferred by the nationalization crisis, the Bank of Australasia and the Union Bank had finally amalgamated in 1951 to form the Australia and New Zealand Bank (ANZ). In the same year the Queensland National Bank was absorbed by the NBA.[93] In both cases a significant number of employees were involved, and in spite of the ANZ's assurances that "no one would lose in pay, pension, security of employment or prospects of employment",[94] there was considerable staff disquiet. Before the ANZ merger, the Australian manager of the Bank of Australasia had written to London warning of this and instancing the earlier takeover of the Australian Bank of Commerce by the BNSW.[95] In the ANZ, unrest was generated by fears of pension anomalies, reduced promotional prospects, the interruption, even cessation, of expected career paths, and forced transfers and even fear of redundancies as a result of branch nationalization. Additionally, those generally older employees with strong bank loyalties realized that the merger would bring an increasingly bureaucratic structure, employment anonymity, and employee loss of identity and security: "the stubborn stuff of illogical but gracious loyalties", as the ANZ's general manager labelled it.[96] It appears that the insecurity and discontent engendered by the merger encouraged a number of ANZ employees to join the ABOA. While the overall male union density of Victorian bank officers rose by less than 2 per cent between 1950 and 1952, that of the new ANZ increased by more than 10 per cent.[97] Clearly the ABOA was now seen as not only capable of advancing bank officers' interests but also of protecting and maintaining existing conditions and security.

The fifties had seen a dramatic acceleration in the ABOA membership's militancy. This was translated into action through belligerent· and eventually successful union tactics. In part, this new militancy was a reaction to the equally rapid changes in banking industry philosophy, structure, and operations. More importantly, it was a function of bank employees' dissatisfaction, arising from further loss of purchasing power and increasingly onerous working conditions. Some older officers also believed that changes in the industry and the wider community had effected a reduction in society's earlier high esteem and respect for them. Until this time, these officers had felt that membership or active union involvement would have been seen by society as inconsistent with the bank officer's prestigious position. For some, the removal of this constraint was sufficient for them to join the union, while others, stripped of society's approval, were readily convinced that only the ABOA provided any real protection against the new harsh realities of the industry. Others sought to replace the advantages formerly accruing from social approbation with better salaries and conditions.

There were two interesting facets of this militancy. In previous years the few examples of employee resistance to the banks had been generated and carefully fostered by union leaders. Not surprisingly, these isolated incidents had been largely unsuccessful. By the middle of the fifties, however, it was the rank and file who were insisting on better salaries and conditions and who were demanding their union take new initiatives to obtain them. Certainly the ABOA's new leadership, skilled, outspoken, and with none of the ingrained inhibitions of early leaders, played a key role in the decade's events. But this was markedly different even from that played by Paterson in the first stage of militancy, immediately after the war. Now Foster and Williams were using their talents to organize and co-ordinate campaigns, rather than to launch and stimulate bank officers' resentment towards their employers. One example of this was the support provided to ACSPA — a body designed to improve the logistics of union operation and activity and which was to be a vital adjunct to white-collar unionism.

This new bank officer militancy was also remarkable for its lack of any ideological base.[98] Those who saw this militancy as a result of Williams's ability to inculcate his own political views into bank officers, and to exploit the union for his own political ends, have misread the situation. In fact he was at pains to ensure that his own party political views did not impinge on his duties or influence his union involvement. Not only would this have destroyed much of the credibility and trust he had built up, but also the nationalization crisis had shown that ABOA members were determined to maintain the union's apolitical stance. Ever the realist, Williams also knew they would be even less likely to tolerate ABOA support for the Labor Party than for the non-Labor parties. Clearly the ABOA rank and file's militancy had quite pragmatic roots — engendered by continuing grievances and realization that they could only be redressed by more direct and vigorous action than that previously used. The gains and successes that soon followed the use of these tactics further convinced ABOA members of the wisdom of their methods, and comparisons with the insipid performances of most of the other state unions provided further reinforcement. By the end of the decade there were some signs that members of these other unions were less prepared to tolerate the aberrations and ineffectiveness of their leaders. However, these leaders still held sufficient power and control over union resources to remain dominant. Soon this authority was to crumble, making the ABOA's long-cherished dream of a single union covering all private bank officers a reality.

Before entering upon this, it is appropriate to discuss the ABOA's struggle to have Saturday morning banking abolished. This had gone on for much of the fifties and was not achieved for some years yet. It too was important to ABOA militancy, providing both a grievance and unifying factor for the membership and allowing the union leadership to further develop and refine their industrial tactics.

Notes

1. Their union density was 95.4 per cent, a result of the bank's deduction of subscriptions from salary and the enthusiastic leadership of Barratt and Simmons (*Bankers Journal*, 8, no. 11 [Nov. 1948] :7)
2. *SABOJ* 27, no. 1 (Aug. 1949): 5. The South Australian premier, Thomas Playford, fearing wage and condition increases won by SBSA employees would flow to other state public servants, constantly reinforced the trustees' decision not to concede.
3. There were three reasons for this: members could not avoid levies struck to finance court cases; it prevented the banks' counsel using resignation rates to the detriment of the union; and it was a counter to the timidity of senior officers who otherwise might resign under pressure from bank management.
4. BOASA revoked Barratt's life membership and sent him an account for some years' membership fees. This petty claim was dropped only when the ABOA, after conferring life membership on him, threatened BOASA with legal action.

5.   So strong was their fear of political intrusion that Gaunson had been encouraged to stand for the federal presidency against Paterson, who still carried the scars of nationalization. However, Paterson's endeavour, skills, reputation, and initative were clearly superior, and he won comfortably.

6.   Among other activities was his long-term secretaryship of the Sandringham branch of the Labor Party and of numerous state and federal election campaigns in Melbourne's southern suburbs. Williams's actions during the traumatic Labor Party "split" of the mid-fifties provide some measure of this political commitment. Converted to catholicism in mid-life, he had become devoutly religious and a leading member of the church community. Yet he chose not to join the newly formed Democratic Labor Party but to remain with the Australian Labor Party, a decision that placed both him and his family under enormous pressure. A forthcoming biography by J. D. Hill, traces Williams's philosophy and industrial and political career.

7.   For example, BOAWA had conducted a survey before the nationalization furore. To the question, "at the next Federal election will you support the Labor Government or the Opposition, or are you at present undecided?, 64 per cent replied that they would vote for the conservative opposition, 26 per cent the government, and 10 per cent were undecided (*Westralian Banker* 21, no. 10 [July 1946] : 9; and 21, no. 11 [Aug. 1946] : 2).

8.   For example, letters in the *Bankers Journal* 6, no. 2 (Nov. 1946): 11-13.

9.   *Bankers Journal* 6, no. 1 (Oct. 1946): 1.

10.   *Westralian Banker* 21, no. 11 (Aug. 1946): 10.

11.   *Bankers Journal* 8, no. 11 (Nov. 1948): 5.

12.   *Westralian Banker* 24, no. 11 (Nov. 1949): 7.

13.   *Bankers Journal* 9, no. 4 (Apr. 1949): 7.

14.   Ibid., 7, no. 7 (July 1947): 7.

15.   In Queensland, 163, or 18 per cent, of the 907 bank officers who returned from the war had resigned within twelve months (*Queensland Bank Officer* 27, no. 11 [Jan. 1947] : 4).

16.   Between 1945 and 1950 the total number of Victorian branches had increased by 201, or 15 per cent. The proportion of branches in city and suburban areas rose from 40.9 to 42.8 per cent of total branches (see app. 1).

17.   *Bankers Journal* 9, no. 1 (Jan. 1949): 2.

18.   *Bankers Journal* 10, no. 1 (Jan. 1950): 2.

19.   Ibid.

20.   Ibid., 9, no. 8 (Aug. 1949): 18.

21.   Ibid., 10, no. 2 (Feb. 1950): 9.

22.   The union's counsel, too, had earlier ruefully commented on the inadequacy of this consent award (UBOA of NSW meeting, 6 September 1947, p. 3).

23.   (1949) 48 AR (NSW) 511. De Baun did establish what was in effect an industry basic wage by providing a margin of £52 over the state basic wage for the twenty-one year clerk.

24.   *Bankers Journal* 9, no. 11 (Nov. 1949): 2.

25.   *Bankers Journal* 9, no. 11 (Nov. 1949): 3.

26.   *Commonwealth Parliamentary Debates*, 23 February, 1950, p. 52.

27.   *Australian Insurance Staffs Federation* v. *Ajax Insurance Company Ltd. and Ors* (64 CAR 224).

28.   Paterson to secretary of Victorian branch, 17 March 1950, letter in ABOA archives.

29.   *Argus*, 16 November 1949, p. 2.

30.   *Bankers Journal* 10, no. 9 (Sept. 1950): 5.

31.   C. W. Larner, vice-president of Federal Council, in *Bankers Journal* 10, no. 9 (Sept. 1950): 3.

32. *The Australian Bank Officals Association* v. *Ballarat Banking Company Ltd and Ors* (71 CAR 497) at 503.

33. Australian manager of Bank of Australasia to London, confidential letter no. 3662, 9 February 1951, in ANZ archives.

34. *Bankers Journal* 11, no. 2 (Feb. 1951): 3.

35. Ibid., p. 7.

36. Australian manager of Bank of Australasia, cable to London, 15 February 1951, in ANZ archives.

37. This reasoning was based on hard-won knowledge that higher rates appearing by consent prejudiced argument in further cases, and the possibility that if the freely discussed concept of wage pegging was introduced, then the lower formalized rates would apply.

38. President's annual report to the Victorian branch, 13 October 1951, in *Bankers Journal* 11, no. 11 (Nov. 1951): 3.

39. *Bankers Journal* 11, no. 7 (July 1951): 1.

40. Ibid., 12, no. 2 (Mar. 1952): 18.

41. Even by 1955, more than 55 per cent of Victorian branches were still located in rural areas (see app. 1).

42. The ABOA, with the cajoling of Williams, agreed to joint action with the ACTU but was unable to convince other members of the Kindred Organizations of this, so that the union had to be content with a donation of £250 to the ACTU campaign, an action that would have earlier been unthinkable *Bankers Journal* 12, no. 8 [Nov. 1952]: 5).

43. For analysis of the Arbitration Court's rationale and actions regarding wage setting in the federal jurisdiction in the fifties, see K. Hancock, "The Wages of Workers", *Journal of Industrial Relations* 11, no. 1 (Mar. 1969): 17.

44. *The Trustee Companies Officers Association* v. *Bagot's Executor and Trustee Co. Ltd and Ors* (79 CAR 232) at p. 241.

45. Ibid., p. 244.

46. *The Commonwealth Public Service Board* v. *The Australian Third Division Telegraphists and Postal Clerks Union and Ors* (81 CAR 20) at p. 23).

47. ABOA pamphlet, November 1954, copy in ABOA archives.

48. See, for example, the *New South Wales Banker* 14, no. 2 (Feb. 1955): 5, and the *Queensland Bank Officer* 36, no. 11 (Jan. 1955): 1.

49. *Queensland Bank Officer* 37, no. 2 (Apr. 1955): 1.

50. *SABOJ* 32 no. 6 (Jan. 1955): 5.

51. *Bankers Journal* 15, no. 5 (July 1955): 8.

52. *Westralian Banker* 30, no. 4 (Apr. 1955): 1.

53. Obviously the Arbitration Court had not accepted the import of the 1949 De Baun judgment that officers beyond the fifth year of service should receive a margin.

54. *Bankers Journal* 15, no. 5 (July 1955): 2.

55. *Australian Bank Officals Association* v. *Australia and New Zealand Bank Ltd and Ors* (83 CAR 659).

56. In 1956, following a successful High Court challenge, the Arbitration Court was restructured into the Arbitration Commission, carrying out conciliation and arbitration processes, and the Commonwealth Industrial Court, whose function was to interpret and enforce the resultant awards.

57. Memorandum from R. D. Williams to the chairman of the ABA, 11 December 1956, in *Bankers Journal* 17, no. 1 (Jan. 1957): 5.

58. *Bankers Journal* 17 no. 5 (June 1957): 5.

59. Ibid., p. 4.

60. For example, in mid-1957 managers and senior officers of the ANZ held a large meeting to express their dissatisfaction at their salaries. They promised

full support for any union efforts in this direction (*Bankers Journal* 17, no. 6 [July 1957] : 3).

61. Minutes of 1957 ACSPA conference, in *Bankers Journal* 18 no. 6 (July 1958): 9.
62. *Banker* 17, no. 6 (June 1958): 1.
63. Executive's annual report to the fortieth annual conference of UBOA of NSW, in *Banker* 18, no. 3 (Mar. 1959): 5.
64. *Bankers Journal* 18, no. 10 (Nov. 1958): 1.
65. Ibid., 19, no. 5 (May 1959): 29.
66. Ibid., p. 21.
67. Ibid. Though social attitudes to working wives were already undergoing considerable change, there was, among banking employees and the banks themselves, a strong feeling that officers placed in this position were under some stigma. This was highlighted by the shocked editorial accompanying the publication of a survey in Western Australia showing that 51 of 150 officers in the head office of one of the banks had working wives, and was a further example of the conservatism still existing in the industry (*Westralian Banker* 34, no. 6 [June 1959] : 6).
68. ABOA general meeting, 5 May 1959, reported in *Bankers Journal* 19, no. 5 (May 1959): 5-7.
69. *Age*, 6 May 1959, p. 5.
70. *Bankers Journal* 19, no. 5 (May 1959): 7.
71. Ibid.
72. Banks circular to officers, 28 May 1958, reprinted in *Bankers Journal* 19, no. 6 (June 1959): 10.
73. *Bankers Journal* 19, no. 7 (July 1959): 19.
74. *Sheet-Metal Working, Agricultural Implement and Stovemaking Industrial Union of Australia and Ors* v. *Metal Trades Employees Association and Ors* (92 CAR 793).
75. *The Bank Officials (Federal) Award No. 654. of 1958.*
76. In a series of events not dissimilar to those in Victoria in 1919, the Hobart Savings Bank's autocractic general manager, R. W. Freeman, had commanded his employees not to join the union. After much cajoling more than 70 per cent did sign ABOA application forms, but Freeman confiscated them. A series of surreptitious meetings followed, and the matter was only concluded after Williams guaranteed the bank's employees union protection and warned Freeman of the implication of any further meddling with union recruitment.
77. *Bankers Journal* 19, no. 7 (July 1959): 11.
78. *Westralian Banker* 30, no. 5 (July 1955): 12.
79. *Banker* 18, no. 3 (Mar. 1959): 5.
80. See, for example, *SABOJ* 31, no. 10 (May 1954): 152. Before state and federal elections, this journal contained full-page advertisements, numerous articles, and other signs of support for Liberal Country League and Liberal Party candidates.
81. *Bankers Journal* 20, no. 1 (Dec. 1959): 12.
82. *Westralian Banker* 32, no. 3 (Mar. 1957): 10.
83. Ibid., 33, no. 12 (Dec. 1958): 20.
84. Apart from the ES&A, which established its own company, the other banks chose to purchase equity in existing hire-purchase companies. This had the advantage of not involving them in the administrative and policy problems of embarking on a new type of business.
85. *CBC Annual Report to Shareholders* 1957, extract printed in *Bankers Journal* 17, no. 7 (Sept. 1957): 7.
86. *Bankers Journal* 18, no. 2 (Mar. 1958): 7.
87. ABOA annual conference minutes, 1958, p. 12.

88. For example, in 1955 Victorian Public Service entrants with similar educational qualifications to bank recruits were paid 8.5 per cent more, a differential that remained after six years of employment.

89. Report on age distribution of officers, 1958, in ABOA archives. It should also be noted that of the 50 per cent less than thirty, almost half were females and so ineligible for promotion.

90. Appendix 3 and Victorian division of ABOA current records.

91. General manager of Bank of Australasia to London, confidential letter no. 3293, 28 March 1949, in ANZ archives. There was also a fear that increases at the lower end of the scale would prompt the Arbitration Commission to respond favourably to a union claim for a general salary increase.

92. *Bankers Journal* 15 no. 1 (Feb. 1955): 1.

93. Whereas the former was necessitated by the long-term effects of introspective management and misplaced emphasis on rural rather than urban expansion, the latter resulted from the NBA's desire to expand operations.

94. Butlin, *Australia and New Zealand Bank*, p. 432.

95. Australian manager of Bank of Australasia to London, 21 December 1946, letter in ANZ archives.

96. General manager of ANZ to London, private letter no. 5, 25 January 1952, in ANZ archives.

97. Appendix 3 and Victorian division of ABOA records. Later, Hore was adamant that non-members from the Union Bank had joined to seek protection from the merger's uncertainties (interview 12 October, 1973).

98. The decade had seen most bitter divisions within both the industrial and political labour movements, as the Democratic Labor Party, with considerable catholic church support, sought to purge a perceived Communist threat. There is little evidence, documented or verbal, that this confrontation occurred in the ABOA to any marked degree during this decade, though in later years it was to pose problems in some states.

Interstate Conference of Bank Officers Association — Perth 1950.

Seated left to right:
S. E. Card, New South Wales Secretary (Life Member)
R. A. McKell, New South Wales President (Life Member)
C. B. Jones, New South Wales
Obscured — (Unknown lady — perhaps Minute Secretary)
E. S. Saw, Western Australian Secretary (Life Member)
G. E. L. Throssell, Western Australian President (Life Member)
G. Scott, Western Australia
T. B. Smith-Ryan, Western Australia
B. E. Adkins, Queensland (Life Member)
K. H. Laidlaw, Queensland Secretary (Life Member)
R. Gibson, Queensland President (Life Member)
C. W. Larner

Standing Left to Right:
J. J. Williams, Western Australia (Life Member)
E. H. Cook, South Australia (Life Member)
D. Thomas, South Australia
T. J. Richardson, Western Australia
E. R. Henning, South Australian President
W. E. Dagnall, Western Australia
R. D. Williams, Victorian Secretary (Life Member)
G. J. Hodson, Tasmania (Life Member)
J. H. O. Paterson, Victoria (Life Member)
J. D. Gaunson, Victorian President (Life Member)
A. Powell, Victoria

A. E. Hore and R. D. Williams visit Tasmania in the early 1950s.

R. D. Williams and S. V. Barratt cement relations between the ABOA and its new South Australian Branch, 1950.

7 The Five-Day Week Campaign: 1948–63

Saturday Morning, oh Saturday Morning!
An extra hour in bed, a nice slow breakfast.
A stroll down the street, a haircut, a glass or two
    (in the saloon bar of course).
A little gardening, or a nap, then polish the boots,
    whiten the pads, and ready for the afternoon's fray.
Ah! the expectation - the sweet sound of leather on
    pigskin, or on willow – I can hear it all.
Yes I can hear the crowd as the team bursts onto
    the ground, as the first cover drive bounces from the pickets.
Yes I can hear it all from where I crouch over the ledgers
    and pass-books in the Bank.
Maybe I'll make the match in an hour or so?
Maybe!!

[Letter from BOA member – April 1936]

The ABOA's campaign to win the five-day week for its members ran over a period of almost fifteen years and is worthy of detailed and separate treatment for a number of reasons. Firstly, it demonstrates that the ABOA was now becoming an effective and aggressive trade union – something that could not have been said of it in the pre-war period. Secondly, these long-running events indicate that the ABOA's leadership and rank and file now had a willingness to pursue a goal over a long period of time. The abolition of Saturday banking had been long desired by bank officers, and on several occasions before the Second World War the union leadership had made tentative and desultory attempts to have branches closed on Saturday mornings, but these had been dismissed out of hand by the banks. However, during the fifties and early sixties, and in the face of industrial and political opposition of the highest order, leadership and rank and file refused to concede defeat and were eventually successful. This ability to pursue an issue over a lengthy period and to translate dissatisfaction into overt opposition is perhaps the best indication of union maturation.

Thirdly, the campaign contained two further elements that confirmed the changing character of the union. One was a willingness to continue to press for changes to banking hours which, on the surface at least (and certainly as incessantly repeated by the press), might be perceived as inconsistent with the needs and wishes of the public. For bank officers who had earlier been most sensitive about their esteemed place in society and long record of service to the public, this was a significant change. The second interesting element was the readiness with which bank officers moved into the political arena, participating in boisterous public meetings, writing to newspapers, lobbying political parties and individual politicians, and threatening to use the bank officers' collective vote to bring about legislative change. The abolition of Saturday banking was eventually achieved by political means, and victory would not have been possible had the ABOA maintained its pre-war apolitical stance.

The final reason for treating this campaign separately is the need to explain why the ABOA, the most efficient and belligerent of Australian banking unions, was in fact the last to achieve a five-day working week for its members. This situation, seemingly so inconsistent with the pace-setting role played by the ABOA in winning improved salaries or conditions, in general resistance to bank initatives, in ACSPA formation, and in bank union amalgamation requires some explanation, particularly of those political events in other states which were so crucial to the campaign's eventual success. It is for these reasons that the ABOA's tactics and actions to achieve the abolition of Saturday morning banking is treated as the central issue of this chapter.

Over a period of many years the ABOA had frequently though unsuccessfully asked the banks to abolish Saturday morning banking. In return they offered to work extra hours on Friday evening. There were numerous arguments for and against the five-day week. These were presented with considerable emotion and fervour though often little clarity, all of which reflected the subjective basis of so much of the debate. During the long-drawn-out campaign, there were many variations; however, certain basic arguments can be discerned, and a brief discussion of these may help to explain the intensity with which the issue was fought out.

Bank employees had always been disgruntled at having to work on Saturday mornings. Even though by the end of the Second World War branches closed by 11.30 a.m., this had done nothing to appease officers denied a full Saturday away from work. Others complained that this earlier closing was of little benefit, for the considerable though varying amount of time required to complete the morning's transactions after the branch closed meant that organized Saturday recreation was still usually impossible. Another argument of bank employees grew from a perception of themselves as professional employees. From this premise they claimed that few other professionals worked on Saturday morning, and those that did were well compensated. Later, after the banks had defended their opposition to Saturday closing with arguments of resultant cost increases, the ABOA emphasized the positive effect on labour productivity; two full workless days would do much to restore the morale and effectiveness of bank officers, victims of strains and tensions resulting from post-war staffing shortages. The union was also quick to claim that the abolition of Saturday banking would aid industry recruiting.

The demand for the five-day week posed a dilemma for the banks. Total banking hours would not be reduced by Saturday closure, operating costs would fall marginally, and as in the immediate post-war period they faced little competition from non-bank savings institutions, then seemingly they had nothing to lose from the five-day week. Before the war, their jealous defence of managerial prerogatives and resistance to change, particularly that which was union inspired, had meant that the issue had never been seriously considered. After the war, as the ABOA's militancy and demands grew, the banks increasingly found themselves defending a policy that was of no benefit to them. They were in fact opposing Saturday banking on behalf of their customers, particularly retail traders. So though never in enthusiastic agreement with the retailers' arguments, the banks were, for several years nevertheless, forced into strenuous support of these. The argument most frequently used against Saturday closing revolved around the resultant extent of public inconvenience, particularly for those in full-time employment, who would be unable to carry out their banking. The ABOA's suggestion that branches remain open late on Fridays was not seen as a satisfactory compromise. There were numerous other arguments why the public would be inconvenienced; the perishability of food and shortages of groceries over the weekend being just two of these. These frequently reduced the argument to the level of trivia, with the union making suggestions such as bringing pay day forward in the week, and quoting at length statistics on the number of ice chests and refrigerators in Victorian homes!

Retail traders had other though less frequently expressed reasons for opposing the five-day week. Though they used the "public inconvenience" argument to justify their support of the *status quo,* it was these other reasons that inspired their lobbying of government and pressure on the banks. These grew from a fear that the abolition of Saturday banking would reduce sales and profitability. They believed that some customers, unable to obtain cash on Saturday morning, would thus be unable to shop. Others, who normally combined their banking and shopping activities, would not bother to go out unless they could do both. Though unsupported by an analysis of shopping habits, retailers placed considerable store in these. They also raised queries relating to security of cash taken on Saturday morning and the availability of change, all of which the union tried to rebut with practical suggestions for alterations to banking practices. However, these suggestions did little to appease the retailers, for underlying their opposition was also a fear that if bank officers obtained a five-day week, shop assistants would agitate for a similar concession. Arguments, particularly those of "public inconvenience" against the five-day week, received extensive exposure through a sympathetic media. In Victoria this was most evident in the publications of the Herald and Weekly Times group. Media support was a result of close social and business links between media proprietors and some large retailers. This was backed up by the retailers' readiness to outline to the media the effects of reduced trading on their considerable advertising outlays.

These, then, were the major issues that were often clouded by the industrial and political events surrounding the ABOA's campaign to win the five-day week. Revitalized in the late forties by Paterson, and eventually carried to fruition by Williams and Foster, this campaign forms an important part of ABOA history. It provided further examples of the increasing militancy of bank officers and encouraged the development of new industrial tactics. As with other examples of militant action in this period discussed in chapter 6, this militancy was increasingly now being internally generated, a result of bank officer dissatisfaction at having to work on Saturday mornings. In the five-day week campaign the union was forced into the political arena, where it encountered considerable political expediency and procrastination. The issue also stimulated previously unknown levels of support from other state unions, particularly in the latter stages of the campaign. Though much of this support was inspired by a fear that an employer or government victory over the ABOA must eventually worsen their own situation, the reduced animosity between unions, and the success of their first serious attempt to work together, was important to union amalgamation plans, which were already unfolding.

Some Early Mistakes

Sir, — I was very amused to see one or two sub-branches complaining about the Five Day Week campaign. The trouble is that some of these country sub-branches are dominated by managers, and when they get up and complain about such a thing as closing on Saturday mornings, the staff hold their tongues, because if they support closing they will be accused of:—
1. Being a loafer.
2. Being hostile to the clients.
3. Being a "Red Ragger".
4. Giving lip to the boss.
I see that Swan Hill "considers it its duty to cater for the convenience of the farming community, and public in general". Like h--- it is! The duty of all sections of the A.B.O.A. is to cater for the interests of bank officers. Well, let Mr. Hyland's party look after the squatters, and the Chamber of Commerce look after the business people. And for heaven's sake let us stop being "the mugs" in the

community, whether it is in salaries, hours of work or anything else.
  –   Yours etc., HAD IT.
      [Letter to Editor – *Bankers Journal* 8, no. 11 (Nov. 1948):5]

The introduction in 1948 of the forty-hour week for most Australian industry stimulated bank union agitation for the abolition of Saturday morning work.[1]   Paterson, eager to press the issue, convinced the executive to join with seventeen other unions from insurance, retail, and clerical areas to form a Five Day Week Committee. He soon regretted this, for it quickly became apparent that the unions involved had different goals.   The ABOA and AISF wanted to abolish Saturday morning work, while retail unions, knowing this to be impracticable in their industries, intended to claim for Saturday penalty rates. Paterson nevertheless remained on the committee, for already he considered it likely that the matter would be decided at the political rather than industrial level and so would require a united campaign. In retrospect this was a mistake, for the intensity and success of the retail traders' campaign made it difficult for the public and most politicians to distinguish between the effects of the closing of banks and the closing of shops of Saturday morning, a situation not helped by the ABOA's membership of the joint Five Day Week Committee.   This confusion was to hinder the ABOA's chances of success for some years.

As a first move the committee enlisted the support of Victorian Labor opposition leader John Cain and approached the state minister for labor. Paterson's fears were confirmed when the minister, in refusing to countenance the committee's proposal, emphasized the possibility of illegal shopping outside hours and the dire consequences resulting from late-night shopping.   His comment that "shorter hours were all right for the well to do, who could afford refrigerators, but the man in the street and his wife were worthy of some consideration",[2]   further convinced Paterson of his mistake and, together with the continuing strain of the nationalization crisis, persuaded him to defer any further action.

In mid-1949, armed with the Victorian Wages Board decision that legislative amendment rather than tribunal decision would be needed to effect the five-day week, the Five Day Week Committee wrote to all state parliamentarians seeking support. Paterson had initiated this move because he now knew that under the Commonwealth Bills of Exchange Act banks were required to open on Saturday mornings unless state legislation existed to include Saturdays as bank holidays. Encouraged by the replies of Labor opposition members, the committee again approached the minister for labour.   Ignoring their arguments, he offhandedly suggested they return to the Arbitration Court.   Paterson's belief that "if the subject had been brought up by a militant union, the request would have been a demand, and a refusal not accepted",[3] was wry recognition of the government's lack of interest and the timidity of the unions involved. The government's refusal to intervene and the inability of the Arbitration Court to hear the matter now left Paterson confused and uncertain of future tactics.

A further appeal to the premier, T. T. Hollway, was prompted by legislative change in New Zealand. The cursory dismissal of this plea, together with developments in Tasmania, where it seemed that all banks would soon be closed on Saturday, persuaded Paterson to abandon a joint approach, and he led an ABOA deputation to the premier. After outlining the problems of Saturday morning work for bank officers, Paterson again argued in vain that only the state government could initiate change, particularly as neither the Victorian Commonwealth Bank branches nor the State Savings Bank were subject to federal awards. The ABOA then wrote to the ABA, claiming that not only would "the increased leisure improve productivity and compensate for the increased load caused by a shortage of recruits, but also if Saturday morning work was abolished then more recruits would be attracted to the industry".[4] This was designed to appeal to the banks whose staffing shortfalls limited their operations and expansion. Though hardly surprised by the premier's further refusal, the union was disappointed by the banks' reiteration of already well worn "public inconvenience" arguments to justify their rejection of the proposal.[5]

Though not hopeful of success, Paterson decided on one more approach to the Arbitration Court. This was an issue that bank officers felt strongly about, but their historical timidity still prevented significant manifestation of their anger. Unlike his successors, Paterson did not know how to use the banks' and government prevarication to incite more overt displays of dissatisfaction. Consequently he had little alternative other than to return to the traditional battleground. His slim hopes of an award variation were quickly snuffed out when it was found that the 1938 claims, upon which the current award was based, contained no reference to a five-day spread of hours. It was therefore necessary to create a fresh dispute by issuing a new log of claims, and it was not until mid-1950 that these came before Commissioner Murray-Stewart as part of the long-running case already discussed.[6] Paterson expounded the union's numerous arguments against Saturday work. In resisting this claim the banks' counsel had the ready support of retail traders, several of whom provided lengthy evidence to the court. This opposition was superfluous, for in the confusion that marked the case, the question of Saturday work fell by the wayside.

It was the new secretary, Williams, anxious to prove his worth, who reactivated the issue. Concerned at the frequency and durability of the "public inconvenience" arguments, he decided to test their validity. In mid-1950, and with tacit bank approval, he initiated a survey of the number of transactions carried out by branches each trading day. Though imperfect, for it relied upon the volunteer efforts of the union members, the survey did show that in the two hours that banks were open on Saturday mornings, they conducted only 40 per cent less business than on an average week-day.[7] This was a serious tactical error by Williams, for he had provided his opponents with evidence that the public would be inconvenienced by Saturday closing. Though the ABOA was quick to claim that much of this business could be done on week-days, and the provision of night-safe facilities for retailers would also reduce Saturday morning transactions, the results had done considerable damage to the union's case. Williams then proposed that branches be manned for an hour and a half each Saturday morning just to receive retailers' cash. The banks quickly dismissed this but did agree to close half an hour earlier at 11 a.m. This was a concession made not to the union but rather to the governor of the Commonwealth Bank, who had agreed to the CBOA's request for earlier closing. The private banks grudgingly accepted the need to maintain uniform banking hours and did likewise.

Little occurred for the next two years, because of Paterson's lower union profile, Williams's involvement in the aftermath of the Murray-Stewart case, and then his marshalling of forces for the next salary case. Williams also realized that any combined approach with retail unions would founder on the rocks of "consumer convenience" and so was prepared to allow the old Five Day Week Committee to wither away before renewing the campaign.

In mid-1958 Williams adroitly used the five-day-week issue to involve the rank and file in the salary campaign. An uncharacteristically boisterous meeting initiated the "Service Without Saturday" campaign, demanded the closure of branches on Saturdays, and reaffirmed their willingness to open on Friday evenings. Knowing that the Victorian government would not allow the closure of private banks while the State Savings Bank and the Commonwealth Bank remained open, Williams had invited the SSBOA and the CBOA to join the campaign. The meetings' resolutions and the enthusiasm with which they were accepted drew sharp criticism from sections of the media, and the first shots in what was to be a long-running battle between the ABOA and the *Herald* and *Sun* were fired.

Saturday closing was also an important issue among the members of state unions. In New South Wales, where organized opposition of retailers and public seemed less, discussions with the banks had led to an agreement to survey the extent of customer disadvantage should Saturday banking be abolished. Queensland secretary Laidlaw had been taken aback by the state Industrial Court's refusal to approve an application by the Shop Assistants Union for late shopping hours on Friday evening in lieu of Saturday work. That Laidlaw saw this decision as preventing him from pursuing the five-day week for his members was a further example of his growing introspection, inertia, and reliance upon the initiative of other unions.

In Western Australia, BOAWA sought its members' attitudes by simply asking whether they were in favour of a five day-week in the banking industry. A significant 91 per cent of the 1,325 ballot papers issued were returned, with 94 per cent of these in favour.[8]   Consequently, S.E.I. Johnson, a former bank officer and BOAWA member and now a Labor member in the Western Australian Legislative Assembly, agreed to propose a private member's bill to abolish Saturday morning trading.[9] There was opposition from not only the expected quarters but also from some bank officers. Even the possibility of no weekend work could not quell their distrust of Johnson's motives, which were "seen as a very astute move on the part of the Labor Party to woo bank officers unsuspectingly into the Socialist camp".[10]   In South Australia, members of the South Australian branch of the ABOA led the fight for the five-day week and were supported by CBOA members.   BOASA's attitude was "Our Association is not in favour of public meetings being held on the five day week, as it is our considered opinion that they would be prejudicial to our cause and would tend to antagonise public opinion".[11]   Though BOASA was not represented on the state's Five Day Week Committee, a number of trading bank officers were unofficially involved in the campaign.

By the early fifties the ABOA leadership, and to a latter extent leaders in other states, knew that the five-day week was of real concern to their members.   They were only partially aware of the strength of the opposition who, with some justification, highlighted the question of public inconvenience should Saturday banking be abolished. Delays would be inevitable and success was far from assured, for the need for legislative amendment dictated that each union must separately and tediously pursue the five-day week.

The First Glimmerings of Hope

Williams and Foster, now intent on applying maximum political pressure but aware of continuing bank officer distaste for the political arena, decided to seek support.   Accordingly they approached the SSBOA and the Victorian division of the CBOA, and in early 1955 the Combined Bank Officers Five Day Week Committee took over the organization of the Service Without Saturday campaign. With a state election in the offing, it was decided to poll all candidates. The result was that 38 per cent of candidates (nearly all Labor contenders) favoured the abolition of Saturday banking, 14 per cent (all from the Liberal Party) declared their opposition, and the remaining 48 per cent failed to reply.[12]   These results, together with candidates' comments, were prominently displayed in the *Bankers Journal*, with an invitation to members to note these re-actions and to vote accordingly. Given the nature of the replies, this was really a recommendation to members to vote Labor, which in the light of the presumed political attitudes of bank employees was a new and daring move by Williams. Yet, there was no discernible adverse membership reaction, a measure of the growing intensity of feeling over Saturday work and the changing views of bank employees.

Following the elections, another deputation to the new premier, Henry Bolte, was rebuffed, and this forced a change in tactics. The committee sensed now that the banks themselves were ambivalent about Saturday morning banking but were under considerable pressure from their customers not to relent. Accordingly the committee decided to seek penalty rates for Saturday work,[13] which would increase the costs of opening on Saturdays and so they hoped, would convince the banks to join them in supporting the five-day week. This strategy was later to be successful, but for now Commissioner Portus refused, claiming that under the Bills of Exchange Act the banks had no option but to open on Saturday and so should not be penalized.[14] However, most importantly he added:

If a five day week is to be prescribed for the banking industry, it should be prescribed by Parliament, as Tasmania has done by closing banks on Saturdays. Alternatively [Federal] Parliament, if it thinks fit, should release the banks from their obligation under the Bills of Exchange Act to remain open on Saturdays. In the latter case, assuming that no agree-ment could be reached between the two parties, an industrial tribunal would then be in a position of deciding whether a five day week should be prescribed.[15]

The ABOA appealed, and though the Full Bench confirmed Commissioner Portus's decision,[16] it concluded that this did not "imply rejection of the proposition that in appropriate circumstances it may be proper to prescribe extra remuneration to those whose occupations reasonably in-volve Saturday morning duty within their standard hours of work".[17] So in December 1957 the ABOA again asked Commissioner Portus to apply penalty rates. In the light of the Full Bench's statement, he agreed and varied the award so that all Saturday morning was to be paid at time and a quarter.[18]   Another factor in his decision was that Tasmanian officers worked a five-day week yet received the same salaries as Victorian officers. The award variation was estimated to cost the banks more than £140,000 per annum,[19] and this additional operating cost immediately influenced their attitude towards Saturday banking. For example, at a meeting with the Australian Council of Employers Federation, the banks' representative, while reassuring retailers that the banks felt they must provide a service to the public on Saturdays, made it clear that if penalty rates became "more burdensome, the banks' position in the matter may call for redetermination".[20]   Were it not for their knowledge that the Commonwealth Bank and various State Savings Banks were heavily involved in savings banking and so anxious to remain open on Saturday morning, it is likely that the private banks would have now agreed to Saturday morning closing.   The ANZ's general manager noted potential benefits: "A worthwhile saving in operating costs, particularly in Saturday penalty rates, and staff turnover could be expected to reduce with resultant increase in overall efficiency".[21]

Aware that any further progress must come from the political arena, the ABOA then decided on a deliberate political campaign. Though sure that the rank and file were angry and upset and that this could be translated into further militancy, Williams believed there were still significant constraints upon this militancy. His editorial comment summed this up: "The goal can be obtained either by saying we won't work Saturday mornings . . . or through legislation enacted in the state parliaments. It would be fair to assume that bank officers are not yet ready to strike . . . the only course to adopt is to vote for that political party which will undertake to introduce legislation to give a five day week".[22]   The latter part of this was made more in hope than any real conviction that bank officers would vote for the Labor Party in large numbers. As previously discussed, few bank employees had yet developed any ideological class-based militancy compatible with support for the Labor Party.

Again however the turmoil surrounding a salaries case delayed further action, and it was not until January 1960 that the committee met Premier Bolte. They outlined developments in other states, stressing the commission's view that legislative change was required and that the banks would not object to this.   Though criticized by a few frustrated and angry union members, this relatively conciliatory approach was adopted because the committee was anxious to avoid "widespread antagonistic publicity from Melbourne's monopolised press", which, some felt, headlined into action "at the snap of Bourke Street's fingers".[23]   This justification, while conceding the crucial role played by the media in the five-day-week campaign, was also a tacit recognition that there was still no other practical alternative.   The premier's ambiguous reply, in stressing the need for amendments to the Commonwealth's Bill of Exchange Act, failed to rouse ABOA members to anything more than angry muttering and was further evidence that union members were not yet prepared to adopt stronger tactics.

The ABOA had made some gains in the Arbitration Commission, and now had a potential ally in the banks. However, its members were less interested in compensation for Saturday morning than in obtaining a five-day week. To win this it was clear that legislative amendment was required, and at this level the union had been conspicuously unsuccessful. They now looked to the experiences of some state unions who, in spite of less aggressive union reputations, were making strenuous and sometimes successful attempts to sway various state governments.

In Western Australia, Johnson had again proposed legislative amendments, and BOAWA members were urged to contact their local members: "Make sure every other one on your staff does likewise – pack the public gallery and show we mean business".[24] The amendments passed through the Labor-controlled lower house but were rejected in the upper house, where the non-Labor parties held sway. After the state Industrial Court decided that it did not have the power to abolish Saturday morning banking, BOAWA asked Johnson to try again. In an attempt to forestall upper house rejection, the Labor government established a select committee. After taking copious evidence, a majority of the committee recommended that the Bank Holidays Act be amended to make every Saturday a bank holiday in the state,[25] but the upper house again rejected the amendments. The party political nature of debate and the continued eagerness of some politicans to view all banking issues emotively are evidenced by a Liberal member's conjecture that he "would be interested to know whether there [was] any connection between a move such as this and the ultimate nationalization of the trading banks".[26]

In mid-1957 Johnson returned to the fray, with BOAWA eagerly joining the political battle by providing members with addresses of all parliamentarians, along with instructions to maintain the pressure.[27] Again after passing quickly through the lower house it was rejected in the upper house. Some angry union members then suggested that in the next state elections BOAWA should organize active support for the party that included the five-day week in its electoral platform. This clearly meant support for the Labor Party, and a resolution to this effect was only narrowly defeated at a general meeting late in 1957. Here was confirmation of some change in bank employee attitudes, similar to that discerned by Williams in Victoria. Certainly bank officers were still relatively conservative, both industrially and politically; nevertheless, it was now clearly possible to arouse their militancy and antagonism by reminding them of the shortcomings of their employment. In Western Australia, as in the ABOA, leadership skills were important, not in stimulating unrest but rather in publicizing grievances and co-ordinating the resulting campaigns.

A little earlier the SBSA-dominated South Australian Five Day Week Committee had vainly approached Liberal premier Thomas Playford with a proposal to work Friday evenings in lieu of Saturday mornings. They then asked the leader of the opposition to sponsor amendments as Johnson had done in Western Australia. This angered the BOASA executive, who felt it was "an insult to the intelligence and political integrity of bank officers to suggest that they would be prepared to sell their votes to gain some personal benefit".[28] Members of the state's BNSW sub-branch also recoiled at this proposed link with the Labor Party, which, they considered, sought to destory them "by means of nationalization or strangulation of private trading banks".[29] However, encouraged by rank-and-file agitation, including that of many trading bank officers, the Five Day Week Committee pressed on with numerous media releases and frequent approaches to politicans of both major parties. Many BOASA members were dissatisfied with their union's non-involvement, and they finally forced a plebiscite. A total of 70 per cent of ballots issued were returned, and 96 per cent of these favoured the abolition of Saturday morning banks and called for BOASA's direct involvement in the campaign.[30] Chastened, BOASA then grudgingly provided delgates for the Five Day Week Committee, as long as the committee first approached Liberal politicians. No government member, however, would sponsor appropriate amendments, and the committee finally turned to D. A. Dunstan, member for Norwood in the lower house. In August 1957 he presented a bill,[31] but it was defeated on party lines.

BOASA was now in an awkward position, for members of the South Australian branch of the ABOA were already receiving Saturday morning penalty rates. Additionally, there were strong rumours that the ABOA was about to try to extend its coverage to South Australia private bank officers. Given BOASA's miserable industrial record and the existence of Saturday morning penalty rates in the ABOA award, BOASA leaders understandably feared their membership's reaction to ABOA overtures. Hesitantly they made one of their infrequent approaches to the banks and were pleasantly surprised when the banks agreed to pay penalty rates. Important to the banks' decision was concern that they "should not un-necessarily jeopardise the position of the South Australian Association [BOASA] by running the risk that the ABOA's application for extension of ambit [would] be successful".[32] The banks' anxiety to preserve the malleable and conservative BOASA leadership was yet another reflection of concern at the ABOA's growing militancy.

These increased operating costs in another state finally convinced the banks to reject continuing retailer pressure and to support Saturday closure. Accordingly they asked Premier Playford to expedite appropriate legislative change. The question of electoral success was also not unim-portant, for as Ewing had written to Williams: "With a very slender majority, at least four vulnerable seats, and the elections only four months away it is still possible that we may succeed."[33] Then after the Five Day Week Committee hinted they would recommend bank officers support the Labor Party, which had already promised to abolish Saturday banking, Playford acted. To lessen the wrath of other state governments, he elicited a meaningless promise from the committee that other ABOA and CBOA branches would not regard the amendment as a precedent. Then when Dunstan again introduced an amendment to close banks on Saturdays, the way was left open for Playford to propose a further amendment that banks should remain open on Friday evenings until five o'clock.[34] The amendments passed smoothly through both houses, the strong support given them in the upper house by Sir Arthur Rymill, chairman of the Bank of Adelaide, reflected the changed bank attitudes resulting from the introduction of penalty rates. Saturday morning branch closure was delayed while the private banks negotiated with the Commonwealth Bank for the closure of its agencies on Saturday mornings. The Commonwealth Bank had claimed that these were conducted in post offices and private businesses and so should not be forced to close. Finally on Saturday, 9 January 1960, all banks doors in South Australia remained closed.

In Western Australia, Johnson, after yet another attempt to have the Bank Holidays Act amended, had lost his seat in the 1959 state elections. The victorious Liberal premier further dimmed BOAWA's optimism by agreeing only to include the matter on the agenda for the next Premier's Conference, and the abolition of Saturday banking in that state seemed as far away as ever. But late in 1960 the state government underwent a surprising change of heart. Influenced by events in South Australia and constantly harried by editor J.J.Williams in the *Westralian Banker*, they offered a compromise. If the union would agree to give up two statutory holidays, the government would guarantee suitable legislative change. As the first of these holidays — Coronation Day, was celebrated on the same day as another public holiday, and the second was one which had not been observed for twenty-five years, the union had little to lose, and the Bank Holidays Amendment Bill was enacted in September 1961.[35]

Before the 1958 Queensland elections, Country Party leader, Frank Nicklin promised if elected to introduce the five-day week. Following his party's success, this proved rather embarrassing, for the UBOA of Q and the CBOA immediately demanded he fulfil his promise. In the meantime retail traders had mounted a strong campaign of opposition to Saturday morning closing. The Queensland government then sought a way out of their predicament by asking the state Industrial Court to inquire into the issue. Their recommendation that trading banks should close but savings banks remain open on Saturday morning posed administrative and staff problems for the private banks, whose branches now conducted both forms of banking. This together with the continued strenuous opposition of retail and commercial employers prevented any immediate action on the recommendation. However, J.D.Herbert, a former ES&A officer and UBOA of Q committeeman who was now in the parliament, lobbied his Liberal and Country Party colleagues before a joint party meeting which Premier Nicklin insisted must approve any legislative change. This together with Herbert's advice to the union that country branch managers should assuage the fears of Country Party members was sufficient, and Saturday closing legislation was passed in March 1961.[36]

Consistent with its post-war torpor, the UBOA of NSW did not show any active support for Saturday closing until the late fifties, and even then it was the New South Wales division of the CBOA which led the way. Once into the fray, however, the union showed unusual determination, even encouraging rank-and-file involvement. Card almost incredulously wrote: "When our campaign was fully mounted with the 'rank and file' massing in behind the spearhead, the opposition we had so long met from a few calamity howlers in the early days suddenly collapsed. . . . if we band together and really fight together instead of leaving the job to the other fellow, we become a force that is very hard to stop."[37]

Early in 1960 the New South Wales Five Day Week Committee received a favourable reaction from the chief secretary, C. A. Kelly, and the Liberal opposition leader, R. W. Askin, a former Rural Bank officer and UBOA of NSW executive member. The committee circularized all bank staff, urging support for a five-day week, and more than twelve thousand letters arrived at Parliament House.[38] This, plus the results of an earlier conference with bank representatives which indicated that the banks approved of Saturday morning closing, provided the committee with ample ammunition to approach the chief secretary again, and he agreed to prepare legislation. After delays caused by a referendum to decide the future of the Legislative Council and the stout resistance of retailers, the legislation eventually passed smoothly through both houses,[39] and on Saturday 13 January 1962, New South Wales banks opened their doors for the last time on Saturdays. Though the involvement of the media had been considerably less than in Victoria, the union executives' pleasure was tempered by some press criticism: "There was no public demand for the change, quite the reverse. Only the bank officers wanted it, and they were shrewd enough to play the politicians off against each other. . . . they ignored the fact that if workers in other service industries had adopted and enforced the same selfish attitudes urban life would come to a halt at weekends."[40]

Lesser men than Williams and Foster may have been bitter at this apparent travesty of justice – that all state unions had now obtained the five-day week. Over the years it had been these unions which had shown little industrial awareness, had failed to activate or respond to rank-and-file interests, and increasingly had relied on the ABOA winning salary increases which were then incorporated into state awards. But the ABOA leadership spent no time on recriminations; rather, they set about analysing the key to the state unions' success. Central to this had been growing bank support for Saturday closing, very much a function of increased costs of Saturday operations. As this was also true of Victorian banks, the answer clearly lay in the political sphere. In Queensland and New South Wales the state

Labor governments had been sympathetic to arguments for Saturday closing, and in South Australia and Western Australia the unions had been able to exploit a volatile electoral situation.

An examination of the Victorian scene revealed an apparently bleak future for Saturday closing, for certainly in the short run these favourable political elements were missing. The Liberal government was comfortably ensconced, with a sound majority in each house. In addition, Premier Bolte's personal animosity towards Williams and his legendary intransigence contrasted with the pragmatism of South Australian and Western Australian premiers. An extra barrier was the resistance of retail traders, whose influence over the state government was apparently considerable and who certainly had a compliant press available to promote and publicize their opposition. Melbourne, the commercial capital of Australia, seemed determined to defend Saturday morning banking. The ABOA leadership knew that to succeed they must muster all the rank and file's latent militancy in an extension of a now blatantly political campaign.

A Tough Battle in Victoria

The ABOA's final drive for the five-day week had started in 1961, which was a state election year in Victoria. Union determination was sharpened by the refusal of Premier Bolte to reappoint Williams as a commissioner of the State Savings Bank, a position he had held for fourteen years. This was nothing more than a venting of political spleen, for though originally a political appointee, Williams had since brought the same capacities to this job as to his union work. Trenchant criticism by the ABOA only increased the premier's obstinacy and set him on a collision course with the union.

The new campaign began with a huge meeting which demanded legislative change and overwhelmingly resolved that "officers be requested to support candidates whose Party [would] undertake to introduce legislation".[41] In the following weeks a fighting fund was established, numerous well-attended country meetings were held, and political parties were approached. The ALP eagerly agreed to legislate if elected, but the Country Party, hopeful of forming a coalition government with the Liberals, refused to be committed. Premier Bolte was in a quandary; on the one hand there was the insistence of retail traders who were traditional Liberal supporters that he must not relent, and on the other Williams's rather convincing argument: "There are in round figures 15,000 bank officers in Victoria. With their wives, families, adult sons and daughters, fathers and mothers, their minimum voting potential must be 30,000. Add friends and this could double, 60,000 nearly an average of 1,000 votes in each state electorate. These are really compelling statistics to those in marginal seats."[42] Bolte stalled for time by seizing on an earlier union statement that the abolition of Saturday morning banking in New South Wales was imminent. He pointed out the competitive disadvantage that Victorian industry would face should his government amend banking hours before New South Wales, and glibly invited the committee to get in touch with him again when this undertaking had been fulfilled. "The Victorian Government will be prepared to have your request re-examined," he said.[43]

In the months leading up to the election, Bolte frequently reiterated that Saturday banking would be abolished in Victoria when New South Wales did likewise. At an election meeting in the Prahran Town Hall he told a group of querulous bank employees, "You boys have nothing to worry about – you will get the five day week as soon as New South Wales does."[44] Soon after the Liberals were comfortably returned to power, and with news that legislation was about to be submitted to the New South Wales Parliament, the committee confidently reapproached the premier. His response that they must now wait for the New South Wales legislation to be enacted and that any further publicity would only harm the union's claim was chastening. Only his reassurance that "it would be an untenable position if Victoria were to be the odd state out with banking days different to those of the rest of the states",[45] stifled the rank and file's anger. By December 1961 the New South Wales legislation had been passed and the committee again met Bolte. He was more than equal to the occasion: "Having in mind that Parliament will be rising in the very near future . . . there is no prospect of introducing the appropriate legislation into Parliament at this juncture."[46]

Outraged by this duplicity, bank officers flocked to a rowdy meeting. A number of speakers urged direct action, but the committee's recommendation that the government be given one more chance to legislate was finally adopted, though only after assurances were given that if satisfaction was not achieved, a ballot on direct action would be taken. Committee president Quirk also produced a statutory declaration detailing Bolte's earlier promise that bank officers would get the five-day week when New South Wales officers did, as a counter to press reports that the premier denied having made such a promise.[47] Even sections of the daily press now approved of the proposed change. The ABOA, pleasantly surprised by this unexpected support, made much of an *Age* editorial comment:

> The Premier [Mr. Bolte] is showing a strange reluctance to face the facts on the bank staffs' claim for a five day banking week. . . . since the principle of no Saturday work in banks has been established in every other state, Victoria can hardly stand out any longer. . . . it may be regrettable that another service to the public will disappear, but the bank staffs have a just claim to a five day week. . . . the Government should face the facts and give a firm assurance to bank staffs that it will introduce the necessary legislation as soon as possible.[48]

In February 1962 the banks gave a further boost to the campaign by publicly declaring their support for the abolition of Saturday banking and its replacement with later closing on Friday evening.[49] This was forced by increased administrative expenses and wage costs resulting from penalty rates, together with almost incessant ABOA press statements, and the ever-growing restiveness of their employees. Again the opposing forces rallied, but now without the banks' support they were forced into the open. Melbourne's lord mayor, Maurice Nathan, used the still readily accessible columns of the *Herald* to warn Victorians of the dangers of Saturday closing.[50] Williams cynically noted: "Cr. Nathan's appeal would have carried more weight as a disinterested action were it not for the fact that he is Managing Director of Patersons . . . a large Bourke Street store."[51] Other retail traders' associations, the Victorian Employers' Federation, and the Chamber of Commerce also spoke out and wrote to any media outlet prepared to support them. The *Herald* had made much of Gallup Poll results which showed that 80 per cent of the Victorians sampled wanted savings banks to stay open on Saturday morning, and 77 per cent wanted trading banks to do likewise.[52] After criticizing the nature of the poll, the ABOA turned it to their own ends. The nation-wide poll showed that in Tasmania, where the five-day week had now operated for years, only 15 per cent wanted the banks to reopen on Saturdays, a sure sign, the union claimed, that Saturday closing did not inconvenience the public.[53]

Bolte's dilemma worsened after he reluctantly took a proposal before the parliamentary Liberal Party only to see it soundly rejected. Yet another deputation was told that he was "surprised and disappointed. He would go to the Party again, but not until he was sure of sufficient support to win the issue."[54]

In early April 1962 the issue was again rejected by government members. With Victorians now the only bank employees still working on Saturday mornings, and with Bolte about to leave on a lengthy overseas trip, drastic action was needed. The committee organized a mass meeting on the steps of Parliament House after work on 7 April. More than six thousand employees attended this "organized walk" and "bank men and girls from all the Melbourne city offices and many from suburbs streamed in their thousands through the peak traffic".[55] An impromtu meeting was held in the Treasury Gardens, which forced the adjournment of parliament. The premier refused to address the noisy crowd, but opposition leader C.P. Stoneham did so. After all union speakers had advised caution about taking direct action, it was moved: "Having explored every conciliatory avenue known to us over a period of sixteen years to try and obtain this reform, we now declare that, should there be no definite assurance that five day week legislation will be introduced into the Parliament of Victoria this session, there is no alternative but to take direct action, and we pledge our support for a stoppage of work."[56] This resolution, accepted with wild enthusiasm and without a single dissenter, marked yet another stage in the militancy of bank employees.

Though Premier Bolte's reply was non-committal, he convinced the party to institute a board of inquiry to be headed by O. J. Gillard, QC. The committee's indignation at further delay was supported by the *Age*.

> The stock of pretences for procrastination has dwindled to the shabbiest and thinnest of all. Suddenly the State L.C.P. has decided that there are not enough facts on which to base a decision. So after 15 years in which sufficient fact, information and opinion to fill a library have accumulated, a board of inquiry is to be established. By accepting the party room recommendation the Government is accepting a subterfuge. Experience, not only in Australia, but overseas shows that a five day bank week is practicable and convenient.[57]

The unions were also angry that they had not been involved in establishing the inquiry's terms of reference, which, they claimed, were heavily loaded in favour of business interests, who had helped the acting premier, Arthur Rylah, draw them up. The ABOA decided to boycott the inquiry and Rylah, anxious to resolve the politically embarrassing issue, offered to amend the terms of reference. Federal Council, drawing strength from the tough-talking Victorian branch, spurned this, recommended a ban on all Saturday work after 19 May 1962, and called upon the CBOA and the SSBOA to support them.[58] While the latter unions decided on a plebiscite to confirm this action, the ABOA leadership, confident that the rank and file were now sufficient angry to take direct action, decided that a plebiscite was unnecessary. Reinforcing their determination was the response of other blue- and white-collar unions who offered help with pamphlet distribution and picketing. The Victorian division of ACSPA called a special meeting to pledge its support, and the Melbourne Trades Hall Council also declared its support for the ban,[59] a statement that worried some older and more conservative ABOA members.

The banks, now under direct threat of a work stoppage, could no longer equivocate, although they hoped that the federal treasurer would solve the problem by declaring Saturday a bank holiday under section 68 of the Banking Act. They sent letters to all staff pointing out that the banks were legally compelled to open on Saturday mornings and stressing the need for staff co-operation and loyalty.[60] They also warned of the implications of direct action. The general manager of the ANZ concluded: "I look to each and every member of the staff to have no part in strike action or to seek to achieve a quite desirable reform by employing means which will lower the standing of the bank officer and will leave a stigma for years to come."[61] He asked employees to declare in advance whether or not they would work on 26 May, and managers were instructed to report to head office any staff who were absent, "the obvious implication being that they would suffer in their employment for loyalty to their Association".[62] With many politicians now seeking to make political capital, A. A. Calwell, leader of the federal opposition, claimed that "this crude pressure banks were putting on their staffs could sow the seeds of future bitterness and leave a legacy of hate and suspicion".[63]

It was now clear that both the state government and the banks were relying upon the Gillard Inquiry results to provide a way out of the impasse, and as it was likely that the union would be subpoenaed to appear anyway, the union removed its boycott. In a tactical move the ABOA, the only union in the committee with access to an industrial tribunal, applied to the Arbitration Commission for implementation of a five-day working week. They also asked that any Saturday work be regarded as overtime, payable at double rates and for a minimum of four hours. With hearing of this claim set down for 24 May, the union decided to defer the work ban planned for the following Saturday, which Williams assured members was "not backing away from the issue, but giving the processes of discussion one last chance".[64] Soon after the hearing began, Commissioner Portus adjourned to allow the parties to confer privately. Here Williams and Foster expanded on a number of proposals for Saturday closure which the banks agreed to consider. But the following week they advised the ABOA that their counsel believed that these would still require legislative amendment.

In the meantime, the Gillard Inquiry had heard evidence from fifty witnesses.[65] Although much of the retailers' evidence retraced now familiar paths, there were some fascinating sessions. In one of these, Lord Mayor Nathan, ostensibly speaking on behalf of the City Council and the citizens of Melbourne, but upon questioning found to be representing only his own commercial interests, had his arguments closely scrutinized in a joint attack by Williams and Drew Aird, the ABA's counsel. While awaiting the inquiry's results, Williams and Foster, knowing that a favourable decision must still be supported by legislative amendment, strove to maintain the campaign's momentum. They warned: "Employing bodies have said outright that this is more than just a battle for an industrial reform for bank officers in Victoria, should we fail then other reactionary efforts will follow."[66]

In late July the inquiry's results were announced, and it was recommended that Victorian banks close on Saturday mornings and remain open until 5.30 p.m. on Friday evenings.[67] After largely dismissing the likelihood of "public inconvenience", the decision emphasized the importance of a common commercial practice throughout Australia: "Officers in Victoria are of the same skill, qualification and standard as in other states and employed by the same employers in doing the same banking work in the same form of organisation as in other parts in Australia, and industrially there appears to be no sound reason for treating them differently in Victoria."[68] As a result of this, the Liberal and Country Party parliamentary parties agreed in September 1962 to legislate in principle for the abolition of Saturday morning banking, subject to the banks agreeing to close later on Fridays, either at 5.30 or 6.00 p.m. The unions, however, favoured 5.00 p.m. closing, and, surprisingly, so did the banks. Not only did they desire uniformity with other states for administrative reasons, but also because of the number of time-consuming tasks that could only be done after the branches closed. Williams reminded those unionists touched by the banks concern for them that under the existing award, meal allowances had to be paid to all officers working after 6.10 p.m.

Following conferences between the government, the committee, and the ABA, it was finally agreed that branches would shut on Saturday mornings, would open at 9.30 a.m. rather than 10 a.m. on weekdays, and would close at 3.00 p.m. Mondays to Thursdays and at 5.00 p.m. on Fridays.[69] To cater for retailers' cash security, branches would accept locked cash bags for custody until 5.30 p.m. on Fridays. The State Savings Bank and the Commonwealth Bank agreed to these conditions, the legislation passed through both houses,[70] and on 5 January 1963, after years of frustration, Victorian bank officers worked their last Saturday morning.

Although the success or otherwise of the planned strike cannot be assessed, it is interesting to examine the effect of the proposal upon union membership. In the month following 10 May, when the Saturday work ban was first mooted, 265 new members (an additional 4.6 per cent) joined the Victorian branch.[71] There was no membership drive under way, and this flow of new members must be seen as a sign of approval of the union's activities. Foster certainly was totally convinced. "The Association is strengthened quantitatively and qualitatively by these events."[72] The abolition of Saturday morning banking had been an issue of real importance to the bank officer; it had been denied them by employers, the Arbitration Commission, and the federal and state governments. The campaign's events, disappointments, and successes were important factors in the growing militancy and aggressiveness of the ABOA rank and file. The ABOA leadership demonstrated continuing skill in mobilizing and channelling it into organized industrial conflict. The culmination of this in work stoppages and a strike is pursued in a later chapter.

Notes

1. Earlier there had been some discussion after the Tasmanian Labor government had in 1937 enacted legislation compelling the Saturday morning closure of most shops and offices in Hobart and Glenorchy, since when at least some ABOA members had enjoyed the luxury of a five-day week.
2. *Age*, 16 March 1948, p. 3.
3. *Bankers Journal* 9, no. 3 (Mar. 1949): 5.
4. Letter to ABA, reproduced in the *Bankers Journal* 9, no. 5 (May 1949): 2.
5. Letter from acting chairman of the ABA to the ABOA, 19 May 1949, in ABOA archives. Laidlaw later summed this up as "Bourke Street [i.e., the retail traders] cracking the whip over Collins Street [i.e., the bankers] and the bankers had to submit" (*Queensland Bank Officer* 31, no. 8 [Oct. 1950] : 1).

6. See "New Campaigns and Tactics" in chapter 6.
7. *Bankers Journal* 9, no. 9 (Sept. 1950): 19.
8. *Westralian Banker* 27, no. 3 (Mar. 1952): 3.
9. Bank Holidays Act Amendment Bill 1952, *Western Australia Parliamentary Debates*, vol. 131, p. 877.
10. *SABOJ* 30, no. 4 (Nov. 1952): 55.
11. BOASA minutes, 16 September 1953, p. 211.
12. *Bankers Journal* 15, no. 4 (June 1955): 8.
13. A claim the ANZ Bank estimated would cost them more than £300,000 a year if settled in the ABOA's favour (general manager ANZ to London, letter no. 56, 13 July 1956, in ANZ archives).
14. *Australian Bank Officials Association* v. *Australian and New Zealand Bank and Ors* (86 CAR 163).
15. Ibid., p. 165.
16. *Australian Bank Officials Association* v. *Australia and New Zealand Bank and Ors* (86 CAR 569).
17. Ibid., p. 573.
18. *Australian Bank Officials Association* v. *Australia and New Zealand Bank and Ors* (88 CAR 598).
19. From records in ABOA archives.
20. General manager of ANZ to London, private series no. 20/1958, 3 March 1958, letter in ANZ archives.
21. Ibid., no. 77/1958, 17 October 1958, letter in ANZ archives.
22. *Bankers Journal* 18, no. 3 (Apr. 1958): 1.
23. Ibid., 20, no. 8 (Aug. 1960): 4.
24. *Westralian Banker* 30, no. 10 (Oct. 1955): 7.
25. Report of Select Committee to Inquire into the Hours Worked in the Banking Industry, reprinted in the *Westralian Banker* 31, no. 10 (Oct. 1956): 5–11.
26. Bank Holidays Amendment Bill, *Western Australian Parliamentary Debates*, vol. 144, 14 November 1956, p. 2242.
27. *Westralian Banker* 32, no. 7 (July 1957): 7.
28. *SABOJ* 33, no. 8 (Mar. 1956): 7.
29. Ibid.
30. BOASA minutes, 17 March 1957, p. 2.
31. Holidays Act Amendment Bill, *South Australian Parliamentary Debates*, 21 August 1957, p. 410.
32. ANZ Staff Department Memo, 3 February 1958, in ANZ archives.
33. Ewing to Williams, 10 September 1958, letter in ABOA archives.
34. Holidays Act Amendment Bill, *South Australian Parliamentary Debates*, 15 October 1958, p. 1217.
35. Bank Holidays Act Amendment Act, *Western Australian Parliamentary Debates*, 3 October 1961, p. 1423.
36. Holidays Act Amendment Act, *Queensland Parliamentary Debates*, 21 March 1961, p. 2889.
37. *Banker* 20, no. 4 (May 1960): 7.
38. Ibid., no. 2 (Mar. 1960): 21.
39. Banks and Bank Holidays (Amendment) Act, *New South Wales Parliamentary Debates*, 12 November 1961, p. 2119.
40. *Sydney Morning Herald*, 8 January 1962, p. 2.
41. *Bankers Journal* 21, no. 2 (Apr. 1961): 2.
42. Ibid., p. 23.
43. Letter from H. E. Bolte to ABOA, 1 May 1961, reproduced in the *Bankers Journal* 21, no. 4 (June 1961): 6.
44. *Bankers Journal* 21, no. 5 (Aug. 1961): 3.

45. Report of meeting between premier and ABOA, 4 October 1961, in the *Bankers Journal* 21, no. 7 (Oct. 1961): 6.

46. Letter from H. E. Bolte to Five Day Week Committee, 29 October 1961, reproduced in the *Bankers Journal* 21, no. 8 (Nov. 1961): 7.

47. Statutory declaration of J. H. Quirk dated 4 December 1961, reproduced in the *Bankers Journal* 22, no. 1 (Feb. 1962): 10.

48. *Age*, 7 December 1961, p. 2.

49. *Bankers Journal* 22, no. 2 (Mar. 1962): 5.

50. See, for example, *Herald*, 6 February 1962, p. 1.

51. *Bankers Journal* 22, no. 2 (Mar. 1962):29.

52. *Herald*, 1 March 1962, p. 2.

53. *Bankers Journal* 22, no. 2 (Mar. 1962): 30.

54. Report of deputation to Premier Bolte, 17 Mar 1962, in *Bankers Journal* 22, no. 4 (June 1962): 6. This prompted Federal Council to resolve that "Mr. Bolte, having failed to redeem a definite promise and now relying on the fact that the LCP Parliamentary Party has overruled him should take the honorable course and resign his office as Premier and Leader of the LCP" (FCM, 27 May 1962, p. 296).

55. *Bankers Journal* 22, no. 4 (June 1962): 8.

56. Ibid., p. 9.

57. *Age*, 3 May 1962, p. 2.

58. FCM, 9 May 1962, p. 311.

59. Melbourne Trades Hall Council Minutes, 17 May 1962, p. 2.

60. The ABOA sought legal opinion on the banks' responsibility. This opinion, that any legal obligations under the Bills of Exchange Act could quite simply be removed by the actions of the banks themselves, was then used to try and influence the banks to oppose the implementation of the inquiry.

61. General manager of ANZ to staff, 16 May 1962, copy in ABOA archives.

62. *Bankers Journal* 22, no. 4 (June 1962): 10.

63. *Bankers Journal* 22, no. 3 (May 1962): 11.

64. ABOA letter to all members, May 1962, copy in ABOA archives.

65. Williams had encouraged Alan Tymms, president of the SSBOA, to lead the union case. He was a strong amalgamation advocate, and Williams wanted to boost his prestige in the SSBOA and so increase the chances of them joining the ABOA.

66. *Bankers Journal* 22, no. 4 (June 1962): 13. In both New South Wales and Queensland there was considerable interest in Victorian events, and both journals carried regular chronicles of these. Though one would be tempted to believe that this new-found enthusiasm for ABOA actions was a result of fresh union thinking, it is much more likely that the state unions were fearful that the inquiry's rejection of the five-day week concept would encourage further attempts in their own states for a return to Saturday morning banking (see, for example the, *Queensland Bank Officer* 44, no. 5 [July 1962]: 2).

67. *A Board of Inquiry on The Five Day Banking Week in Victoria* (Melbourne: Government of Victoria, 1962).

68. Ibid., p. 89.

69. The earlier opening was to be for a trial period of twelve months but lasted until a concerted industrial campaign brought about its end in 1978.

70. Bank Holidays (Saturday) Act, *Victorian Parliamentary Debates*, 12 September 1962, p. 100.

71. Appendix 3 and ABOA Victorian division records.

72. *Bankers Journal* 22, no. 4 (June 1962): 13.

8   An Australia-Wide Union at Last

There is no line of demarcation in our business as bankers, therefore there can really be no separation in our interests. No state is self contained as far as the lives of bank officers are concerned, because the man of Kalgoorlie may next month find himself at Newcastle or Townsville. The ideals of bank officers are greater than sectionalism.

> [From L.P. Harrisons's address to Victorian,
> Tasmanian, and New South Wales bank
> officers in *Australian Banker* 1, no. 1
> (Sept. 1924): 1]

This is madness! Australian bank employees are represented by five separate unions (if that is what you could call those to the north of here). Only the ABOA has anything resembling industrial muscle — that is why the others now dwell on our every move. There is little co-operation, just a lot of jealousy, bickering and dilly-dallying. It's a wonder the banks don't make mincemeat of the lot of us.

> [R.D. Williams to S.V. Barratt, 3 June 1954]

From the inception of Australian banking unionism, the amalgamation or "federation", of the several unions into one Australia- wide union had been a goal frequently discussed and pursued by the ABOA. The ABOA's early bumbling attempts to take over the state unions have already been discussed. There were two major impediments to amalgamation: (a) the state unions' belief that their tribunals provided superior salaries and conditions, and (b) the determination of incumbent union secretaries to retain their autonomy, power, and influence. Problems of causality make analysis of the first impediment difficult. In earlier years the willingness of various state Labor governments to influence the composition of industrial tribunals and to intervene directly to introduce favourable legislation supported the state unions' views.[1] However, by the midfifties the ABOA's aggressive pursuit of members' interests and the development of ACSPA and its "margins" campaigns, together with the inertia and incompetence of the UBOA of NSW, meant that bank officer initiatives and gains were now largely attributable to the ABOA.

The extent of union leader antipathy, distrust, and jealousy has frequently been mentioned. Williams, in speculating on amalgamation overtures to the UBOA of NSW, commented, "I feel positive that any initial approach on this important but touchy matter should come from one of the States who could not be branded as desiring something for their own ends . . . I agree with you, personalities must be out . . . For my Association or for me to pursue it too persistently at this stage would only raise unnecessary barriers".[2]   The dramatic post-war changes in ABOA philosophy and actions intensified these interstate rivalries, and the union's militancy, success, and growing rank-and-file support resulted in state union leaders becoming increasingly defensive and insecure. Until the late forties there had been only minimal interstate co-operation between unions, and then only when catastrophe loomed. Fault for this had not always lain at the door of state unions. Before the war, the ABOA's federal registration had continually reassured its leaders that any amalgamation would be carried out on its terms, with the state unions merely becoming ABOA branches. This attitude was frequently reflected in dictatorial and abrasive approaches to other unions and when coupled with the ABOA's lacklustre and complacent leadership, aborted all amalgamation attempts.

After the war, however, the increasing industrial expertise of the banks and their stronger resistance to union claims, together with the disappointing 1949 De Baun award in New South Wales, firmed the ABOA's resolve to work for greater co-operation and unity. Feelers were put out to the state unions, and branch presidents Hodson and Barratt assisted Williams to write a number of journal articles supporting amalgamation.[3] Barratt also used events of the ABOA 1953 federal conference, when branch representation was doubled, to assuage BOAWA and BOASA fears that their identities and interests would be submerged following an amalgamation. "There were many Victorians present . . . their readiness to consider the interests of smaller and weaker members is the outstanding prerequisite of a successful federation."[4]

In early 1953, confident that earlier ill-will had dissipated, the ABOA suggested to BOASA that they amalgamate with the South Australian branch. To forestall objections, they advocated fresh branch elections, and told Cook that branch secretary Ewing would step aside for him. BOASA could also retain its assets and most of its subscription revenue. But the ABOA was wrong, for the defection of SBSA officers obviously still rankled. "The ABOA must realise that New South Wales and Queensland have always been bitterly opposed to federation, and that South Australia and Western Australia, having once experienced its disadvantages, are not likely to be easily tempted to return."[5]   Williams, saddled with the sins and omissions of earlier years, could only plead, "To rely on something which happened thirty years ago as a reason for rejecting amalgamation today shows a lack of progressive thought — separate colonies in Australia were quite adequate in the horse and buggy era."[6]   Inhibited by a commitment given to the Arbitration Court not to recruit South Australian trading bank officers, the ABOA could do nothing more.

The issue again surfaced in 1954 at an interstate conference called to discuss the restoration of margins. The banks' refusal to negotiate prompted ABOA delegates to urge further consideration of a united approach through amalgamation. This was rejected by the other unions, and the ineffectual Commonwealth Council of Bank Officer Associations was reconstituted. But the ABOA refused to join and drew the wrath of other unions by issuing claims on the banks, which, the other unions complained, pre-empted their negotiations. The ABOA then sent a series of pamphlets to all Australian bank officers. Although these merely set out how bank officer margins had shrunk compared with those of blue-collar workers, the real intent of the ABOA was clear.[7] Convinced that the positive aspects of amalgamation had not been presented to rank-and-file unionists in other states, the ABOA used these pamphlets to imply just how ineffective and costly separate state unionism was. The response from state union leaders was predictable. Laidlaw was quick to question Williams's motives: "The move is for power and more power which could very possibly lead to the one organisation being eventually undermined by political or any such control. Members only have to read the press reports of the doings in other big unions to see how serious a position could obtain."[8]

Williams and Foster, frustrated by the state unions resistance, then decided on more direct action. In their next Arbitration Court case they succeeded in having the federal award extended to bank officers in the Australian Capital Territory and the Northern Territory. The reciprocal agreement with other unions relating to members transferring interstate was cancelled, and ABOA members were instructed to remain in the union rather than join the relevant state union upon transfer.

At the 1955 UBOA of NSW annual conference the president, McKell, increasingly worried by the ABOA attempts and incursions, delivered a paper attacking amalgamation on several grounds.[9] These included the logistical expense for state unions, the deleterious effects upon executive members' personal careers, and the loss of autonomy suffered by state unions.[10] McKell also emphasized the reduced decision-making power of institutional sub-branches and consequent inability to represent their members' interests adequately. He argued that a federally structured union would only be able to represent a homogeneous mass of employees and not take account of differences in conditions of employment between banks. But underlying all of this was the feared loss of state autonomy. It had been conceded that federal registration was a prerequisite of any viable amalgamation, and as the ABOA already held federal registration, state leaders worried that Williams and Foster would dominate the proposed new union. This was in spite of Williams's promise: "The ABOA is completely genuine in its aim of Federation. Although it possesses, by virtue of its registration in the Commonwealth Arbitration Court, an advantage, its Executive members are quite prepared to vacate office and permit a fresh election under the provisions of a mutually agreed constitution".[11]

Disturbed by the approval given McKell's attack, the ABOA decided to enlist the support of BOAWA, where there had been some signs of support.[12]   Foster went to Western Australia and, at a general meeting called to discuss the issue, stressed that state unions should retain local registration and use the local courts whenever appropriate.[13] Foster also pointed out that the major industry cases had been fought by the ABOA or the UBOA of NSW, the results then flowing to other state unions. He argued that this had not represented real autonomy anyway and concluded: "We ask you to help us to form an organisation in which the Western Australian bank officer will have a say and play his full part in deciding just what sort of a future we intend to seek."[14] The ABOA then agreed to obtain legal opinion on the technical problems involved in amalgamation.   This   opinion made it clear that amalgamation was straightforward,[15]   yet BOAWA's fear of the increasing militancy and aggression of the ABOA under Foster and Williams was still too great, and they eventually rejected the ABOA's proposal.

In 1956 similar discussions were held with BOASA. A highly critical report by the president, Wills, again concentrated on state union loss of autonomy: "Certainly we would have representation in such a body, but would our numerical strength allow us to be other than a weakening voice?[16] Foster's rebuttal of Wills's arguments was not printed in the South Australian journal, and it was not surprising that the South Australians refused to consider further amalgamation discussions. Yet another blow was the SSBOA's decision not to join the ABOA despite the strong links already forged in the five-day week campaign. On 9 October a small general meeting supported the motion of the SSBOA's secretary that it was not in their best interest to amalgamate with the ABOA.[17]

Again in 1958, encouraged by the SSBOA's continuing enthusiastic support for the abolition of Saturday banking, the ABOA suggested amalgamation. The SSBOA was to elect its own officers, retain its own assets, funds, and journal, and to negotiate its own salaries and conditions subject only to Federal Council approval. But again the ABOA was rebuffed, and the SSBOA's comment, "We await with interest the outcome of the log of claims recently served on the banks",[18] drew scathing criticism from Foster. This comment highlighted the SSB's recent practise of adjusting salaries in line with those in the private banking industry. This reversed the pattern of earlier years and led Foster to claim that the SSBOA was now riding on the ABOA's back:

The SSBOA is to a great extent linked with the Bank, and at least 95 per cent of its activity is devoted to sporting and social affairs. As a reader of *The Savings Weekly* for over thirty years, I have no hesitation in saying this, because more space is devoted to a visit of the management to country areas, or to a validictory social or to a football match in one issue than is devoted to industrial matters in the course of a whole year.[19]

The eagerness of Foster and Williams to have the SSBOA join the ABOA was not only based on a desire to increase membership. In spite of ineffectual leadership, the SSBOA's rank and file had given several indications of increasing though uncoordinated restiveness and resistance to their employers. The ABOA leaders saw this as complementing the attitudes of a large proportion of their own membership. In particular, amalgamation would improve chances of success in the five-day week campaign, now being waged at the political level, for the ABOA would be able to speak on behalf of all Victorian bank employees.

Relations with the UBOA of NSW worsened when the ABOA discovered that the New South Wales union had communicated with other state associations "suggesting a conference in Sydney to discuss the activities of the ABOA towards amalgamation",[20] and had not issued an invitation to the ABOA. Consequently by mid-1958, with the ABOA in seemingly irreconcilable conflict with the other banking unions, the prospect of one union covering all Australian private bank employees seemed more remote than ever. Yet within the space of a few years this had occurred.

The turning point came in December 1958 when the New South Wales Industrial Court handed down a new UBOA of NSW award.[21] This provided only minimal male scale increases, the female scale was unaltered because of pending state "equal pay" legislation, and allowance increases still only brought them up to the federal award level. Williams was quick to exploit this poor result:

The award completely explodes the myth that has erroneously built up the New South Wales Industrial Court and the De Baun determinations as the best standards for Australian bank officers. Until bank officers realise that united action through an Australia wide association is the only way to improve working conditions, they will continue to have these industrial "insults" hurled at them.[22]

Foster also chimed in to maintain the superiority of the federal award. He stressed the difficulties facing bank officers trying to win margin increases from the state courts and quoted Justice De Baun's observation when handing down the award: "I am afraid it is true right throughout industry . . . that through an inordinate increase in the base rate, people in the less skilled occupations have successded in having their remuneration increased at the expense of the people in the higher grades . . . There is simply nothing we can do about it."[23]

The banks then offered the ABOA the same miserly marginal increases as provided by the De Baun award. These were rejected out of hand, and the extensive and aggressive campaign discussed earlier was mounted. Using newly learned tactics, including mass meetings, strike threats, and extensive publicity, the ABOA in conjunction with ACSPA forced the banks to concede margin increases of more than 33 per cent, a remarkable achievement. The ABOA's top of scale salary became £1,470, compared with the UBOA of NSW's £1,300. The ABOA leaders' superior negotiating ability, their enthusiasm to involve the rank and file, and their willingness to use some industrial muscle were in striking contrast to the methods of the other state leaders. In the events that followed, this was to be crucial, for now a major argument of the state unions, that local court awards were superior to federal awards, was clearly invalid.

Significant leadership changes in some states also favoured amalgamation. BOAWA's new president, J. J. Williams, was by 1959 providing open support.[24] In South Australia the conservative and limited Wills and Cook had gone. The latter had been BOASA secretary when the SBSA officers broke away, and Wills had become president in 1951, largely on the basis of his earlier anti-nationalization activities. They had both been strong critics of the ABOA's increasingly militant approach and still bitterly complained about its foray into South Australia in 1949. In mid-1959 the new executive members, president K. R. Byerlee and secretary E. S. Johnson, supported moves for a plebiscite on amalgamation. Of the 1,603 replied, (67 per cent of the membership) − 1,533, or 96 per cent − favoured some form of amalgamation.[25] A committee formed of BOASA, South Australian branch of the ABOA, and ABOA representatives began developing proposals for discussion. However, these received scant attention from the UBOAs of New South Wales and Queensland who had already drawn up another set of guidelines designed to minimize ABOA influence. These emphasized that the role of the federal organization should be to "Determine the policy of the Federation in industrial matters relating to rates of pay, conditions of employment and hours of work, state association members would retain their own existence and registration; and whilst some general policy-making power was to exist, the federal organisation was to have no power of enforcement over recalcitrant state associations."[26]

Both the ABOA and BOAWA refused to co-operate with the new body, seeing it as of no more value than the other scorned interstate associations and conferences. Laidlaw, fearful and on the defensive, increased the tension when warning his members of the ABOA's motives, after they had

sent pamphlets throughout Australia outlining how they had won large
marginal increases. Laidlaw dredged up the familiar bank officer bogies of
involvement with blue-collar workers, the supposed links between ABOA
leaders and the Labor Party, and the prospect of being forced to strike.

> No doubt you have seen the latest bulletins issued by the Victorians.
> They seem to thrive on this dirty work. Who do they think we are? A
> lot of numbskulls to fall for this type of propaganda? Queenslanders are
> loyal to their Association which has done so much for them and which
> carries our confidence. These bulletins are only "commo" stuff to try
> and confuse the issue. They don't want unity — they want dictatorship
> — heaven help us if we ever get into their hands.[27]

In New South Wales in response to the poor De Baun award and the
ABOA's continuing pressure for amalgamation, the CBA sub-branch
decided to poll their members. The result, not mentioned in UBOA of
NSW minutes or journal, showed overwhelming support for some form
of unified industry union.[28]   Card and McKell were now having
difficulty containing the groundswell of dissatisfaction manifesting itself
as support for amalgamation. So the BNSW sub-branch's decision to
support amalgamation along ABOA lines was a body blow to the UBOA
of NSW executive, for they now had little choice other than to support
amalgamation. The important remaining questions in Card's and McKell's
minds were what type of amalgamation would result, what power and
authority would the resultant federated body have, and how could the
ABOA's influence best be minimized?

Amalgamation discussions continued at an interstate conference in April
1960, and the ABOA eventually convinced the other unions to poll
members as BOASA had done. Unionists were to be asked whether they
favoured "an Australian wide association of bank officer associations,
embracing all present bank officer organisations in Australia as state
branches, with appropriate registration in Commonwealth and State
Courts".[29] While this still left the question of the actual type of organization open, there were two important implications. BOAWA now openly
supported the ABOA and its type of amalgamation, with state unions becoming ABOA branches. Additionally, each state was now committed
to testing its members' feelings, and a positive reaction would necessarily
restrict McKell, Card, and Laidlaw's obstructionism.

BOAWA was the first to hold the plebiscite. Of the 2,145 papers issued,
1,588 — more than 96 per cent of the 1,650 returned — favoured amalgamation.[30]   The CBOA, which had participated in discussions to date,
was next;   their members convincingly opposed amalgamation.[31]   This
was surprising, because their 1958 Annual Conference had passed a
resolution supporting close liaison with other bank unions. However,
little more than lip service had been given to this, even inquiries from
other unions regarding Commonwealth Bank salaries and conditions re-

ceiving scant attention. Influential and conservative sections of the CBOA strongly advocated a "no" vote, and the wording of the question had been altered to give the impression that the independence, autonomy, and still superior bank salaries and conditions were threatened by amalgamation.

Voting in other states was delayed while the UBOA of NSW and UBOA of Queensland procrastinated by seeking legal advice on several issues. With success seemingly close, Williams and Foster were prepared to placate the state unions by also agreeing to wait. The first question asked was whether the banks could force extension of the federal award to cover all bank officers following amalgamation. The ABOA's legal adviser, J.H. Wootten, felt this was possible,[32] for once the new body had obtained a federal award, no state award could supplant it without the banks' consent. The second contentious point was whether state branches of a federal organization should, or could, retain their separate state registration. Wootten advised against this, because if the rules of the state and federal bodies varied, or if different office bearers existed in each body, factional disputes were possible.[33] This opinion further depressed McKell, Card, and Laidlaw, for they had still envisaged some type of loose "federation" that would allow them to retain their autonomy.

In early 1961 the remaining plebiscites were conducted. In New South Wales, 58 per cent of ballot papers issued were returned and 94 per cent of these favoured amalgamation; similarly in the ABOA, 64 per cent were returned and less than 2 per cent opposed the proposal.[34]   Most gratifying to Williams and Foster was the SSBOA result. President Brian Kincade and former president Alan Tymms, convinced of the need for amalgamation after their five-day week campaign experiences, had been active in the ballot preliminaries. Their membership returned 48 per cent of the issued voting papers, and 83 per cent favoured amalgamating with the ABOA.[35]

In Queensland, the procrastination and resistance continued. Much of Laidlaw's obstinacy arose from a fear that amalgamation would deprive the union of its treasured compulsory unionism clause if they were forced into the Arbitration Commission's jurisdiction.   This would be a considerable blow to the union leadership, who for years had relied upon compulsion rather than endeavour and industrial relations expertise to guarantee membership and finances. Laidlaw was also still suspicious of the ABOA leadership and continually stressed a preference for the Australian Council of Bank Officer Associations, an organization he knew could never be dominated by the ABOA. Both he and the president, W.T.Code, were increasingly irritated by the apparent approval of many UBOA of Queensland members for the ABOA's enthusiastic and aggressive approach which had recently brought them large salary increases as a result of the ABOA/ACSPA salary campaign. In May 1960, at a small general meeting, a group of these members, weary of the UBOA of Q's inaction and paternalism, resolved that the union donate five hundred pounds to the ABOA.[36] Desperate to prevent this, Code and Laidlaw obtained a solicitor's opinion questioning the legitimacy of such action. A special meeting was then called to rescind the resolution, but to the executive's dismay it merely confirmed the earlier decision.

Humiliated and resentful, the UBOA of Q leadership launched an all-out attack on the ABOA and amalgamation proposals, using all the union's resources to encourage a "no" vote. By the time the ballot was finally held in April 1961, Queensland officers had been convinced "federation" automatically implied loss of access to the state court, though few were clear why this would disadvantage them. Even so, the size of the negative vote was surprising and reflected the executive's uncharacteristic zeal. Of the 72 per cent of the voting papers returned, 87 per cent opposed unification.[37]

In mid-1961, with all bank unions other than the UBOA of Q and the CBOA supporting amalgamation in principle, an interstate conference was held to settle upon the form of organization. Foster outlined how the state unions could become branches of the ABOA. He was adamant that the ABOA would not countenance being dissolved and reregistered as a body covering all states. This would be administratively difficult and might allow the FCU, which was actively organizing in the general clerical area, to step into the breach and recruit temporarily non-unionized bank officers. Foster then dealt at length with some of the fears besetting the states. He showed that with the current structure of Federal Conference the states could out-vote ABOA representatives anyway.[38]

In the ensuing debate the ABOA was strongly supported by BOAWA delegates, while Card argued for the loose, non-binding type of federation long preferred by the UBOA of NSW. After considerable procedural manoeuvring, it was finally resolved (with the UBOA of NSW dissenting) that "there should be a Federal Association with branches in the States concerned, and to attain this position members of the present State Associations should join the ABOA, as the federal body, through the formation of branches in New South Wales, South Australia and Western Australia".[39] Conference concluded with what seemed to be an agreement that state associations other than Queensland would move rapidly to join the ABOA, while maintaining their present state registration and awards.

Six months elapsed before the unions met again. In the meantime several mechanical problems — capitation fees, conference representation, and the amalgamation of BOASA and the South Australian branch of the ABOA — had been solved. The New South Wales executive had done nothing while awaiting further legal advice on the retention of state registration. It waited also, one suspects, in the hope that some further barriers might arise. The logic and actions of Card and McKell over the whole issue are often difficult to understand. They had been strong amalgamation opponents for several years, yet it had been Card's motion at the 1960 conference that led to the holding of state plebiscites. Now with amalgamation looming they were again vocally opposed.[40] The New South Wales leaders realized that the concept of a non-binding "federation" was unlikely, and that it was logical that the federal office should be in Melbourne, where four of the six major trading banks had their head offices. So even had they been able to muster the numbers to win the chief executive positions, the centralization of activities in Melbourne would have been inconvenient.

In Queensland, interest in amalgamation had waned following the plebiscite results, and the UBOA of Q had held only observer status at the conferences just discussed. But Laidlaw had now retired in favour of his son, Ray, who though still opposed to unification with other states, lacked his father's deep-rooted dislike of the ABOA. Nor was he as obsessed with maintaining the parochial power base and its attendant comforts developed over so many years by Laidlaw senior. In the short run, Queensland's isolation was of little importance to amalgamation planning, for Card and McKell's ability to prevent Foster and Williams from appealing directly to the UBOA of NSW rank and file ensured a continuation of the stalemate.

However, amalgamation opponents had reckoned without the resourcefulness of BOAWA president J. J. Williams. Though he did not totally agree with the mechanics of amalgamation as proposed by the ABOA, his conviction that only a combined union approach could adequately protect and advance bank officer interests overrode this, and a bold tactic was devised. Aware that the banks now favoured a single federal award for all their employees, Williams forced their hand by issuing a log of claims. He felt sure that this would not only reflect the new spirit of the Western Australians but would break the deadlock. The banks replied:

> Formal service of this log or for that matter a log in any other state or restricted jurisdiction will almost certainly precipitate the service by the banks on all Associations of their staff of a federal log of claims designed to bring the whole of Australia within the scope of a Federal Award. In the circumstances it has occurred to us that it may suit your committee for the banks to meet representatives of all Bank Officer Associations rather than your committee alone.[41]

At one stroke the whole complexion of amalgamation manoeuvring had changed, for the employers had made it clear that they too supported and encouraged amalgamation.

The success of Williams's tactic was due to two factors. The ABA was concerned about the proliferation of awards and agreements in different jurisdictions. This not only created logistical problems, but, it was felt, still allowed the ABOA and the UBOA of NSW to build on awards from the other jurisdictions. With the growth of bank officer militancy in Victoria and Western Australia, it was feared that this "leap-frogging" effect could escalate. The relative militancy of the ABOA executive also concerned the ABA. Believing that amalgamation was inevitable and desirable, they were anxious to restrict the power and influence of Foster and Williams in the new body. They felt that if amalgamation took place on ABOA terms, and if the new body proved effective and viable, then the positions of Foster and Williams could only be strengthened. However, if the other more conservative state unions amalgamated and organized themselves quickly, they might have sufficient numbers to control the enlarged union. Accordingly, ABA representatives met informally with UBOA of Q committee members, chosen supposedly because of their lack of sympathy with the ABOA and current refusal to amalgamate. A letter from the UBOA of Q to the other banking unions outlines what happened:

> One of the Staff inspectors stated in so many words, and to which the other staff inspectors agreed — what we want is to form a strong and virile active Bank Officers Association and it is here where we are relying on the state branches of a federal organization to take over control and have an Association run by bank officers for the welfare of bank officers and not run for the benefit of one man with political ambition and greed.[42]

Proof of the changing attitude of Queensland's new union leadership was given by secretary R.K. Laidlaw's reply to the banks that they "were indignant to think that the banks wanted the State Associations to be their pawns in seeking the control of the ABOA for their own purposes."[43]

With the banks' intentions now clear, the state unions hastily summoned a conference, Foster and Williams attended and were emphatic that the ABOA would not oppose any bank move to extend the federal award Australia wide. They then withdrew, leaving the states (and the UBOA of NSW in particular) to ponder the realization that should the ABOA not contest the banks' move, then on the basis of legal advice it was unlikely that the states would be able to maintain separate registration, let alone separate state awards. However, a futile motion expressing opposition to federal award extension was accepted by unions other than BOAWA, and extensive criticism made of the ABOA. Williams tersely replied: "It is highly regrettable that workers' associations should be opposing one another, but the ABOA is a federal body with a federal award, and it would be a contradiction of its policy to do anything that might prevent the establishment of an Australia-wide association of bank officers.[44]

As expected and hoped for by the ABOA and BOAWA, the banks then served claims on all private trading bank officers in Australia.[45] This costly exercise intimidated and frightened the state unions and many of their members, both because of its harsh nature and implications. Among its provisions were those providing for the employment of part-time workers, restrictions on overtime eligibility and payments, and the reduction or abolition of a wide range of allowances. The salaries and conditions in the industry were to operate unchanged for five years "without alteration in favour of employees despite any changed circumstantes or enhancement in standards in other industries or awards".[46] The ABOA immediately called upon its members to ready themselves for battle, whilst Card vainly pleaded with the banks not to force amalgamation. In addition to fears already discussed, he was worried at the possible breakaway of Rural Bank of NSW employees. These officers operated under superior conditions to those in either state or federal awards, and Card feared that in order to retain these benefits they would choose to remain outside either jurisdiction. This would significantly reduce the membership of the UBOA of NSW, or if the worst came to the worst of the New South Wales division of the ABOA. Card asked the banks to remember the loyal service of bank officers and the crucial role they had played in defeating the bank nationalization legislation. He pleaded: "Now, after all this history, the banks turn on their loyal servants in New South Wales and treat them in a fashion that at a minimum is undignified and unprecedented, and in my view, a disgrace to the industry."[47]

The Queensland executive, now under direct threat, tried to rouse their membership to reject amalgamation again. Not only had the banks' log been issued "in order to shanghai them into the federal sphere"[48] but it was nothing less than an "attempt to nationalize members under a federal award".[49] Whether the membership knew this was an empty and irrelevant use of the dreaded nationalization threat is unknown, but this last-ditch attempt failed. Within a month the UBOA of Q's official posture had been changed and it had agreed to join the federal body. One reason for this change of heart lay in a legal opinion obtained by the UBOA of NSW.[50] According to this, the ABOA's decision not to oppose the banks' application for federal award extension taken in conjunction with its federal registration and the Australia-wide nature of private trading banking, would be sufficient to convince the Arbitration Commission that jurisdiction existed to hear the case. Resignedly the UBOA of NSW had sent notification to all members that the extension of the award would not be opposed and that they would now co-operate to build an enlarged federal union.[51] Amalgamation ABOA sytle was now certain, for the ABOA already had the support of BOAWA, BOASA and the SSBOA.

In December 1962 the ABA claims came before Commissioner Portus. After finding that an industrial dispute did exist between the ABA and the various unions, he turned to the question of whether a federal award could be applied to all private bank officers. Legal counsel for each union then assured the commissioner they would not oppose this action, and he stated his preparedness to bring down such an award. Shortly afterwards, when Williams announced that the SSBOA would also join the ABOA as a separate division, the amalgamation of Australian private bank officer unions was substantially complete. However, although the amalgamation and the form it would take were now determined, the actual entry of some state unions was considerably delayed while rule changes were made and administrative detail attended to.

Already Williams and Foster had established considerable authority over the new body. In part this was because they had prepared and were in charge of the current salary case, the newly amalgamated unions' first venture. But it was also apparent that they held superior administrative and tactical skills. One incident reflects their control and illustrates that though leaders in other states still held considerably less militant views, these were of little importance and would not unduly hinder union actions. In mid-1963, following lengthy and largely fruitless salary negotiations with the banks, the ABOA tried more direct tactics. A half-page advertisement was run in major daily newspapers in all states,[52] which argued that the banks' "miserly" 5 per cent margin increase offer would further swell already huge bank profits and in turn would allow the establishment of other profitable bank enterprises. It condemned the banks, who were "spearheading the attack on all the one million white collar workers in Australia by the attack on the salary rates of their own employees",[53] The advertisement concluded by urging bank officers to attend mass meetings to "demand salary justice in 1963". State union leaders were angry both because of the advertisement's content and because Williams had not even bothered to consult them. They claimed that this attack on the banks would alienate the public and make the transfer of members from state unions to ABOA divisions more difficult. BOAWA president Williams wrote to the *Westralian* repudiating much of the advertisement's content,[54] and there were a number of comments from disgruntled state union members. For example, from South Australia: "Please accept my resignation from the Association which I joined in 1920. Now that you have allied yourself with the Communists I feel I want no further part of your affairs. Like everyone else I want a salary rise but don't believe the way to get it is to try and whip up public feeling against the banks."[55]

The ABOA remained unperturbed that some state leaders believed their pre-amalgamation fears of ABOA dominance and militancy were already being realized. Williams and Foster were confident that most rank-and-file members still wanted unification, and having tasted the fruits of militancy would now not allow their state leaders to renege. More pragmatically, Williams knew the state unions had irretrievably tied their fortunes to those of the ABOA by abdicating responsibility for the preparation and presentation of the current case. Williams scornfully dismissed the grumbling criticism and reminded the other unions that at an earlier conference on salaries they had agreed that the ABOA had full discretion in the case. Typically, he then made capital from the situation: "This break in public relations between the Associations can only give satisfaction to the banks and lead to the jeopardising of the position of the bank officers' claims before the Arbitration Commission."[56] With this statement Williams simply closed the debate, leaving state union leaders in no doubt that they had indeed entered into an industrial pact and arena somewhat more rigorous than they had previously known.

Little seemingly remained other than for the state unions to formally become ABOA divisions. In June 1963, BOAWA president Williams became an ABOA member, heralding the entry of that union, followed shortly afterwards by the formation of the South Australian division of the ABOA. But there was still considerable delay in Queensland and New South Wales, in part owing to their desire to retain state registration. In Queensland there was also pressure to hold on to the compulsory unionism clause, and the rank and file received little encouragement to sign on as ABOA members.[57] Card and McKell did not have the compulsory unionism straw to grasp, but given the potential complexity and problems of a single organization operating under two sets of rules, and the possibilities of internal conflicts among these rules,[58] they still hoped for a last-minute reprieve. So it was not until 1966 that the UBOA of NSW finally joined the ABOA to complete the amalgamation. After more than forty-five years, the dreams of some of the pioneers of banking unionism had almost come true. There were now only two unions, the ABOA and the CBOA, representing Australian bank officers.

The important question of who would lead the ABOA remained to be resolved. Just before the admission of New South Wales members, federal secretary Williams and assistant secretary Sanders had been re-elected and did not have to face re-election for five years. This left the federal presidency, two vice-presidential positions, and the treasureship to be contested. Whichever group won these positions would hold the balance of power, and given the divergent attitudes of the two major divisions, Victoria and New South Wales, this outcome would be vital in determining whether the ABOA's aggressive tactics would continue. The elections took place at the 1966 Federal Conference, where for the first time all state divisions were officially represented. Again these elections reflected the superior organizational skills of the ABOA leaders. Foster had a comfortable victory over McKell for the federal presidency. This was an interesting result, for not only did he obtain the "hard core" support of Victorian, Tasmanian, and Western Australian delegates, but he also picked up a number of votes from Queensland and New South Wales delegates. These defections occurred despite the caucusing of the New South Wales delegates, who had agreed before the conference to support their own candidates. McKell and Kincade were elected vice presidents, and Remington added further to Victorian numbers by winning the treasurer's position. If union leadership was to be as important to future ABOA actions as it had been in the past, then a continuation, even extension, of its already forceful and militant approach could be expected.

The conservatives were not yet totally vanquished, and much of the balance of the conference was taken up with controversy over the extent and nature of ABOA militancy. Two issues had brought this to the fore. The first was the ABOA's affiliation with ACSPA and most particularly this latter organization's frequent critical statements on Australian involvement in the Vietnam War. Williams, secretary of both organizations, strongly defended ACSPA and the ABOA's affiliation with it, emphazing its co-ordinating ability and importance as a peak organization. Other delegates warned that its openly political statements were in contravention of the union's supposed, though recently ignored, non-political stance. A compromise resolution, that any ACSPA socio-political statements should be in line with the predetermined policies of its affiliates, was finally accepted. Williams and Foster were unperturbed and confident that white-collar militancy, some of it ideologically based, was now beginning to spread through other ACSPA affiliates. Consequently they did not feel that this conference resolution would unduly limit their plans to use ACSPA both as the spearhead of white-collar salary and condition improvements, and more idealistically, to improve the quality of Australian life.

The other debate concerned the possibility of strike action. This was prompted by the Victorian division's frequent discussion of direct action, and also because of events in Brisbane during Federal Conference. At a mass meeting called as part of the 1966 salaries campaign, Queensland members had an opportunity to hear the Foster and Williams duo at first hand. Foster's refusal to assure a questioner that stop-work meetings would not be held in banking hours, and Williams's statement that the ABOA would win salary increases at any cost, brought an excited and enthusiastic response. A motion from the floor that should negotiations fail then a stop-work meeting be held was passed by a large majority. Back in Conference the New South Wales delegates attacked Foster and Williams's "eloquent deception" and the stop-work resolution, querying whether, in the "cold light of the banking chamber", bank employees would in fact be willing to strike. McKell led the attack competently; instead of exploiting the emotive implications of bank employee stoppages concerning status, prestige, and employer loyalty, he argued that a stoppage at this stage would only play into the banks' hands. He claimed this would give them the opportunity to take the matter to the Arbitration Commission, from where few significant concessions had been obtained in recent times. Williams retorted that McKell's analysis assumed that direct action would fail and that employers would not concede and so force the ABOA to the commission. Though Conference was stalemated on the issue, an amendment to provide that secret ballots would be mandatory before striking was still defeated. It was then resolved that following the failure of conciliation and arbitration, direct industrial action could be taken where such was "initiated and/or approved by members in a practical form at the time the action [was] comtemplated".[59] Though few delegates other than Williams and Foster knew what it really meant, this was a significant victory for the proponents of militancy. While allowing for the expression of rank-and-file unrest, it still gave Federal Executive considerable flexibility in the timing of direct action and similar industrial tactics.

The advantages of amalgamation became apparent as the events of the turbulent later sixties unfolded. The ABOA had significantly increased its bargaining power, for its leaders could now confront the banks and the Arbitration Commission on behalf of all private and state bank employees. No longer would the timidity and lack of industrial strength of one union hamper the success of others. Also, although each division maintained its own leaders and secretariat, activities such as journal production, campaign co-ordination and operation, case presentation, and policy development were centralized. This not only made for greater efficiency but left the significant decisions in the hands of union leaders who had demonstrated a real capacity to extract concessions from the banks.

Notes

1. Two examples of this are the introduction of compulsory unionism in Queensland and a form of child endowment in New South Wales.
2. R. D. Williams to G. Throssell, 13 June 1951, copy in ABOA archives.
3. See, for example, *Bankers Journal* 11, no. 3 (Mar. 1951).
4. Annual report of South Australian branch of the ABOA, 1953, reprinted in the *Bankers Journal* 13, no. 10 (Nov. 1953): 12.
5. *SABOJ* 30, no. 8 (Mar. 1953): 113.
6. *Bankers Journal* 13, no. 3 (Apr. 1953): 2.
7. Pamphlets reprinted in the *Bankers Journal* 14, no. 9 (Dec. 1954): 7, and 15, no. 1 (Feb. 1955): 3.
8. *Queensland Bank Officer* 36, no. 12 (Feb. 1955): 4.
9. Reprinted in the *Banker* 15, no. 3 (Apr. 1956): 6–8.
10. BOASA had earlier echoed these sentiments and fears. "Distance and time would preclude direct state representation and would force us to rely on Victorian proxies" (*Bankers Journal* 13, no. 3 [Apr. 1953] : 7).
11. *Bankers Journal* 13, no. 3 (Apr. 1953): 9.
12. The *Westralian Banker* had contained several member letters favouring amalgamation (for example, see vol. 29, no. 4 [Apr. 1954] : 4–5), and had also reprinted Harold Foster's plea for unity.
13. He justified this later statement (which could have been construed as evidence of the superiority of state court awards), by saying, "If it was decided to seek a new award, and it was thought likely that the New South Wales Court for example was the best avenue, then our New South Wales Branch, which would

be registered in the Court, could make the application, with the full moral and financial backing of the whole Association" (speech by H. W. Foster to members of BOAWA, 15 March 1956, reproduced in the *Bankers Journal* 16, no. 3 [Apr. 1956]: 14).

14. *Bankers Journal* 16, no. 3 (Apr. 1956): 14.
15. Opinion of G. Gowans, QC, reproduced in *Westralian Banker* 31, no. 5 (May 1956): 4–5.
16. *Bankers Journal* 16, no. 8 (Nov. 1956): 18.
17. The voting was 42 to 34 (*Bankers Journal* 16, no. 8 [Nov. 1956]: 19).
18. *Bankers Journal* 18, no. 3 (Apr. 1958):8.
19. Letter by H. W. Foster to the SSBOA, published in the *Bankers Journal* 18, no. 4 (May 1958): 14.
20. *Bankers Journal* 18, no. 7 (Aug. 1958): 7.
21. *New South Wales Industrial Gazette* 131, no. 2 (Nov. 1958): 2116.
22. *Bankers Journal* 18, no. 11 (Dec. 1958): 6.
23. *New South Wales Industrial Gazette* 131, no. 2 (Nov. 1958): 2119.
24. See, for example, the *Westralian Banker* 34, no. 7 (July 1959): 1.
25. *Bankers Journal,* 19, no. 8 (Aug. 1959): 12.
26. Rules of the proposed Federation of Australian Bank Officer Associations, reprinted in the *Bankers Journal* 19, no. 9 (Sept. 1959): 25.
27. *Queensland Bank Officer* 40, no. 9 (Nov. 1959): 4.
28. There was an 80 per cent return of ballots with 93 per cent in favour (*Bankers Journal* 19, no. 5 [May 1959]: 4).
29. Minutes of interstate conference, Adelaide, April 1960, p. 7.
30. *Westralian Banker* 35, no. 8 (Aug. 1960): 7.
31. Of the ballots returned, 6,442 opposed the CBOA joining the ABOA and 3,508 were in favour (FCM, 26 Oct. 1960, p. 177).
32. Opinion of J. H. Wootten, 15 September 1960, copy held in ABOA archives.
33. Williams and Foster, while pressing for a form of amalgamation that would have restricted state autonomy, did agree that retention of state as well as federal registration was desirable. They knew there were certain advantages in state registration arising from favourable state legislation, such as automatic cost of living increases in the New South Wales court and compulsory unionism in Queensland.
34. *Bankers Journal* 21, no. 1 (Mar. 1961): 31.
35. *Westralian Banker* 36, no. 2 (Feb. 1961): 11.
36. *Queensland Bank Officer* 41, no. 4 (June 1960): 2.
37. Ibid., 42, no. 5 (July 1961): 21.
38. Existing membership of state branches (or divisions, as they became known) at June 1961 meant Conference, the union's proposed supreme decision-making body, would have the following representation:

New South Wales	23
Victoria	17
South Australia	8
Western Australia	6
Tasmania	3
	57

(*Bankers Journal* 21, no. 4 [June 1961]: 19). Throughout these manoeuvres, the ABOA leadership were aware of and accepted the possibility that after amalgamation they might lose control of the new union. Foster's comments here were, however, couched in the knowledge that it was unlikely that the state associations would vote in a bloc, as the ABOA now seemed assured of the support of both BOAWA and the SSBOA.

39. Minutes of Interstate Conference on Federation, Sydney 6 June 1961, p. 11, copy held in ABOA archives.
40. Williams later expressed the view that Card and McKell had blundered tactically by not joining the federal body at this early stage. He argued that had they done this before he and Foster had shown the other union leaders the necessity and benefits of aggressive leadership, then the New South Wales officials might have gathered enough votes to win the presidency and secretaryship (interview with R. D. Williams, 17 July 1979).
41. Letter from Associated Banks to BOAWA, 27 July 1962, reproduced in the *Bankers Journal* 22, no. 5 (July 1962): 29.
42. Letter from the UBOA of Q to the ABOA, 12 August 1962, in ABOA archives. R. D. Williams, for so long a thorn in the bank's side, was undoubtedly the person referred to here.
43. Ibid.
44. *Bankers Journal* 22, no. 7 (Sept. 1962): 13.
45. Interestingly, the banks had discussed such action many years previously (see confidential letter no. 1767, superintendent of Bank of Australasia to London, 8 August 1936, in ANZ archives). It appears the only factor preventing the banks issuing claims on all staff then was the ill will and concern that would be generated among staff, something of apparently less importance to the banks in the post-war era.
46. Banks' Log of Claims on All Employees, 10 September 1962, reprinted in the *Bankers Journal* 22, no. 8 (Oct. 1962): 7-8.
47. *Banker* 21, no. 5 (Sept. 1962): 9.
48. *Queensland Bank Officer* 43, no. 7 (Nov. 1962): 8.
49. Ibid., no. 6 (Oct. 1962): 1.
50. Opinion of J. H. Wootten to the UBOA of NSW, October 1962, reproduced in the *Banker* 21, no. 6 (Nov. 1962): 305.
51. Circular reprinted in the *Banker* 12, no. 6 (Nov. 1962): 5-6. Both procrastinating unions had also been reminded by their solicitors that if their resistance continued, it was likely that "federation" would come anyway, initially merely by the establishment of ABOA branches in each state. Both unions knew that ABOA membership was attractive to many bank officers in New South Wales and Queensland. The inevitable consequence of these new branches would be the demise of state unions and their current leaderships.
52. See, for example, the *Age,* 26 July 1963, p. 6.
53. Ibid.
54. *Westralian,* 29 July 1963, p. 6.
55. Contained in letter from BOASA to the ABOA, 26 August 1963, in ABOA archives.
56. ABOA letter to all state associations and divisions, 21 August 1963, copy in ABOA archives.
57. At October 1965 there were still fifteen hundred UBOA of Q members (some 27 per cent), who had not joined the ABOA (*Queensland Bank Officer* 45, no. 8 [Oct. 1965]: 7).
58. This problem had bedevilled Australian industrial relations for several years and had frequently led to considerable internal union conflict (see, for example, 127 CAR 1397).
59. Minutes of 1966 ABOA federal conference, Brisbane, 20-24 June 1966, item no. 83, p. 26, copy in ABOA archives.

9 Two Important Campaigns of the Sixties and Early Seventies

And I can give you this assurance. This Association of bank officers will not join the Trades Hall, nor will it carry out actions or oppose the employer as do unions of manual workers, for that is unbefitting of professional men. Above all, this Association will not indulge in, or be associated in any way with the strike or any other tactics distasteful to the honorable traditions of banking.

[E. C. Peverill, at first general meeting of BOA, September 1919]

The period following amalgamation was one of frenetic ABOA activity. Now representing private bank officers in all states, the union needed all the unity, strength, and finance this provided to maintain the momentum of the fifties and to translate continuing bank officer militancy into effective action. The period encompassed two major union offensives which provided ample opportunity for this. First were the lengthy and bitter struggles to obtain salary increases. These resulted in nation-wide stop-work meetings, and finally in the previously unthinkable action — a strike of ABOA members. Second was the ABOA's welcome though long-delayed attempt to protect and advance the interests of female members.

Not all of the union's initiatives were well planned or carried out with total conviction, yet each played a crucial role in the ABOA's development and were further demonstrations of the ever growing militancy of an increasing number of members.

Salary Campaigns — Stop-Work and Strike

The background to the 1963 salaries case has been briefly discussed in the context of union amalgamation. Originally made possible by the banks' unprecedented issuing of a log of claims on each of their employees, it was aided by the ABOA's refusal to oppose bank attempts to bring all bank employees under an Australia-wide award. At the initial Arbitration Commission hearing, Williams argued that the ABOA case should be a test case because of the extent of white-collar margins' compression in recent years. Following supporting applications from ACSPA and the ACTU, the president of the commission, Sir Richard Kirby, eventually agreed, but a series of negotiations both inside and outside the commission made little headway. Relations were further soured by the union's refusal of the banks' request not to communicate negotiation details to members. The ABOA "made it clear they would brook no interference with their rights ... and that members would be fully informed".[1]

In July 1963 the banks unilaterally adjusted salary rates by applying marginal increases ranging from 10 per cent for clerks down to 5 per cent for managers. This was a response to continuing recruiting problems and an attempt to pre-empt the ABOA's application for marginal increases, in line with the overall 10 per cent recently granted in the pace-setting metal trades.[2] The banks' decision to pay marginal rates less than those in the blue-collar area had tacit commission support: "It does not follow automatically that there should be a directly proportionate increase for high margins as for low margins. ... In our view it is true to say that such a course favours those on high salaries as against those on low salaries."[3] The union was incensed: "It's a downright insult to bank officers — an act full of trickery."[4] Even the passive BOASA executive was moved to write to Williams: "to express our admiration of your restraint on 4 July when the banks made their insulting offer".[5]

The ABOA eventually succeeded in having a full-scale work value inquiry held. This had barely got under way when the Reserve Bank announced marginal increases of 10 per cent and a fifty-pound loading. ABOA hopes for a quick flow-on of this were shattered, however, when Commissioner Portus told them that H.C. Coombs, governor of the Reserve Bank, had stated: "Central banking functions and operations of the Reserve Bank differ significantly from the functions and operations of the commercial banks."[6] Williams, convinced this statement had been inspired by the private banks, asked Commissioner Portus either to ignore it or to allow him to question Coombs in the commission. Meanwhile the Commonwealth Bank had acceded to CBOA pressure for similar increases, as had the State Savings Bank of Victoria.[7] Rejuvenated, the ABOA suggested further negotiations, and in late December, with little fuss, the first truly federal award, covering all private bank officers in Australia and providing for £1,600 at the top of the scale,[8] came into being.

Throughout this struggle Williams had continued to promote ACSPA, and the number of white-collar unions affiliated to it had continued to grow. More than ever Williams saw the affiliation of white-collar unions with ACSPA as merely a forerunner to eventual ACTU membership. However, he also knew that this was still anathema to most white-collar union leaders and members, his own still being no exception.[9] (Ironically, the amalgamation of ACSPA and the ACTU eventually occurred just a few months after Williams's death in 1979, and it is perhaps fortunate that Williams was not to know that his own union was the only significant ACSPA affiliate whose membership voted not to join the ACTU.) Williams's strong links with the ALP allowed him some access to A.E.

Monk, president of the ACTU, and its secretary, H. J. Souter. He also had a close personal relationship with R. J. Hawke, who was appointed ACTU research officer in 1958. Consequently he knew that his own personal enthusiasm for ACTU–ACSPA co-ordination was not necessarily reciprocated by the ACTU leadership or its affiliates.

Indeed, in these early years of ACSPA, with memories of the actions of some white-collar union leaders during the turbulent Labor Party "Split" of the mid-fifties still fresh in their minds, Monk and Souter were very suspicious of the motives of ACSPA affiliates such as the FCU. This wariness was enhanced by the traditional doubts of blue-collar unionists about the courage, tenacity, and dedication of these white-collar "professional associations", as they viewed them. The dour Souter, unfamiliar with the constraints facing white-collar union officials, frequently reminded those seeking his support for ACSPA initiatives that ACTU membership was always open to them, and if they really wanted the protection and support of a peak organization, then this indeed was the logical step. Their unwillingness to accept this invitation only further increased the ACTU leadership's apprehension. In addition, some ACPSA activities, such as the White Collar Festival Week of November 1961, with features including folk-singing, a concert in Hyde Park, and discussions on the writing of the trade union histories, were regarded with some amusement and even ridicule by the hard-nosed ACTU leadership. Even some ACSPA leaders were concerned that Baker's enthusiasm had impaired the organization's credibility with affiliates, blue-collar unions, and even employers. Consequently, Allsop, Williams, and Richardson were at pains to point out that issues such as child endowment, salaries, superannuation, the means test, working hours and leisure, equal pay, and the health of office workers formed the major areas of ACSPA interests.

In fact ACSPA had already broken some new ground for the union movement. The first formalized discussions of the impacts of technology had occurred at ACSPA's Automation in the Office Conference in December 1958, and shortly afterwards the National Office Code, outlining the minimum conditions that employers should provide for white-collar workers, was prepared. In March 1961, a pamphlet, "Equal Pay — A White Collar Problem", was released following a Federal Conference on this issue. However, these initiatives had not yet convinced blue-collar union leaders of the veracity and genuineness of all ACSPA affiliates.

Williams, with his "grand vision" of a single peak organization covering all Australian unions ever uppermost, continued to work slowly towards building the credibility of ACSPA with its own affiliates, blue-collar unions, and the ACTU. A further step in this direction was the establishment in 1962 of a joint committee to co-ordinate blue- and white-collar submissions to the Arbitration Commission. This committee, composed of representatives of the ACTU, ACSPA, and (at the insistence of Monk and Souter, who were still suspicious of the intentions of some ACSPA affiliates) the High Council of Commonwealth Public Service Organizations, was in reality very much a result of Williams's commitment to a single peak organization. A measure of the ACTU leadership's early apathy was their frequent non-appearance and apparent lack of interest in meetings of the committee. Yet Williams never lost sight of his goal, and in readily forgiving the ACTU representatives' absences, merely reiterated an eagerness to work more closely with the blue-collar unions.

Williams's control of ACSPA was now even more complete, for his experience, both in politics and the ABOA, had confirmed his belief that the individual prepared to do the mundane tasks of establishing working procedures and setting out agenda could very much control an organization. In this he was aided by a finely honed ability to "count heads" and to draft resolutions that provided "something for everybody", a factor crucial to the survival of ACSPA. He was also fortunate that the ABOA award, with its automatic eighteen-year scale and classification system for all bank officers, was essentially a single, industry-wide instrument and hence relatively straightforward to administer. In contrast, some other white-collar union secretaries were faced with multiple and complex awards covering their members. It was only this that made it possible for Williams to cope with the increasing work load created by ACSPA's continuing expansion, while still maintaining a sometimes still quite despotic control over the ABOA Victorian branch and Federal Council.

In 1963, following Richardson's resignation, Williams selected John Paterson, a young commerce graduate and Labor party supporter, as ACSPA research officer. The unimpeded manner in which Paterson was able to go about his work was in sharp contrast to the control Williams had exerted over his ABOA staff. This reflected an exaggerated admiration and respect for those with formal qualifications as well as recognition that Paterson, with his academic leanings and lack of enthusiasm for organizational affairs, did not represent a threat either to ACSPA's future viability or direction or to Williams's own position. Again his eagerness that Paterson should always co-operate with and, where necessary, provide material to the ACTU indicated Williams's desire that ACSPA work closely with the blue-collar peak organization.

For the first time the Australian white-collar union movement was now generating significant quantities of industrial information, and ACSPA affiliates were beginning to use this in their salary claims. In addition, ACSPA representatives were regularly appearing in Basic Wage and margin cases before the Arbitration Commission, and Williams and Allsop were even appearing there on behalf of individual affiliates.

In mid-1965 the ABOA adopted new salary policies by asking the commission to award increases in junior salary rates and equal pay for female juniors. In doing this they hoped to reverse a worrying decline in union density by enticing more young clerks into the union. The banks reiterated their opposition to equal pay (an issue discussed further a little later), emphasizing the significant differences in the work of junior males and females. For example, while there were no female tellers, 69 per cent of the eighteen hundred male juniors in Victoria and Tasmania were tellers for some or all of the working day.[10] This statement encouraged the ABOA to concentrate on their application for minimum rates for tellers. In arguing this case, Williams laid stress on the changing nature of banking. In earlier times a bank clerk was not appointed teller until in his late twenties, when the incremental scale compensated him for the increased skill and responsibility required. However, with the introduction of new banking machinery and growing post-war recruiting shortfalls, male clerks were being appointed tellers at much younger ages. Whereas in 1958 the proportion of Victorian tellers under the age of twenty-one was 12 per cent, by 1965 it was 36 per cent.[11]

In March 1966 Commissioner Portus awarded a 2 per cent increase to junior males, based upon comparative wage justice rather than changed work value. In rejecting equal pay claims, he outlined what was to become a familiar argument: although male juniors generally sought to make a career in the bank and made consequent sacrifices, "the girls do not regard their work as much as a career but rather as a job which is convenient for them in the locality in which they live".[12] This, he claimed, resulted in males doing tasks requiring greater skill and responsibility. As regards special tellers' allowances, the commissioner again ignored work-value aspects to emphasize the disincentive effects upon staff morale of allowances for specific types of bank work, for to alter the salary structure so "would be to produce discontent amongst bank officers who were transferred to or from telling work".[13] The ABOA came away even further disenchanted with the commission and with a renewed desire to use the membership's restiveness to seek salary increases directly by negotiation.

On the award's expiry in late 1965, the union served a claim for 30 per cent marginal increases. Aware of growing senior officer discontent as the compression of internal industry relativities continued, they also sought to extend and increase classification categories and rates. Williams was at pains to point out that whereas most Australian employees had some compensation for shrinking margins from over-award payments, this was not so for bank officers. As evidence of this he tendered a survey showing that the average over-award payment for male bank employees was $1.59 and females 34 cents; in comparison, in the metals industry this figure was in excess of $12.00.[14] Large Australia-wide protest meetings and a salaries campaign, to which union members donated more than $32,000,[15] ensured wide publicity. This, coupled with Federal Executive's ability to mobilize support in all states, ensured a quick hearing and consent decision. Junior clerks received a 12 per cent increase and others on the scale 10 per cent.[16] A result of the ABOA's claim for improved senior officer salaries was the introduction of a new classification for managers of branches with more than sixteen hands, and average increases of 15 per cent to all classified officers.[17]

The union's new strategy had been confirmed in this early part of the sixties, and the ABOA was now fully aware that conciliation and arbitration processes available in the commission offered few returns unless supported by external campaigns. Clearly, the gains made had been a result of membership agitation, well publicized and supported by the leadership. Both union leaders and rank and file alike now knew that any significant salary increases would have to be won outside the commission and that the mounting resistance of the banks would require more militant and determined tactics.

In April 1967, even though the award would not expire until June 1968, Federal Conference instructed Federal Executive to prepare a claim for a 25 per cent salary increase. Though no reasons were provided for this, and later events showed it certainly was not an ambit claim, the 25 per cent figure quickly became an "article of faith" with union leadership and membership. This single-mindedness was to be of great significance in the bitter struggles of the next three years.[18] Only later, after the campaign was well advanced, did the union provide some justification for the 25 per cent claim. In a cleverly prepared and frequently published table, the ABOA demonstrated that for the twenty-one-year-old clerk, the claimed increase would mean an additional $607 per annum, just equalling the total over-award payments of the metal fitter, with whom the union now claimed equivalence for the twenty-one-year-old bank officers' rate.[19] This use of blue-collar wage rates reflected Williams's view that only in this way was success possible. Implicit in his plans was a belief that bank officers would now accept closer links with manual workers and would be more prepared to use traditional blue-collar tactics to win similar concessions.

Spurred on by rank-and-file approval, and all too aware of the banks' delaying skills, Federal Executive demanded that the salary issue be determined separately rather than be included in any package of claims, where some part of the increase might be "traded off" in negotiations. Foster also sought to allay older members' fears about the claim's legitimacy by preparing another pamphlet outlining how the banks' increasing profitability would ensure that the salary increase was not inflationary.[20] Conscious of the still conservative attitudes of New South Wales division leaders in particular, he stated: "It would be nonsense to think that worthwhile progress can be made merely by 'argument' in the Conciliation Commission and other tribunals, no matter how skilled our advocates may be. It is just as silly to suggest that any good can come from negotiation behind closed doors."[21]

In mid-1968, with the claim already fifteen months old and with rank-and-file discontent mounting, spasmodic negotiations began. The banks, realizing that industry and labour market changes merited some salary increases, were nevertheless determined to obtain some quid pro quo. They pressed for union concessions in staffing allocation so as to facilitate the usage of recently introduced banking technology. After these discussions eventually broke down, the ABOA activated the next stage of the salary campaign. To those division leaders who questioned the mass meetings, heavy media advertising, and floods of pamphlets, Williams had some hard-learned advice to offer: "Any union or association which goes cold to arbitration gets 'cold' results."[22] Mass meetings held around Australia reflected considerable differences of opinion, and clearly amalgamation had not solved all problems arising from forty years of separate state banking unionism. In New South Wales, resolutions merely supporting the salary campaign echoed the historically timid attitudes of the old UBOA of NSW. In Western Australia and Victoria, however, a number of meetings enthusiastically endorsed the use of new aggressive tactics. For instance, at Shepparton the meeting gave "authority to the Executive to take any additional action and if necessary the action to be taken in our employers' time".[23] This enthusiastic support for direct action heralded another stage in ABOA history and developing militancy. There had been earlier isolated membership calls for direct action, but apart from the culmination of the five-day week campaign in 1962, these had been confined to aggressive minorities at Melbourne meetings. Consequently these latest demands, unanimously approved by rank and file from country centres and a division other than Victoria, were most significant.

Exhilarated, Williams and Foster persuaded Federal Executive to maintain the momentum with further copious press releases and advertising. This prompted a *Sun* headline, "Wage Strike May Hit Banks",[24] which brought immediate response from several quarters. The Victorian and Western Australian divisions immediately promised Williams full support in any action he wanted to take, while the New South Wales division, and the BNSW sub-branch in particular, complained bitterly that the ABOA should be seen as even contemplating such action. In a circular to all branches the BNSW urged its staff not to stop work and rejected Foster's claim of surplus profits in the industry.[25] Also a group of BNSW senior officers, purportedly independently, though later events indicated that they acted with covert bank support, wrote: "We deplore the continued articles in the Sydney press which infer that bank officers are contemplating industrial action. We prefer to rely on legal action through the Arbitration Court, and emphasise that we have no intention of participating in any strike action."[26] This clash over union policy on strike action was soon to erupt in open conflict within the ABOA.

The escalation of the ABOA's campaign had forced the banks to reopen negotiations, and they made a confidential offer which amounted to a 9.7 per cent increase in the top of the scale award rate. However, as a result of externally generated wage increases granted earlier in 1968 and not incorporated into the award, actual rates paid now exceeded award rates by 4.9 per cent at the top of the scale. Consequently, the banks' offer amounted to less than a 5 per cent increase on existing salaries. This difference between award and actual rates not only confused later salary negotiations but also made any salary agreement virtually impossible. To some extent now victims of their own propaganda, Federal Executive could do little other than reject the offer. They did this with some reluctance, for the size of the original claim was now embarrassing to them. Williams and Foster were now engulfed in the rank and file's enthusiastic insistence, and at a large mass meeting held on 25 November 1968 there was general agreement that nothing less than 25 per cent would be accepted. To the relish of the press, the meeting added that it must also be retrospective to July, and unless "achieved within fourteen days, this meeting calls on our Executive to hold mass meetings in all States without delay, if necessary, during working hours".[27]

The next morning negotiations recommenced, with the banks offering a larger interim increase pending the results of a work value case, provided the union refrained from further threats of direct action.[28] Card, reiterating the fears of the BNSW sub-branch, and spurred on by this rash of publicity and threats, seized upon the sub-branch's suggestion of a referendum on strike action. Unaware of his own membership's hardening attitudes, he was anguished when the NSW division committee refused to support such a referendum.[29]

With rank-and-file pressure continuing to grow, further negotiations saw the gap between the banks' offer and the union claim narrowed to less than 3 per cent on actual rates, or 8 per cent on award rates. Williams now knew that no compromise was possible, so often and so fervently had the rank and file agreed that nothing less than 25 per cent was sufficient. This was unfortunate, for a relatively small concession by the union would no doubt have permitted the banks to make an acceptable offer at this point. So it was that on 10 December 1968 the historic decision was made to "refuse the latest offer and to inform the membership of negotiations to date at meetings to be held at 9.00 a.m. . . . in all capital cities and other centres".[30] These stop-work meetings were set down for 18 December, and in all states other than New South Wales, planning for the meetings went ahead smoothly.

Meanwhile the banks, desperate to head off the stop-work meetings, had lodged an application with the Arbitration Commission for award application of a 10 per cent increase, believing this would appease union members. This was hastily brought on the next day but only resulted in a confrontation between Williams and bank counsel, Aird. Williams was annoyed by Aird's claim that rejection of the offer was not in the rank and file's interest and his insistence that the ABOA refrain from further industrial action. But it was Aird's condescending advice to Commissioner Portus that he should stand ready to invoke the penal sanctions of the Conciliation and Arbitration Act that finally infuriated Williams, and he walked out of the hearing. As the date of the stop-work meetings drew inexorably closer, the executive of some divisions were clearly having second thoughts. Card had already convinced the New South Wales division executive to hold the meeting after work. The South Australian division, their apprehension resurfacing, did likewise. In Tasmania there was also hesitancy, but in spite of secretary Hodson's remonstrations it was eventually agreed to hold the stop-work meetings as planned.

On 16 December Federal Executive met for one of the most crucial meetings in ABOA history. After confirming that the proposed action was not in defiance of the union's constitution, they instructed the New South Wales division to comply with the executive's decision and to arrange mass meetings for 18 December.[31] Anticipating Card's refusal, a number of executive members had already resolved to support intervention for the purpose of arranging and conducting such meetings. High drama followed as Card informed the meeting that the New South Wales division committee had reaffirmed its decision not to hold a stop-work meeting. McKell, believing his federal presidency conflicted with his position as New South Wales division president, offered his resignation.[32] Delegates from the Victorian and Victorian State Savings Bank divisions had caucused the day before to discuss this possibility. They had agreed they would not allow themselves to be blackmailed by the New South Wales division delegates and would be prepared to accept this resignation if necessary. Sufficient other executive members thought likewise and so, after only six days as federal president, McKell resigned.[33]

The conflicting attitudes of ABOA division leaders towards militancy were now in the open. Worse, the banks were now provided with an opportunity to reduce the effectiveness of the stop-work meetings or perhaps even prevent them going ahead. In this, the banks' traditional supporters were again to the fore. For example, the Sydney *Sun* had rushed into print with Card's statement: "Irrespective of any decision of the meeting in Melbourne, the New South Wales Branch will not in any circumstances support the holding of mass meetings in working hours. This amounts to, and is in fact strike action."[34] The South Australian division, led now by H. Becker, currently a Liberal state parliamentarian, also lived up to their legendary timidity and in deciding not to hold the stop-work meeting fell back on the tame excuse that a suitable venue could not be found at short notice. However, rank and file support continued to grow, and Federal Executive again called on unionists within reasonable distance of the capitals to stop work and go to the meetings. To members contemplating this previously unthinkable action, the union also tried to provide reassurance:

> No industrial law of any kind is being broken. This Association will reimburse members any salary deduction which any bank may impose for time lost in attending the meeting. We are confident that our action is necessary to win just salary increases for officers of all banks in all

states at a time when banks are making record profits and we look to every member for their utmost support in this first industrial action in fifty years.[35]

The stop-work meetings finally went ahead in all states other than New South Wales and South Australia. In Melbourne some three thousand bank officers could not even obtain admittance to the Town Hall, and large numbers also attended in Brisbane and Hobart. Williams had now convinced Federal Executive that the claim should be reduced to 20 per cent increase on actual rates, arguing that this was equivalent to 25 per cent on award rates anyway, and was more likely to elicit a favourable bank response. At the stop-work meetings, some officers, obsessed with the incessantly repeated 25 per cent claim, were dissatisfied by the amended claim, seeing it as at least partial defeat. These members were, however, somewhat appeased by the union's determination to obtain retrospectivity of the claim. Common motions to this effect were passed at all meetings. These concluded with the threat that unless the banks agreed within a month, further mass meetings and direct action would be held.[36] Encouraged by the outspokenness of the eastern states, the Perth meeting went further by insisting on total retrospectivity and specifying strike action if this was not granted. Federal Executive, elated by the success of the stop-work meetings, approached the banks again but were nonplussed by their limited reaction and demand that the union put its proposals in writing.

Confusion over the banks' response to this audacious union action and uncertainty regarding how to exploit the apparent willingness of the rank and file to strike only partially masked another problem for the ABOA. Of considerable importance was the need to discipline the wayward New South Wales and South Australian divisions. Failure to do so could only result in a return to the earlier uncoordinated state actions, apathy, and lack of success, an unpalatable thought for those who had worked so long and hard to achieve amalgamation.

New South Wales presented the major problem. Not only was this the largest division, but the rift ran much deeper. Though some division members opposed Card's dominance and even suggested establishing a new division committee, Federal Executive finally resolved that the New South Wales division committee be "asked to give an unqualified assurance that it [would] abide by the decisions of Federal Executive".[37] Certain New South Wales division committeemen, including McKell, indicated they would resign from the ABOA if this happened. But neither this threat nor the division committee's claim that direct action was in conflict with the views of members, the Conciliation and Arbitration Act, and the ABOA's rules elicited any sympathy from the Federal Executive. In another delaying tactic, the division considered holding a plebiscite to determine membership attitudes to stop-work meetings, an action at odds with their earlier disdain for the rank and file. Federal Executive decisively and swiftly forbade this, and with McKell unwilling to pursue the matter further, Card's obsessive opposition to the ABOA now alienating most other division committee members, and clear indications of support for direct action from the New South Wales rank and file, the Federal Executive quickly regained control.[38] In South Australia, Williams had shrewdly allowed the division committee to draft face-saving resolutions, ensured Federal Executive's acceptance of them, and in this way had put down the rebellion.[39]

The ABOA had gained from its first foray into direct industrial action, for Federal Executive's control over the divisions had been confirmed. More importantly, there was now acceptance by some division leaders and most rank and file that direct industrial action was both appropriate and necessary under certain conditions. In future confrontations with the banks, this was to increase the union's bargaining power and confidence and would guarantee even more membership support. An indication that the employers were concerned at the union's new industrial strength and anxious to minimize the risk of further confrontation was their dropping of an application to deduct pay from those who had stopped work. This and the fact that no officer who stopped work was, at least overtly, victimized or discriminated against by the banks were for many members signs that the costs of direct industrial action were not necessairly as high as had long been feared.

At a compulsory conference the next month the union reiterated its salary demands. The banks countered with an offer of an interim increase of 11.5 per cent while a work-value case was carried out, and Commissioner Portus surprisingly announced that he would arbitrate, using the banks' 11.5 per cent interim offer as a basis.[40] This dismayed the banks, for it would again allow the ABOA to stir up unrest and so influence the commissioner before he began hearing evidence. Further stop-work meetings were announced, but these were called off at the last moment, following the victory of more moderate members in Federal Executive, who had argued that over-use of stop-work meetings would only reduce their effectiveness. This, plus earlier reversals in the commission, prompted the assistant federal secretary, Sanders, to warn: "The arbitration system is loaded with conservatism and therefore leans towards preserving the status quo — precisely what the employers want. Those members who criticised the Association's creation of bargaining counters by means of abrasive publicity and 'stop work' threats are just ignorant of the realities of industrial bargaining."[41]

Sander's remark was more than timely, for the salary campaign had faltered as a result of the inertia and conservatism of these federal executive members, the distractions of the equal pay case running simultaneously, and the apparent satisfaction of at least part of the rank and file at the banks' offer of 11.5 per cent, which had been converted into an interim award by Commissioner Portus.[42] This illustrates the pragmatic source of bank officer militancy. They had forced significant concessions from the banks, using their new-found industrial strength. At least for the time being they were content, having obtained some 16 per cent of the 25 per cent original claim, and were unwilling to stop work again. This resulted partly from naivete and unfamiliarity with these new industrial tactics, but basically it reflected the lack of any ideological or class basis to most officers' militancy.

A little later, in a vain attempt to retrieve the campaign's lost momentum, Williams wrote to all members outlining the long-running events, the perfidy of the banks, and the continuing loss of bank officer purchasing power.[43]   In mid-year, fitful negotiations again foundered on the question on confidentiality, but suggestions for further stop-work meetings and prosecution of the banks for award breaches were rejected by Williams and the Federal executive as now lacking rank-and-file support.

In September 1969 the parties returned to the Arbitration Commission with the union's argument now centred on the question of retrospectivity of the balance of the original claim, which they estimated at 12 per cent. Considerable technical argument followed, but Commissioner Portus eventually declined to issue a formal order. This angered the ABOA, which viewed it as commission support for the banks' attempts to avoid the restrospectivity claim. Rank-and-file memories of earlier gains were now fading fast, and the question of retrospectivity provided an additional specific grievance to concentrate renewed member discontent. Federal Executive accordingly instructed divisions to prepare plans for stop-work meetings, and this time all but the New South Wales division responded quickly and positively.

In the face of escalating bank officer dissatisfaction, Commissioner Portus directed the parties back into conference. Federal Executive instructed negotiators Williams and the new federal president, Remington, that the 12 per cent claim, and retrospectivity of this to March 1969 were sacrosanct and no compromises could be considered.[44] Reinforcing this was a Victorian division resolution that if negotiations broke down and the federal executive did not immediately institute preparations for direct action, then the Victorian branch should be allowed to organize industrial action in that state.[45]   Though this too was a direct challenge to the federal executive's authority, Williams and Remington saw it rather differently. Not only did the resolution sum up the feelings of an increasing proportion of the rank and file in other states (and that of Williams and Remington too in an individual capacity), but its firmness would be of benefit in negotiations.

The conferences continued but made little progress. The banks, though seemingly determined not to concede, were becoming increasingly anxious as direct industrial action loomed. For example, the general manager of the BNSW wrote at length to all staff urging them not to strike even if the dispute was not settled.[46] In a barely veiled threat he asked staff "to   consider the damaging effects which disruptive industrial pressure tactics create in employer/employee relations".[47] The following day the bank sent a further circular to all managers setting out instructions should the strike eventuate. Managers were to keep records of absences and to deduct salary "in a manner to be advised in due course."[48] The ABOA leadership, though concerned that these statements would inhibit older officers in particular, were nevertheless sure that the rank and file were now thoroughly roused again. Remington, settling quickly into his role, had commented:

> Bank officers throughout Australia are on the verge of taking action to demonstrate their impatience with the banks continued tactical manoeuvring inside and outside the Arbitration Commission, to deny their workforce a reasonable salary structure. Young and old bank clerks alike are ashamed to tell their friends how poor their salaries are. They believed when they went into banking that it was a prestigious and at least semi-professional job . . . now they are disillusioned and they won't take it lying down.[49]

Negotiations were officially declared failed on 31 October, and the next morning's press carried large advertisements urging bank officers "not to attend for work on Monday next November 3rd, 1969".[50]

There were two reasons for calling the strike so quickly. The day following the planned strike, Tuesday 4 November, was Melbourne Cup Day, when city and suburban branches would be closed, and this would heighten the disruptive effects of the stoppage. More importantly, Federal Executive feared that any delay would allow senior management and branch managers sympathetic to the banks time to convince or even coerce staff not to strike. This was a compelling argument to Federal Executive members, already apprehensive whether a significant number of bank officers would take the ultimate step of refusing to work. Their decision to call the strike sooner rather than later seemed justified when the BNSW sub-branch of the New South Wales division cabled all BNSW branches. "Executive Wales Staff Council do not endorse possible strike action. Stand with us. Letter following."[51] In the light of earlier discussion on the lack of success of staff associations in the Australian environment, there would seem to have been little reason for union concern. However, the BNSW had encouraged and promoted their sub-branch (or Staff Council), in order to maintain a high level of *esprit de corps* in the face of significant depersonalization in the industry, and it did wield significant authority with the bank's employees. The ABOA, who had earlier forbidden the council's involvement in industrial activities, moved quickly. Williams, after confirming that the telegrams had been sent on the bank's private telegraphic account, went on the offensive. First he sent telegrams to all BNSW branches outlining the Staff Council's earlier promise not to intervene in industry affairs. He also wrote a scathing article in the *Australian Bank Officer* under the heading "An Undertaking Dishonoured", where he bitterly denounced the Staff Council's leadership.[52] Williams then used his close links with the ACTU and ACSPA to condemn the action publicly. In his desire to discredit the BNSW Staff Council he in fact overreacted, and under threat of legal action he was forced to retract certain statements. Despite this, the staff association's credibility was at least partially destroyed and four of its leaders resigned from the ABOA. The bank also stood convicted of duplicity in the eyes of many of its employees, this in spite of some evidence that a number of them opposed strike action.[53]

In the interim, the first strike by Australian bank officers had occurred. In spite of strenuous bank attempts to play down its effects, it was evident that many bank officers had struck. The only measurement of strike effectiveness available was the number of branches that did not open for business. This did understate the strike's effect, for in many cases only the manager came to work, while a number of suburban branches were opened by senior staff sent out from head office. Yet in Victoria and Queensland, more than 60 per cent of branches were closed and another 30 per cent opened with only skeleton staffs, and in Western Australia and South Australia 85 and 75 per cent of branches did not open.[54] In New South Wales, more than half the branches remained closed, a surprisingly high figure given Card's lack of co-operation and the opening of a large proportion of BNSW branches.[55] In Tasmania, more than 50 per cent of branches opened, though many of these were only staffed by managers.[56] In one well-reported incident, the Tasmanian division secretary led more than twenty members of the Hobart ES&A branch out of the bank. As could be expected, the extent of country branch closures was less, though still surprisingly high.

Over the next few weeks the ABOA went to considerable lengths to justify its actions and reassure jittery and concerned members. This was partly motivated by an increase in resignations. For example, in the Victorian branch the resignation rate increased by more than 3 per cent between December 1969 and February 1970.[57] In the same period, however, 750, or 8.1 per cent of total membership, joined the division, many of them encouraged by the ABOA's firm stand.[58] Nationally more than three thousand bank employees joined the ABOA in the two weeks following the strike.[59] Those who queried the union's refusal to hold a plebiscite on strike action were told by Federal Executive that the resultant delay would have enabled the banks to place their staff under intolerable pressure. The ABOA took a hard line with senior officers who had "scabbed". For example, the Victorian division suspended the membership of conference delegate J. H. R. Bayliss for twelve months because he had worked on the day of the strike.[60] They also graciously assumed that the younger officers who had not struck had been coerced by senior staff, and in gently remonstrating with these young clerks urged them "in true solidarity and new sympathy to remit something to the ABOA salaries' campaign".[61] Conscious of how the campaign had floundered the year before, the union leadership was now determined to maintain the momentum. This was not difficult, for unlike the previous year, members had not yet gained anything from their direct action. Well attended follow-up meetings were held in all state capitals except Sydney. At all of these an overwhelming majority favoured further strike action if either the 12 per cent claim or retrospectivity was denied them. The banks, clearly shocked at the success of the strike, then invited the ABOA to present a work-value case. Commissioner Portus, in a change of heart which only further convinced the Federal Executive of the importance of direct action even in the context of arbitration stated that any salary increase granted would be retrospective to 1 March 1969.[62]

When the work value case began in December 1969, Williams emphasized the industry's intensified competition which had increased officers responsibilities and workloads. He also highlighted the rising incidence of bank hold-ups, the lack of over-award payments, and the reduced purchasing power of younger officers, all of which had been reflected in an extensive national survey of salaries and conditions conducted earlier in the year.[63] When handed down, the new salary rates (averaging 6 per cent at the top of the scale), while retrospective to March 1969, were almost identical with the rates the banks had actualy been paying for some time.[64] Though the union's public protestations were predictable, they were at least partially satisfied. The leadership, using elaborate mathematics, could claim significant satisfaction of the original 25 per cent claim, now nearly three years old. Retrospectivity had been obtained, but most importantly the union had finally demonstrated to an initially disbelieving employer that it had now shaken off its historical docility. As well, those executive members still uneasy at the use of direct action were appeased, for the final result had come by way of arbitration. There were few rank-and-file members, however, who did not realize that it was their own determination and preparedness to strike that had won the day.

In contrast with the turmoil of 1969, the salary case of 1970 was a low-key event. Both parties were keen to avoid confrontation. The union was anxious to reassure members that direct action would not necessarily be a frequent tactic. For their part, the banks, still shocked at the involvement of so many of their staff in a strike, were eager to reach a peaceful settlement and avoid further direct action. With the assistance of Commissioner Portus, a salary increase averaging 7 per cent was amicably settled upon.[65]

By 1971, this euphoria and self-satisfaction had waned, and rank-and-file pressure persuaded the union to claim a 10 per cent salary increase. In late 1971, after the banks refused this claim, Commissioner Portus referred it to a Full Bench. The banks were supported by the Commonwealth government and the Public Service Board. In highlighting the key role that the ABOA award now played in the Australian white-collar salary structure, the parties urged the Full Bench to ignore Williams's argument for salary increases based on 9 per cent increases in certain manual industries. The Full Bench, in providing for average scale increases of only 6 per cent,[66] indicated that they too were aware of the importance of the ABOA award to other white-collar salaries.

The union's rank and file were far from content, and Federal Executive responded by ordering another round of stop-work meetings to demand the additional 4 per cent in the form on an over-award payment. At the Melbourne meeting on 16 February 1972, younger officers suggested a more sophisticated use of their industrial strength in the form of bans on the handling of cheques.[67] These bans, applied by Victorian trading and savings bank employees, lasted for three days and proved most successful. Before the end of the second day, the Melbourne clearing house was forced to close. Though not as disruptive as a strike, this did considerably impair bank operations and had the advantage of not carrying the same public opprobrium, a factor still of some consequence to many members. This rank-and-file initiative in the development of new industrial tactics was a further indication of their heightened militancy and the fact that this militancy was now largely internally generated rather than stimulated by union leaders. A measure of the banks' concern and the industry's deteriorating industrial relations climate was their application for the insertion of a "stand-down" clause in the award, but Commissioner Portus deferred this. In negotiations that followed, a compromise was reached, with the banks withdrawing their application and agreeing to expedite the hearing of the 4 per cent claim and the ABOA instructing its members to withdraw the cheque bans.[68]

The usual flurry of bank circulars had accompanied the cheque ban, and their content worried some older officers. For example, the general manager of the CBC lashed his staff:

> Disappointment or disagreement with properly constituted authority is no justification for denying that authority. Neither is it justification for confrontation with your employers. For bank officers, such behaviour is out of character with the more responsible attitude demanded of them by the Banks and public alike. Furthermore, I would hope that those who took part will have reflected by now on the impact that such behaviour could have had on their career prospects.[69]

This final statement prompted the ABOA to ask the banks to destroy statements of intent regarding strike action which they had earlier demanded from their employees.[70]

The union's claim for the additional 4 per cent, now linked with argument for award restructuring, came before the same bench later in the year. Again the Commonwealth intervened to urge the commission to limit the possibilities of flow-on into the white-collar sector, an argument at least partially accepted, for an average 2½ per cent salary increase was granted, providing for £5,434 at the top of the scale.[71]

The ABOA's actions of the late sixties and early seventies, which revolved around salary claims, had continued and extended its increasingly militant philosophy. Significantly, however, whereas earlier the union leadership had clearly led the way, it was now the rank and file's refusal to compromise on optimistically established goals· that prompted the stop-work meeting and strike. This determination also marked union initiatives later in the seventies, though it was noticeably missing in much of the controversy over equal pay for females. This issue, running concurrently with events just discussed, initially cast much of the leadership in a less than favourable light and reinforced the ABOA's male domination and orientation. Yet this too provided an opportunity for the rank and file to demonstrate its militancy. The issue eventually forced union leaders to reassess their attitudes and to make significant change to their policies and actions toward female members. For these reasons it forms an integral part of ABOA history.

There is little doubt that the ABOA remained one of Australia's leading white-collar unions, whether measured by its rate of unionization, willingness and ability to protect its members, continuing commitment and support for ACSPA, or key role in the periodic wage flare-ups that marked the sixties and early seventies. Even though other ABOA state divisions did not possess the militancy or aggression of the Victorian division, the ABOA was still overall a stronger union than the other major ACSPA affiliates. However, this was now beginning to change.

The relative importance of the ABOA among Australian white-collar unions had been a result of two factors. Firstly, the bank officer, because of his prestigious position in society and the nature of his work, had historically enjoyed both the considerable esteem of other white-collar workers as well as a significant salary advantage over them. Secondly, particularly during the fifties the ABOA leadership, by dint of its skills and initiative, had been able to harness the growing militancy of bank officers; this had enabled the ABOA to make salary breakthroughs which then flowed on to other white-collar unions. Both of these factors were, however, now changing. The prestige of bank employees was diminishing as new technology altered the nature of the banking task, limiting the career base of the industry and changing the source of its recruitment.

The ABOA's role as generator of white-collar wage increases had actually been changing since the mid-fifties, when the white-collar unions were first able to take advantage of margins increases won by metal trades unions. The increasing ease with which these increases flowed to the white-collar sector resulted not directly from the ABOA's militancy or ACSPA's development, but rather from the unique role played by AAESDA. While itself about to face considerable technologically induced upheavals, AAESDA did have the advantage of close links with blue-collar workers and with the pace-setting metal trades unions in particular. This resulted both from its location within the Australian industrial relations structure (it was in fact a member of the Metal Trades Federation) and because a considerable proportion of its members had formerly been blue-collar workers. For example, a number of draughts-men had been fitters, and many of the engineers in AAESDA had earlier been skilled metal tradesmen. At the leadership level, E.G.Deverall, a former draughtsman, was for a time Victorian secretary of AAESDA and had in fact introduced Allsop to Williams. He later left AAESDA to be-come research officer but in the following years was at pains to maintain the link between AAESDA and the metal trades unions. In this he was aided by the fact that the AAESDA award applying to technical grade AAESDA members working in the metals industry was, after 1947, part 2 of the Metal Trades Award. Consequently, metal industry wage increases flowed through to these technical grades, from where other white-collar unions could, if sufficiently aware and competent, go about translating these into their own awards. The ABOA was still of con-siderable importance, however, for not only did they have greater strength in Victoria (where AAESDA was relatively weaker), but also had the oft-discussed administrative and organizational skills which enabled them to be the first white-collar union to follow up on the increases.

The AISF, always less able to attract members, faced continuing organ-izational problems as the insurance industry rationalization of the seventies got under way. Still financially impoverished, it had only just begun to acquire the professional leadership and organization that had marked the ABOA since the fifties. P.W.Reilly had been federal president since 1969, and K.H.McLeod federal secretary since 1962, and both were still fully engrossed in building up a stronger union infra-structure. Since 1970 Reilly has also been federal president of ACSPA, and understandably this had been a factor in McLeod playing a larger role in ACSPA events. Also the new administrative and industrial officer, W.J.Richardson, who had been appointed following Paterson's resignation in 1968, began to take over some of the ACSPA organizational work. He too attempted to involve the AISF leadership in ACSPA affairs.

The Municipal Officers' Association (MOA), another significant white-collar union, still suffered from organizational problems resulting from the dispersal of their members across numerous public and private industries. After some early enthusiasm for ACSPA (MOA secretary L. Carter was its first treasurer), this union had been forced to devote its resources to winning salary increases from the Victorian government, which was anxious that wage increases should not be generated in state instrumentality areas. The New South Wales Teachers Federation had also lost some of their earlier prominence in ACSPA, and the fact that they received little support from the Victorian Teachers Union also hindered their efforts to represent schoolteachers more adequately in ACSPA.

In the areas of workers' defence against technology, union education, and pursuit of social issues such as opposition to the Australian troop commitment in Vietnam, ACSPA was clearly leading the blue-collar trade union movement, and its leaders now believed they had something to contribute to the ACTU.   Certainly from an international perspective, ACPSA was quite remarkable, for few other labour movements had been able to organize white-collar workers effectively, let alone draw them together into a reasonably cohesive body.   At another level, the rapid introduction of new technology into areas of office and white-collar work brought with it not only threats of redundancy, job downgrading, and insecurity but also the possibilities of jurisdictional and demarcation disputes between unions.   These added further urgency to the need for some co-ordinating organization.   In increasing the blurring of distinctions between blue- and white-collar work, these changes also provided Williams and Reilly with more arguments why ACSPA affiliates should join the ACTU so as to allow some overall perspective on these potential problem areas.   Following R. J. Hawke's election as ACTU President in 1969, Williams who was a personal friend and staunch advocate of Hawke's more progressive industrial policies, was even more enthused about a merger of ACSPA with the ACTU.

Through the early seventies the ABOA continued to play a key role in ACSPA, and ACPSA certainly was still very dependant upon the drive of Williams and the resources provided by the ABOA. For example, ACSPA's positon on the federal Labor Party's Consultative Council was largely a result of Williams's political contacts and the fact that he had been a key figure in the revamping of the Labor Party's industrial relations policy. Then when the Labor Party won federal government in late 1972, ACSPA through Williams, was able to obtain direct access to cabinet and to the various relevant government departments.

Yet to the casual observer it might have seemed that the ABOA's role in ACSPA had considerably diminished. Williams in fact had chosed to lower the ABOA's to date very high profile in ACSPA, a response to some internal union discord following the increase of right-wing and "grouper" influence, particularly in the Queensland and State Savings Bank division. One criticism of Federal Executive and federal officers made by these groups was that scarce and costly union resources were being expanded on ACSPA affairs, with neither short-run nor long-run benefits for ABOA members. Certainly Williams was now devoting more time that ever to ACSPA affairs, for Sanders had taken over a considerable part of the federal office workload, and since 1967 Victorian division affairs had been in the capable hands of ex-BNSW officer H. K. Salter. However, Williams not to be so easily deterred from his "grand vision", reacted not by any reduction in commitment but rather by merely minimizing the emphasis and publicity formally given to the ABOA's involvement in ACSPA. The *Australian Bank Officer* carried fewer reports of ACSPA activities and mentioned less frequently the benefits of ACTU affiliation, while Williams was also at pains to play down his own role in the frenetic industrial-political events of the early seventies.

A Tardy Defence of Female Members

Females have no place in our Association, which is an organisation for promoting professionalism amongst bank officers. The work of females is of an inferior standard, and they do not desire a banking career, but join the Bank to make some pin money and to snare a husband. In doing so they deny men of work. Their giggling and tittering disturbs the serious business of the banking chamber, makes customers uneasy and the junior clerks are distracted from their work.

I urge you to reject their membership of the BOA, for to accept them would be to approve of their employment in the Bank.

[Letter to the BOA, June 1936]

Before the First World War, private trading banks had employed few females, some banks in fact maintaining an entirely male staff. This was due to an oversupply of suitable male recruits as well as the conservative attitudes of bank management. The onset of the war and the enlistment of large numbers of male bank officers opened the way for increased female employment, yet this employment was severely restricted, both in scope and duration. S. J. Butlin writes of the Bank of Australasia:

The Bank was opposed to women as bank employees, and only the inability either to get through work with a depleted staff, or to recruit male substitutes brought a change of view . . . Finally, advice that women had been satisfactory in head office employment (in London) brought reluctant acquiescence. Thereafter women were employed more extensively, but were never allowed custody of cash, were required to resign on marriage, and were kept away from direct contact with customers.[72]

Though these female officers were competent, they were almost all displaced by returning servicemen at the conclusion of the war, and for almost two decades the proportion of female officers remained at less than 10 per cent of total staff. The emphasis on banking as a career industry, the relative stagnation of the industry for much of this period, the continuing availability of suitable male recruits, and the consistent unwillingness of many bank managements to employ more female clerks all served to perpetuate the existing employment structure. Consequently few females, even after many years of faithful service, received a salary above the top of the established eight-year scale.

Aversion to the employment of females was not confined to the banks. One male officer wrote:

The presence of two or three lady assistants has an unsettling effect on those male members of the staff who do not possess a well balanced temperament and it is sometimes conducive to frivolity, even in office hours, and petty jealousies and slackness in discipline, which things do not make for efficiency in the working of an office . . . the offices in which there was an all male staff ran more smoothly and satisfactorily than those in which lady clerks are also employed.[73]

Another officer, more concerned with employment opportunities than threats to the chastity of his fellow staff, wrote: "These rosebuds set with little wilful thorns are employed not to break the monotony in the routine life of male officers, but because they are paid less, keep down working expenses and so increase half yearly dividends."[74] A glance at comparative salary rates confirms this, for a considerable differential existed. For example, in 1930 the male scale ran to £412 at the eighteenth year, while the eighth-year female scale peaked at £170, equivalent only to the fifth year of male service. That the banks continued to employ so few females despite this is proof of their strongly held belief that banking should remain a male preserve. A leading Adelaide banker had earlier noted, "Banking is so intricate, and a profession of such magnitude, that I cannot really see a woman taking a place in the branches."[75]

Consequently it is hardly surprising that the BOA executive, whose conservatism and prejudices very much mirrored bank management and membership alike, gave little thought to organizing the industry's female employees. In fact there is no evidence that female BOA membership was even discussed by the executive, despite the UBOA of NSW's willingness to enrol females. Here Sydney Smith, always prepared to place increased membership and improved finances before finer scruples, had encouraged female membership by winning some salary increases. Smith's motives became crystal clear after the banks wrote asking for union attitudes towards retrenchment of females. Smith proposed to the executive that "in the case of all women non-members, their names be furnished to the banks with approval to dispense with their services".[76]

In 1937 two factors finally forced the BOA to open its membership to females. One was the growing proportion of females employed by the banks, a result of the introduction of ledger machines to supplement the only other technologically advanced feature of the banking chamber of the period — the typewriter. Between 1930 and 1937 the proportion of females in the Victorian private banking industry had risen from 7 per cent to 12 per cent: "The machines are in most cases worked by women specially recruited for the work, but in some banks women clerks and typists already on the staff have been trained to use the machines."[77] The other factor was the rather pointed query by Judge Dethridge during the "Ogilvie Case" why female employees could not be union members.

The union reluctantly called a meeting of females to invite their membership. Two happenings indicate the true state of affairs. Firstly, at the annual general meeting in September 1937, the well-supported motion that "females be excluded from membership" was only withdrawn when the secretary advised that to continue to exclude female bank officers from union membership would not only endanger the ABOA's registration with the Arbitration Court but would also possibly permit another organization to recruit in the industry.[78]   Secondly, the wording of Smith's circular to lady clerks announcing the meeting alternatively bullied and patronized. He concluded: "Lack of interest on the part of any young lady to be present . . . may result in her case being omitted in any future agreement and her interests will not be protected."[79]

Even the employment of females on a large scale during the Second World War and the retention of many as a result of post-war branch expansion found the union still willing to do little more than accept their union dues. "If the girls do the job they should be paid for it. That's a good reason why all lassies should be in the Association"[80] was typical of remarks of the time. Even in 1953 Federal Conference resolution to press for equal pay was only a counter to the employers' claims for a reduction in the male basic wage and a cut in the female rate from 75 to 60 per cent of the male basic wage, rather than a result of concern that females were discriminated against.

The discriminatory 1920 "equal pay" award clause had been confirmed and extended by a number of later judgments. In the 1938 arbitration fiasco the following clause had been added: "Where female clerks are employed on such work as typing, shorthand, indexing, filing, recording, branch remittances, current account or tellers cash books, or the working of any mechanical appliances, they may be paid the rates prescribed for female typists."[81]   By 1951, with women also now carrying out a number of new tasks, the addition of ledger keeping to this clause further extended the banks' discretion to use female labour at lower rates. Increasingly, however, even this extensive list of female tasks was honoured only in the breach by employers faced with continual branch expansion, considerable technological advances, and an inability to recruit sufficient male clerks. Additionally, the significant salary differential provided the banks with a further incentive to employ more females. By 1960, not only was there an average 25 per cent differential, but the female scale still ran only to the tenth year.[82] With an increasing number of females carrying out work either designated male tasks or not categorized at all, the argument increasingly revolved around the question of "equal pay for equal work". In 1959, amendments to the New South Wales Industrial Arbitration Act had theoretically provided that females performing male tasks should be paid male salaries. This gave impetus to ABOA and ACSPA equal-pay attempts, though again the ABOA's motives were suspect.

It is appropriate to note here that Foster and Sanders, whilst appearing to support the historical dominance of males so frequently enunciated by Williams, in fact had quite different views. However, their awareness that most of the male membership felt little affinity for the plight of female bank employees, that Federal Executive was a totally male preserve, and that the dominant Williams remained adamant that women had little place in the work force convinced Foster and Sanders to adopt an alternative stratagem. In essence this was to accept historical prejudices and outwardly to support the traditional arguments for increasing female rates, on the basis of eliminating competition for male employment rather than equal pay for equal work. For example, in 1961, with fears of unemployment rife, Foster astutely summed up the male rank and file's antipathy towards female salary increases: "When quite considerable numbers of men are laid off or put on short time, as is the case in many industries in Australia at this juncture, the threat posed by cheap female labour should rouse self interest in those males who can see no virture in the other just arguments in favour of equal pay".[83]

When ACSPA sent a deputation to Premier Bolte vainly suggesting he legislate for equal pay, it was hardly surprising this did not include an ABOA representative. In 1962, when the BNSW appointed a few female tellers and paid them at male rates, there was a surge of anger. "This Association opposes the employment of female tellers on the principle that the position of teller has always been regarded as a position exclusively reserved for the male officers."[84] Clearly, much of the union leadership and its male members saw this as a further inroad into male preserves.

The issue of equal pay for equal work came to a head in the 'Cameron Case" in 1963. Joyce Cameron, a devoted ANZ employee for many years, was the centre of a controversy which resulted in the banks reluctantly agreeing to pay male rates to females carrying out male duties.[85] By the late fifties Miss Cameron, with considerable ability and application, had risen to the position of manager's clerk in one of the ANZ's largest city branches, a position never before held by a female and for which she received a salary above the female award rate. Around this time she also joined the ABOA and brought to her union involvement the same willingness and enthusiasn. By the early sixties she had been elected to the Victorian division committee and have been a member of several deputations to the bank. Here she was received with a mixture of amusement and patronization and was often told "Girls shouldn't belong to unions, the bank will look after you." She was the first woman elected to the Federal Executive, where her positive contributions surprised and even embarrassed some male delegates. She was critical of the domination of the ABOA's leadership by men and the union's consequent obsession with male demands. In her pragmatic fashion, she saw little chance of improved female salaries while the Australian trade union movement remained such a strong male preserve, interested only in promoting male interests. Her unwanted notoriety arose, however, not from her union involvement but as a result of ANZ actions.

In 1964, in the face of mounting ABOA criticism of its alleged underpayment of females, the ANZ had surveyed their usage in the bank and were shaken at the number carrying out male duties yet still receiving only female rates. To forestall union action, the bank removed females from jobs where blatant award breaches were occurring, and Miss Cameron returned from vacation to find she had been transferred to more mundane work. Distressed, she contacted Williams, who convinced her to allow this to be used as a test case. Any sympathy she still held for the bank was soon destroyed as negotiations dragged on and she came under increasing intimidation to proceed no further. However, the daily phone calls from senior administrative staff, frequent entreaties from branch management, and offers of employment as a teller all failed to sway her. Finally Williams, exploiting the bank's hatred of publicity by threatening to take a case to common law or the Commonwealth Industrial Court, was able to negotiate an agreement. Miss Cameron was to be employed in a similar capacity as previously and was to be paid male rates, although the bank insisted that this be paid in the form of female salary plus special allowance. This was at least a partial victory, for it was now confirmed that females doing male tasks should be paid at male rates. However, the greater problem was that new technology and banking practices were creating jobs that were not specifically designated male but which would encroach on traditionally male employment areas.

In April 1966 a lady members' convention was held, presided over by Miss Cameron, now chairwoman of the Ladies Advisory Committee.[86] Arising from this, Federal Executive eventually formulated a salary structure to allow for equal pay for equal work. Simply put, the plan was to categorize five areas of female employment, based upon degrees of skill and responsibility. The banks were in a quandary, for though anxious to recruit more females, they were concerned at the higher salaries that must result from such a scheme. They countered with a scheme that had no categorization, would provide greater flexibility in the use of female employees, and would be considerably less costly. The ABOA refused this and rather reluctantly agreed to join the Equal Pay Campaign recently established by ACSPA.[87] Within the ABOA, attitudes of male chauvisism and neglect of female employees' interests built up over years were still strong.

In mid-1967 the ABOA, in attempting to exploit an Arbitration Commission decision in the textile industry,[88] argued that female tellers, now being used in increasing numbers, should be paid male teller rates. This argument was ignored, though it did give Williams an opportunity to remodel the scheme for categorization of female work. The new proposal was that males and all females other than those doing basic machining, typing, and stenographic work should be paid the same rates. This embodied an awareness that some females would not wish to make a career in the industry but would be content to carry out traditional female work. Though a significant proportion of females would still earn less than men, there seemed to be some appreciation that "banking was a career for both

men and women without discrimination".[89]   It was also a sign that the
ABOA's support for equal pay was now a little more sophisticated than
the earlier simple defence of male employment. Citing the United States
experience, Williams maintained that the development of a dual labour
market, with an ever increasing group of part-time and casual female
workers forming the bottom tier, was inimical to long-term female banking
employment. However, caution should again be used in interpreting this
apparent concern over female career prospects, for this was actually a
result of growing anxiety at the low level of female union density and
fear that it would fall even further.[90]   Also, while expressing hopes for the
growth of female banking careers, the union leadership was still only
vaguely aware of the disabilities facing females in the male-oriented industry. So when the federal executive authorized a letter of appeasement
to the male membership, it seemed that nothing had changed. They
justified their actions in terms such as: "All the banks, benefiting from
the lower rates for female labour, have increased the number of girls
employed by 36 per cent, and this proportion will continue to increase
while female rates are low."[91]

In spite of these statements, the ABOA's traditional policy towards
female bank clerks was undergoing slow change. Increasing female discontent, based on their treatment by banks and union alike, now found
a more receptive audience among some younger Victorian division
committeemen and Federal Executive members. It was this group,
together with Foster and Sanders, who were to the fore in the flurry of
activity following a union survey on female duties and salaries, which again
showed a large number of females carrying out duties beyond the scope
of the award.[92]   The union offered to support any females wishing to
claim back pay for extra duties, and then asked the banks to grant
increases equal to the male margin in areas where females were carrying
out specified male tasks. The banks, though refusing to discuss the "equal
pay for equal work" principle, did in some cases agree to pay male rates to
these women. However, they were at pains to reiterate that changing industry conditions made it imperative that even more females be allotted
traditionally male tasks.   The question came before the Arbitration
Commission in late 1967, but lengthy procedural delays, exacerbated by a
shift in the ACTU's equal pay campaign tactics, followed. Fitful discussions were only resumed after the union threatened to prosecute the
banks for some of the more glaring award breaches revealed by the survey.

The ABOA's lack of strong commitment to female interests was still
evident as negotiations drifted on through 1969. After agreeing that the
extent of change required the phasing in of any equal pay scheme over at
least three years, discussion revolved around bank proposals to list female
duties and to pay those females doing all other work at an intermediate
rate. The banks, after offering immediate female salary increases, strenuously argued that females doing general banking work did not require

the same skills as males and so should receive only the intermediate rate. Their enthusiasm for this lesser rate was based on a need to use females in these new areas, rather than a wish to accommodate the small proportion of females at present receiving male rates.[93]   Chances of compromise were further reduced when the federal executive resolved to make no further concessions.[94]   In this they were following a federal conference resolution that the principle of equal pay for equal work must not be sacrificed.[95]

It was the banks who took the offensive by announcing, with regard to technological and structural changes occurring in the industry, "Avenues of promotion can be opened to females without jeopardising male employment."[96] Obviously they were keen to use the ready availability, adaptability, and flexibility of female recruits at significantly lower salary levels. In particular they were anxious to staff the expanding administrative complexes and data-processing centres with females.   The suddenness of this proposal to restructure the female award surprised ABOA leaders and dictated a change in policy direction. Instead of pursuing the female claims separately, they incorporated them into the general 1968 claims discussed earlier, an action with few short-term benefits for females. However, it did result in the deferral of this bank proposal, one that Williams and Foster realized also had far-reaching implications for male career structures.

In the interim, the union had agreed it could do little to prevent the establishment of new banking tasks, most of which were done by females. Consequently they decided to protect those traditionally male areas, such as telling, now being "invaded" by females. Again using the earlier survey results, the ABOA pressured the banks into paying male rates and up to a year's back pay to women proved to have been engaged on male duties.[97] The banks, careful to avoid any connotations that they had accepted the concept of equal pay, labelled these as "special allowances". While using this to encourage other females to join the ABOA, Williams was also anxious to justify the union's aggressive action: "We can only ask for up to a year's 'backpay' yet most of the female officers concerned have been in their present job for years and so it can be easily seen that the banks have gained the services of these officers at much lower rates of pay than was their entitlement."[98]

When the equal pay case came before Commissioner Portus in early 1969, he awarded the same percentage increases to males and females but left the question of equal pay for equal work unresolved.[99] The union then agreed to incorporate their claim into the test case to be presented by the ACTU. As this case began, the banks' actions indicated their determination to resist equal pay provisions. After the Full Bench rejected the banks' claims that earlier statements supporting equal pay by the members of the bench disqualified them from hearing the case, this question of jurisdiction came before the High Court.

Anxious to obtain female support for the flagging general salary campaign, Williams set about wiping out memories of the ABOA's earlier lack of interest and inertia:

> This irresponsibility of these employers is far worse than a stoppage of work by union members and it is hoped that all interested in industrial affairs will understand what is taking place. It is suggested that equal pay could cost the economy and employers $600,000,000 a year. The truth is that this is the amount by which female workers in Australia are subsidising the economy and building up the profits of employers.[100]

This rhetoric concealed fears of Williams and Sanders that in an industry with complex classification and duty structures such as banking, the introduction of equal pay provisions would be difficult, for it was often impossible to define precisely just what was male work when new jobs were being created so rapidly. Meanwhile, the High Court had rejected the employers' application and the case recommenced in April 1969. The banks again intervened to ask that the banking industry be exempted from the test case. The Full Bench agreed, on condition that equal pay in the banking industry be the subject of a separate hearing. A favourable test case decision, in setting down a timetable for the implementation of equal pay and abolishing salary discrimination based on the employees' sex,[101] heartened the ABOA but destroyed any chance of compromise with the banks. There was now little chance that less committed members of Federal Executive would be able to trade off equal pay provisions in return for concessions of more benefit to males.

At the commission hearing, the banks presented a more refined argument against equal pay. They argued that in areas such as telling and ledger examining, equal pay would create anomalies for males. Females, because of their relative immobility, would be appointed to these positions at a later age than would males, yet under the incremental salary scale would receive higher salaries for doing the same work as the men. Williams countered by suggesting a cut-off point at the seventh year of adult service. This, together with the fact that two-thirds of female bank employees were less than twenty-one, and of the remainder, almost half were typists or machinists, meant that less than one in five females would have actually received full male rates.

In its judgment, the Full Bench confirmed ABOA fears that equal pay provisions could not readily be applied to an incremental salary scale.[102] The Full Bench agreed with the banks' contention that female tellers did not perform the range of work carried out by male tellers. Accordingly, all new female tellers were to be paid at male rates only up to the seventh year of adult service, and females employed on other general banking tasks received no increase. Increases in machinist and typist rates were rejected, as was the claim for equal pay for juniors. By instituting a separate scale for ledger supervisors and examiners, the Full Bench also accepted the banks' argument that females came to these jobs later in their careers than males, so that the banks were paying more for their services. This, the Full Bench claimed, not only reduced female promotional opportunities but added significantly to banks' costs.[103]

Over the next few months the precise details of this scheduling of female labour was determined. A few females received full male rates, a further 10 per cent were to be paid an intermediate rate, but the vast majority were still to receive normal female rates.[104] Although the ABOA had fought a largely unsuccessful battle to limit the categorization of female work, they had prevented the replacement of the incremental scale with a job-based grading scheme. While this would have removed some discrimination against females, the changing nature of banking employment would have trapped most females and a number of males in its lower grades and thus established a dual labour market. It is doubtful whether Williams understood the full implications of the employers' proposal, but this hardly mattered. The mere suggestion of doing away with the male-oriented salary scale in the interests of some female workers was totally repugnant to the ABOA leadership. They knew that male rank-and-file members, many of whom were totally dependent upon the incremental scale for salary increases, would not countenance its abolition.

Meanwhile, the union had decided to proceed with the long-threatened prosecutions of certain banks for award breaches. The three banks concerned tried to have these set aside until after the commission proceedings just discussed. The Commonwealth Industrial Court rejected this, arguing the banks were proposing that employers could break an award in the hope of having it altered in their favour retrospectively.[105] The court sat for nine days, and the four women concerned suffered considerable strain under the bank counsel's lengthy cross-examination. In its judgment, handed down in February 1970, the court agreed that each female performed duties that should have been paid at male rates.[106] However, in the case of the three ledger examiners, the court conceded that there could have been some doubt, so that the banks' refusal to pay male rates could not be regarded as openly flouting award provisions. However in respect of the other woman, a Brisbane travel consultant, the court was more critical. "In our view the liability to pay male rates was clear and ought to have been acknowledged before these prosecutions were launched."[107]   Accordingly, the court imposed a token penalty and, as with the other cases, awarded salary retrospectivity. Remembering the delays and reversals of the previous three years, it is not surprising that the union made much of these decisions. Most of the February 1970 edition of the *Australian Bank Officer* was given over to a report of the cases. Williams's editorial summed up the relief and justification felt by leaders and rank and file alike: "The banks because of their resolute opposition to any review of female positions and salary standards over the past three years forced the Association to take this issue to the Industrial Court . . . it handed down a judgment in the four award breach cases which was almost 'perfect' from the Association's point of view."[108]

For many union members these prosecutions had been almost as disturbing and raised as many doubts as had the recent strike. Though growing out of an industrial issue, the quasi-criminal atmosphere and proceedings of the prosecutions had added a dimension lacking in Arbitration Commission appearances, the scene of previous legal challenges to the banks. Bank officers had seen their employers placed in a new, even humiliating, light, and while the ABOA's action was a logical extension of bank officer militancy, it had left many of them uneasy. Older officers, conditioned by years of paternalism and managerial dominance, found this further breaking down of traditional bank authority particularly difficult to come to terms with. Others, conscious that their union had now reached a level of confrontation with employers that could only intensify, were concerned at the implications of this for their working relationship and future in the bank. At another level, a number of these members still doubted the wisdom of taking such extreme action on behalf of females whose existence in the industry and union they still questioned. So although the verdict provided justification and perhaps some consolation to these members, particularly considering the ABOA's other recent aggressive actions, it failed to dissipate all their concern.

There was, however, one group of members who felt no such remorse, those in fact who had sponsored and encouraged the prosecutions, who earlier had demanded aggressive union action on a number of fronts, and whose attitudes reflected the beginnings of a new, ideologically based militancy. Led by Sanders, they were generally younger and less constrained by years of industrial conditioning and saw female salary discrimination as yet another issue to be used to reduce the banks' control and dominance. The existence of this group helps explain Williams's support for the prosecutions, seemingly at odds with his earlier reluctance to pursue female interests. His enthusiasm for the prosecutions was not the result of a new conviction that the union should defend female bank employees, for philosophically he still saw their place as being in the home and their employment as only temporary. Rather, he now grasped this as an issue to be used to further diminish the banks' authority while promoting the ABOA's image among bank officers, the public, and other unions. In the excitement of victory his continuing male orientation was revealed as he apologized to the male membership for having pursued female interests. "We assure male members that the ABOA has not gone exclusively feminine . . . we have over 10,000 female members to look after."[109]

These prosecutions marked another stage in bank officer militancy. Clearly they did not have the wholehearted support of all members, yet that they went ahead reflected the growing power of a group of members and leaders determined to challenge and reduce the banks' control. The success of the prosecutions increased the influence of this group while further straining already tense relations between banks and union.

The actual introduction of equal pay in the banking industry lies outside the scope of this discussion, as it was not achieved until 1975. This came as a result of the ACTU's second test case before the Arbitration Commission, which established a timetable for the progressive implementation of equal pay, starting no later than December 1973.[110]

The ABOA's post-war militancy and aggression had been eventually reflected in its equal pay campaign. Initially, however, the union's response to threats posed by large numbers of females entering the industry were limited by its long-term male orientation. In the latter stages of the campaign came a new determination to seek improved female salaries for more honourable reasons than in earlier years. This allowed the ABOA to use tactics formerly only employed in pursuit of its male membership goals. These tactics, developed and refined in the conflicts of the late sixties and early seventies, were to become more frequent and acceptable in events of the later seventies. Having now achieved some measure of genuine industrial unionism, as indicated by the offensives discussed in this chapter, it may have been expected that the ABOA's progress and success would continue. There were, however, significant impediments to this, and one of these was the gradual resurgence of the divisions' independence, leading to some reduction in Federal Executive's control and authority.

In the years just before amalgamation, most state union leaders had believed that they were merely joining some type of loose federation of bank officer unions, where they would retain significant autonomy and a separate existence. The ABOA leadership, while anxious that the UBOA of NSW and UBOA of Q retain state registration and hence access to their respective state tribunals, really wanted, and had achieved, an amalgamation of the state unions with the ABOA. For example, UBOA of NSW members were required to join the ABOA, an already federally registered union, not some new federation of bank employee unions to which their state union would have been affiliated. Thus the state unions disappeared as separate entities, becoming divisions of the ABOA in just the same way as the Victorian, Tasmanian, and South Australian branches had become ABOA divisions.

Clearly these new divisions were largely to provide administrative convenience. Consequently, following amalgamation, though some state leaders remained disgruntled, there were few changes to the ABOA's formal union structure. The existing structure, consisting of the Federal Executive and division committee of management, was retained and the already registered ABOA rules were adopted.[111] As a result only the federal component of the ABOA held corporate status and thus was legally entitled to hold property and to sue and be sued, and the divisions were only able to control assets through their trustees. More importantly, the division committees of management and full-time division officials were now under the formal control of Federal Conference. The Annual (and after 1970, biennial) Conference had been expanded, with delegates elected by each division depending on membership.[112] Conference still remained the ultimate policy-making body, and annual leadership elections were also held at Conference, with the federal secretary and assistant federal secretary positions decided every five years (and after changes in federal legislation in the mid-seventies, every four years).

As in the past, the implementation of Conference policy, along with the handling of national industrial problems, was in the hands of Federal Executive. In line with the expanded membership, Federal Executive, which now met monthly, was made up of a federal president, two vice-presidents, federal secretary, assistant federal secretary, and treasurer, who formed the Federal Officers Group. As well it included a representative elected from each division, usually the president, except where he was already a federal officer. Within the Federal Executive, the crucial relationship was that of the formal head of the ABOA, the federal president, with the federal secretary, its chief executive. For some years after amalgamation, Williams and Foster continued their already lengthy association, and their rapport, complementary characters, and ability to work together were contributing factors to Federal Executive's efficiency and control over the ABOA in the latter part of the sixties. The formal relationship between Williams and McKell lasted but a few days, and conjecture as to the result is of little value. However, McKell's successor, Remington, extroverted, articulate, and aggressive, had been influenced by Williams and had much in common with him, and this enabled the positive and effective relationship between the federal president and federal secretary to continue.

Formally then, the division committees of management were obliged to carry out the directives of Federal Executive (or requests, as they were described in the rules) and, through it, the decisions of Conference. Through the 1960s, the Federal Executive, and particularly its full-time officers — Foster, Williams, and Sanders — did retain significant control over the divisions. They ensured that those Conference policies which they thought of most importance were put into train at the division level (as indicated, for example, in the events of the salary campaigns of the late 1960s).

However, by the early 1970s, and particularly after Williams left the ABOA, the divisions began to exert considerably more autonomy. No longer could Federal Executive expect that conference policy or its own decisions would be automatically implemented by the divisions. An example of this was the Rural Bank division's moves to settle new industrail agreements with the bank's management without Federal Executive's endorsement. Another was the State Savings Bank division's 1976 decision to ignore a Conference decision requiring it to co-operate with the

Victorian division in a campaign not to open branches before ten o'clock. The divisions had always controlled the election of their own Conference delegates and committees of management and the employment of their full-time officials, but this kind of refusal to obey Conference policy was a new phenomenon.

The Federal Executive's increasingly limited control over division actions in fact reflected its lack of a power base. Full-time federal officials had no separate division membership to appeal to, no separate group of articulate, committed allies who could effectively communicate with the rank and file at the grass-roots level. However, division officials could use these groups to subvert or even obtain the members' mandate to ignore Federal Executive decisions. Additionally, division officials, when called upon to implement Conference policies with unpleasant repercussions, or those seemingly inconsistent with the demands of some of their member-ship, were apt to lay the blame at the feet of the "Federal Executive down in Melbourne".

A further complicating factor had been the emergence of another division, this one covering employees of the Rural Bank of New South Wales. Before April 1968, members of this state-owned bank had formed a branch within the New South Wales division. However, with a long history of separate negotiations and discussions with their own bank, Rural Bank union leaders soon realized that their interests were not being adequately represented either within the New South Wales division or at Federal Conference or Federal Executive. Financial limitations had been the main impediment to separate division status, and these were overcome when the Rural Bank agreed to provide premises and seconded the secretary, G. R. Ayres, and an office assistant to work full time for the new division. The bank's financial support for the division, also reflected in their suggestion that union subscriptions be deducted from salaries, did concern the ABOA's federal leadership by reminding them of similar earlier employer attempts to subvert union determination by forming house associations. In the now rapidly changing intra-union environment, however, there was little that Williams and other federal officials could do about this.

So the increased assertiveness of the divisions by the early 1970s was not just a function of Williams's reduced control over divisions or Sanders's more democratic style of management, nor of their lack of control over the appointment of some perhaps antipathetic, lack lustre, unsympathetic, or even antagonistic division officials, but also of changing circumstances. In most divisions, small but influential interest groups had emerged, some of them espousing more militant philosophies than those developed at Conference. Others with covert National Civic Council affiliations sought to divert the ABOA towards the extreme Right, and even some, particularly in states where the BNSW was strong, were actually tools of the banks. In a number of cases the activities of these groups had considerable impact upon division officials.

Not surprisingly, then, there were times when the division officials, their own positions very much dependent upon the good graces of these groups, had felt compelled to ignore or had refused to put into practice certain Conference and Federal Executive decisions. Additionally, as division elections became more competitive, full-time division officials became keener to handle as much of their own industrial relations as possible, only handing on to the Federal Executive those situations which were difficult or those liable to reduce their prestige and electoral appeal.

A contributing factor in the ABOA's successes to this point had been Federal Executive's control over division actions. This authority was now lessened and was inhibiting the union's ability to cope with new pressures. Other impediments to the ABOA's continuing success are discussed in the following chapter.

Notes

1. ABOA pamphlet "Free Enterprise Pranks", July 1963, p. 7, copy in ABOA archives. The banks' frequent attempts to ensure confidentiality resulted from the ABOA leadership's ability to whip up and sustain membership support with strategically timed pamphlets and press releases.
2. *Amalgamated Engineerion Union* v. *Metal Industries Association of South Australia and Ors* (102 CAR 138).
3. *Federated Clerks Union of Australia* v. *Public Service Board and Ors* (94 CAR 812) at p. 828.
4. H.W. Foster, ABOA newsletter, 23 July 1963, copy in ABOA archives.
5. E.S. Johnson to R.D. Williams, 11 July 1963, letter in ABOA archives. At this stage Williams was not noted for his retiring manner either before the commission or in negotiations with the banks. Perhaps BOASA hoped this reaction was an indication of his mellowing.
6. *Australian Bank Officer* 23, no. 6 (c) (Nov. 1963): 1.
7. The CBOA had been able to apply considerable pressure because of the delicately poised situation in the House of Representatives, where the Liberal - Country Party government held a majority of only one seat. A number of public service unions had threatened to campaign against the government at the impending election unless granted marginal increases at least equal to those in the blue-collar sector.
8. *Australian Bank Officals Association* v. *Australia and New Zealand Bank and Ors* (105 CAR 443).
9. As he noted himself, "The majority of the members of the associations regarded the ACTU and the trade union movement as tied to the labor side of politics. Little did they realise that if every trade unionist voted Labor, the ALP would hardly ever be out of government" R.D. Williams *"White Collars Make Council", Labour History* (Australia), no. 6 (May 1964), p. 32.
10. *Australian Bank Officials Association* v. *Australia and New Zealand Bank and Ors* (113 CAR 812) Transcript p. 64.
11. Ibid., p. 139.
12. Ibid., p. 815.

13. Ibid., p. 817.
14. ACSPA survey on over-award payments, 1966, copy in ABOA archives.
15. *Australian Bank Officer* 26, no. 4 (b) (Oct. 1966): p. 1.
16. *Australian Bank Officials Association* v. *Australia and New Zealand Bank and Ors* (116 CAR 64).
17. Ibid.
18. These events are discussed in some detail in L. N. Riches, "Coming of Age: Salary Campaigns of the Australian Bank Officials Assocation, 1968 and 1969" (Melbourne: ABOA, 1976).
19. ABOA pamphlet, March 1968, copy in ABOA archives.
20. H.W. Foster, "Bank Salaries in 1968 – Some Factors for your Consideration", copy in ABOA archives.
21. Ibid.
22. *Australian Bank Officer* 28, no. 5 (Sept. 1968): 1.
23. Ibid., no. 6 (Oct. 1968): 3. An earlier Western Australian meeting had also supported direct industrial action.
24. Melbourne *Sun*, 7 November 1968, p. 3.
25. BNSW circular to all branches, 14 November 1968, copy in ABOA archives.
26. Letter from BNSW sub-branch members to ABOA, 11 November 1968, in ABOA archives.
27. Report of meeting in ABOA archives.
28. Report of negotiations, 26 November 1968, in ABOA archives.
29. New South Wales division minutes, 3 December 1968.
30. Federal Executive minutes, 10 December 1968, p. 4.
31. Ibid., 16 December 1968, p. 8.
32. McKell had just become federal president upon the retirement of Foster. He felt himself to be placed in a most invidious position because of the statements of some New South Wales division delegates (interview with R.A. MacKell, 18 August, 1981).
33. Federal Executive minutes, 16 December 1968, p. 6.
34. *Sun*, 16 December 1968, p. 3.
35. Federal Executive minutes, 23 December 1968, p. 1.
36. Reports of stop-work meetings in the *Australian Bank Officer*, January 1969 (special issue), pp. 1-4.
37. Federal Executive minutes, 23 December 1968, p. 1.
38. Riches, "*Coming of Age*", pp. 38-43, details the way in which Federal Executive asserted its power over the New South Wales division.
39. Federal Executive minutes, 23 December 1968, p. 2.
40. Full details of these negotiations are given in the *Australian Bank Officer* 29, no. 1 (Mar. 1969): 1-2.
41. Ibid., p. 3.
42. *Australian Bank Officials Association* v. *Australia and New Zealand Bank and Ors* (127 CAR 802).
43. Letter to all ABOA members, reproduced in the *Australian Bank Officer* 29 no. 2 (Apr. 1969): 1-4.
44. Federal Executive minutes, 2 October 1969, p. 2.
45. Victorian division minutes, 19 August 1969, p. 43.
46. Letter from general manager of BNSW to all staff, 28 October 1969, copy in ABOA archives.
47. Ibid.
48. Circular from general manager of BNSW to all branch managers, 29 October 1969, copy in ABOA archives.
49. ABOA pamphlet, October 1969, copy in ABOA archives.
50. See, for example, the *Age*, 1 November 1969, p. 4.
51. Cable dated 30 October 1969, copy in ABOA archives.

52. *Australian Bank Officer* 29, no. 8 (Nov. 1969): 3.
53. The South Australian sub-branch of the BNSW Staff Council had earlier asked its members whether they favoured strike action. Seventeen per cent said they did, while the balance of the 294 replies opposed this. It should be noted, however, that 38 per cent of this latter group were not ABOA members (survey on strike action, South Australian sub-branch of BNSW Staff Council, October 1969, copy in ABOA archives).
54. *Australian Bank Officer* 29, no. 8 (Nov. 1969): 2-3.
55. Ibid.
56. Ibid.
57. Victorian division minutes, November and December 1969 and January and February 1970, folios 61, 66, 71, and 79.
58. Ibid.
59. Federal Executive minutes, 18 November 1969, p. 3.
60. Victorian division minutes, 17 February 1970, folio 79, p. 2.
61. *Australian Bank Officer* 29, no. 8 (Nov. 1969): 4. A continuing decline in the union density of younger clerks may have also influenced the ABOA's moderate response.
62. It should be pointed out that Williams believed the banks had discussed the matter with the commissioner and encouraged him to grant retrospecivitiy so as to avoid further direct action (interview with R.D. Williams, 15 March 1979).
63. ABOA national survey of bank officers, 1969, copy in ABOA current files.
64. *Australian and New Zealand Bank* v. *Australian Bank Officials Association and Ors* (130 CAR 938). Actual rates had again crept ahead of award rates as a result of national wage increases and the banks' recent application of small over-award payments.
65. *Australian Bank Officials Association* v. *Australia and New Zealand Bank and Ors* (135 CAR 531).
66. *Australian Bank Officials Association* v. *Australian and New Zealand Bank and Ors* (141 CAR 1294).
67. Report of meeting in the *Australian Bank Officer* 32, no. 1 (Mar. 1972): 1-2.
68. Full details of these negotiations are reprinted in the *Australian Bank Officer* 32, no. 1 (Mar. 1972): 3.
69. CBC general manager's circular to all staff, 24 February 1972, copy in ABOA archives.
70. Federal Executive minutes, 21 February 1972, p. 15.
71. *Australian Bank Officials Association* v. *Australia and New Zealand Bank and Ors* (144 CAR 844).
72. Butlin, *Australian and New Zealand Bank* p. 364.
73. *Bank Officials Journal* 1, no. 2 (July 1921): 13.
74. Ibid., 3, (Aug. 1921): 3.
75. *Adelaide News* 9 February 1924, p. 12.
76. *Bankers Journal* 3, no. 1 (Jan. 1922): 3.
77. *Queensland Bank Officer* 16, no. 12 (Feb. 1936): 4.
78. Minutes of Victorian branch annual general meeting, 22 September 1937, p. 189.
79. ABOA circular to female staff, 27 October 1937, copy held in ABOA archives.
80. *Bankers Journal* 13, no. 5 (June 1953): 9.
81. *Australian Bank Officials Association* v. *Bank of Australasia and Ors* (39 CAR 1012) at p. 1014.
82. See, for example, *Australian Bank Officials Association* v. *Australia and New Zealand Bank and Ors* (94 CAR 461), clause 6 (b), at p. 463.

83. *Bankers Journal* 21, no. 4 (June 1967): p. 14. A further example of the union's male orientation had come earlier when the president and secretary of the Ladies Advisory Committee (formed in 1956) had nominated as Federal Conference delegates. Their resounding defeat was a warning that the membership still regarded females warily and certainly saw them as unacceptable in the union leadership hierarchy.
84. *Bankers Journal* 22, no. 4 (Sept. 1962): 4.
85. Interviews with Miss Cameron (25 July and 4 August 1979) and R.D. Williams (16 February and 4 March 1979) provided the basis for this discussion.
86. Neither the formation of the advisory committee nor the staging of the convention marked any significant change in the ABOA's attitude to females. Rather, they were a result of the determination of a few females from each division. This is confirmed by the ABOA's procrastination over and eventual shelving of a proposal to appoint a full-time secretary for the advisory committee. Similarly, Williams's support of Miss Cameron should not be seen as a step forward in thinking on female issues. Williams had fought the bank primarily in defence of male interests, and because it provided an opportunity to inflict a defeat on the employers at a time when salary increases were difficult to obtain.
87. For a full discussion and analysis of this and later equal-pay campaigns, see L.N. Riches, "The Struggle for Equal Pay in the Australian Private Banking Industry 1966-1975" (Melbourne: ABEU, 1980).
88. *Australian Textile Workers Union* v. *Victorian Chamber of Manufacturers and Ors* (119 CAR 329).
89. *Australian Bank Officer* 27, no. 3(b) (July 1967): 3.
90. As at December 1966 Victorian division female union density was 39.1 per cent, while the male figure was 74.8 per cent (see app. 3). The real union rationale was confirmed by the ABOA's actions following the banks' refusal of their proposal. They wrote to all females, highlighting the banks' intransigence and appealing to them to join the union (letter from ABOA to all female bank officers, 3 August 1967, copy in ABOA archives).
91. Letter reproduced in the *Australian Bank Officer* 27, no. 3(b), (July 1967): 3.
92. ABOA survey on female duties and salaries, September 1967, copy in ABOA archives.
93. As at mid-1968, only 1 per cent of female Victorian division members would have qualified for the intermediate rate under the banks' proposed list of duties (derived from material in ABOA current files). All other females would have received female rates. This indicates that this scheme was a rather crude bank attempt to subvert the "equal pay for equal work" argument of the ABOA.
94. Federal Executive minutes, 9 July 1968, p. 8. It is perhaps significant that Williams, who had shown little of his characteristic initiative, zeal and determination in this whole question, was not at this meeting.
95. Federal Conference minutes, June 1968, p. 13. The resolution also instructed negotiators to seek the granting of equal opportunity for females in promotion. Though this was later to be of some importance, it was merely a bargaining tactic at this stage.
96. Chariman of Banks Arbitration Committee to ABOA, 31 July 1968, letter in ABOA current files.
97. More than sixty female unionists received salary increases averaging a thousand dollars per annum and a further thousand dollars in back pay (*Australian Bank Officer* 28, no. 5 [Sept. 1968]:5).
98. *Australian Bank Officer* 28, no. 5 (Sept. 1968): 5.
99. *Australian Bank Officials Association* v. *Australia and New Zealand Bank and Ors* (128 CAR 215).

100. *Australian Bank Officer* 29, no. 1 (Mar. 1969): 4.
101. *Australian Meat Industry Employees Union* v. *Meat and Allied Trades Federation of Australia* (127 CAR 1142).
102. *Australian Bank Officials Association* v. *Australia and New Zealand Bank and Ors* (132 CAR 349).
103. Ibid., at p. 355.
104. From records contained in ABOA current files.
105. *Australian Bank Officials Association* v. *Bank of New South Wales, Australia and New Zealand Bank, and English Scottish and Australian Bank* (131 CAR 857).
106. Ibid., p. 859.
107. Ibid., p. 882.
108. *Australian Bank Officer* 30, no. 2 (Feb. 1970): 2.
109. Ibid., p. 3.
110. *Administrative and Clerical Officers' Association, Commonwealth Public Service* v. *Postmaster General and Ors* (147 CAR 172).
111. Separate sets of rules for the New South Wales, Queensland, and Rural Bank divisions were initially registered with appropriate state industrial tribunals to suit state susceptibilities and to try to "keep a foot in the door" for possible industrial gains at state level. However, this had little influence on either the ABOA's structure or its operations, nor on the dominance of the federal award.
112. For example, at the 1972 Conference the Tasmanian division had two delegates, Western Australia four, South Australia five, Victorian State Savings Bank six, Victoria twelve, Rural Bank of New South Wales four, New South Wales thirteen, and Queensland six.

Rees (Barney) David Williams

Harold William Foster

Robert Arthur McKell

Keith Henry Remington

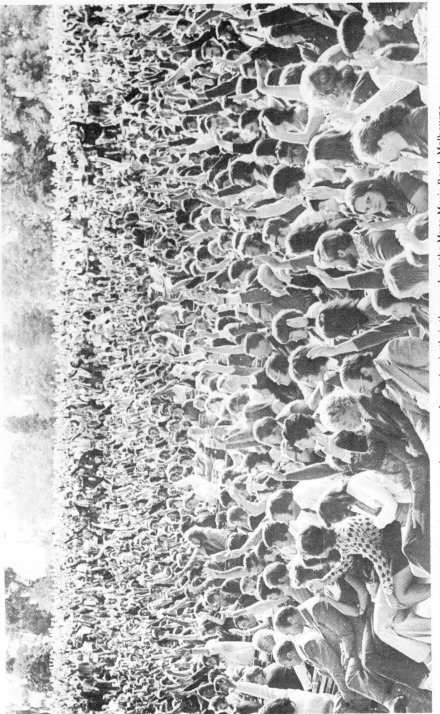

Young bank employees attend a stop-work meeting in their thousands at the Myer Music Bowl, Melbourne.

The march down Collins Street.

The Collins Street March led by ABOA officials.

10 Some New Problems, and a Partial Solution

"There is no need to wear a red tie and sing 'Solidarity', but demand a fair deal and see that you back your Association in getting it".
[Letter to *Australian Banker* 2, no. 29 (Jan. 1927) : 4]

In the previous chapter the ABOA's aggression throughout the sixties was highlighted. Paralleling this was considerable industry change, which placed in doubt the viability and future of the union. This was reflected in an alarming decline in union density. For example, between 1960 and 1971, Victorian division male union density fell from 82 per cent to 68 per cent, and female density from 54 per cent to 39 per cent (see app. 3).[1] Reasons for this included the continuing centralization of the industry, the increasing youth of the industry's work force, and the increasing proportion of females entering the industry. At another level, rapid technological change was ultimately seen by both union and membership as threatening bank employment. These changes forced some defensive actions from the ABOA, though the late reaction to technological change was to limit the available protection for bank employees. The union, however, did solve the problem of dwindling union density by obtaining a form of compulsory unionism in the industry.

The Changing Face of Banking

Considerable changes in the structure of the industry, the location of bank officers, and the type of work they did had significant influences on the operations and membership of the ABOA. The first of these structural changes was the declining importance of rural branches. It was not until 1960 that the number of branches in Melbourne exceeded those in the rest of Victoria (see app. 1). However, this is not an accurate measure of staff location, for country branches were generally smaller, transacted less business, and so needed fewer staff than urban branches. Even so, by 1960, 43 per cent of male and 39 per cent of female staff were still working in rural areas.[2] A rapid decline followed, and by 1973 only 21 per cent of male staff and 14 per cent of female staff were employed in rural branches. Earlier it was mentioned how the ABOA's membership was limited because a large proportion of bank officers worked in dispersed branches with only infrequent contact with other clerks. What then was the effect of an increase in the proportion of bank officers working in urban branches and head offices? To explain this it is necessary to remember that the degree of upward job mobility existing in the industry at different times has been a factor influencing male union membership. That is, when few promotion opportunities existed, there was a tendency for the bank clerk to turn to the union to protect and increase existing salaries and conditions. The major variable affecting the availability of promotable positions was the rate of new branch openings. Appendix 1 shows that the rate of branch openings and hence the opportunity for promotion has varied considerably over the years, and a brief historical analysis of this variable is useful.

Between 1900 and 1910 there was a 36 per cent increase in the number of Victorian branches, but between 1910 and 1920 this increase was negligible, indicating a sharp reduction in promotion opportunities. Appendix 1 shows that the number of rural branches increased by 41 per cent between 1900 and 1910, but decreased by 6 per cent between 1910 and 1920. As younger staff normally received their first promotion to a rural branch, it was these officers whose promotion prospects were most limited by this net closure of rural branches. While the increase in suburban (29 per cent) and city branches (9 per cent) between 1910 and 1920 did offset the decrease in rural branches, these were promotion positions available only to older officers. This also helps explain why younger rather than older members were instrumental in the formation of the ABOA.

Two other periods are worthy of brief discussions with regard to promotion and unionization. From 1920 until 1930 there was a small increase in the number of rural branches, but branch closures resulting from the economic depression more than offset this, so that by 1940 there were fewer rural branches than in 1920. Lack of promotional opportunities arising from this was a contributing reason for the relatively high rate of unionization in the period. Between 1940 and 1945, branch rationalization effected a 15 per cent decline in rural branches. However, this had little immediate impact upon the degree of upward job mobility because of the large number of bank officers in the armed forces. Then between 1945 and 1955, the number of rural branches grew by 28 per cent. When coupled with the rapid expansion in other areas of the banking industry, this indicates that a high level of upward job mobility existed. This would normally have reduced the rate of unionization, but appendix 3 shows that this did not occur, for the rate of ABOA male unionization actually increased from 81.9 to 84.0 per cent.[3] The primary reason was that the majority of those bank officers in a position to receive promotion were older officers who had been in the ABOA since before the war. Their delayed promotion was due largely to the lags in the promotion system caused by the stagnation of the 1930s and the Second

World War manpower problems. So far as upward job mobility after 1955 is concerned, the declining relative importance of rural branches reduced promotion prospects for younger officers, which exerted a favourable influence upon the rate of unionization.

Urbanization of the branch banking structure facilitated unionization in another way. It allowed easier contact with potential members, travelling time and costs were reduced, and with relatively fewer members in isolated branches, greater rank-and-file support for union actions was possible. For example, the mass meetings of the sixties exerted considerable pressure on the banks mainly because of the large numbers of city and suburban-based officers who flocked to them. Increased bank employee centralization also facilitated greater union strength and unity. It was mentioned earlier that rural branch officers, in only infrequent contact with other clerks, were more subject to anti-union employer pressure. As more bank officials came to work in suburban branches, where daily contact with other unionists took place, unionization became easier. Frequently direct stimulus both to join the ABOA and to become active in the union was evident. This interaction has been labelled as the "proximity effect" by Shister,[4] who saw it as an important ingredient in union growth. Increased member urbanization also made it possible for a greater number of potentially active and interested unionists to become involved in union affiars, usually centred on the Melbourne office. There was also a favourable impact on union recruiting, as enthusiastic members influenced other potential members. This had some impact on the age composition of the union hierarchy and so upon the union's decision-making. Before the war Federal Council and the Victorian committee (in fact the same officers), were made up of older senior officers.[5] By 1973, although a number of Victorian division committee members were managers and senior officers, they had achieved this position at a much younger age, and there was a sprinkling of officers still receiving scale salaries. This was reflected in the average age of the division committee, which was less than thirty-eight years.[6]

The decreasing proportion of rural-based bank officers had another important though less discernible impact upon unionization and union militancy. This related to the bank employee's perception of his status and position in society. The rural or small-town bank officer has always occupied a position of appparently greater social importance than has his urban-based counterpart. In country areas, where fewer people were employed in tertiary industry, where there was extensive use of overdraft facilities, and where these financial affairs were controlled by one or two bankers, these officers were viewed as having considerable status and prestige in the immediate community. Certainly urban-based officers carried out similar tasks and had similar responsibilities, but this was not so apparent to the community. Additionally, the anonymity of urban living meant that bank-officer perceptions of their status and prestige in society were not confirmed or reinforced as frequently as those of rural officers. A result of this was that rural-based officers had been less willing than suburban bank officers to join the ABOA, because of the views that bank clients might hold of them (the generally unfavourable attitudes of the rural populace towards banking unionism have been discussed earlier), and because of their own view of their position in society. To the extent that rural-based branch officers held these attitudes, the decline in the proportion of officers located in these areas favoured overall union membership.

The steady, often spectacular, increase in the number of suburban and city branches had further impacts on union growth. Appendix 1 shows that in 1920 there were 124 suburban branches, making up 20 per cent of total bank branches. Almost all of these branches have continued to operate but have had little impact on union growth. This is because these branches were largely confined to what became inner suburban areas and have not expanded their levels of business activity greatly, either because of lack of population increase in the area or because of the changing nature of banking requirements. Any trading bank expansion in the inner suburbs was to service secondary and tertiary industry banking needs rather than to provide personal banking services. This latter type of banking requires a considerably higher ratio of staff to customer than does the servicing of industry. Consequently, most inner suburban branches have shown little staffing growth,[7] so that any favourable unionization effect from this area has been minimal.

Of greater importance to unionization was the opening of new city and suburban branches. Appendix 1 shows that the number of these branches more than trebled between 1920, when 19 per cent of male bank staff worked in these branches, and 1973, when the proportion of bank officers in these branches had risen to 40 per cent. Just as inner suburban branch staffing requirements were affected by the nature of the banking carried out in these branches, so too have the staffing requirements of new branches been influenced. Generally established in newer suburban residential areas, their major function has been to service individual customers. This more labour-intensive form of banking has required large numbers of staff, all potential unionists.

However, a rapid expansion in urban branches later had some negative impacts for unionization. First was the effect upon promotion. Between 1945 and 1973 there was an increase of 155 per cent in the number of city and suburban branches (see app. 1). This created a demand for more managers and accountants, a demand only met by a rapidly increasing rate of promotion. For example, the average age for first managerial appointment in the NBA in 1973 was thirty-six, whereas before the Second World War few appointments were made before forty-five.[8] In addition, these branches were on average considerably larger than rural branches,[9] which meant that new senior classified positions such as accountant and assistant manager also were created and became available for promotion. Second, rapid city and suburban branch expansion resulted in the rate of inter-branch transfers in urban areas also increasing, as the staff requirements of a much larger number of branches fluctuated. This limited the unionization effect created by staff centralization by reducing the constant peer pressure frequently required to convince younger staff of the benefits of union membership. Suburban and city branch expansion also limited unionization because of the higher proportion of married females employed in city and suburban branches than in rural branches. For example, in the NBA in 1973, 34 per cent of females working in country branches were married, while in suburban and city branches this proportion was 51 per cent.[10] Whereas 45 per cent of unmarried female NBA employees were in the ABOA, less than 20 per cent of married females were union members.[11]

The final structural change of importance to unionization was the growth of large administrative departments designed to co-ordinate expanded branch banking activities and to house newly established services and departments. Until the late sixties the rate of increase in employees in these complexes was relatively slow. In 1967, 12 per cent of male private trading bank staff worked in administrative headquarters, but by 1973 this proportion had increased to 34 per cent; for females the proportion rose from 17 to 31 per cent. What did this imply for ABOA membership? Literature relating to the English experience outlines how the development of large administrative complexes resulted in an increase in the unionization rates of employees from these areas.[12] This was so because the atmosphere and working conditions in these larger, more bureaucratic structures contrasted sharply with the smaller, traditionally paternalistic branch banking environment. Unionism was encouraged because this bureaucratization, with its accompanying task specialization, destroyed what the clerk believed was his individual responsibility to his bank and his close relationship with the acceptance of management: "Such an organizational structure inevitably discourages individual action in favour of collective action, since decisions of the employer, about salaries for example, apply impersonally to all members of a group."[13]

The effect of this head office expansion upon the growth of the ABOA was overtly not dissimilar to that of other banking areas. However, this is quite misleading, for the rate of union recruitment from these areas (as distinct from the actual level of unionization) was considerably less. Because of the relatively recent establishment and development of these areas, most male staff had considerable prior branch experience. Consequently they had already been exposed to unionism under more favourable conditions, and were frequently already ABOA members before transferring to head office.

The effect of bureaucratization upon the ABOA is more discernible from an examination of the unionization rates of clerks under twenty-four years. These clerks (who had spent most if not all of their career in the head office and so were more typical of the employees under discussion in the literature) had an extremely low unionization rate, that for males being 24 per cent and for females 22 per cent. Consequently the ABOA experience would seem to be in direct contrast with the British experience. There are several factors that help account for this. One relates to the problems encountered in organizing and recruiting in these areas. Organizers experienced some difficulty in making initial contact with young head-office staff. Whereas in branches the organizer could approach the accountant, who was responsible for staff matters and general branch operation, to arrange a discussion with potential recruits, there was no equivalent position in the administrative complexes. Consequently initial contact with recruits was difficult. The organizational structure and task deployment of head office operations also made it difficult for organizers to interview and discuss union membership with potential members. Also, the general atmosphere of anonymity common to bureaucratic organizations further limited recruitment, because it reduced the opportunities for enthusiastic union members to influence non-members, a factor very evident in the suburban branches yet inhibited in the large complexes by their very size and organizational structure.

The growing preponderance of younger bank officers in these areas, a result of recruiting shortfalls and the changing nature of bank tasks, also influenced unionization. The banks' most urgent manpower need now was for clerks with only rudimentary skills; consequently they could use recruits with no branch experience. The result was that an increasing proportion of head-office employees had not worked in branches and so had little or no contact with ABOA organizers. As the rate of growth of staff in these areas between 1967 and 1973 was three times faster than the rate of growth in suburban and city branches, not only were current unionization levels reduced, but the long-term growth rate of the ABOA was impaired.

Most industry structural changes discussed to date had both favourable and unfavourable implications for ABOA growth. What was the net effect of these structural changes? This can best be examined through an analysis of the five most relevant variables arising from changes in the industry's structure: (1) the rate of promotion; (2) the ease with which union organization, co-ordination, and recruiting could be carried out; (3) the extent of employee centralization and bureaucratization; (4) the degree to which interactions between individual officers existed; and (5) the type of banking activities as they affected the banks' ability to use young, inexperienced staff with lower unionization propensities.

Firstly then, the rate of promotion, where analysis reveals considerable change over the cause of time. Initially the absolute decline in the number of rural branches between 1910 and 1920, by limiting promotion opportunity, was undoubtedly important to union formation. In the period 1920-45 rural branch banking continued to decline and the rate of expansion of suburban and city branches was limited, which favoured union growth. In later years, however, the relative decline in the proportion of rural branches was more than offset (with regard to promotion) by the establishment of suburban branches. Added to this there was subsequently a dramatic growth of specialist positions in newly created head office departments, and the continued expansion of suburban and city branch banking, the development of new banking techniques, and further diversification of the private trading banks into new areas increased the rate of creation of promotable positions. So the changing rate of promotion, while favourable to union growth in earlier years, goes some way towards explaining the decline in the rate of unionization after 1960.

The second factor was the ABOA's ability to unionize industry recruits and to organize and carry out union activities. The high proportion of dispersed rural branches had initially impeded union formation, but the relatively slow expansion of city and suburban branches until the Second World War had a favourable though limited effect upon ABOA growth. Rapid post-war urban branch growth then assisted union growth, so that this is seen as increasingly favouring unionization.

The third factor of importance — the rapid urbanization of bank officers resulting from the expansion of head offices and administrative complexes, particularly after the mid-sixties — was largely unfavourable to ABOA growth. There were two reasons for this. Sheer size and the administrative design of these areas made organizing and recruiting difficult, and fragmented work tasks and bureaucratic work systems limited the ability of enthusiastic union members to convince other bank officers of the benefits of ABOA membership. This factor also helps explain the decline in ABOA union density after 1960.

The degree to which union members could influence other bank clerks to join the ABOA was the fourth factor arising from the industry's structural change, for this variable is seen as being responsive to physical working location, environment, and conditions. Again the increase in the proportion of bank clerks in city and suburban branches, where the size and operations of the branch favoured a relatively higher level of personal interaction, and where union gains were more readily discernible and discussable, is seen as favouring union growth. In the sixties, however, two factors arose which reduced the value of the structural changes to the growth rate of the ABOA by reducing the opportunities for involvement and interaction between bank officers. These were (a) the development of large administrative complexes and (b) the expansion of some of the city and suburban branches in particular areas to such an extent that they too no longer provided an environment conducive to increased union-ization.

The final implication for unionization arose from changes in the type of labour required by the banks, resulting from new diversified banking activities and technology. As a result of this the banks were able to use young, inexperienced clerks and even those short-term employees who in earlier years would not have even been considered suitable. This was a critical factor in inhibiting the growth of the ABOA in the sixties, for the union found itself unable to recruit many of these young employees, particularly those females working in administrative complexes and electronic data processing (EDP) centres. The situation is discussed in the following section.

An Increasingly Young Industry Work Force

The age structure of male bank officers has shown considerable change over the years. Of the three age categories into which male bank officers may be grouped, junior clerks, those under twenty years, con-stitute the first. This group, of some importance in the union's early years, became insignificant in the 1930s but grew rapidly in the post-war period. The second category, made up of those officers aged twenty to thirty-nine, after a period of numerical significance fell away in the post-war years; since then they have increased in importance again. The third category, those over forty, were an important component of the work force when the ABOA was formed and remained so through the Depression and the years before and after the Second World War when recruiting was limited. Since that point they have steadily declined as a proportion of the total work force.

The industry's dramatic post-war expansion forced the banks to recruit school-leavers in such numbers that by 1973 almost 30 per cent of their male employees were less than twenty, [14] and this was critical to ABOA growth. Shister [15] claims that younger workers, particularly those in career industries, have a strong propensity to unionize. Compared with older workers, their shorter period of service reduces commitment and loyalty to the employer; their resentment of arbitary management treat-ment is higher; fear of victimization or loss of accrued benefits is less: and chances of finding and adapting to alternative employment are better. These, taken together with the fact that young Australians had grown up in a period when unionism was acceptable, legitimate, and a normal adjunct to employment, would suggest that a union should have little trouble organizing in an industry with an increasing proportion of young workers, However, in the NBA this group had in 1973 a unionization level of only 23.6 per cent, while the overall male figure for the bank was 67.1 per cent. This seems to contradict Shister's argument. However, a further variable, the high turnover rates of young bank officers, must be included. Until 1950 turnover rates had been low. Little data is available, but in 1925 the ABOA calculated that turnover was of the order of 3 per cent.[16] This is consistent with industry circumstances of the time: relatively few alternative employment situations existed, and bank officers still enjoyed considerable status and occupational prestige. In the 1930s the turnover rate continued to remain low owing to economic conditions that virtually eliminated alternative employment possibilities.[17] However, the male turnover rate then increased sharply from 8 per cent to more than 11 per cent.[18] In addition, whereas in 1955 the proportion of those under the age of twenty leaving the industry had been 65 per cent, by 1973 it had grown to 88 per cent. This high turnover rate restricted unionism in two ways. Firstly, these highly mobile young officers saw little reason to join an organization that provided protection for their long-term rather than immediate interests. Secondly, many of them were in the industry for such a short period that union organizers had no opportunity to make contact.

The four major reasons for male resignations were salary levels, lack of opportunity for promotion, insufficient job satisfaction, and frequency of transfers. There were two reasons why young clerks rather than older ones, made up the bulk of these resignations. Specific banking industry skills were of little relevance to most other occupations, and this immobilized most officers who had been in the industry for any length of time. The cheap personal and housing finance so readily supplied by the banks to the employees also reduced labour mobility, so that any officer contemplating resignation had to not only find another position paying a similar salary but also an alternative source of low-cost finance. Consequently, banking employees with more than four or five years service were generally effectively locked into the industry. The high turnover rates of young clerks (almost 88 per cent of all resignations in 1973), helps explain both why Shister's hypothesis that unionization was positively related to bureaucratization was not borne out by the ABOA's experience, and also why the ABOA's union density rate continued to fall.

A further important reason for the decline in the ABOA union density levels was the unwillingness of female bank employees to join the union. Appendix 3 shows that between 1946 and 1973 the proportion of female employees in Victorian private trading banks had increased from 20 to 35 per cent, but the level of female unionization had fallen from 49 to 42 per cent. Though the male unionization level had also fallen for reasons already discussed, it was still significantly higher than the female level. Most importantly, an increasing proportion of females were continuing to enter the industry. Rapid growth of specialized banking services, centralized administrative centres, and data processing complexes had encouraged female employment in two ways — by creating jobs more suited to and more competently handled by females,[19] and by reducing the proportion of bank staff coming into direct contact with the public. Until the late sixties, banks were still reluctant to place females in jobs requiring extensive dealings with bank customers. Consequently the increasing proportion of jobs sited in the anonymity of large administrative head offices further encouraged their use of females.

Several reasons why female unionization rates are invariably lower than male in the same industry have been provided.[20]   These include female apathy and the supplementary income and transitory nature of some female employment.   Examination of banking industry data suggests further reasons for low female union densities in the industry, particularly between 1960 and 1973, when the female union density rate fell from 54 to 42 per cent (see app. 3). The first of these was the long-term attitude of the ABOA leadership and most male members towards females. The result of this long-term indifference, discussed in the previous chapter, was that few females viewed the union as capable or even willing to provide assistance and protection, and so saw little reason to join. From 1937, when the ABOA had first grudgingly enrolled females they had been only tolerated, while the union had concentrated on preserving male employment, salaries, and conditions. The equal pay campaign indicated that the ABOA still maintained this male orientation and that actions ostensibly carried out on behalf of females were really in defence of male interests. In areas such as female scale extension, career opportunities, and promotion there had been only minimal union interest or action.   Certainly there was considerable bank opposition to such initiatives, but in the eyes of female bank officers this did not excuse the ABOA's refusal to develop and pursue coherent policies for advancing female employment conditions.[21]

The second factor accounting for low female unionization rates was the youth of much of the female work foce. The unionization rate of junior NBA males was, at 23.6 per cent, very similar to that of junior females (22.2 per cent).[22] It is important to note, however, that while more than 56 per cent of NBA female staff were under twenty, less than 30 per cent of male staff were in this age group, so that the problem of low junior female unionization rates was of more consequence.

There were two main reasons why young females had a low unionization rate, just over one-third that of older females. The first was the exceptionally high turnover rate of these young female clerks, which in 1973 was more than 75 per cent.[23] They thus had neither incentive nor opportunity to join the union. This high turnover rate resulted from the full employment maintained almost continuously in Australia after the end of the Second World War. Even more significantly, rapid growth of the tertiary sector had meant a constant demand for female employees with several years of secondary education. This excess demand allowed young females to leave the industry relatively freely and with little fear of lengthy unemployment. While male resignations resulting from better salaries and greater opportunities available elsewhere were relatively higher, irregular hours of work and family reasons accounted for a larger proportion of female resignations.

The recruiting processes used by the banks provide a further explanation. From the mid-sixties almost all female recruits came directly from the fifth year of secondary school to this, their first full-time employment. As it took considerable time for a young clerk to accumulate any degree of industry expertise, and because an alternative job normally required a set of general rather than specific skills, the penalty incurred in leaving the bank for other employment was small. Consequently a large number of young females spent a relatively short period in the industry,[24] many of them in banking areas where it was difficult for union organizers to contact them.[25] Female union recruitment was further inhibited because the ABOA did not employ their first female organizer until 1973, choosing instead to leave recruiting largely in the hands of an elderly male union official.

The second explanation for low female unionization rates lies in the type of work done by female bank clerks. R. M. Blackburn argues in *Union Character and Social Class* that if the employment commitment of females is low, the rate of unionization will also be low.[26] Moreover, if their employment required training and development of specific skills, offered some promotional prospects, and was of a career nature, there was a greater tendency for females to join unions as part of their overall commitment to employment. The extent of tedious, mundane, low-skill tasks performed by female clerks has already been mentioned; however, a brief summary, and more particularly some indication of the changes in these tasks, allows an evaluation of the trend in female employment commitment. Crucial to this was new and rapidly expanding banking technology, which established a set of new banking tasks by segmenting existing jobs and in other areas introduced work of an even more simple and mechanistic nature than previously. The batch clerks' job of balancing account credit and debits remained, but ledger machinists' tasks were simplified even further. The reduction in banking skills were exemplified by the work done in the new data processing areas, where some tasks were even reduced to the stamping of vouchers. This was reflected in low unionization rates. For example, in the NBA's centre (where the average age was twenty-three years), the level of unionization (at 20 per cent), was considerably less than the average rate of female unionization.[27] While this was partly due to the difficulties of union recruitment and organization in these areas, there is sufficient evidence to suggest that the low skills required did tend to reduce employment commitment and to inhibit willingness to unionize.[28] The frequently monotonous work contrasted with the broader range of skills required in branch banking, particularly in the smaller branches, where females were called upon to carry out duties either normally done by males or by a number of females in larger branches.

The argument that higher skill requirements and usage brought increased employment commitment, which in turn was a factor leading to higher levels of unionization, is supported by the fact that NBA female unionization in country and provincial branches (where the logistics of union recruitment remained difficult) was 59 per cent and 67 per cent respectively, whereas in the urban branches the corresponding figure was 31 per cent.[29]   Certainly some part of these higher branch unionization rates was due to reduced alternative employment opportunities in country areas, but that is not sufficient to explain the considerable difference. Yet the union could draw little satisfaction from these higher female unionization rates in rural areas, or even the relatively high unionization rates of adult females.   Rural banking was shrinking proportionately, and adult females formed a declining proportion of the industry's work force.

New Machines Bring New Problems

A number of young ladies are being trained to work the new machines, and the male ledger keepers will soon be booking their passages to, at the best, the smaller country branches, or alternatively will be looking for a new job.
[*Queensland Banker* 11, no. 3 (May 1930): 14]

Another problem of increasing importance in the latter part of the sixties, one inextricably bound up with the problems of female employment and of declining union densities, was the extent and rate of technological change.   This problem was to be endured, not overcome, and was to present the union with possibly its greatest long-run threat, one that from the union's view-point still has no apparent solution.

Before 1930 the typewriter had been the only labour-saving piece of machinery in general use in the industry. Even this had been regarded with some apprehension:

Ever since the nimble typewritten sheet began to replace the stiff, stodgy, pompous old pass book, there have been protests from the conservatively minded. Men of respectability it is felt should not be shocked by sudden confrontation with the naked, but not always lovely truth. The capital complaint is its indecent lack of reticence. Every word and figure is clearly legible, and there is no pretending that this £20 to a wine merchant is £10 to a society for the prevention or the propagation of something, or that which looks very like Hotel Metropole should in face read Hotel for Missionaries.[30]

However, most tasks, such as the maintaining and balancing of ledgers, were still done by hand.   By the early thirties there were rumours of new banking machinery and contrasting views on the effects of its introduction. On the one hand was relief: "The tediousness of old fashioned ledgerkeeping will soon be a thing of the past . . . No longer shall we hunt the elusive account that was out of order; no longer shall we have those pleasant little evening parties on Monday night, 'hunting the difference', which so added to the joy of ledgerkeeping".[31]   But reported effects of its introduction in the United Kingdom, coming amid fears of retrenchment in the Australian industry, caused some consternation: "Only a few months ago the Bank of England, as a result of having installed automatic ledger-posting machines, found it necessary to dispense with the services of 1000 men, ranging in age from 26 to 34, simply because the machines were doing their work, and it had no employment for them.[32] A letter from Tasmanian secretary W.T. Crosby illustrated this concern: "I advise that the CBA and the ESA in Hobart and Launceston intend to install American ledger posting and cash-book machines, and ask what action is necessary to stop such an unfair practice, as it is considered that the installation of these machines will mean further retrenchment of staff".[33] The banks too were aware of the implications: "Experience of machine posting has proved it to be satisfactory," wrote the superintendent of the Bank of Australasia to the London head office, "and I shall lose no opportunity of installing it when economy of staff can be effected by doing so."[34]

Union fears and management expectations were largely groundless, for the Australian branch-oriented banking structure did not lend itself to the exploitation of this new technology. To employers the attractiveness of this equipment was its ability to process large numbers of transactions rapidly. Consequently, whereas large "city" banks in the United States of America and England had sufficient business and transactions to take advantage of the cost-saving benefits of the new equipment, the smaller Australian trading banks, still carrying out most of their business in a multitude of small rural and suburban branches, could not do so. This industry fragmentation, coupled with the relatively small amount of banking business carried out in the Australian pre-war economy, meant that the large capital outlays required were not justifiable. Additionally, there were communication and transport difficulties involved in importing new technology and expertise, problems compounded by uncertainties generated in the economic depression.

Just before the Second World War most banks did eventually install rudimentary ledger machines. While the manpower drain caused by the war ensured there were no redundancies, the recruitment of large numbers of females just as this new machinery came into operation was significant. Their efficiency, coupled with lower female salary rates, soon convinced the banks of the desirability of continuing and extending female recruiting in the post-war period. Even then the introduction of more advanced proofing, ledgerkeeping, and adding machines did not threaten banking employment. For even though it was believed that "these semi-automated machines resulted in one less clerk being required in a seven-handed branch and two less in larger branches",[35] the industry's ever-increasing manpower requirements more than offset this.

In the late fifties the proposed introduction of electronic data processing applications spurred the ABOA to action. Following an ACSPA conference on office automation, the ABOA gave evidence at an inquiry into the effects of technological change conducted by the New South Wales Industrial Commission.[36] Here the banks' argument for increased mechanization and their operation by females centred on a need to process the burgeoning quantities of vouchers and documentation now being generated in branches and administrative centres. This view conflicted with the ABOA's belief that the banks were employing increasing numbers of females mainly because of the significant salary differential. The ABOA's proposals emphasized the need for joint consultation and that the employer should provide both early warning and justification of any proposed technological change. Their submission made detailed comment on retraining and redundancy requirements and on relocation allowances. More generally they argued for the introduction of the thirty-five-hour week and an extra week's annual leave, as well as making a case for sharing in any productivity increases and for tripartite discussions of the effects of automation on employee health and well-bearing. Significantly, however, this was still couched in terms of broad approval. "Nothing but good can come from automation provided it is handled properly."[37] This was the first considered statement by the ABOA on the subject, and one very much at odds with their later views. Williams and Sanders, who was to be responsible for much of the union's policy and actions in the area, also saw the question as one that might be turned to the union's short-run benefit. This was evidenced by their inclusion of recommendations for the abolition of Saturday morning work and a demand for increased wages to encourage recruitment, issues they were already pursuing in other quarters.

For their part, the banks were encouraged by results in areas where technological innovation had already occurred. For example, in the ANZ, where by 1961 almost all of the 550 branches had been equipped with ledger machinery, economies on staff costs were believed to be in excess of £500,000 per year.[38] In advising branch managers of anticipated staffing effects of a soon-to-be-installed computer, the bank's general manager stressed that these would be achieved by attrition and reduced recruiting rather than retrenchments.[39] The lower staffing levels were to be calculated by the newly introduced Work Measurement Unit, whose goal was the establishment of a "scientific yet practical formula for accurately determining branch complements in relation to volume of work".[40]

The mid and late sixties brought rapid banking technological developments, but this still largely supported the functions of bank clerks rather than replaced them. However, the banks then indicated that they intended to computerize many of their routine operations, because their attempts to overcome backlogs by extending clearing house operating hours and introducing shift work had encountered considerable union opposition. The ABOA, now increasingly worried and conscious of the experience of the SSBOA, which had earlier found itself presented with a *fait accompli* on shift work following that Bank's introduction of a computer, challenged employer claims that this would provide a better service to the public. They argued that the banks had only just realized that the new technology could only justify its costs if used to the maximum. The union was able to insist that only volunteers should work shifts, shift loadings should be paid, strict limits should be imposed on the length and timing of shifts, and females working shifts should be provided with free transport home. These limitations not only increased costs considerably but largely prevented the faster transactions so desperately needed by the banks. By introducing electronic communication techniques, the banks, as well as expediting their own operations, had hoped to take better advantage of short-term money markets. Faster transaction transferral, by minimizing liquid funds required for the banks' "float", would make this possible.

To date, the nature of technological change, in the context of seemingly endless industry expansion, had hidden any negative employment effects. Consequently the ABOA leadership, preoccupied with the more immediate problems of salary campaigns and female employment, seemed unaware of the threats posed by new technology and had not developed a coherent policy. There was, however, some concern at developments in other industries. Of particular importance was an arbitration case involving technologically induced redundancy in the oil industry, and finally the Arbitration Commission was asked to rule on the effects of technological change upon employees.[41] While the commission did give a commitment to intervene in the "interests of industrial justice", action was limited to a direction to the parties to confer on the question of greater levels of prior consultation, rather than an agreement to award permanent employment rights or the establishment of standards to be followed in such situations.

This decision, coinciding with further developments in banking technology, now brought considerable union anxiety. First was the unease arising from renewed forecasts that duties including ledgerkeeping and telling would be eliminated. For example, the BNSW had announced a computerized communication network linking its main volume centres. Although initially this was to handle only clearings, current and savings account transactions, and general ledger work, the ABOA believed it would soon be extended further. Additionally, "on line" teller terminals were to be provided in selected branches so that all account transactions would be handled centrally. Also of concern were the problems already surfacing in the rapidly growing data processing centres, where poor working conditions, far from encouraging unionization, were having the opposite effect.

The ABOA reacted by again resurrecting proposals for joint consultation. The banks agreed to the establishment of institutional sub committees which were to be advised of any new or changed processes in time for adequate investigation, consultation, and representation. The union's enthusiasm was tempered by the banks' insistence that all matters be treated confidentially and that these committees should not delay plans for change nor have the power to demand changes — in effect that the committees be emasculated. However, the ABA's assurance that "although unlikely to occur, the provision of opportunities for retraining in new skills and techniques in employment in other areas in the same organisation would be carried out wherever possible"[42] allowed the ABOA to accept the banks' ultimatum.

Another problem lay in the structural inadequacies of the federal award. It was now evident that an incremental scale was inappropriate in an industry where employee duties and responsibilities were being so altered by technological change. No longer did a clear career path, based upon on-the-job training and the gradual development of skills, exist. Increasingly young clerks were being given tasks previously done by officers with years of experience and requiring considerable levels of skill and responsibility. Anomalies were created when older clerks received higher salaries for carrying out similar work, or in some cases work of less importance. After much discussion, the union suggested that some form of salary grading be introduced so as to base salaries on duties rather than years of service. Experience, job complexity, extent of supervision, initiative, judgement and responsibility requirements, and even the ability of the individual to avoid losses to the bank and to make personal contacts with clients, were now, as never before, vital to successful banking. The union argued that these criteria should form an explicit part of salary determination, but that a modified incremental scale should be retained for those officers who for one reason or another did not progress into this career system. This was obviously designed to protect male members, already under threat from the increasing number of females in the industry.

The banks showed little enthusiasm for this proposal. This was because the ABOA's emphasis on career structures was at odds with the type of industry labour market the banks were encouraging and which they believed was emerging. Technological advances and changes to banking techniques, emphases, and areas, in eliminating some positions and creating others, were stimulating the formation of a dual labour market. There would continue to be a demand for some senior staff with policy and decision-making skills and able to carry out sophisticated banking tasks. However, these positions would increasingly be filled by the recruitment of staff with specific skills, rather than those traditionally trained in the branches. The lower part of the dual labour market would comprise the generally younger, predominantly female staff who would operate the new banking machinery.[43] In the banks' view it was neither feasible nor desirable that this latter group should be provided with any form of career salary structure. As well, with the high turnover rates common to this ever-growing lower portion of the dual labour market, the upper ranges of the existing scale would contain relatively few employees, which would allow further salary savings.

By late 1971 the inadequacies of the banks' operating systems were apparent. One manifestation of this was the excessive levels of overtime being worked, as shown by a comprehensive survey of unionists in EDP centres.[44]   The banks' response to union protests again was to suggest the introduction of part-time employees, but the ABOA angrily rejected this. They argued that the low morale and productivity of part-time workers, the effects on promotion of full-time employees, and the problems created by using part-time workers in branches militated against their use. The union was understandably anxious to protect full-time employees, for the nature of branch banking, with peaks in activity occuring on particular days and at certain times during the day, required the banks to maintain higher branch staff establishments than would otherwise be necessary. The ABOA was concerned that improved staff flexibility made possible by the use of part-time workers would affect both the employment and promotion of full-time employees. Williams and Sanders were also aware of the longer-term implications for the union of having a significant proportion of part-time workers in the industry. Not only would they generally have less commitment (and perhaps less reason) for union membership, but the nature of their employment would make their recuitment most difficult.[45]

In 1972 industry recruitment fell for the first time since the war. Though this was later determined to be a result of recession-induced business downturn and recruiting-technique imperfections, the union proclaimed this to be the result of technological changes. They sought to quantify this through a survey of ANZ branches where data processing techniques had been introduced. The results showed that in the 147 branches surveyed there had been a significant reduction in staffing establishments.[46]   On average, those branches of four hands or less, already operating at minimum staffing requirements, lost no staff; those up to six hands lost one; branches up to twelve hands lost two; and in the larger branches at least three fewer staff were needed. Because branch managerial salaries were based on staff establishments, the union was also concerned that "silent downgradings" would result. Choosing to ignore the survey's several limitations, the union then used these results to support their now increasingly strenuous opposition to further technological advances, both in negotiations and in later appearances before the Arbitration Commission.

This resistance, and the industrial conflict it generated, lies beyond the scope of this discussion. By the end of the seventies the union, faced with technological change which now threatened the careers and even employment of banking employees, was desperately and largely unsuccessfully trying to defend its members' interests. Like several other Australian white-collar unions, the ABOA had failed to appreciate both the rate of technological change and its impact on employment. Though their early compliant attitudes and later mild opposition and appeals for joint consultation had now given way to outright confrontation and rejection of the increasingly sophisticated banking technology, the ABOA faced huge, perhaps insurmountable, problems. In the short run, however, the more immediate crisis of a continuing decline in union density had to be solved.

A Solution to Declining Union Density

The net effect of the centralization of an ever younger work force was that union density had fallen almost continuously since the early sixties, as shown by appendix 3. New technology and the nature of banking operations dictated that the proportions of young male and female clerks would continue to increase. As these were the employees the union found most difficult to unionize, the ABOA's future as a strong representative industrial union appeared bleak.

This rapidly declining rate of industry unionization highlighted the ABOA's lack of full-time organizers. Over the years, the union had occasionally used retired officers or even union leaders to carry out spasmodic recruiting drives. Clearly full-time organizers were now needed to overcome the inertia, even resistance, of potential members, to make contact with young employees soon after they entered the industry, and in the absence of an effective shop steward or office representative system, to provide a link between the union and the rank and file. However, partly owing to lack of finance, the first permanent organizers were not appointed until 1969, years after the union density decline had begun. These full-time organizers, former bank officers and members of institutional sub-branches, had shown considerable enthusiasm and interest in union activities. Their relative youth brought initial difficulties, particularly with some senior officers. However, their credibility improved as bank employees came to see the benefits of being able to air grievances and obtain some union assistance. The organizers also played an important role in reducing the rate of resignation, which had risen sharply following the union's first direct action.

Resignations from the union were of some concern.[47] A survey of

Queensland members who resigned in 1972 and 1973 provide a number of reasons for union resignation and indicate some of the problems facing the union.[48] Of the 115 males who had resigned, 24 per cent had left the industry, a figure that reinforces earlier comments regarding the implications of high industry turnover rates for unionization; 25 per cent had resigned following approaches by a debt collector regarding unpaid union dues; and a further 14 per cent left claiming they could obtain most benefits of unionism without being members. Of the remainder, 10 per cent indicated they had received a higher appointment and that union membership was now either unnecessary or embarrassing. This concerned union leaders, for it indicated some diminution in the potentiality of the "manager-member" thesis. Only 2 per cent left because of opposition to the ABOA's militant stance, which suggests that the union's aggressive attitudes did not foster a significant number of resignations. The only available evidence whether this militancy discouraged recruits from joining comes from division secretaries and organizers.[49] Here there is a unanimous view that the ABOA's militancy was a positive factor in union recruitment, and that but for this there would have been an even lower rate of unionization in the industry. In other words, industry bureaucratization and high bank clerk turnover rates, accentuated by increasing levels of female employment, were the dominant reasons for the union's inability to enrol industry recruits.

Over the years the ABOA had made sporadic attempts to have a union-security clause inserted in the award, and to have the banks deduct union subscriptions from members' salaries (known as a "check-off" provision). Williams was constantly reminded of the benefits of check-off, for the SBSA branch of the South Australian division had enjoyed this since 1957 and at December 1972 had a unionization rate in excess of 90 per cent.[50] Also in the SSB division, where check-off had also existed for many years, the unionization rate at December 1972 was 91 per cent for males and 70 per cent for females.[51] Check-off did solve many union recruitment and operational problems. It aided recruiting by eliminating the organizer's need to press for subscriptions at the same time as trying to sign up a new member. Besides, the regular and smaller salary deductions were not such an immediate or severe financial strain on the new member.[52] In latter years the extent of the problem can be gauged from the action of the Victorian division, which in 1973 issued almost five hundred demand drafts on members who had been unfinancial for more than a year.[53] This always created ill will, led to further resignations, and involved the expenditure of scarce union resources. All of this, plus the lack of any office representative system, meant that the implementation of check-off would greatly assist union finances.

The banks had always refused ABOA requests for check-off, arguing this was administratively impossible. Finally, in 1971 the ABOA formally asked the Arbitration Commission to insert such a clause. In spite of bank argument that this was not an industrial matter, Commissioner Portus claimed he did have jurisdiction to hear the claim, an opinion quickly denied by the High Court.[54]   The chief justice, Sir Garfield Barwick, summed up the court's view: "In my opinion the demand that the employer should pay out of earned wages some amounts to persons nominated by the employee is not a matter affecting the relations of employer and employee".[55] Here the matter rested for nearly three years.

Most early ABOA attempts to obtain some form of preference in employment for their members had been forced by Laidlaw's loud and frequent trumpeting of the virtues of the compulsory unionism clause in the UBOA of Q.s award. Until 1970 few unions had been able to make use of the relevant section of the Conciliation and Arbitration Act.[56]   However, in 1971 the Federated Clerks Union succeeded in having a new type of preference clause inserted in their federal award,[57] which gave preference to unionists in the engagement, promotion, and retention of employment. This decision paved the way for other unions to seek preference clauses in the federal jurisdiction, and in October 1973 the ABOA served a claim for preference on the banks.

At the same time, private negotiations between the ABOA and the banks were under way. These had been instituted by the employers, who had expressed a willingness to facilitate the introduction of a form of compulsory unionism and to make check-off facilities available if the ABOA did not pursue the preference clause. The banks' desire to avoid preference was largely influenced by the career nature of the industry itself and particularly by the increasing specialization of banking tasks, which together with the relative decline of branch banking had brought the need to provide specialized training for some employees. As the commission would almost certainly grant a preference clause similar to that already won by the Federated Clerks Union, the banks appreciated that the question of union membership could impede their promotional plans for selected employees. They also knew that the introduction of a preference clause would in the long run result in almost total unionization in the industry anyway, which was no more than they were willing to concede to the ABOA by way of a compulsory unionism clause.

Williams, Sanders, and Remington supported the banks' propositions, for the prospects of increased union membership and financial security overwhelmed their doubts that the acceptance of compulsory membership would create a problem - that of turning conscripted members into convinced supporters of union policies and activities.[58]   The ABOA leadership also believed that preference clauses were most effective in circumstances where there was a large proportion of non-members. Because preference was of most value to career-oriented males already established in the industry, (whose unionization rate had always been in excess of 70 per cent anyway), rather than to younger males or females with high turnover rates, they felt that the advantages accruing to the union from the insertion of a preference clause were limited.

The banks were also willing to apply check-off procedures, a decision which at one stroke removed the ABOA's financial problems. In early 1974 an agreement was finalized. As from 1 July 1974, virtually all recruits would be compelled to join the ABOA, and the banks were to deduct union subscriptions from members' salaries fortnightly. In return the ABOA agreed to "refrain from taking any actions . . . to obtain preference for its members".[59] The effect upon union density was dramatic. For example, by mid-1975 the Victorian division male unionization rate had increased from 70 per cent at December 1972 to 78 per cent, and the female rate from 40 per cent to 77 per cent.[60]

The ABOA, now with few membership or financial worries, looked to the future with some confidence. However, the union and new secretary Sanders were to face problems previously unknown to banking unionism. In the next few years, the rigors of ever-increasing technological change, new and more capital-intensive banking practices, and an extensive economic recession were to tax ABOA resources and initiatives sorely.

This history has emphasized the two phases of ABOA development. The first two decades saw the hesitant, often fearful formation and growth of an association of white-collar workers. The second stage, beginning immediately before the Second World War, was remarkable for the development of militancy, initially by union leadership but eventually among a good proportion of the ABOA's rank and file. Throughout this history, the implications of the economic, social, legal, technological, political, historical, and geographical contexts in which the union, its membership, and its leadership worked have been highlighted. More particularly, emphasis has been placed upon changes in these environmental variables in seeking to explain the gradual transformation of a conservative and timid association of bank officers into a militant and aggressive trade union.

Banking was traditionally a career industry, with a hierarchical and paternalistic structure reinforcing the authority and absolute control of bank management. The banks' recruiting techniques ensured not only that new officers were from quite specific socio-economic groups but that they would also be amenable to extensive regimentation. This, coupled with the extraordinarily high levels of managerial prerogatives held by the banks, made unionization extremely difficult. In fact, union formation and early survival was very much the result of a few determined officers taking advantage of favourable Australian industrial legislation. Not surprisingly, the union's ability to win concessions over and above those grudgingly granted by the Arbitration Court was severely limited.

Paralleling and very much influencing this development was the question of union leadership. In early times union leaders, apart from the incompetent Maher and the irascible and self-centred Sydney Smith, very much mirrored bank employees' long-held characteristics. Conservative, and inhibited by a lifetime of subservience to their employers, these leaders were incapable of taking advantage of economic conditions favourable to union successes. Limited gains were made, but even the introduction of a lengthy automatic salary scale resulted from external events and conditions rather than from union initiatives. Similarly, fortuitous circumstances were largely responsible for the relative improvement in bank officer salaries during the economic depression of the early 1930s. As well, the lack of challenge to the employers' dominance and dictatorial control over their staff, in diminishing the union's credibility in employers eyes, made later initiatives most difficult to implement. The first significant change in the nature of ABOA leadership came during the Second World War, with the replacement of the meek and elderly leadership by younger and considerably less constrained bank officers. By 1945 J. H. O. Paterson had emerged as the first of several vigorous and combatant ABOA leaders.

This new leadership, together with rapidly changing economic, social, and technological factors, provide an explanation for the dramatic postwar shift in ABOA philosophy and tactics. The militancy and employer opposition were initially well in advance of what the rank and file would have of themselves considered. Accordingly there was some resistance, for issues such as the ABOA's nationalization stance, Williams's appointment, formation of a new branch, and restructuring of the union held few immediate or even apparent advantages for the rank and file. Worse, in the face of extensive bank opposition and the disinclination of the Arbitration Court to support wage earners' claims, there were few salary increases in this immediate post-war period. Consequently this was a most difficult period for Williams and Foster, the leaders who succeeded Paterson. With their skills as yet unproved, and holding views considerably more radical than those of the membership at large, they depended for survival on their success in continually reminding the rank and file of the inadequacies of banking employment. However, neither Williams nor Foster viewed militancy as an end in itself but rather as the means of achieving specific goals. In doing this they correctly gauged the temper of members, and the increasing ease with which they later roused the rank and file was testimony to the effectiveness of their approach. This also ensured that the ABOA's militancy remained very much pragmatically based, and by the mid-fifties their persistence and aggression had forced such concessions from employers so as to eliminate any challenge to their leadership. To their advantage also was that despite their own ideologically based opposition to employers, both men still sensibly refrained from publicly airing these feelings and resisted temptations to develop ABOA policy more in accord with their personal beliefs.

A further important facet of bank officer militancy was the gradual change in its source. Whereas rank-and-file unrest had initially been generated and maintained by the leadership, now, with shifts in industry recruiting patterns, in the nature of banking, and in society's view of bank employees, the basis of bank officer militancy underwent a subtle change. By the early sixties the increasing number of dissatisfied officers and the now obvious success of more aggressive tactics in the face of continuing bank intransigence persuaded many bank officers of the necessity for further strong and belligerent actions. This change was first reflected in the increased enthusiasm with which members embraced the union's salary initiatives and the eventually successful assault on Saturday morning banking. Another result was the rash of new tactics and initiatives suggested and implemented by the rank-and-file.

By the late sixties it was also possible to discern a shift in the nature of the militancy of some bank employees. For the first time their opposition and resistance to the banks contained an ideological element. Though issues of salary, promotion, and conditions still remained of singular importance for most, other more active members now displayed elements of class-based antagonism, founded on a generalized resistance to employers and the "employing class". In part this reflected the increasing youth of the work force, a result at first of rapid industry expansion and later of the onset of rapid technological change. Though most young male and female clerks had little interest in union actions or even membership, those who did become involved proved to be considerably more radical and outspoken than older members. Their brief service had left them less inhibited and conditioned by the industry's environment, and this, together with a lower perception of the role and status of bank officers in modern society, allowed them to form a small, aggressive group, to the forefront in the planning and execution of the stop-work meetings and strike at the end of the sixties.

Leadership approval of this development reflected their attitude towards rank-and-file involvement. The ABOA's early history had been marked by leadership indifference, even impatience with membership requests or attitudes. In contrast, post-war leaders showed a considerable determination to search out membership views and to encourage rank-and-file involvement in the settlement of grievances. Williams and Foster did not see this as diminishing their own authority or impinging on their leadership, but rather as consistent with the needs of a strong, viable trade union. It also allowed them time to establish sound administration, order member priorities, refine and implement tactics, and carry out the extensive and frequent negotiations and arbitral work the ABOA's expansion and success demanded.

Recognition of the membership's latent power was a significant factor distinguishing the ABOA from the state unions in the post-war period and was an important ingredient in the ABOA's absorption of these unions. Both the UBOA of NSW and the UBOA of Q had now lost all vestiges of their original energy and initiative which had placed them in the vanguard of Australian banking unionism. Nearly all state unions suffered from well-ensconsed leadership that was either incompetent, apathetic, or intent on using the union for ends other than its stated industrial goals. Understandably these leaders were apprehensive of the threat posed by the ABOA and were trenchantly opposed to its philosophy or style of operation. Their survival in the post-war era was made possible by two factors. First, the long-standing respect that bank officers held for any authority, be it ever so paternalistic, and second the ease with which state union leaders could incorporate ABOA gains at the federal level into their own state awards. Eventually, however, the ABOA's militancy and strength was reflected in such significant gains and inroads into the banks' managerial prerogatives that the deficiencies of state union leaders could no longer be concealed. Membership dissatisfaction grew rapidly, and within a few years rank-and-file pressure had forced all state unions into the ABOA.

This engulfing of the state unions provided considerable financial and administrative advantages and increased the ABOA's bargaining power. However, as events in New South Wales in the late sixties showed, the ABOA was at times restricted by continuing conservatism among members and leaders of some of its new divisions. That the union overcame these problems and moved into the seventies as one of Australia's foremost white-collar unions was a measure of the superiority of its federal leadership and the militancy and determination of its Victorian "hard core" membership, which had been maturing for some years.

As a result of common economic and legal factors, the development of a number of other Australian white-collar unions mirrored and to some extent followed that of the ABOA. However, this history is distinguished by significant differences in the technological, social, historical, and geographical contexts, and it is the reaction of the ABOA, its membership and leadership, to these changing circumstances which has been highlighted. The manner in which the ABOA has attempted to cope with the economically and technologically induced vicissitudes of the latter part of the seventies should properly form the basis of another story.

Notes

1. For part of the sixties the ABOA had divisions in all states. However, for several reasons only Victorian division data are used in this analysis. Firstly, there is no membership data at all for some state unions (later divisions), and for others the data are of a most partial nature (or, in the case of Queensland, are biased by the existence of a compulsory unionism clause until 1966). Also the amalgamation of the state unions with the ABOA, running over a period of more than five years, further impaired the limited membership data of state unions. Secondly, as only the Victorian figures are available for the whole period, and

these have been used throughout the balance of the discussion, then it does seem reasonable to continue this practice. Thirdly, while there are some minor differences between membership patterns in different states, there are also considerable similarities. (Interviews with R. D. Williams, 18 May 1973; K. Salter and T. Mason [Victorian division] 9 December 1973; L. Hingley [Queensland division] 14 January 1974; and J. Harlow [South Australian division], 26 August 1974.)

2. This and other data relating to the location of Victorian private bank employees has been compiled from *AIBR* vols. 44, 74, 84, 91, and 97 – that is, December 1920, 1950, 1960, 1967, and 1973 – also records of private trading banks and of the ABOA.

3. Union density figures are artificially inflated between 1939 and 1945 by the ABOA's practice of retaining all enlisted members on "the books". To give a more accurate account, the union's density figure for 1946 rather than 1945 is used.

4. J. Shister, "The Logic of Union Growth", *Journal of Political Economy* 6, no. 5 (Oct. 1953): 422. This was also supported by several ABOA leaders, including A. E. Hore (13 September 1973), and H. W. Foster (11 May 1973).

5. For example, the average age of the Victorian committee of management in 1925 was fifty-six years (compiled from various union documents and VCMM).

6. Compiled from Victorian division minutes, 1972 and 1973.

7. NBA branch staffing schedules indicate the lack of growth in staffing needs of inner suburban branches. For example:

	1920	1973
Clifton Hill	5 males	5 males/2 females
Fitzroy	5 males	5 males/1 female

Source: NBA records.

8. Interview with L. Smith, personnel officer, NBA, 16 November 1973. The average age at which manager appointments were made in 1935 and 1936 was fifty-two years (compiled from union material prepared for the 1938 arbitration case and held in ABOA archives).

9. An analysis of NBA branches at October 1973 reveals that the average staffing establishment of rural branches (excluding six provincial city branches), was 4.5 staff, that of suburban branches 8.9 staff, and city branches 13.6 staff. In 1920 these figures were 2.9, 4.9, and 8.3 respectively (prepared from material in ABOA archives, and ABOA Victorian division current files).

10. Records of ABOA and NBA and membership files of ABOA Victorian division.

11. Union organizers have also frequently commented on the difficulty of recruiting married women (interview with ABOA organizers, 14 November 1973).

12. See G. S. Bain, *The Growth of White Collar Unionism* pp. 72–81; R. M. Blackburn and K. Prandy, "White Collar Unionisation: A Conceptual Framework", *British Journal of Sociology* 16, no. 2 (June 1965): 111–22; D. Lockwood, *The Black Coated Worker* (London: Allen and Unwin, 1958).

13. Blackburn and Prandy, "White Collar Unionisation", p. 117.

14. ABOA records.

15. Shister, "Logic of Union Growth", pp. 421–22.

16. Extracted from VCMM correspondence in ABOA archives.

17. In 1937, 110 Victorian bank officers left the industry (including 35 who retired or died). With an average of 4,310 employees in the private banking industry in 1937, the turnover rate was 2.5 per cent. (Data from various documents in ABOA archives.)

18. Private bank and ABOA records.

19. From the banks' view point some part of this "suitability" also lay in significantly lower female salary rates, as discussed in the previous chapter.

20. The following provide considerable analysis of this issue: Blackburn, *Union*

Character and Social Class, pp. 122–24; S. Lewenhak, *Women and Trade Unions* (London: Ernest Benn, 1977); E. Ryan and A. Conlon, *Gentle Invaders: Australian Women at Work, 1788–1974* (Melbourne: Nelson, 1975), pp. 145–76; Shister, "The Logic of Union Growth", pp. 421–22.

21. Ths point was confirmed in discussion with ABOA female organizer Maryann Hore (16 March 1974) and Joyce Cameron (17 August 1979).
22. NBA and ABOA records.
23. Interview with L. Smith, personnel officer, NBA, 26 November 1974.
24. In fact more than 60 per cent of females leaving the NBA in 1973 had been employed for less than twelve months (interview with L. Smith, 26 November 1974).
25. As Blackburn says of the English experience, "The failure of these young women to join is not because of dislike of the organisation, or because of lack of interest, but because they leave banking before they have actually taken the step of joining" (Blackburn, *Union Character and Social Class,* p. 124).
26. Blackburn, *Union Character and Social Class,* p. 56.
27. Compiled from NBA and ABOA Victorian division records. Male employees in data processing centres work under similar conditions to females. Blackburn's thesis that this work situation leads to reduced commitment and lower rates of unionization is also borne out by the fact that NBA male employees in these centres had a unionization rate of 26 per cent, compared with the average male unionization figure for the bank of 67 per cent.
28. This view was supported by ABOA female organizer Maryann Hore (16 March 1974).
29. Compiled from NBA and ABOA Victorian division records.
30. *Australian Banker* 2, no. 2 (Feb. 1927): 1.
31. Ibid., 6, no. 4 (Apr. 1931): 13.
32. Ibid., 7, no. 8 (Aug. 1932): 1.
33. Tasmanian branch secretary to Federal Council, FCM, 12 April 1933, p. 25.
34. Confidential letter no. 1229, 23 October 1930, in ANZ archives.
35. "ABOA Special Report on New Banking Machinery", August 1952, p. 3, copy in ABOA archives.
36. Inquiry into Recent Mechanisation and Other Technological Changes in Industry and Other Matters (New South Wales Industrial Commission), No. 58/307, 1960.
37. Joint ABOA/ACSPA submission to inquiry into Recent Mechanisation, p. 10.
38. ANZ general manager's annual review, 1961, p. 3.
39. Private series letter no. 73/61, 14 September 1961.
40. ANZ general manager's annual review, 1961, p. 4.
41. *Federated Clerks Union of Australia* v. *Golden Fleece Petroleum Limited and Ors* (122 CAR 339).
42. Letter from ABA to ABOA, 24 August 1971, in current ABOA files.
43. For an analysis of the development of dual labour markets in Australian white-collar industries, see P. Gilmour and R. D. Lansbury, *Ticket to Nowhere: Education, Work and Training in Australia* (Ringwood, Vic.: Penguin, 1978).
44. Survey of ABOA members in EDP centres, 1971, original held in ABOA current files.
45. Eventually in 1975, and in the face of trenchant union opposition, the ABOA award was varied to allow for up to 3 per cent of total industry employment to be part-time. Part-time employees were to be used only as tellers, and the union instructed its members to report any incidents of part-time workers "giving a hand out at the back of the counter" (*Australian Bank Officer* 35, no. 2 [July 1973]: 1). The union continued to refute bank claims that the part-time tellers would allow better customer service. In the light of a circular from the CBA to its managers, which raised doubts about the vitality of part-time tellers, the

ABOA urged all members to "make it clear to their branch managers that they do not want part-time female tellers at their branch . . . if in spite of this situation a part-time teller is appointed at your branch the ways in which she is being disadvantaged and used up should be made very clear to her" (ibid., p. 2).

46. ABOA survey of ANZ branches, 1972–73, copy in ABOA current files.
47. In 1973 the rate of resignation from the Victorian division was more than 8 per cent (ABOA Victorian division records).
48. "Reasons Provided for Resignations of Male Officers from the Queensland Division of the ABOA 1972–73", copy held in ABOA Queensland division files.
49. Ibid.; interviews with R. D. Williams (21 September 1973); L. Hingley, Queensland division (14 January 1974); J. Harlow, South Australian division (26 August 1974); M. Hore, Victorian division organizer (9 December 1974).
50. Data from ABOA current files.
51. Ibid.
52. For example, in 1924 more than 43 per cent of the union membership had been unfinancial for more than twelve months, so that more than £1,100 was outstanding (VCMM, 29 July 1924, p. 33).
53. Interview with A. S. Mason, secretary ABOA Victorian division, 4 April 1974.
54. *R. W. Portus and Anor* ex parte *Australia and New Zealand Banking Limited and Ors* (127 CLR 353).
55. Ibid., p. 357.
56. For a history and analysis of preference clauses in the federal jurisdiction, see I. G. McDonald, "Some Aspects of the Union Security Provisions in the Australian Conciliation and Arbitration Jurisdiction" (M. Admin. thesis, Monash University, 1975).
57. *Federated Clerks Union of Australia* v. *Altona Petrochemical Co. Pty Ltd, IIB*, vol. 26, no. 6, June 1971, p. 1352.
58. At the 1974 Federal Conference, Sanders, who had recently become federal secretary, following Williams's appointment as a deputy president of the Arbitration Commission, made this point very strongly.
59. Unregistered agreement between the Australian Bank Officials Association and Australian Bankers Association.
60. Appendix 3 and membership records of ABOA Victorian division.

Appendix 1

Location of Victorian Private Trading Bank Branches, 1900–1973

Year	Rural Branches		Suburban Branches		City Branches		Total Branches		Proportion of Branches in City and Suburbs %
	Number	% Change over Previous Period	Number	% Change over Previous Period	Number	% Change over Previous Period	Number	% Change over Previous Period	
1900	342		77		20		439		22.1
1910	481	+40.6	96	+24.7	21	+ 5.0	598	+36.2	19.6
1920	452	− 6.4	124	+29.2	23	+ 9.5	599		24.5
1925	478	+ 5.8	141	+13.7	37	+60.8	656	+ 9.5	27.1
1930	482	+ 0.1	193	+36.9	51	+37.8	726	+10.7	33.6
1935	460	− 4.6	198	+ 2.6	53	+ 3.9	711	− 2.1	35.3
1940	449	− 2.4	236	+19.2	54	+ 1.9	739	+ 3.8	39.2
1945	378	−15.9	207	−12.3	55	+ 1.9	640	−13.4	40.9
1950	424	+12.2	257	+24.2	60	+ 9.1	741	+15.8	42.8
1955	483	+14.0	332	+29.2	62	+ 3.3	877	+18.4	44.9
1960	474	− 1.4	401	+20.8	80	+29.0	955	+10.0	51.2
1965	511	+ 7.8	533	+32.9	92	+15.0	1136	+19.0	55.0
1973	512	+ 0.2	572	+ 7.3	96	+ 4.3	1180	+ 3.9	56.5

Source: AIBR, vols. 24, 34, 44, 49, 54, 59, 64, 69, 74, 79, 84, 89, 94 and 97 (Dec. 1900, 1910, 1920, 1925, 1930, 1935, 1940, 1945, 1950, 1955, 1960, 1965, 1970 and 1973).

Note: For this appendix, branch agencies are expressed as equivalent to one-fourth of a branch. For example, the NBA in 1920, with 86 country branches and 24 country branch agencies, has been credited with a total of 92 country branches.

Appendix 2
Money and Real Wages of Clerks, Accountants, and Managers in Victorian Private Trading Banks, 1880–1939

It was not until September 1920 that a formal salary scale was established in Victorian private trading banks. Even then it covered only clerks and not branch accountants or managers. As knowledge of money and real wage levels and movements was of importance to an analysis of the development and growth of banking unionism, this appendix has been constructed. It was compiled from the salary histories of more than three hundred Victorian officers from the Bank of Australasia (a Melbourne-based but London-owned bank), the NBA (with its head office in Melbourne), and the CBC (which has headquarters in Sydney). Salary has been taken to include any bonuses paid to staff but not travelling, housing, or living away from home allowances.

To allow for the incremental nature of salaries which accompanied promotion to more responsible positions in the industry, six groups of officers, each of fifteen to eighteen officers, were chosen from each bank. These groups comprised officers who entered the industry in 1880, 1890, 1900, 1910, 1920, and 1930. Each group, or intake, then contained approximately fifty officers. The salaries of intake members for each year were then averaged. These results for each intake have been kept separate, for any attempt to average out the salaries of, say, all bank clerks in a particular year would have provided a significant upward bias and distortion of salary levels. The salaries accruing to promotion (as the clerk progressed to accountant and manager), are consequently shown. Because promotion occurred at different times in the bank officer's career, the size of accountant and manager samples varies. In general, a minimum sample size of fifteen was adhered to.

A further important component of this research was to calculate real wage levels for the different groups of bank officers. To this end the Australian retail price index developed by Bambrick was used, with the base year recalculated to 1910=100.[1]

1. S. Bambrick, "Australian Price Levels 1890–1970", *Australian Economic History Review* 13 (Mar. 1973): 57.

Table 1. Money and Real Wages of Bank Clerks 1910–39

Year	Retail Price Index 1910=100	1890 Intake: Money Wage (£ s. d.)	1890 Intake: % Change in Money Wage	1890 Intake: Real Wage Index 1910=100	1900 Intake: Money Wage (£ s. d.)	1900 Intake: % Change in Money Wage	1900 Intake: Real Wage Index 1910=100	1910 Intake: Money Wage (£ s. d.)	1910 Intake: % Change in Money Wage	1910 Intake: Real Wage Index 1920=100	1920 Intake: Money Wage (£ s. d.)	1920 Intake: % Change in Money Wage	1920 Intake: Real Wage Index 1930=100	1930 Intake: Money Wage (£ s. d.)	1930 Intake: % Change in Money	1930 Intake: Real Wage Index
1910	100.0	242.18.0		100.0	164. 7.0		100.0	63.10.0		100.0						
1911	106.0	257.19.0	6.2	100.2	174. 1.0	5.9	99.8	79. 8.0	25.0	118.0						
1912	115.0	270. 0.0	4.7	96.7	190. 0.0	9.2	100.5	91. 7.0	15.1	125.1						
1913	113.5	273.15.0	1.4	99.3	197. 7.0	3.9	106.0	104. 8.0	14.3	144.9						
1914	119.5	291. 0.0	6.3	100.2	219.14.0	11.3	111.9	118.19.0	13.9	156.7						
1915	132.8	294. 0.0	1.3	91.1	227. 3.0	3.4	104.1	133.18.0	12.6	158.8						
1916	135.8	307.10.0	4.6	93.2	235.19.0	3.9	99.1	145. 0.0	8.3	168.6						
1917	144.8	311. 5.0	1.2	88.5	246.10.0	4.5	103.6	160. 8.0	10.9	174.4						
1918	155.2	285.12.0	-8.2	75.6	252.18.0	2.6	99.1	165. 0.0	2.9	167.4						
1919	174.6	295.10.0	3.5	69.6	257.10.0	1.8	89.7	173. 6.0	5.0	153.7						
1920	177.6	321.16.0	8.9	74.6	311. 9.0	21.0	106.7	226. 0.0	30.4	200.4	76. 2.0		100.0			
1921	161.2	327.13.0	1.8	83.7	318.11.0	2.5	120.2	241. 3.0	6.7	235.6	98.13.0		151.9			
1922	158.2	332.19.0	1.6	86.6	326. 1.0	2.3	125.4	269.11.0	11.7	268.3	107. 3.0		157.7			
1923	158.2	344. 1.0	3.3	89.5	338. 3.0	3.7	130.0	281.17.0	4.6	280.6	117. 4.0		178.1			
1924	159.7	361. 8.0	5.0	93.2	359.15.0	6.4	137.1	304.13.0	8.1	300.4	139. 9.0		203.3			
1925	161.2	370.12.0	2.5	94.6	367.18.0	2.2	138.9	315.10.0	3.6	308.2	162.14.0	16.7	235.0			
1926	161.2	378.10.0	2.1	96.7	370.11.0	0.7	139.9	332. 4.0	5.3	324.5	211.16.0	30.2	305.9			
1927	164.2	383. 4.0	1.2	96.1	375. 3.0	1.3	139.0	351.15.0	5.9	337.4	231. 3.0	9.1	327.7			
1928	165.7	388. 3.0	1.3	96.4	382. 1.0	1.8	140.3	371. 9.0	5.6	353.0	244. 7.0	5.8	343.3			
1929	165.7				389. 9.0	1.9	143.0	386.17.0	4.2	367.7	260.11.0	6.6	366.0			
1930	152.2				393. 4.0	1.0	157.2	391.19.0	1.3	405.5	279. 2.0	7.0	426.9	72.12.0		100.0
1931	145.3				351.10.0	-10.6	147.3	344. 3.0	-8.4	389.3	263.10.0	-6.0	419.3	73. 3.0	-0.6	98.7
1932	140.3				353.12.0	0.6	153.4	345. 7.0	0.3	404.5	266.19.0	1.5	442.9	81.12.0	13.1	115.6
1933	140.3				348. 7.0	-1.5	156.1	341.11.0	0.9	400.2	265. 0.0	-0.7	439.7	98. 2.0	20.2	138.9
1934	140.3				351. 1.0	0.8	152.2	365. 5.0	2.4	410.0	268. 4.0	1.2	445.0	111.12.0	13.8	158.0
1935	141.8							379. 1.0	3.9	421.0	308.18.0	15.2	507.1	134. 3.0	20.2	188.0
1936	146.3							382. 0.0	0.8	411.2	344. 0.0	11.4	547.4	172.13.0	28.7	234.5
1937	149.3							397. 1.0	3.9	418.8	389. 6.0	13.2	607.0	196. 6.0	13.7	261.2
1938	152.2							413. 6.0	4.1	427.6	409.11.0	5.2	626.4	220.11.0	12.4	287.9
1939	156.7							418.13.0	1.3	420.7	417. 3.0	1.9	619.7	265.12.0	20.4	336.8

Table 2. Money and Real Wages of Accountants 1910–39

Year	Retail Price Index 1910=100	1880 Intake Money Wage £ s. d.	1880 Intake % Change in Money Wage	1880 Intake Real Wage Index 1910=100	1890 Intake Money Wage £ s. d.	1890 Intake % Change in Money Wage	1890 Intake Real Wage Index 1910=100	1900 Intake Money Wage £ s. d.	1900 Intake % Change in Money Wage	1900 Intake Real Wage Index 1910=100	1910 Intake Money Wage £ s. d.	1910 Intake % Change in Money Wage	1910 Intake Real Wage Index 1920=100	1920 Intake Money Wage £ s. d.	1920 Intake % Change in Money Wage	1920 Intake Real Wage Index 1934=100
1910	100.0	300.10.0	—	100.0	196. 5.0	—	100.0	158.12.0	—	100.0						
1911	106.0	308. 6.0	2.6	96.9	208.15.0	6.4	100.3	161. 8.0	1.8	96.0						
1912	115.0	311.14.0	1.1	90.3	213. 0.0	2.0	94.3	170.12.0	5.7	93.5						
1913	113.5	323. 6.0	3.7	94.9	227. 0.0	6.6	101.9	189. 3.0	10.9	105.1						
1914	119.5	331.14.0	2.6	92.5	235. 0.0	3.5	100.2	198. 6.0	4.8	104.6						
1915	132.8	345. 0.0	4.0	86.6	250. 5.0	6.1	95.9	204. 3.0	2.9	96.9						
1916	135.8	350. 5.0	1.5	85.9	262.10.0	4.9	98.5	220. 6.0	7.9	102.1						
1917	144.8	366.14.0	4.7	84.4	270.10.0	3.0	95.1	226. 8.0	2.8	98.6						
1918	155.2	368.10.0	0.5	78.6	280.15.0	3.8	92.1	230.12.0	1.9	93.7						
1919	174.6	371.14.0	0.9	70.9	285.10.0	1.7	83.3	235.15.0	2.2	85.1						
1920	177.6	420. 5.0	13.1	78.7	331.11.0	16.1	95.1	268.14.0	13.9	95.4						
1921	161.2	438. 3.0	4.3	90.5	360. 5.0	8.7	114.0	284. 3.0	5.6	111.1						
1922	158.2	441. 4.0	0.7	92.8	378.15.0	5.1	121.9	305.17.0	7.6	121.9						
1923	158.2	446. 7.0	1.2	93.9	382. 7.0	0.9	123.2	317.11.0	3.8	126.6						
1924	159.7	454. 3.0	1.8	94.6	388.18.0	1.7	124.1	328. 6.0	3.4	129.6						
1925	161.2	460.11.0	1.4	95.1	397.10.0	2.2	125.6	337. 8.0	2.8	132.0						
1926	161.2				403. 6.0	1.5	127.5	348. 6.0	3.2	136.2	336. 7.0	—	142.2			
1927	164.2				420.15.0	3.9	130.6	361. 9.0	3.8	138.8	356. 8.0	6.0	148.2			
1928	165.7				428.12.0	4.2	131.8	376.11.0	4.2	143.3	370. 4.0	3.9	152.5			
1929	165.7				438.13.0	2.3	134.9	392.11.0	4.3	149.4	389.18.0	5.3	160.6			
1930	152.2				446.19.0	1.9	149.6	410. 7.0	4.5	170.0	419. 3.0	7.5	188.0			
1931	145.3				402.19.0	-9.8	141.3	368. 4.0	-10.4	158.7	378. 4.0	-9.8	176.5			
1932	140.3				411. 7.0	2.1	149.4	371. 9.0	0.9	166.9	381. 6.0	0.8	185.5			
1933	140.3				416.13.0	1.3	151.3	378. 3.0	1.8	169.9	388. 0.0	1.8	188.8			
1934	140.3				424.11.0	1.9	154.2	390.11.0	3.3	175.5	392. 9.0	1.2	191.0	361. 8.0	—	100.0
1935	141.8							397. 9.0	1.8	176.7	403. 7.0	2.7	194.2	369. 9.0	2.2	101.2
1936	146.3							406. 3.0	2.2	175.0	416. 5.0	3.2	191.4	368.11.0	4.6	101.0
1937	149.3							414. 8.0	2.0	179.5	428. 7.0	2.9	195.9	398.11.0	3.1	103.5
1938	152.2							433. 7.0	4.6	179.5	456. 6.0	6.5	202.0	416.12.0	4.5	106.1
1939	156.7							442.11.0	2.1	178.1	458.10.0	0.5	199.8	423.19.0	1.8	104.9

Table 3. Money and Real Wages of Branch Managers 1910–39

Year	Retail Price Index 1910=100	1880 Intake			1890 Intake			1900 Intake			1910 Intake			1920 Intake			1920 Intake		
		Money Wage (£ s. d.)	% Change in Money Wage	Real Wage Index 1910=100	Money Wage (£ s. d.)	% Change in Money Wage	Real Wage Index 1910=100	Money Wage (£ s. d.)	% Change in Money Wage	Real Wage Index 1910=100	Money Wage (£ s. d.)	% Change in Money Wage	Real Wage Index 1910=100	Money Wage (£ s. d.)	% Change in Money Wage	Real Wage Index 1920=100	Money Wage (£ s. d.)	% Change in Money Wage	Real Wage Index 1934=100
1910	100.0	288. 1.0		100.0	264. 5.0		100.0	215. 6.0		100.0									
1911	106.0	298. 7.0		97.7	277. 5.0		99.0	218.10.0		95.8									
1912	115.0	307.10.0		92.8	285.17.0		94.2	221.14.0		89.6									
1913	113.5	319. 7.0		92.7	298. 9.0		99.6	215. 0.0		88.1									
1914	119.5	325.14.0		94.6	300.17.0		95.0	214.13.0		83.3									
1915	132.8	346.13.0		90.6	310. 5.0		88.4	227.17.0		79.8									
1916	135.8	350. 2.0		89.5	321.17.0		89.7	234. 7.0		80.2									
1917	144.8	365.16.0		87.9	326.11.0		85.4	251.17.0		80.9									
1918	155.2	379. 3.0		84.8	341. 6.0		83.3	260.10.0		78.0									
1919	174.6	393. 7.0		78.2	368.17.0		79.9	275. 7.0		73.2									
1920	177.6	430. 8.0	9.4	84.1	425. 3.0	15.3	90.6	301. 5.0	12.7	78.8									
1921	161.2	439.11.0	2.1	94.7	441. 8.0	3.8	103.6	324. 1.0	7.6	93.4									
1922	158.2	449.13.0	2.3	98.7	457. 8.0	3.6	109.4	341. 6.0	5.3	100.2									
1923	158.2	458. 1.0	1.9	100.5	468.11.0	2.4	112.1	358.11.0	5.1	105.3									
1924	159.7	470. 3.0	2.6	102.0	479.11.0	2.4	113.6	371.13.0	3.7	108.3									
1925	161.2	476.12.0	1.4	102.6	485.15.0	1.3	114.0	392.16.0	5.7	113.2									
1926	161.2				493.11.0	1.6	115.9	415. 8.0	5.4	119.7	402. 8.0	5.8				150.3			
1927	164.2				518.14.0	5.0	119.5	433. 7.0	4.3	122.6	411. 6.0	2.2				150.8			
1928	165.7				539. 1.0	3.9	123.4	451. 1.0	4.1	126.4	421.16.0	5.0				153.2			
1929	165.7				551. 7.0	2.3	125.9	464.15.0	3.0	130.3	449.12.0	7.0				163.3			
1930	152.2				573.10.0	4.0	142.6	477.17.0	2.8	145.8	457.18.0	1.9				181.1			
1931	145.3				518.14.0	-9.6	134.2	429.15.0	-10.1	136.4	410.11.0	-10.3				168.9			
1932	140.3				524. 9.0	1.1	141.5	433.17.0	1.0	143.6	415. 6.0	1.1				178.2			
1933	140.3				531.17.0	1.4	143.5	439. 4.0	1.2	145.4	421. 0.0	1.4				180.6			
1934	140.3				543. 1.0	2.1	146.5	451.10.0	2.8	149.5	434. 7.0	3.2				186.4	369.11.0	—	100.0
1935	141.8							456. 7.0	1.1	149.5	441.13.0	1.7				187.3	373. 3.0	1.0	99.9
1936	146.3							463.15.0	1.6	147.2	449.11.0	1.8				185.0	378.10.0	1.4	98.2
1937	149.3							469. 2.0	1.2	145.9	455.19.0	1.4				183.8	391. 4.0	3.4	99.5
1938	152.2							495.12.0	5.6		479. 3.0	5.1				189.5	424.11.0	8.5	105.9
1939	156.7							510. 3.0	5.0		491.10.0	2.6				188.8	436. 8.0	2.8	104.3

Table 4. Comparison of Real Wages Paid to Unskilled Workers, Skilled Workers, and Bank Clerks, Accountants, and Managers, 1910–39

Year	Average Unskilled Minimum Weekly Wage (s. d.)	Real Wage Index (Unskilled Worker) 1910=100	Average Skilled Minimum Weekly Wage (s. d.)	Real Wage Index (Skilled Worker) 1910=100	Real Wage Index of Clerks (Weighted Average) 1910=100	Real Wage Index of Accountants (Weighted Average) 1910=100	Real Wage Index of Managers (Weighted Average) 1910=100
1910	39. 3	100.0	55. 4	100.0	100.0	100.0	100.0
1911	43.11	105.7	58. 3	99.3	98.9	98.1	97.9
1912	45.10	101.5	62. 5	99.4	103.1	92.9	92.5
1913	46. 7	104.8	63.11	101.8	106.8	100.8	95.5
1914	47. 5	101.1	64. 9	97.9	100.6	99.2	91.3
1915	49.11	95.7	66.11	91.1	98.5	93.5	86.7
1916	51. 5	96.5	69. 7	92.6	96.6	95.9	86.9
1917	55. 1	96.9	71. 0	88.6	97.1	92.7	85.1
1918	60. 9	100.1	76. 9	89.4	89.2	88.7	82.4
1919	68. 1	99.5	81. 8	84.5	81.1	80.2	77.7
1920	78. 8	113.0	101. 0	102.8	70.1	86.6	87.3
1921	84. 9	134.2	107. 2	120.1	86.4	108.6	87.3
1922	83. 3	134.2	102. 9	117.4	88.3	108.6	105.0
1923	89.10	144.3	108. 8	124.1	92.1	110.5	107.7
1924	86. 4	137.9	108.11	123.2	69.6	91.3	95.1
1925	88. 1	140.5	110. 4	123.7	74.4	94.8	98.1
1926	90. 1	143.9	112. 1	126.6	85.2	98.9	102.4
1927	92. 3	143.3	112. 1	121.7	88.9	101.6	104.8
1928	89. 7	137.8	111. 7	125.0	92.8	104.8	107.9
1929	92. 9	142.8	114. 7	129.6	97.9	109.7	111.3
1930	87. 6	146.7	109. 2		110.1	126.4	125.0
1931	70. 1	123.6	88. 6	109.3	106.3	118.3	117.1
1932	68. 3	124.1	85. 8	110.3	112.0	124.4	123.4
1933	67. 6	122.7	86. 0	110.8	111.1	126.6	125.0
1934	69. 2	125.6	89. 8	115.5	109.3	126.6	128.3
1935	71. 5	128.6	92. 7	118.0	116.0	129.6	118.0
1936	74. 5	130.1	95. 0	117.4	116.8	129.9	116.4
1937	80.10	138.2	104. 7	126.6	125.9	129.9	115.7
1938	82.11	138.9	107. 3	127.5	130.0	130.7	119.8
1939	84. 6	138.4	108.11	126.4	128.0	135.4	119.7

Source: Unskilled and skilled minimum average wages: years 1910–13, appendixes B and C of annual report of the chief inspector of shops and factories to the Victorian Parliament, VPP, 1896–1915. Years 1914–39, D. W. Oxham, "Unskilled and Skilled Wages", *Economic Record* 26 (1950): 112.–18.

Appendix 3

Union Membership and Density, Victorian Division of the ABOA, 1919–73

Year (Dec.)	Male Union Members	Males in Victorian Private Trading Banks	Male Union Density %	Female Union Members†	Females in Victorian Private Trading Banks	Female Union Density %	Overall Union Density %
1919	473	2,821	16.8	n.a.			
1920	1,373	2,936	46.8				
1921	1,987	3,813	52.1				
1922	2,207	4,196	52.6				
1923	2,279	4,260	53.5				
1924	2,435	4,336	56.2				
1925	2,571	4,390	58.6				
1926	2,651	4,431	59.9				
1927	2,925	4,582	63.8				
1928	2,916	4,634	62.9				
1929	2,968	4,453	66.7				
1930	3,067	4,396	69.8				
1931	3,004	4,250	70.7				
1932	2,960	4,146	71.4				
1933	2,927	4,120	71.0				
1934	2,898	4,137	70.1		332		
1935	2,695	4,103	65.7		329		
1936	2,830	4,230	66.9		310		
1937	2,871	4,325	66.4		317		
1938	2,906	4,414	65.8		315		
1939	3,054	4,534	67.4	40	380	10.5	63.0
1940†	3,033	3,964		75	467	16.1	
1941†	3,087	3,483		215	774	27.7	
1942†	3,186	3,278		295	1,183	24.9	
1943†	3,307	3,064		358	1,364	26.2	
1944†	3,292	2,986		341	1,344	25.4	
1945†	3,212	3,274		282	1,096	25.8	
1946	3,186	3,889	81.9	474	978	48.5	75.2
1947	3,465	4,031	86.0	388	862	45.0	78.7
1948	3,478	4,187	83.1	315	1,074	29.3	72.1
1949	3,804	4,380	86.8	512	1,382	37.0	74.9
1950	3,844	4,567	83.0	557	1,647	33.8	70.8
1951	4,299	4,783	89.9	1,026	2,039	50.3	78.1
1952	4,331	5,114	84.7	1,182	2,409	49.1	73.3
1953	4,423	5,139	86.1	1,233	2,396	51.5	75.1
1954	4,505	5,304	84.9	1,202	2,354	57.1	74.5
1955	4,775	5,683	84.0	1,289	2,534	50.9	73.8
1956	4,909	5,988	82.0	1,362	2,689	50.7	72.3
1957	4,978	6,184	80.5	1,365	2,781	49.1	70.8
1958	5,103	6,374	80.1	1,515	3,073	49.3	70.1
1959	5,135	6,673	76.9	1,528	3,374	45.3	66.3
1960	5,512	6,718	82.0	1,876	3,481	53.8	72.4
1961	5,578	6,796	82.1	1,805	3,674	49.0	71.1
1962	5,865	7,387	76.9	1,818	3,793	47.9	67.1
1963	5,749	7,643	75.2	1,681	3,884	43.2	64.4
1964	5,814	8,034	72.3	1,697	4,031	42.0	62.2
1965	6,074	8,148	74.3	1,789	4,363	41.0	62.8
1966	6,218	8,308	74.8	1,804	4,613	39.1	62.1
1967	6,347	8,589	73.8	2,050	4,781	39.9	62.8
1968	6,409	8,802	72.8	2,073	5,139	39.7	60.8
1969	7,303	9,247	78.9	2,508	5,286	47.4	67.5
1970	6,766	9,573	70.7	2,330	5,343	43.6	61.0
1971	6,847	9,993	68.5	2,133	5,387	39.5	58.4
1972	7,149	10,227	69.9	2,173	5,486	39.6	59.3
1973	7,539	10,427	72.3	2,359	5,636	41.9	61.6

Source: ABOA records in archives and current files. Private bank records.

Notes: * This division was earlier known as the Victorian branch of the BOA and later the Victorian branch of the ABOA.

† The ABOA's policy of retaining all enlisted members on its membership rolls between 1940 and 1945 renders male union figures for this period rather meaningless.

† No females were admitted to the union until 1939.

Bibliography

BOOKS

Allen, V. L. *Militant Trade Unionism.* London: Merlin, 1966.
———. *The Sociology of Industrial Relations.* London: Longman, 1971.
Anstey, F. *The Kingdom of Shylock.* Melbourne: Fraser and Jenkinson, 1916.
Arndt, H. W., and C. P. Harris. *The Australian Trading Banks.* Melbourne: Cheshire, 1968.
Atkinson, M. *The New Social Order: A Study of Post War Re-Construction.* Melbourne: Macmillan, 1919.
———. ed. *Australia, Economic and Political Studies.* Melbourne: Macmillan, 1920.
Bain, G. S. *The Growth of White Collar Unionism.* London: Oxford University Press, 1970.
Baker, J. *Communicators and Their First Trade Unions: A History of the Telegraphist and Postal Clerk Unions of Australia.* Sydney: Union of Postal Clerks and Telegraphists, 1980.
Bendix, R., and S. M. Lipset, eds. *Class, Status and Power.* London: Routledge and Kegan Paul, 1970.
Blackburn, R. M. *Union Character and Social Class: A Study of White Collar Unionism.* London: Batsford, 1967.
Blainey, G. *Gold and Paper: A History of the National Bank of Australasia Limited.* Melbourne: Georgian House, 1958.
Blum, A. A. *Management and the White Collar Union.* Research Study No. 63. New York: American Management Association Inc., 1964.
Butlin, S. J. *Australia and New Zealand Bank.* London: Longman Green, 1961.
———. *Foundations of the Australian Monetary System, 1788-1851.* Carlton, Vic.: Melbourne University Press, 1953.
———. *War Economy 1939-42.* Canberra: Australian War Memorial, 1954.
Butlin, S. J., A. R. Hall, and R. C. White. *Australian Banking and Monetary Statistics, 1817-1945.* Sydney: Reserve Bank of Australia, 1971.
Butlin, S. J., and C. B. Schedvin. *War Economy, 1942-1945.* Canberra: Australian War Memorial, 1977.
Caiden, G. E. *The A.C.P.T.A.: A Study of White Collar Public Service Unionism in the Commonwealth of Australia, 1885-1922.* Canberra: Australian National University Press, 1966.
Campbell, E. W. *History of the Australian Labor Movement.* Sydney: Current Book Distributors, 1945.

Congalton, A. A. *Status and Prestige in Australia.* Melbourne: Cheshire, 1969.

Crisp, L. F. *Ben Chifley.* Melbourne: Longmans, 1961.

Crowley, F., ed. *A New History of Australia.* Melbourne: Heinemann, 1974.

Cyriax G., and R. Oakeshott. *The Bargainers: A Survey of Modern Trade Unionism.* London: Faber, 1960.

Dahrendorf, R. *Class and Class Conflict in Industrial Society.* London: Routledge and Kegan Paul, 1959.

Dale, J. R. *The Clerk in Industry.* Liverpool: Liverpool University Press, 1962.

Davies, A. A., S. Encel, and M. J. Berry, eds. *Australian Society: A Sociological Introduction.* Melbourne: Longman Cheshire, 1977.

Doeringer, P. B., and M. J. Piore. *Internal Labour Markets and Manpower Analysis.* Lexington, Mass.: D. C. Heath and Co., 1971.

Foenander, O. de R. *Industrial Regulation in Australia.* Carlton, Vic.: Melbourne University Press, 1965.

Forster, C. *Industrial Development in Australia, 1920–1930.* Canberra: Australian National University Press, 1964.

Giblin, L. F. *The Growth of a Central Bank.* Carlton, Vic.: Melbourne University Press, 1951.

Gilmour, P., and R. D. Lansbury. *Ticket to Nowhere: Education, Work and Training in Australia.* Ringwood, Vic.: Penguin, 1978.

Gollan, R. *The Commonwealth Bank of Australia: Origins and Early History.* Canberra: Australian National University Press, 1968.

———.*Revolutionaries and Reformists: Communism and the Australian Labour Movement, 1920–1955.* Canberra: Australian National University Press, 1975.

Healey, B. *Federal Arbitration in Australia.* Melbourne: Georgian House, 1972.

Henig, H. *The Brotherhood of Railway Clerks.* New York: Columbia University Press, 1937.

Higgins, H. B. *A New Province for Law and Order.* London: Dawson, 1968.

Holder, R. F. *Bank of New South Wales: A History.* Sydney: Angus and Robertson, 1970.

Humphreys, B. V. *Clerical Unions in the Civil Service.* Oxford: Blackwell and Mott, 1958.

Hutson, J. *Six Wage Concepts.* Sydney: Amalgamated Engineering Union, 1971.

Juddery, B. *White Collar Power: A History of the ACOA.* London: Allen and Unwin, 1980.

Klingender, F. D. *The Condition of Clerical Labour in Britain.* London: Martin Lawrence, 1935.

Lang, J. T. *Why I Fight.* Sydney: Labor Daily Limited, 1934.

Lewenhak, S. *Women and Trade Unions.* London: Ernest Benn, 1977.

Lockwood, D. *The Black Coated Worker.* London: Allen and Unwin, 1958.

Louis, L. J. *Trade Unions and the Depression.* Canberra: Australian National University Press, 1968.

Louis, L. J., and I. Turner. *The Depression of the 1930s*. Melbourne: Cassell, 1968.

Mackay, A. L. G. *The Australian Banking and Credit System*. London: P. S. King, 1931.

McKinlay, B. *A Documentary History of the Australian Labor Movement, 1850-1975*. Melbourne: Drummond, 1979.

Martin, R. M. *Trade Unions in Australia*. Ringwood, Vic.: Penguin, 1975.

Mawson, P. *A Vision of Steel*. Melbourne: Cheshire, 1958.

May, A. L. *The Battle for the Banks*. Sydney: Sydney University Press, 1958.

Murphy, D. *Ken Laidlaw: A White Collar Union Leader*. Brisbane: Australian Bank Employees Union, 1979.

Portus, J. H. *The Development of Australian Trade Union Law*. Carlton, Vic.: Melbourne University Press, 1958.

Prandy, K. *Professional Employees: A Study of Scientists and Engineers*. London: Faber, 1965.

Rawson, D. W. *A Handbook of Australian Trade Unions and Employers' Associations*. Canberra: Australian National University Press, 1973.

Roberts, B. C., R. Loveridge, and J. Gennard. *Reluctant Militants: A Study of Industrial Technicians*. London: Heinemann, 1972.

Ryan, E., and A. Conlon. *Gentle Invaders: Australian Women in Work, 1788-1974*. Melbourne: Nelson, 1975.

Sawer, G. *Australian Federal Politics and Law, 1929-1949*. Melbourne: Melbourne University Press, 1963.

Schedvin, C. B. *Australia and The Great Depression: A Study of Economic Development and Policy in the 1920s and 1930s*. Sydney: Sydney University Press, 1970.

Scott, E. *Official History of Australia in the War of 1914-1918*, vol. II, *Australia During The War*. Sydney: Angus and Robertson, 1936.

Seidman, J., J. London, B. Karsh, and D. L. Tagliacozzo. *The Worker Views His Union*. Chicago: University of Chicago Press, 1958.

Shann, E. O. G., and D. B. Copland. *The Battle of the Plans*. Sydney: Angus and Robertson, 1931.

——— .*The Crisis in Australian Finance, 1929 to 1931*. Sydney: Angus and Robertson, 1931.

Sheridan, T. *Mindful Militants*. Cambridge: Cambridge University Press, 1975.

Sinclair, K., and W. G. Mandle. *Open Account: A History of the Bank of New South Wales in New Zealand*. Wellington: Whitcombe and Tombs, 1961.

Sturmthal, A., ed. *White Collar Trade Unions*. Urbana, Ill.: University of Illinois Press, 1966.

Sutcliffe, J. T. *A History of Trade Unionism in Australia*. Melbourne: Macmillan, 1921.

Sykes, E. I., and H. J. Glasbeek, *Labour Law in Australia*. Sydney: Butterworths, 1972.

Turner, I. A. H. *Industrial Labour and Politics*. Canberra: Australian National University Press, 1965.

Walker, E. *The Australian Economy in War and Reconstruction*. New York: Oxford University Press, 1947.

Walker, K. F. *Australian Industrial Relations Systems*. Melbourne: Oxford University Press, 1970.
Wright Mills, C. *White Collar: The American Middle Classes*. New York: Oxford University Press, 1956.

MONOGRAPHS

Butlin, S. J., A. R. Hall, and T. D. White. "Australian Banking and Monetary Statistics, 1817–1945". Reserve Bank of Australia Research Department, Occasional Paper no. 4A. Sydney: Reserve Bank of Australia 1971.
Caiden, G. E. "Public Employment Compulsory Arbitration in Australia". Ann Arbor, Mich.: Institute of Labor and Industrial Relations, University of Michigan–Wayne State University, 1971.
Cupper, L. "Technical School Students' Attitudes to Trade Unionism". Melbourne, 1977.
Martin, R. M. *White Collar Unions in Australia*. Monograph no. 5. Sydney: Australian Institute of Political Science, 1965.
Mobbs, C. L. "Conciliation Can Work: A History of the Commonwealth Bank Officers Association". Sydney, 1968.
Riches, L. N. "Coming of Age: Salary Campaigns of the Australian Bank Officials Association 1968 and 1969". Melbourne: Australian Bank Officials Association, 1976.
———."The Struggle for Equal Pay in the Australian Private Banking Industry 1966–1975". Melbourne: Australian Bank Employees Union, 1980.
Williams, R. D. "Harold Foster and the ABOA". Melbourne: Australian Bank Officials Association, 1978.
———."Pev was the Founder". Melbourne: Australian Bank Officials Association, 1979.
———."Dick Hore and the ABOA". Melbourne: Australian Bank Employees Union, 1979.

ARTICLES AND PERIODICALS

Allen, V. L., and S. Williams. "The Growth of Trade Unionism in Banking". *Manchester School of Economic and Social Studies* 28 (Sept. 1960): 298–318.
Anderson, G. "Wage Reductions in Australia's National Emergency". *Economic Record* 7 (May 1931): 117–21.
Australasian Insurance and Banking Record, 1880–1977. Melbourne: McCarron Bird and Co.
Bain, G. S., and R. Price. "Who is a White-Collar Employee?". *British Journal of Industrial Relations* 10, no. 3 (Nov. 1972): 325–39.
Bambrick, S. "Australian Price Levels, 1890–1970". *Australian Economic History Review* 13 (Mar. 1973): 57–71.
Bankers' Insurance Managers' and Agents Magazine. London: Waterlow and Sons.

Blackburn, R. M., and K. Prandy. "White Collar Unionisation: A Conceptual Framework". *British Journal of Sociology* 16, no. 2 (June 1965): 111–22.

Caiden, G. E. "Some Problems of White Collar Unionism in the Commonwealth Service". *Public Administration* 35, no. 3 (Sept. 1966): 233–51.

Copland, D. B. "The Economic Situation in Australia 1918–1923". *Economic Journal* 34: 23–38.

Dufty, N. F. "The White Collar Unionist". *Journal of Industrial Relations* 3 (Oct. 1961): 151–56.

Fogarty, M. P. "The White Collar Pay Structure in Britain". *Economic Journal* 29 (Mar. 1959): 55–70.

Forster, C. "Australian Unemployment 1900–1940". *Economic Record* 41, no. 95 (Sept. 1965): 426–50.

Fristacky, J. M. "Collective Bargaining, Conciliation and Arbitration in Victorian Wages Baords". *Journal of Industrial Relations* 18, no. 4 (Dec. 1976): 309–25.

Hamermesh, D. "White Collar Unions, Blue Collar Unions and Wages in Manufacturing". *Industrial and Labour Relations Review* 24 (Jan. 1971): 159–70.

Hancock, K. "The Wages of Workers". *Journal of Industrial Relations* 11, no. 1 (Mar. 1969), pp. 17–38.

Hartmann, H. "Managerial Employees: New Participants in Industrial Relations". *British Journal of Industrial Relations* 12, no. 2 (May 1977): 37–54.

Hince, K. "Wages Boards in Victoria". *Journal of Industrial Relations* 7, no. 2 (July 1965): 169–81.

Howard, W. A. "Australian Trade Unions in the Context of Union Theory". *Journal of Industrial Relations* 19, no. 3 (Sept. 1977): 255–73.

Hughes, H., and D. W. Rawson. "Collective Bargaining and the White Collar Pay Structure". *Journal of Industrial Relations* 2, no. 3 (Oct. 1960): 75–89.

Isaac, J. E. "The Basic Wage and Standard Hours Enquiry in Australia 1952–53". *International Labour Review* 69 (May 1954): 570–93.
———."The Federal Basic Wage – Margins Case 1965", *Journal of Industrial Relations* 7, no. 3 (Nov. 1965): 225–49.

Kassalow, E. M. "The Prospects for White Collar Union Growth". *Industrial Relations* 5: 37–47.

Keating, M. "Australian Work Force and Employment 1910/11 to 1960/61". *Australian Economic History Review*, (Sept. 1967): 150–70.

Lamour, C. "Women's Wages and the WEB". In *Women at Work,* edited by A. Curthoys, S. Eade, and P. Spearritt, pp. 47–58. Canberra: Australian Society for the Study of Labour History, 1975.

Lansbury, R. D. "White Collar and Professional Employees". In *The Worker in Australia,* edited by A. Bordow, pp. 184–221. St Lucia: University of Queensland Press, 1977.

Macarthy, P. G. "Wage Determinations in New South Wales, 1890–1921". *Journal of Industrial Relations* 10, no. 3 (Nov. 1968): 189–205.

———."Wages in Australia 1891–1914". *Australian Economic History Review* 10 (Mar. 1970): 56–76.

Martin, R. M. "Class Identification and Trade Union Behaviour: The Case of Australian White Collar Unions". *Journal of Industrial Relations* 7, no. 2 (July 1965): 131–48.

———. "Australian Professional and White Collar Unions". In *Australian Labour Relations Readings*, edited by J. E. Isaac and G. W. Ford, pp. 178–88. Melbourne: Sun Books, 1966.

Piore, M. J. "Notes for a Theory of Labour Market Stratification". In *Labor Market Segmentation*, pp. 125–29. edited by R. C. Edwards, M. Reich, and D. M. Gordon, Lexington, Mass.: D. C. Heath, 1975.

Prandy, K. "Professional Organisation in Great Britain". *Industrial Relations* 5: 67–79.

Rawson, D. W. "The Frontiers of Trade Unionism". *Australian Journal of Politics and History* 1, no. 1 (Nov. 1955): 196–209.

Reddaway, W. B. "Australian Wage Policy, 1929–37". *International Labour Review* 37 (Mar. 1938): 314–37.

Shister, J. "The Logic of Union Growth". *Journal of Political Economy* 61, no. 5 (Oct. 1953): 413–33.

Strauss, G. "Professionalism and Occupational Associations". *Industrial Relations* 3, no. 3 (May 1963): 7–31.

———. "The White Collar Unions are Different" *Harvard Business Review* 37 (Sept.–Oct. 1954): 73–82.

Turner, I. A. H. "The Growth of Melbourne". In *Australian Capital Cities*, edited by J. W. McCarty, J. Ward, and C. B. Schedvin, pp. 62–81. Sydney: Sydney University Press, 1978.

Williams, R. D. "White Collars Make Council". *Labour History* (Australia), no. 6 (May 1964): 32–33.

Williams, R. D., and J. Paterson. "White Collar Unionism". *Dissent*, no. 14 (Winter 1965), pp. 40–43.

Yerbury, D. "Technological Change and Industrial Relations in Australia". *Search* 4, no. 7 (July 1973).

Yerbury, D., and J. E. Isaac. "Recent Trends in Collective Bargaining in Australia". *International Labour Review* 103, no. 5 (1971): 421–52.

THESIS

McDonald, I. G. "Some Aspects of the Union Security Provisions in the Australian Conciliation and Arbitration Jurisdiction". Master of Administration thesis, Monash University, 1975.

NEWSPAPERS

The *Age*
The *Argus*
The *Australian Star*

The *Herald* (Melbourne)
Labor Daily
Smiths Weekly
The *Sun News-Pictorial*
The *Sun* (Sydney)
The *Tribune*

GOVERNMENT DOCUMENTS

Federal

Commonwealth Parliamentary Debates
Labour Reports (Commonwelath Bureau of Census and Statistics)
Commonwealth Year Book (Canberra: Australian Bureau of Statistics)
Federal Industrial Registrar's Files (Melbourne)
Royal Commission on the Monetary and Banking Systems (Canberra: Commonwealth of Australia, 1937).

State

A Board of Inquiry on the Five Day Banking Week in Victoria, (The Gillard Inquiry), 1962.
Victorian Year Book (Canberra: Australian Bureau of Statistics, Victorian Office)
New South Wales Industrial Registrar's Files (Sydney)
Queensland Year Book (Canberra: Australian Bureau of Statistics, Queensland Office)

UNION DOCUMENTS

The basic archival source for union material has been the ABOA deposits E2 and E248, in the Archives of Business and Labour at the Australian National University. This material, though copious, has as yet not been fully catalogued. Consequently all references to this material are simply cited as "in ABOA archives". Material relating to more recent ABOA and ABEU activities is held at the federal office, Melbourne, and the Victorian division office, Melbourne.

The journals and some correspondence and records of the now amalgamated state unions are held in various state division offices in other capital cities.

Union material used frequently included the following:

BOA and ABOA, 1919–75

Minutes of BOA committee of management, after 1922 known as the Victorian committee of management (VCMM), and after 1962 as the Victorian Division.

Federal Council Minutes (FCM) 1924–76.

Federal Conference Minutes 1938–1976.
BOA monthly circulars (sometimes known as BOA Bulletins), 1920 and 1921
Bank Officials Journal, 1921–24
The Australian Banker, 1925–41 (in conjunction with the UBOA of NSW)
The Bankers Journal, 1941–63
The Australian Bank Officer, 1963–76
ABOA newsletters, 1963–75
ABOA pamphlets, 1950–75

New South Wales (UBOA of NSW, 1919–65)

All material held in ABEU New South Wales division office, Sydney.
UBOA of NSW minutes, 1919–31, 1934–65
The Bankers Bulletin, 1920–24
The Australian Banker, 1925–41 (in conjunction with the ABOA)
The Banker, 1941–65

South Australia (BOASA, 1920–64)

All material held in ABEU South Australian division office, Adelaide.
BOASA minutes, 1924–64
South Australian branch of ABOA minutes, 1949–62
South Australian Bank Officials' Journal (SABOJ), 1922–59

Queensland (UBOA of Q, 1919–65)

UBOA of Q minutes, 1920–65.
Assorted files
The Queensland Bank Officer, 1920–65

Western Australia (BOAWA, 1920–62)

All material held in ABEU Western Australian division, Perth.
The Westralian Banker, 1924–62

BANK MATERIAL

ANZ Archives, Melbourne

The ANZ Archives, now located at that bank's head office in Melbourne, contain a most comprehensive and well-catalogued collection of the records, circulars, and pamphlets of the Bank of Australasia, the Union Bank, and the English, Scottish and Australian Bank, and to a lesser extent those of the London Bank, the Royal Bank, the Commercial Bank of Tasmania, and the Bank of South Australia. There are also complete records relating to the ANZ Bank. Among the more frequently used Series were:
UB and UA series – Australian manager of Union Bank to London, confidential letters

AB and AB series — superintendent Bank of Australasia to London and
    London manager to Australia, confidential letters
EB and EAB series — Australian manager of the ES&A to London
Y series — minutes of meetings of Associated Banks of Australia
ZB series — general manager of the ANZ to London

Other Bank Archives

Limited amounts of material were also made available from the archives of
the Bank of New South Wales and the Commercial Banking Company of
Sydney, both located in Sydney.

INTERVIEWS

Full-Time Union Officials

P. D. Allsop, federal president ACSPA, 1956-70
H. W. Foster, federal president ABOA, 1953-68
J. Harlow, secretary South Australian division, 1967-79
L. Hingley, secretary of UBOA of Q, 1968-1981; assistant federal secre-
    tary 1981 —
Maryann Hore, organizer, Victorian division, 1973-81
K. H. Laidlaw, secretary UBOA of Q, 1920-60
K. H. McLeod, federal secretary AISF, 1962—
A. S. Mason, assistant secretary victorian division, 1971-73; secretary Vic-
    torian division, 1973—
K. H. Remington, federal treasurer ABOA, 1961-69; federal president
    ABOA, 1969-78
P. W. Reilly, federal president AISF, 1969-81, and federal president,
    ACSPA 1970-79
W. J. Richardson, administrative and industrial officer, ACSPA, 1968-79
L. Riches, federal industrial research officer, 1974-81
H. K. Salter, secretary Victorian division, 1968-73; assistant federal secre-
    tary, 1973-81; federal secretary 1981-
John Sanders, assistant federal secretary, 1959-73; federal secretary,
    1973—
R. D. Williams, secretary Victorian branch, 1950-78; federal secretary,
    1950-73; federal secretary ACSPA, 1956-73

Honorary Union Officials

S. Barratt	L. Byrne
J. Cameron	A. Cilento
J. Don	D. Gaunson
A. E. Hore	R. D. McKell
A. S. McNab	D. Northcott
E. C. Peverill	D. Simmons
	K. Yates

Other Interviews

P. Callinan, industrial officer, Australian Bankers Association
K. Hill, general manager, ESANDA
J. Portus, commissioner, Australian Conciliation and Arbitration Commission
L. Sheckleton, personnel manager, National Bank of Australasia
L. Smith, personnel officer, National Bank of Australasia

Index

Aird, D., 186, 215
Allsop, P. D., 147, 210-11
Amalgamation, early attempts, 39, 40, 68-69, 92; success, 179, 190-207
Arbitration Court: formation, 17-18; proposed abolition, 65-66
Association of Architects, Engineers, Surveyors and Draughtsmen (AAESDA), 224-25
Associated Banks Association, 45
Atkinson, Meredith, 24-25, 49
Australian Bankers Association (ABA), 158, 186-87, 199-200
Australian Bank Officials' Association (ABOA): formation, 11-20; first arbitration appearance, 47-48; and Second World War, 98-106; formation of South Australian Branch, 124; post war changes, 132; and ACSPA, 142, 147, 226-27; formation of ACT and NT Branches, 145; and increasing militancy, 133-34, 139, 149-52, 153-54, 182-87; and other while collar unions, 151-52, 224-25; post war union structure, 154-55; and five-day week, 168-89; and amalgamation of state unions, 190-207; and strikes, 204-205, 219-22; and female bank officers, 102-103, 227-37, 257-60; prosecution of banks, 235-36; post-amalgamation structure, 237-40; and membership problems, 249-56; and young members, 256-60; and technology, 260-66; and part-time workers, 265; and union security clauses, 267-68
Australian Bank Officials Federation (ABOF) 39
Australasian Clerical Association (ACA) 35
Australian Council of Salaried and Professional Associations (ACSPA), 142-43, 147-52, 204, 209-11, 224-27

Australian Council of Trade Unions (ACTU) and ACSPA, 148-49, 151-52, 209-11
Australian Insurance Staffs Federation (AISF), 63, 137, 225

Baker, J. S., 147-48
Bank Employees Protest Committee, 123
Banking industry: structure of, 1-6; and depression, 65-78; and urbanization, 79, 159, 249-56; and Second World War, 98-106; branch rationalization, 99-102; female employment, 102-103, 222-37, 257-60; and Commonwealth Bank, 111-12; bank nationalization, 111-30; post war staff shortages, 134-35; structural change, 158-60, 249-56; growth of savings banking, 158; changing age structure, 256-60; technological change, 262-66; part-time work, 265
Bank Officers: nature of work, 6-11; working conditions, 8-10, 14-16; recruitment, 6-7; promotion, 7-9, 159, 250-51, 252-53; pre award salaries, 10-11; and rationing, 71, 83 n83; and retrenchment, 75, 77; enlistments, 98, 108 n61; declining status of, 135, 251-52; first strike, 219-22; increasing youth, 256-60; and turnover, 256-57; resignations of, 256-57; increasing militancy of, 104-105, 126-27, 212-40
Bank Officers Guild (BOG), 19-20, 27-28
Bank Officials' Association (BOA): formation, 11-20, 24-28; registration, 26-27; First Agreement, 35-38; internal union structure, 42-43; High Court challenge, 47; in 1924, 49-50; at end of depression, 78-80; and 1937 award, 88-94; internal dissension, 90-98; Ogilvie Award